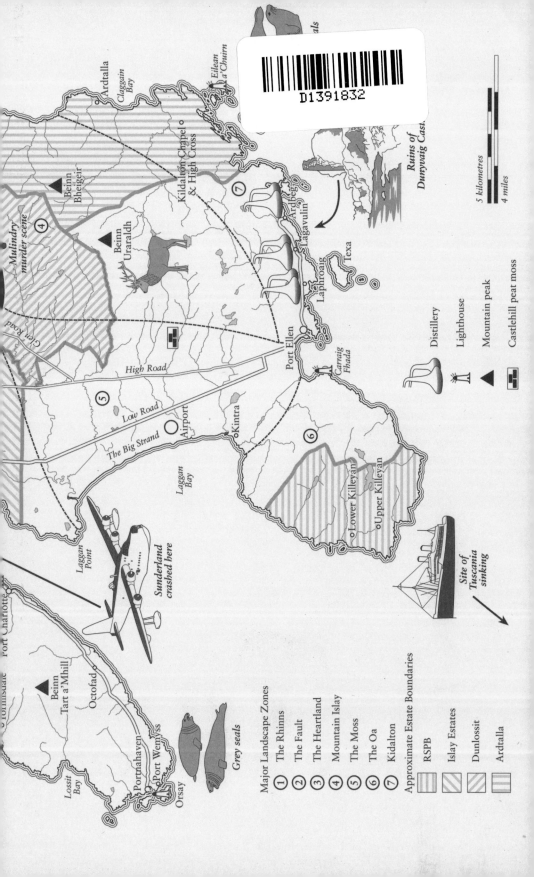

PEAT
SMOKE
AND
SPIRIT

PEAT SMOKE AND SPIRIT

A PORTRAIT OF Islay AND ITS WHISKIES

ANDREW JEFFORD

headline

Copyright © 2004 Andrew Jefford

The right of Andrew Jefford to be identified as the Author of
the Work has been asserted by him in accordance with
the Copyright, Designs and Patents Act 1988.

First published in 2004
by HEADLINE BOOK PUBLISHING

10 9 8 7 6 5 4 3 2 1

Apart from any use permitted under UK copyright law, this publication
may only be reproduced, stored, or transmitted, in any form, or by any
means, with prior permission in writing of the publishers or, in the
case of reprographic production, in accordance with the terms
of licences issued by the Copyright Licensing Agency.

Every effort has been made to fulfil requirements with regard to
reproducing copyright material. The author and publisher will be
glad to rectify any omissions at the earliest opportunity.

Cataloging in Publication Data is available from the British Library

ISBN 0 7472 2735 7

Typeset in Caslon and Gill Sans by Avon DataSet Ltd, Bidford-on-Avon, Warks
Printed and bound in Great Britain by
Mackays of Chatham plc, Chatham, Kent

Headline's policy is to use papers that are natural, renewable and recyclable
products and made from wood grown in sustainable forests. The logging and
manufacturing processes are expected to conform to the environmental regulations
of the country of origin.

HEADLINE BOOK PUBLISHING
A division of Hodder Headline
338 Euston Road
London NW1 3BH

www.headline.co.uk
www.hodderheadline.com

Contents

IN MEMORY OF

Iain Maclean (1913–2003), a gentle Ileach; and 'Murdoch of the Kilt', exciseman, journalist, agitator and fighter for justice for the people of the Highlands and Islands.

Acknowledgements

The author would like to thank the following for their help in the preparation of this book (those whose names appear in italics were kind enough to allow me to record or conduct interviews with them).

ON ISLAY

Douglas Bowman, *James Brown*, Sheila Brown, *Grant Carmichael*, Scott Chance, Wendy Chance, *Suzanne Cobb*, Isabel Coughlin, Simon Coughlin, Dr Elizabeth Cunningham, *Jane Dawson*, Ivor Drinkwater, Ella Edgar, John Edwards, Kay Fleming, *Mark French*, Alec Gunn, *Ben Harrison*, Stephen Harrison, *Iain Henderson, James How, Norrie Kimble*, Christine Logan, Flora MacAffer, *Iain (Pinkie) McArthur*, Lillian MacArthur, *James Macaulay, Lily MacDougall*, Barbara McEwan, *James (Jim) McEwan*, Ann McGill, *Duncan McGillivray*, Susan McGillivray, Mary McGregor, Hilary MacIntyre, *Kirsten MacIntyre, Rae Mackenzie, Angus Maclachlan*, the late *Iain Maclean, Neil MacLean*, David MacLellan, *Gilbert MacLellan, John MacLellan*, Lindy MacLellan, *Victor MacLellan, Ruiradh MacLeod*, Ian (Percy) McPherson, *Gilbert Mactaggart, Sandy Mactaggart, Fiona Middleton, George Middleton*, Irene Miller, *Ian Mitchell*, Donald Morrison, Billy Muir, Ann Newman, *Gus Newman*, Martine Nouet, *Dr Malcolm Ogilvie*, Brian Palmer, Margot Perrons, Hamish Proctor, *Chloë Randall*, Carl Reavey, Jan Reavey, *Mark Reynier, Donald Renwick, Toby Roxburgh*, Colin (Pat) Roy, Jimmy Roy, Sarah Roy, *Blair Rozga, Margaret Rozga, Robin Shields, Billy Stitchell, Jackie Thomson*, John Thomson, *Stuart Thomson*, Richard Woods.

ELSEWHERE

Jim Beveridge, Valérie Blanc, Andrew Ford, Natalie Guerin, Mark Hunt, Bill Lumsden, Iseabail Mactaggart, *Sir John Mactaggart, Lord*

Margadale, Clare Meikle, Matthew Mitchell, Dr Nicholas Morgan, Douglas Murray, Mike Nicolson, Annie Pugh, Andrew Rankin, *Bruno Schroder*, Peter Smith, Bryony Wright.

AND PERSONAL THANKS TO . . .

Paula Eyers, who helped transcribe interview recordings and discovered Islay for herself with characteristic zest and enthusiasm; Anastacia Kirk, who crossed hemispheres to visit Islay and who also generously helped with interview transcription; Laurence Forbin, who regularly brought her sketch pad and her wide smile from Paris to Islay; John Edwards and Ivor Drinkwater, the Port Charlotte irregulars; my dentist George Taylor, for offering me so many restorative glasses of post-surgical Laphroaig over several decades of treatment; all of the distilling companies on Islay, who provided vital help with travel and accommodation; the Museum of Islay Life, whose staff are cited above and whose curating skills made the research into Islay's history and shipwrecks so enjoyable; to Jo Roberts-Miller of Headline, for following this book through from inception to publication; to my father Peter Jefford, for answering my aviation questions so comprehensively; and finally to my brother Stephen Jefford, without whose generosity with air miles this book would have taken even longer to write.

AUTHOR'S NOTE

This book will, alas, contain errors and omissions. I would like to have recorded interviews with many more Ileachs and written a still longer book, but even the patience of publishers has limits. Please ensure that any reprints are as accurate as possible by providing the author with details of errors, no matter how small, via email (text only; no photos or graphics) to andrew@jefford.fsbusiness.co.uk

Thank you.

List of Illustrations

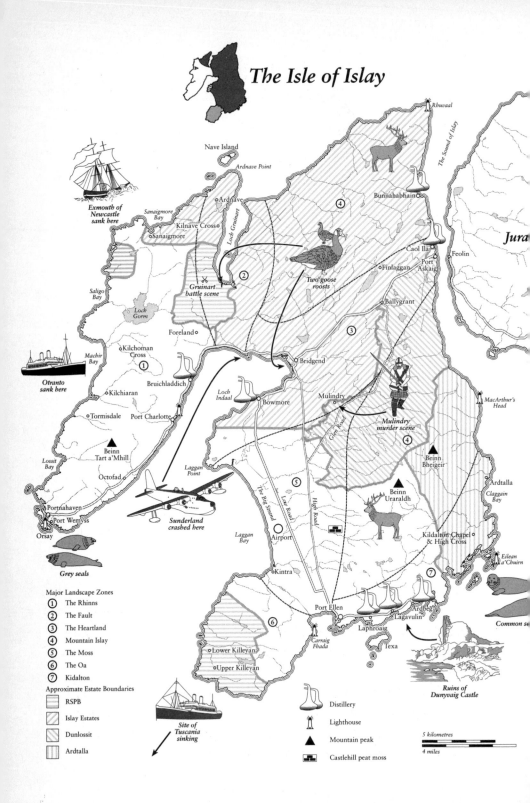

The Isle of Islay

Rhuvaal

The Sound of Islay

Jura

Nave Island

Ardnave Point

Ardnave

④

Bunnahabhain

Exmouth of Newcastle sank here

Sanaigmore Bay

Kilnave Cross

Sanaigmore

②

Caol Ila

Port Askaig

Feolin

Finlaggan

Two'goose roosts

Saligo Bay

Loch Gorm

Foreland

Ballygrant

③

Gruinart battle scene

Machir Bay

Kilchoman Cross

①

Bridgend

Otranto sank here

Bruichladdich

Kilchiaran

Loch Indaal

Bowmore

Mulindry

MacArthur's Head

Port Charlotte

Mulindry murder scene

④

Tormisdale

Beinn Tart a'Mhill

Laggan Point

Beinn Bheigeir

Lossit Bay

Octofad

Sunderland crashed here

⑤

Beinn Uraraldh

Ardtalla

Claggain Bay

Portnahaven

Port Wemyss

Laggan Bay

Airport

High Road

Kildalton Chapel & High Cross

Eilean a'Chuirn

Orsay

Grey seals

Kintra

⑦

Port Ellen

Ardbeg

Lagavulin

Common se

Lower Killeyan

⑥

Laphroaig

Texa

Upper Killeyan

Carraig Fhada

Ruins of Dunyvaig Castle

Major Landscape Zones
① The Rhinns
② The Fault
③ The Heartland
④ Mountain Islay
⑤ The Moss
⑥ The Oa
⑦ Kidalton

Site of Tuscania sinking

Distillery

Lighthouse

Mountain peak

Castlehill peat moss

Approximate Estate Boundaries
RSPB
Islay Estates
Dunlossit
Ardtalla

5 kilometres

4 miles

The Whisky Island

Quiet keys. Dead screens.
One sip: the dusk flight. A mouth,
hot with beating wings.

ON MANY DAYS of the year, you will see nothing. Nothing beyond a grey, clean city dropping away as the swaying aeroplane clambers into the clouds; and then, half-an-hour later, a dark green land, broken by rock, moor and bog, looming out of the cloud vapour as the pilot banks towards a dark, salt-moist runway.

In May, though, on a day of spilling light, this is a journey from compressed time to unfolded time, from urban intensity to lonely Hebridean calm, from the confining geometry of tower blocks to a blue-green archipelago.

The old Shorts SD3-60, a winged box seemingly designed by an ungifted nine-year-old, used to take off with the noisy agitation of a wasp; now the plane is a Saab 340, and it trundles into the sky more calmly. Glasgow, with its sandstone banks, its bus lanes and its tenements, dissipates into lush farmland, a briefly pastoral landscape which swiftly grows sombre as the Bridge of Weir is left behind. Conifers darken the rock; pebbly streams and black ditches incise it; pylons make their bleak, seven-league stride towards the sea. The two little Cumbrae islands are scooped greenly up out of the water to the port side; Bute lies beneath. Rocky, mountainous Arran gleams like a mineral crown out in the Firth of Clyde. The mainland soon surges from the water beneath, though it looks much like another island: this is the dangling tongue of Kintyre, its hillsides combed with ancient peat cuttings and lazy-beds. Low-lying Gigha breaks the water just beyond, a little slip of land which the sea seems ready to lap up at any moment.

In the brilliance of May's sunshine, the plane hangs serendipitously over the Mull of Kintyre, its waters not their habitual turbid grey but a milky jade. There is motion, but there is also stillness; for a moment, this small capsule of sentience is the core of the world, and the passengers and crew bathe in the crystal air which spins about them. The Hebridean flight is briefly Caribbean, Javanese, Moluccan . . . Then the plane turns and banks over Ardmore Point, Islay's first landfall, its quartz sand gleamingly white. For those sitting on the starboard side, the parade of distilleries begins: Ardbeg, Lagavulin, Laphroaig, each announcing itself in stout black lettering of dignified plainness on the white-painted warehouse walls. Over Port Ellen, where the peat smoke from the maltings drifts lazily in the afternoon sun, the plane's aerial trajectory slices the rocky rump of the Oa from the rest of the island. There is water lying in this year's cuttings, down on the moss; before this swiftly moving shadow sweeps over them, they catch reflected sunlight, and glitter briefly. The plane turns and composes itself above Laggan Bay, then creeps stealthily in over the big strand before bumping down on a treacle-dark strip of warm tarmac. The hay sways in the breeze to each side. Even the newly expanded terminal is barely bigger than a village hall; the firemen unload the luggage from the tail and wheel it in on a hand-trolley. The passengers step down, on to Islay.

In every continent, and in most countries of the world, the whisky of Islay is being drunk, now. This island alone provides one-quarter of

Scotland's malt whisky exports. Some is thus sipped neat, and advisedly; but most of it is dissolved in blends – a little trace in a glass of Cutty Sark, a big dash in a Ballantynes, a spoonful or two in every Johnny Walker.

Two Venezuelan oil executives lounge in leather armchairs watching a motor race on television while a multi-coloured parrot flits through the palms outside; a skinny Portuguese and his Galician lover spend a rainy Sunday evening in Braga arranging their postcard collection; a bearded French accountant sits in an aeroplane on the way to a three-month audit in Senegal reading St Augustine. None of them has ever heard of Islay, yet all five are sipping its whisky, and it binds them with threads of pleasure to the world of which all are a part.

Every year, around 25 million litres of whisky (calculated at 40 per cent alcohol by volume) leave the island; if the export and excise revenues on that whisky were to make their way back again, this would be a wealthier part of Britain than Ascot or Henley. As it is, the cars here are old, and nibbled rusty; the houses are small, and not uncommonly damp; little Champagne and less foie gras is sold in Bowmore's Co-op store; there are never quite enough tourists for nine months of the year; farmers have considered suicide.

'That's Ireland over there, you know,' said Jack Phillips to me, as we stood outside the Islay cheese factory one sunny morning in August 1999. He managed the factory – until it closed early the next year, annihilating the island's dairy herds. We looked across to the hazy Antrim hills. Across twenty miles of bright, white-flecked sea; across the journey whisky itself first made, from Ireland to Scotland. Islay was, in all probability, where Scotch was born. This island, with its seven working malt distilleries, all of them creating among the most characterful whiskies available to human sensory apparatus, remains a backbone for blenders to call on, and a lighthouse for whisky lovers. Among malt whiskies, these are more palpably marked with the place of their birth than any others. Savage, stern, uncompromising: Islay is the conscience of Scotch.

It is not just whisky which marks Islay out from all other Hebridean islands. It is one of the most southern (most of the island lies south of Glasgow and Edinburgh), and very nearly the most western of the Inner Hebrides. Few other islands are as fertile as Islay; it has at times been populous. It was the seat of a great medieval sea realm, that of the Lord of the Isles; Lewis, Skye, Mull and the mainland tracts of Ross were all once ruled from Islay. Today it is a quietly resilient community, battered at times by the ruthlessness of economic life, but tenacious and spirited. Whisky may draw our attention to this place; but it is more than merely a whisky island. In the pages which follow, you will find an intimate portrait of each of the island's whiskies, but you will also find a picture of the island itself, its physical fabric, its historical tapestry, its rain, its wind. On Islay, you can leave behind stale metropolitan obsessions, shrill nationalist hysteria, dreary media chatter, the pitiful vacuity of celebrity adulation and hollow, doll-eyed fashion; you can meet people whose faces are lifted by weather, song and struggle rather than by cosmetics and the surgeon's knife; you can find, surrounded by a wilderness of seawater, room to breathe. There is no substitute for making the journey to Islay itself, but for those still waiting for the flight, this book is intended as a diversion . . . with the reek of peat about it.

A word or two on whisky

Fire in the darkness.
Rain patters slates. The promise:
cold bones warmed; eyes lit.

WHAT IS WHISKY? Simple. It is distilled beer. The only way in which the beer brewed to make Scotch whisky differs from the beer which you might have drunk after work last night is that it contains no hops, and is therefore not bitter in any way. (Technically speaking, such beers are defined as 'ales'.)

All of the whisky which comes into being on the island of Islay is malt whisky. That means that the beer from which it is distilled is brewed using one particular cereal grain only: malted barley. When a bottle of malt contains whisky from a lone distillery, it is generally called a 'single malt'. If you blend together a number of different malts, you have what is called a 'vatted malt'.

Whisky need not be distilled from malted barley beer alone; a range of other cereals can be used. Wheat and maize (corn) are two of these; rye is a third, though not in Scotland. When Scotch whisky is principally distilled from wheat and maize, it is known as grain whisky. Most big-brand whiskies, like Johnnie Walker Red Label, Cutty Sark, J&B or The Famous Grouse, are a mixture of grain whisky and malt whisky, usually in a 60–40 mixture. Grain whisky is also distilled differently from malt whisky, using a towering, office-block-sized piece of apparatus called a continuous still. Mixed-grain beer goes in at one end, and a very pure, colourless, high-strength spirit comes trickling ceaselessly out at the other. Grain whisky is more neutral in character than malt whisky, and takes most of its character from the wooden casks in which it is stored.

Grain, malt and blended whisky all qualify as 'Scotch' – provided they have matured in oak casks for at least three years in Scotland, and provided they are bottled at not less than 40 per cent alcohol by volume (henceforth abbreviated to abv).

We can now forget all about grain whisky. Islay means malt, and mostly malt of pungent and reverberative character. Each of Islay's seven major distilleries produces a spirit quite different in character from its neighbours, and some of the distilleries now produce two or even three different styles of spirit. Islay malts are just the kind of thing, in other words, which blenders seek out to give backbone and personality to their blends. Where do their different characters come from?

I don't know. No one does. It's a mystery.

Or, to be more precise, the answer is so complicated as to remain mysterious. For the time being.

When a new distillery is built, the type of malt, the shape of the stills, the way the distillery is run and the casks chosen to age the spirit will make the broad style a predictable one. But precisely what its character will be and exactly how good that spirit will prove is almost wholly unpredictable and a matter of some serendipity. Designing and building a distillery is a gamble. Every distillery is different. It is only after distillation, and after ten or fifteen years' age in wooden casks, that the quality of the spirit will become apparent.

Each of the distillery chapters in this book describes these seven Islay characters in some detail, supported by as much technical analysis as I have been able to extract from their owners. I hope these descriptions will help the reader towards a more intimate understanding of how aroma and flavour in malt whisky are created – though mysteries, be warned, remain. Scotch whisky distillers have been reprehensibly incurious about their craft; they have, historically, resisted research and experiment. Matching precedent and maintaining consistency has been one industry aim; when things have been changed, meanwhile, it has generally been for the purposes of a second aim, which is to cut costs and make more profit for owners and shareholders. I believe a more curious and questing approach could lift the quality of Islay's whiskies higher than it is at present. We do not, yet, have the best of all possible whisky worlds. Complacency benefits no one.

The culture of secrecy which surrounded the Scotch whisky industry until the late 1980s is, happily, dissipating. I have had to ask many questions in researching this book. Most of those who I have asked (and most notably the managers of the seven Islay distilleries) have been enormously helpful, yet some questions remain unanswered. In the majority of cases, this is because the answers are not known, since the research has not yet been done. In a frustrating minority of cases, the answers are known, but the residual culture of Scotch whisky secrecy has kept them locked away in company filing cabinets or computers under the vague excuse of 'commercial confidentiality'. Whisky writers and drinkers are constantly told by distilling companies that flavour is in large part the consequence of still shapes and sizes and distilling practices – yet those same companies sometimes seem unwilling or unable to answer questions about the dimensions of the stills, or provide precise details of those distilling practices. To what end? It is hard to say, since no distillery has ever been, nor could ever be, exactly duplicated.

 This chapter describes how to make malt whisky. Mastering the basics here will help us understand (in later chapters) how Bowmore differs from Bruichladdich, or Lagavulin from Laphroaig.

Let's begin with barley. Raw barley – a handful of grains picked out of the hopper of the roaring harvester in the dust and sunlight of July – would be no use whatsoever to a distiller. Why not? Because it contains starch and not sugar.

Yeasts cannot turn raw barley starch into alcohol. To do so, the yeasts need fermentable sugars. The barley has therefore to be malted.

Malting is a playful deception practised on a barley grain. After an essential post-harvest rest (which the innocent, trusting grain will equate with winter), you moisten it and warm it. The grain thinks that spring rains and the comfort of a sunny day in April have arrived, and it begins to grow. It sends out rootlets (called culms); a nascent grass blade forms inside the grain. Enzymes get to work to turn that starch into the food the growing plant will need.

At that point, you brutally disappoint the grain – by baking it. The process I have just described is arrested. The hopeful rootlets are discarded. The grains, indeed, don't look wildly different to the way they looked before – but they are crunchy, and if you chew a mouthful (as, in visiting a distillery, you may be encouraged to do), you will find them sweet. Yeasts (a microscopic fungus) will gleefully notice much the same thing; they can now make alcohol. So let the brewing of our beer commence: grind the grain, add hot loch water, and soak all those complex, full-bodied and deliciously fermentable sugars out of the malt. This happens in a giant bathtub called a mash tun, and the resulting hot sweet liquid, a kind of nutritious cereal tea, is called wort. The wort travels through a collecting vessel called an underback, and then into a fermenting vessel called a washback. (My apologies for this swarm of technical terms: these and others like them are listed in the glossary at the back of the book, should you want a reference definition at any time.) Then yeast is added – and the washback begins to seethe.

Wait a moment, though: what about barley variety? What about the type of yeast? Isn't the water incredibly important, too? And where does the famous 'peatiness' we all notice in a glass of Lagavulin or Laphroaig come from?

Barley varieties and yeast types do vary in some whisky (or whiskey) cultures, but on Islay all the distilleries are at present using Optic malt, and two standard distilling yeasts called Quest and Mauri (sometimes alone and sometimes in combination). A neutral efficiency is what is sought from both, rather than any distinct stamp of flavour. Barley variety and yeast strains are two matters to which the Scotch whisky industry remains indifferent; this is a state of affairs which I hope will change in the years ahead.

Water, by contrast, is accorded importance by all, and on Islay is prodigiously natural. For five out of Islay's seven distilleries, the water is super-soft and richly peaty: a deep brown in colour and faintly vegetal to the taste. It flows through the heather, leaches out of the bogs, and trickles across the quartzite pebbles which constitute this island's heart before plunging down off the hill to the distillery concerned. In a sixth case (Bruichladdich), all of the above is true save that the pebbles are phyllite and sandstone rather than quartzite.

One of Islay's distilleries, though, is exceptional: Bunnahabhain. Its water source is unpeaty spring water: limpid, bright and colourless, rising through quartzite and dolostone rather than falling as rain then trickling through the vegetation. Do we conclude from this that Bunnahabhain produces Islay's only unpeated whisky?

We do not, for the simple reason that the peat flavour in a whisky does not come from its water. You can make unpeaty whisky using peaty water: Bruichladdich has done it for years. (And so, too, has Caol Ila, though for a whisky which only ever gets used for blending rather than for sale as a single malt.) Whether the peat in the water has any influence at all on the flavour of the whisky is a controversial matter which will be discussed in some of the distillery chapters which follow. 'What is water's effect on the character of the spirit?' Douglas Murray of Diageo, the Scotch whisky giant which owns both Lagavulin and Caol Ila as well as the Port Ellen maltings, sums up the general industry view. 'On a scale of one to one hundred, I would rate it at between one and two.'

Peat flavour does not come from water, then. So where does it come from? The answer is the malt. For thousands of years, peat has been the traditional fuel on Islay, an island with few trees and no coal. Peat was the heat source used to dry the malt – and peat burns smokily. The result was that that smoke (which, as every cigarette smoker should know, is constituted of fine particles of tar) left its trace in the malt. Islay's malts tasted of smoky peat. Drinkers, once they acquired the taste, liked it; so too did blenders, since a dash of Islay malt mixed into their boring grain whisky gave it some character. What was once accidental became deliberate, and the peating of the malt remains an option long after it was no longer necessary. Nowadays, of course, you can specify exactly how peaty you would like your malt to be; peat is a question of recipe, rather than an effect of *terroir* (or 'placeness'). The peatiness of a particular malt is measured in parts per million (ppm) phenols, though you should be aware that there are different measuring methods which give different results: this subject is discussed more fully in the chapters on Peat and on Bruichladdich. Remember, too, that the phenols in the spirit are always lower than they are in the malt, and that they fall further as the spirit is aged. Laphroaig's 40 ppm in the malt become 25 ppm in its new make spirit, for example. They then drop to 8 to 10 ppm in the 10-year-old and 15-year-old, and finish at just 6 ppm in the 30-year-old.

Back to our seething washbacks. After somewhere between 48 hours (Bowmore) and 120 hours (Caol Ila at the weekends), fermentation is finished, and the new beer can be distilled. It is relatively strong: 7 per cent to 9 per cent abv on Islay. As with every other stage of the process, just how quickly or how slowly you ferment the beer, and how clear you allow it to become afterwards, will have an effect on the flavour of the whisky: quick ferments, turbid beer and lower strengths lead to a pungent, spicy character in the spirit, while slow fermentations, very clear beer and higher strengths lead to lightness and finesse. If you visit a distillery and look into a washback, by the way, remind yourself that two-thirds of what you are gazing at will be thrown away during the distillation process – another reason why the water source is perhaps less influential than at first seems likely.

CHATTING WITH COPPER

So: what is distillation? It is the exploitation of a natural phenomenon.

This phenomenon is the fact that different liquids boil at different temperatures. Water, famously, boils at 100°C. Ethanol (alcohol) boils at 78.5°C. If you heat beer to 78.5°C, therefore, the alcohol in it will begin to evaporate, but the water will remain where it is. That alcohol will billow off the warm beer as intoxicating steam. Once this heady steam is cooled, the alcohol will resume its life as a liquid: whisky, in this case.

That is the principle of distillation: gentle heating of an alcoholic liquid, followed by the gathering and the cooling of the steam.

There are, of course, snags. One of them is that ethanol is not the only substance ready to evaporate out of your beer; there are many others, all of which have different boiling points. Methanol, for example, boils at 65°C, and too much of that may leave you blind, as many illicit distillers have found down the centuries to their cost. These undesirable substances need to be separated from the desirable ethanol: purity is the great desideratum. The techniques for doing this have been refined down the years in distilling protocols, as we will find out in a paragraph or two.

A word, too, about another raw material, this time the raw material for most of the distilling equipment: copper. Every malt-whisky stillhouse gleams with copper, often lacquered to a high and beautiful shine. When the stills are puffing away, and the morning sun fills the stillroom, it makes a glorious sight – and the spirity, almost fruity scents and the richly invasive warmth combines with that coppery gleam to give you, the visitor, a sudden moment of joy. Purity, as I said, is the great desideratum, and it is the fine, microscopic hairiness of copper, and its sociable, reactive nature, which makes it such an ideal distilling material. 'If you look at copper under a microscope,' says Douglas Murray, 'it looks like a scouring pad. The result is that, as the spirit vapour passes over it, copper stops that vapour for what we could call a 'chat'. The more slowly the vapour passes over the copper, the more the chemical impurities in the spirit attach themselves to the fine scouring-pad threads. The longer this chat goes on, in other words, the lighter the spirit.'

Malt whisky needs to be distilled twice. Why? Because, technically speaking, the pot stills used for this purpose are crude and ineffective. If obtaining pure alcohol is your aim, then the continuous stills installed in grain-whisky distilleries do a far better job.

Odd – until you realise that pure alcohol is very much not the aim, since pure alcohol would be vodka. What distinguishes malt whisky from vodka is, precisely, its impurities – a bundle of assorted alcohols, esters, aldehydes, phenols and acids which are usually termed 'congeners'. These are precious; these are, indeed, the whole point. And the crude old pot stills, when manipulated with great craft and skill by Islay's stillmen (who are probably at work right now, no matter where in the world or at what time of day you are reading this) are the perfect way to extract just the right bundle of congeners – and eliminate, no less importantly, all the wrong ones. The pot still, if you like, is the bicycle of the distilling world. Technically superseded long ago, but still the greatest and most efficient machine ever invented for the purpose for which it is used.

So what are these two stages? Simple: you do the same job twice. First of all you heat your beer (or 'wash') in what is called a wash still. This process gives you a weak, impure alcoholic beverage called low wines. There is, at this stage, a vast amount of yeasty, alcohol-free leftovers called pot ale (wash stills produce more pot ale than low wines). Most of this, on Islay, goes off to feed the fishes, though Ardbeg's pot ale gets spread on the fields of the island.

You then do the same thing all over again in what is sometimes called a low wines still, but which I will henceforth refer to (for reasons of clarity) as a spirit still. Once again there is a residue, though rather less of it this time, called spent lees. It is mixed with the pot ale before dispersal.

Are the two distilling jobs identical? They are not. Running a wash still is a relatively straightforward operation: you drive off more

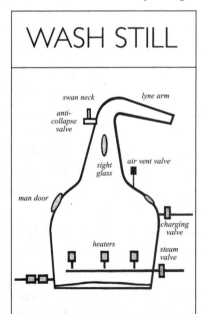

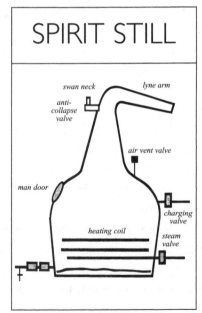

or less every drop of alcohol, plus whatever congeners wish to travel steamily with it, in one operation. This usually begins at around 46 per cent – 50 per cent abv, and finishes at 1 per cent abv or less, giving an average strength of about 21 per cent. The less full you fill your still, and the slower you run it, the finer and lighter in style your final spirit is likely to be.

Running a spirit still is much more complex, since the unwelcome or toxic congeners will be both the first and the last to be distilled; we could casually call these 'baddies'. The desirable alcohol and welcome congeners (or 'goodies') are distilled during the middle part of the run. The standard practical test to detect the end of the baddies and the start of the goodies is to mix equal quantities of water and distillate: if the result is hazy, there are baddies about; but when the result is crystal clear, then you can begin to collect your 'new-make' spirit. The exact point (in terms of alcoholic strength, measured at 20°C) at which you switch on to spirit and later off spirit are known as the cuts, and they vary significantly between distilleries. To make a light, fine, elegant spirit you will once again leave plenty of space in your stills when you fill them, run them slowly, and use relatively narrow cuts towards the high end of the alcoholic spectrum. To make a rich, oily, pungent spirit, you will do the opposite. The narrowest cuts on Islay are those of Bunnahabhain, which comes on to spirit at around 72 per cent and goes off at 64 per cent, though on occasion Bruichladdich's can be as narrow; the broadest cuts are those of Lagavulin, which comes on at 72 per cent and goes off at 59 per cent. Caol Ila is the distillery which cuts on to spirit at the highest point, 76 per cent, running it down to the island's highest cut-off at 65 per cent. So far as I know (though I have not been supplied with the necessary figures for Laphroaig), no stills on the island are filled as full as Lagavulin's spirit stills (95 per cent of capacity) or left as empty as Caol Ila's spirit stills (37–41 per cent of capacity).

We need to take a break for terminology. The precious, salvaged middle part of the distilling run is called the heart, middle cut or spirit cut; it is preceded by the foreshots, sometimes called the heads; and it is followed by the feints, sometimes called the aftershots, tails or tailings. In general, the foreshots are quickly dealt with (foreshot running times on Islay vary from around 10 minutes at Ardbeg and Bunnahabhain to around 45 minutes at Bruichladdich and Laphroaig), while feints take much longer to run off (up to 4 hours 30 minutes at Lagavulin).

What happens, by the way, to the baddies – in other words the combination of foreshots and feints? This is a prize question. The answer is that they are recycled: they are added to the low wines, and redistilled (a fact which in turn explains why the usual strength of the charge of a spirit still is around 26 per cent or 27 per cent, whereas the low wines themselves only measure 21 per cent; it is the foreshots and feints which boost the strength of the charge).

But what then? Surely, after a while, these foreshots and feints would accumulate, forming a surly and toxic gang?

I must have asked this question a dozen times, and I have never had a wholly satisfactory answer; indeed I am beginning to believe that even those of great chemical experience don't fully understand everything which is going on inside a spirit still, let alone a reactive slow-wit like me. The fact is, though, that no such surly and toxic gang ever makes its presence felt. So far as I understand the matter, some of the undesirable elements are reconverted into desirable alcohols; some eventually leave in the spent lees residue in the spirit still; some form into a doubtful sludge which is periodically removed from the tank in which foreshots and feints are collected (called the feints receiver); and some eventually pass into the spirit itself. 'We cannot claim,' says Douglas Murray, 'that all "toxic" alcohols are completely removed and small (very small) levels will remain in the spirit – but at levels which would not be considered harmful.' Indeed these traces may well be vital components of what we, as drinkers, recognise as 'distillery character'. 'After a still has been in production for a while,' says Douglas, 'the chemistry becomes balanced and amount of flavour enhancement and off-flavour removal gets to the point where the true unique distillery character is produced.'

You may, by this stage, be under the impression that all stills are the same. They aren't. They vary enormously in size and shape and those differences will, just like everything else, play their part in making each malt whisky unique. Let's start, though, with the similarities before we move on to the differences.

As the name 'pot still' suggests, all malt-whisky stills look round and ample at the bottom, and grow narrower as they get to the top. They contain steam coils or pans (and sometimes both) to heat the liquid (wash or low wines) with which they are charged. They also have vents – partly for safety reasons, to stop stills collapsing or exploding, but partly also because some highly volatile compounds in the wash or low wines refuse to condense back to a liquid at all, and so have to be vented either before or during distillation.

Once the stillman heats the coils and pans, distillation begins. Vapour begins to rise, like steam off hot soup. Later, the process may get more boisterous and jacuzzi-like, especially in wash stills – which tend to foam in the early stages. Some wash stills have little porthole-like windows through which the excitable wash may be viewed, and devices called 'switchers' to keep it calm and stop it frothing over the top of the still. If it does go charging over the top in liquid form (this is called carryover), the stillman may be in trouble.

Ideally, the vapour rises steadily up to the neck of the still, then passes into a pipe called the lyne arm (sometimes also called a lye pipe), which carries it to the condenser where it will be cooled back into a liquid. Simple, no? Well, it would be, were there not ten thousand minute variants on this process.

CINDERELLA IN THE STILLROOM

There are three fundamental still shapes (see diagram). Plain stills are the most common and will, given a plump pot and a broad neck, provide the least copper contact. It's a hard generalisation to make, though, since some plain stills (like Bruichladdich's spirit stills) have

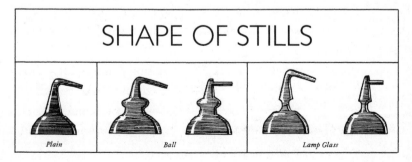

SHAPE OF STILLS

Plain   Ball   Lamp Glass

very long, thin necks which will provide extensive copper contact. In principle, ball stills and lamp-glass stills provide more copper contact than plain stills. Not only that, but they also provide what is called 'reflux'. In other words, they offer a mechanism by which rising vapour is held in check and sent back down again before rising once more – and enjoying, as it does so, more of a chat with the copper. In the case of wash stills, too, the lamp-glass and ball designs allow the stillman more time to react during the initially foamy phase. There are no ball stills on Islay, however, and the only lamp-glass stills are found at Ardbeg (both wash and spirit) and Laphroaig (spirit alone).

The overall size of a still is very important, too, with bigger stills (providing they are not charged too full) providing the most copper contact and the lightest styles of spirit, while smaller stills (especially when charged full) tend to produce heavier, more pungent spirits. The biggest wash stills on the island are those of Bunnahabhain (35,356 litres total capacity) and the biggest spirit stills at Caol Ila (29,549 litres total capacity), while the smallest spirit stills are probably those of Laphroaig (the company was not able to provide the total capacity of the 'teapots' and visitors should note that the figures which have been shown on the signs at the distillery over many years are a fiction: they claimed a capacity of 3,630 litres but the charges alone are 4,700 litres). Without knowing the capacity of Laphroaig's wash stills it is hard to say whose are the smallest on the island, but it seems likely to be either Laphroaig's or Lagavulin's (whose wash stills have a total capacity of just 12,300 litres). The squattest stills are at Ardbeg.

Lyne arms, naturally, vary as well. They may run horizontally from the still; they may rise up from the still; or they may descend from the still. Those which rise will provide a measure of reflux, as you might imagine, depending on how steep an angle is adopted (up to about 30°); those which are horizontal will provide little reflux; and those which descend (to about 20°) will provide no reflux at all, and may even entail carryover. More reflux emphasises lightness and finesse; no reflux and the chance of carryover implies a heavier, nuttier style. 'The vapour from the still is hunting the coldness of the condensers,' says Iain McArthur of Lagavulin, one of the most experienced distillery workers on the island. 'When the lyne arm falls, it is getting siphoned over to some extent. When the lyne arm rises, the vapour has to be pushed over.' The rising lyne arms on Islay are those of Ardbeg, Bowmore (spirit still only) and, particularly, Laphroaig; while the most steeply descending lyne arm on the island belongs to Lagavulin's wash still. Both Bunnahabhain's stills and Bowmore's wash still have straight lyne arms, and the rest descend gently.

That is not, though, the end of the gripping lyne-arm story. Those visiting Ardbeg will discover a bulbous growth hanging off its spirit-still lyne arm, with a tube dropping away from it: this is called (descriptively) a purifier, and is a way of organising a massive dose of reflux every time – to the extent that manager Stuart Thomson says that his spirit is distilled two-and-a-half times. See the Ardbeg chapter for more details.

And so to bed – which, for newly liberated spirit vapour, means a condenser. That is where, in the close confinement of a water-cooled copper tube, the hot spirit vapour turns back into liquid. That is the end of the distilling process.

Poor old condensers. No one knows their internal architecture, not even the distillery managers (they are usually ordered and fitted by the engineers of head office). When visitors troop through the stillrooms on distillery tours, they all gawp at the beautiful stills, but no one pays any attention to those Cinderellas of the whole process, the condensers. Even I feel guilty about them, since despite great efforts I have been able to marshal few statistics about the condensers in Islay's distilleries. For all that, they matter.

Copper contact, as we have discovered, is very important in creating the distinctive characteristics of a malt, and huge amounts of copper contact take place inside condensers. Bruichladdich's, for example, weigh two tonnes each, and contain 210 one-inch copper tubes. No wonder a new one costs three times as much as my car did: £20,000. Their two aspects of greatest consequence are the number and size of tubes inside them (more tubes of smaller bore will once again emphasise finesse and elegance), and the temperature at which they operate, known as the 'recovery temperature'. A higher recovery temperature, as at Caol Ila, will mean slower condensing, more copper contact, and more lightness and finesse; a cooler recovery temperature, as at Lagavulin, will mean quick condensing, less copper contact, and a heavier, sturdier style. It follows that distilleries producing a heavy, punchy spirit prefer to operate in the winter, when recovery temperatures can easily be kept down, whereas those producing lighter spirits are happier with the naturally higher recovery temperatures which summer furnishes. There is, by the way, a primitive condensing alternative still used at some distilleries (like Dalwhinnie or Cragganmore) called a worm tub; there are, though, no worm tubs on Islay.

By the end of the distilling process, as you see, the character equation is already a complex one. Hard to summarise, too, since it is the totality of details which matters rather than individual facts. We'd all agree that Laphroaig is pungent, I would imagine, so it comes as no surprise that its stills are small and (presumably) amply charged. Yet Laphroaig's rising lyne arms and lamp-glass spirit stills are providing reflux and finesse, reinforced by the relatively high recovery temperature which its dual-condensing system provides, and the high number of tubes inside its condensers. Even a pungent spirit needs some lightening finesse, in other words, just as the lightest of spirits would be rather dull without a note or two of pungency buried in it somewhere.

INTO THE FOREST

But the story isn't over yet. The spirit now has to go into an oak cask. Neat – in the case of Bruichladdich, which fills its casks at distilling strength. All the other distilleries on the island, though, add a little water in order to fill at a standard 63.5 per cent – the reason being that casks of whisky have traditionally been traded among companies for blending purposes, and swapping casks of different strengths would make these transactions problematically complicated. (Bruichladdich does not intend to trade in this way but aims to become a 'malt only' distillery.)

Estimates vary as to how important the wood is in the character of the final spirit, but even the conservative reckon it accounts for around 40 per cent of the finished malt's character, while some tree-hugging radicals believe it may be as high as 70 per cent. Wood matters for flavour, and it matters for time, too: malt whisky takes just six days to make, but ten years or more to mature.

Every drop of Scotch, including all the malt made on Islay, is aged in a second-hand cask. For me, this is the most astonishing whisky fact in this or any whisky book. Every drop of bourbon is aged in a brand new cask, and much Cognac and Armagnac are aged in brand new casks, too; most of the world's great wines also climb into new wooden barrels at some point along their journey to the customer. But Scotch is aged in the leftovers.

Is this due to laziness? Lots of second-hand casks are available, after all, since bourbon must, by law, be aged in new wood; no need, therefore, for the Scots to go to the trouble of getting hold of new ones. Is it parsimony? Second-hand American casks cost less than a sixth of what new French ones cost. Or is it, by contrast, a happy accident? Yes, using second-hand wood is easier, cheaper and more environmentally sound than using new wood, but it is also perfect for endowing Scotch malt whisky (and Scotch whisky in general) with the subtlety and nuance which distinguish it. According to Diageo's wood expert Andrew Ford, the company has carried out experiments ageing malt in new American oak. 'Within a year,' he says, 'it is woody and over the top.' Using a huge spectrum of second-hand casks (Diageo alone has 7.4 million of them ageing its whiskies at any one time) creates a kind of dappling effect. It tames and mellows the spirit, speckling it with the extraordinarily allusive notes which wood can provide, but the fact that the most insistent of these have already been leached out in America or in Spain allows the distillery character to emerge, embellished but uncompromised.

There are, of course, drawbacks to the system. Every distillery manager hates being sent poor quality wood (exhausted casks, many times re-used; heavily sulphured casks; damaged casks) since he or she knows that the carefully distilled spirit will fail to live up to expectations if stored in such containers. There is no shortage of disappointing wood used by the Scotch whisky industry, as anyone who has ever tasted a range of cask samples will know. Even the good casks are unpredictable; no two casks are ever truly alike. If new wood were used, this would not be the case; there would be a greater measure of predictability in the ageing stocks. The use of second-hand casks creates a huge amount of work for managers and blenders, since every cask has always to be nosed and assessed before use; coopers are kept busy, too, in looking after, repairing and rejuvenating this vast wooden junkyard. Yet the fact that Scotch blends and malts are as popular as they are around the world is no accident, and the subtlety and finesse which are the legacy of second-hand wood has its role in this.

What is happening during the eight to forty years which whisky passes in a cask? Two things.

The first thing is that the whisky is breathing. This controlled oxidation (not too little, not too much) has a mellowing effect of its own, and can add both complexity and apparently 'fruity' notes to the whisky. Too much, of course, can flatten a whisky completely, which is why some very old single casks can be dully disappointing, and why blenders tend to 'freshen' very old whiskies with younger ones.

The second activity is that the whisky is making exchanges with the wood. Wood contains, among many other substances, hemi-cellulose, which adds sweetness and colour to a spirit; lignin, which adds complexity and can evoke vanilla (artificial vanilla essence, indeed, can be made from wood); and tannins, which add a textural dimension. The charring which American casks receive (and which Scottish coopers reimpose on the casks when they are rejuvenated) emphasises these characteristics, helps deepen colour, and assists in the removal of sulphur compounds. (The lighter toasting which European casks receive makes them less immediately active.) These are all additive effects; but wood can also remove the more unpleasant notes of immaturity from a malt, and act interactively, too, to form acetal, a volatile compound also used in perfumery.

Ah; I nearly forgot the angels and their celebrated share. We could say that a third thing is happening while a malt is passing those long years in dark silence: it is evaporating. In warm, dry America or Cognac, the water evaporates more quickly than the alcohol, therefore the strength of a bourbon or a Cognac rises with age. In cool, damp Scotland, the alcohol evaporates more quickly than the water, therefore the strength sinks with age. In both cases, though, there is some concentration of flavour due to evaporation; since Scotch whisky casks are not topped up, the oxidation effects also increase with age. British

Customs and Excise allow distillers to write off 2 per cent of their inventory (lost to the angels) per year.

There are, of course, different types of cask in use to age the malts on Islay, and each will have a different effect. The fundamental distinction is between ex-bourbon casks and ex-sherry casks. Bourbon casks are made of American oak, *Quercus alba*, whereas sherry casks are made of European oak, *Quercus robur*. The fact that sherry casks have contained sherry of various sorts (dry, yeasty Fino; nutty Amontillado; dark, tangy Oloroso or super-sweet, viscous Pedro Ximenez) is, of course, important, but probably not as important as the fact that toasted European oak will, over long years of ageing, stamp a different character on a malt, making it darker, more brooding, more dense and more fruity than will the often flamboyantly sweet yet light American charred oak, with its vanilla and coconut characters.

Casks, of course, come in different sizes. The American standard barrel contains 180–200 litres; these are often broken down before shipment to Scotland, and when they arrive are remade into hogsheads or dump hogsheads (250 litres). Note, though, that the remade casks are given new ends which are untoasted and uncharred: the effect is therefore different to that of an unbroken barrel. The traditional sherry cask is a 500-litre butt; puncheons also contain around 500 litres, but are slightly rounder in shape than the elongated butts. Since most sherry casks used for ageing Scotch today are commissioned and specially prepared in Spain, ex-sherry hogsheads also now exist.

The malt stays in the barrel for ten years or more; the barrel could then be used again, for what I term in this book, for reasons of clarity, a second fill (though the industry term is a refill). Another decade passes, and that same barrel could be filled a third time (second refill) or even a fourth (third refill). By this point, forty years after its original emigration, it has little left to give to a whisky, and there is no point in giving it a fifth fill. Ready for the bonfire or the garden plants? Not necessarily. It could, at that point, go off back to the cooperage to be rejuvenated. To have its insides scraped back to white wood, in other words, followed by a new charring session. It would then, suddenly, have a lot more to give – and back it goes into the cycle as a rejuvenated cask, ready to serve for another four fills and four decades. In theory, it could then be rejuvenated twice more – giving any cask a potential life expectancy in Scotland of 160 years, though in truth most will fall apart long before this. Even so, American oak casks only spend four years in America whereas they can look forward to at least 50 years in Scotland. Sherry casks can be rejuvenated, too, though when this happens it is not charring which counts; instead, they must be filled with sherry for at least four months before being used for whisky again. When you take into account all of these different life-stages of a cask, plus the fact that they might be made of American or European oak to start with, we are faced with another of malt whisky's complex equations. Diageo alone has 29 different wood bar codes in its maturation software.

When a second-hand cask is used for the first time in Scotland, it will have most to give to a whisky. A smaller cask, too, will have more to give to a whisky than a larger one. All Laphroaig, for example, is now aged in first-fill ex-bourbon American standard barrels, imported whole: that's a recipe for maximum wood influence. Lagavulin, by contrast, goes into third-fill American remade hogsheads: that's a recipe for much more discreet wood influence. Overall, a striking change in wood use for Islay whiskies over the last half-century has been the decline of sherry: only Bowmore (around 14 per cent), Bruichladdich (around 25 per cent) and Bunnahabhain (around 10 per cent) are still using more than 'the odd cask' of sherry-wood. As I prepared this book, I had a chance to taste from many different warehouse casks at all seven distilleries, and many of the casks which are seared into my mind as producing whisky of superb quality . . . were ex-sherry casks. I greatly regret the disappearance of sherry casks in general from Islay, and I hope they return.

What of the future? Every malt whisky drinker is aware of the explosion of wood 'finishes' over the last decade. This trend has been led by Glenmorangie, whose finishes have made choosing a bottle of malt whisky an even more complex affair than it was before – though with that complexity has come a sense of fun, discovery and excitement. What is a finish? This means the transfer of whisky from an ordinary, moderately active cask into a very active, highly characterful cask for the last few months of its maturation. Those months stamp the malt with a distinctive personality twist derived from the cask. 'Finish', by the way, is not a universally accepted term: Diageo calls this technique 'double maturation', and uses it for the Distiller's Edition version of Lagavulin, which spends what manager Donald Renwick calls 'months rather than years' in butts which formerly contained the dark, unctuously sweet Pedro Ximenez sherry. Bowmore is the other main practitioner of this art on Islay at present: its Darkest is finished in sherry wood for two years after 12 in bourbon wood, while Dawn is finished in the same way in port casks and Dusk in Bordeaux wine casks. The highly creative Bruichladdich has also been using a range of rum and wine casks for ageing its spirit since 2000, and it would be surprising if Glenmorangie-owned Ardbeg wasn't up to something similar, too. Time will tell.

EMBRACING THE SKY

So much for wood – but still the character equation isn't finished. The last few paragraphs have focused on the micro-location of the malt, locked into its aromatic wooden prison. What, though, about the macro-location, the place those casks are stored?

There is no more controversial question on Islay than this, so let me summarise the two sides of the argument as fairly as I am able. As you will find out in Chapter Five, Islay's weather is distinctive. It is relatively mild (rarely hot, rarely frosty), highly changeable (four seasons in a day), splendidly wet (between 40 and 60 inches of rain, or around 100 to 150 centimetres, every year), and often stormy. Islay is also an island surrounded by large tracts of seawater, and its prevailing wind blows from the west, where there is no land at all for several thousand miles. Most of the distillers on the island believe that storing whisky in these conditions on Islay for between eight and 40 years will mark the spirit in some way or other. All of the distilleries except two, therefore, claim to mature their proprietory malt from start to finish on Islay (though Ardbeg specifies that its malt may leave the island after ten years).

The two exceptions are Caol Ila (which isn't even filled into cask on the island, but leaves in bulk by road tanker) and Lagavulin (which stores considerably less than 50 per cent of its malt on the island). This is partly for historical reasons: Diageo used to have extensive storage facilities in Campbeltown just across the water on the Kintyre Peninsula, and it also used to own a number of warehouses in Port Charlotte (some have been converted in the Youth Hostel and Wildlife Centre, while the remainder are now owned by Bruichladdich). These locations made sense in the days when distilleries were principally serviced by deep-bellied little boats called puffers. All the casks left the distillery by water, and it was no trouble for the puffer to pootle round a bay or two. In the era of lorry transport, Kintyre in particular made no sense whatsoever, so warehousing in Central Scotland became the corporate (and logistically savvy) solution.

Diageo's experts say that they have compared Islay ageing with mainland ageing and (in the words of Andrew Ford) 'We can't find a difference.' Those who do all their ageing on Islay swear that there is a difference. They point out that Islay is a place where the sea fills the sky, and malt whisky (never, remember, topped up in its cask) embraces that marine air, day and night, for a decade or more. Such a long embrace cannot pass undetected. You, the malt-whisky drinker, must decide who to believe.

Whatever the analytical or sensorial truth, there is also a philosophical and emotional dimension to this question. You buy, let's say, a bottle of Caol Ila's fine 18-year-old from the Islay section of your whisky shop, take it home, open it, pour a dram, and sit down to enjoy it by the fire. If, as you sip it, you leaf through this book only to discover that it has spent just two weeks on Islay compared with 17 years and 50 weeks scattered about various warehouses in Central Scotland, and that all the water used to bring it down to its bottling strength came out of a Central Scotland tap before being demineralised, will you really be satisfied that it is indeed an 'Islay malt'? Personally, I would like to see legislation to ensure that anything calling itself 'single malt' is actually stored throughout its maturation period at its distillery of origin. Which means on Islay, of course, for Islay malts.

Bruichladdich, typically, has upped the ante even further by building its own bottling line. Its malt has thus become the first on Islay to pass its entire life on the island, from the first drop of rain water percolating off the heather flowers on the hill until the last drop of malt is dripped into the bottle before sealing. The 'distillery with attitude' has also implicitly challenged its rivals by becoming the first on the island to bottle its entire range without chill filtering. This self-explanatory procedure prevents malts from becoming hazy once in bottle, though comparisons show that it also robs malts of some of their textural unction and complexity of flavour. More and more malts are now being bottled without chill filtering, including cask-strength versions from those other Islay distilleries which offer them. Abandoning chill-filtering entirely, though, means that the entire range has to be at 46 per cent abv or above to avoid haze problems.

And now . . . over to you. Each of the distillery chapters which follows will detail the complex equation detailed above, filling it out with exemplary flesh. So much for theory.

It is empty, of course, without practice – which is why, as you tackle each chapter, I urge you to arm yourself with a bottle of the Islay malt in question, pour yourself a glass, and only then begin reading.

CHAPTER ONE

Landfall

Dawn light on drenched grass.
Always – the ocean wind: hunched
trees, sung homes, scoured lives.

I WOKE, THIS morning, on the far north-western edge of Europe. Nothing separates Islay and Labrador but the liquid body, moody and restless, of the North Atlantic. The air from the west, too, is sleet-scraped, rain-washed, mist-nourished; only water droplets, in a fan of forms, divide two distant continents. You can feel, as you lie in bed, the shelf edge close at hand; it's not hard, here, to recall the anxiety of those who knew the earth to be square. From where we sleep, London, Paris and Frankfurt are elementally indistinguishable: cities of the plain, stiff with concrete, maggoty with traffic, noisy with need. Here is elsewhere.

Having dressed, I walked outside – and remembered the Aegean. It was a calm morning in mid-November. The sun had just crossed the peaks which lie to the east of the island, unrolling a great golden avenue across the long Atlantic bay of Loch Indaal. The sea to each side of this golden way formed a blue field across which tremulous currents, or the hazards of a quiet breeze, had left sheep tracks. Rock-mass silhouettes in foreground and background cut the sky in a thousand places, and sliced and rearranged the sea into as many coves and inlets, roads and reaches. Why does the stony maze of the Hebrides resemble the scattered seed of the Sporades, the broken spine of the Dodecanese, or the star-fallen chaos of the Ionian islands? Drain the sea and you would see. When water meets a naturally mountainous land, this is the result: a coastline nibbled, fragmented and broken; a sea rock-studded. Greece and Western Scotland are close topographical cousins, distinguished principally by rain, which is why one steps out into the mist in soft green while the other walks naked in brilliant sun.

One of Scotland's many treasures is the fact that it possesses 163 noteworthy islands, and Islay is just one of these. It is not the most southern, and certainly not the most northern. It is neither the biggest nor the smallest, nor the highest nor the lowest; others lie further out into the Atlantic, and others nestle closer to the mother land. An average island, then?

No: Islay has long been styled the 'Queen of the Hebrides'. Rugged Mull and bleak Harris have every right to be jealous of its tracts of fine farming land, while treeless Orkney and distant, northerly Shetland's envy for its relatively mild climate needs little explanation. The snows lie for far longer on lumpy, neighbouring Jura, whose human population has never rivalled Islay's, though the deer roam more thickly there. The Lords of the Isles chose well, both politically and agriculturally, when they decided on Islay to administer their sea kingdom from, as we will find out in Chapter Two.

And, of course, Islay has whisky. There are no certainties here, but it seems probable that the art of distillation reached Scotland from Ireland, and only Kintyre is closer to Antrim than Islay. Macbeth is a name synonymous for most of us, thanks to Shakespeare's paciest play, with murder-stoked ambition, stone-hearted infanticide and a catastrophic dinner party; yet history cast the Macbeths (or Beatons) in an altogether kindlier role: as hereditary doctors to the Lords of the Isles. Whisky was a medicine before it became a recreational drug, and it is possible that it was on Islay that use of this particular medicine was refined. Whatever the truth, it is certain that during the whisky jungle-warfare of the nineteenth and twentieth centuries, where only the fittest distilleries survived, Islay finished the race far ahead of any other island, with seven in business and a great eighth (Port Ellen) just lost. No ordinary seven, either, fashioned merely to slake the oceanic thirst of bulk blenders; but seven of the best.

The purpose of this chapter is to land you on this island, and to show you around. First, though, how do you get there?

You start from Scotland's wet western capital, Glasgow. ('On a clear day,' a joshing Glaswegian once told me, 'you can see your own furniture.') From Glasgow, you head west. The road is a long and winding one; the journey by air is much shorter and simpler. If you draw a direct line from Glasgow to Port Ellen on Islay, you will find that land is succeeded by sea three times, which is why the road to Islay heads north-west for 40 miles out of Glasgow despite the fact that the island actually lies to the south of the city.

It is a journey into wind and mildness. I have left a late-December Glasgow in frost and crossed the 'Rest and Be Thankful' pass which links Glen Croe and Glen Kinglas wearing dark glasses against the sparkling snow, only to watch the presence of the great sea eventually transform that frozen water into a sweet, sodden softness by the time Islay drew near.

There are three places to step on to the island's soil. The ferry, depending on its destiny, may make its way up the Sound of Islay and dock nimbly at the snug little cove of Port Askaig. (The Jura ferry makes its way from Islay to Jura here, too, so this is the crossing those bound for Jura choose.) The second ferry route takes you to the smoky, solemn village of Port Ellen, the axial point between the pretty Kidalton coast with its three distilleries, and the lonely Oa (pronounced 'Oh') with its piping birds and its sad memories. If you land by plane, by contrast, you will find yourself in the middle of Islay's largest peat bog, the Machrie. Depending on the wind direction, the final approach is either low over the sea and across the brown-stained sand; or down from the high land at the island's heart, skimming the Leorin Lochs and casting a shadow over the black glinting puddles in the peat, setting the bog cotton and the reeds waving.

It has been said before, but in its overall outline, Islay resembles a witch. This witch has a fierce, long and resolute chin which juts out into the Atlantic; she has a small nose, a thin neck and a small, peaked cap. Her back is inevitably humped, though this hump culminates in a point. She is stout-bodied, but her hands have been gathered together to form a little fist, and her short legs seem to have been bundled into a sack. Should you wish for a naming of parts, here they are. The chin culminates at Portnahaven; the nose is at Coull; and the peaked cap at Ardnave. The lighthouse at Rhuvaal marks the pointed summit of her hump, while her fists are gathered together at Laggan Point. Those short, stumpy legs are hidden away in the sack called the Oa. Kidalton and Ardtalla mark her unspeakable nether regions. And thus, cat-less and with no sign of a broomstick, she is crouched for eternity, ready to meet the Atlantic and face whatever the jaunty hateful sea cares to throw at her.

In previous lives, this witch was beheaded; time has healed her. That western appendage of the island which resembles her long, chinny head is called the Rhinns or Rinns (meaning 'promontory'). It was once a separate island to Islay, with a sea channel drowning the lowlands of the witch's neck. Geologically the Rhinns is different to the rest of the island; some of its rocks are much older. The southern part of the Rhinns, indeed, brings up to the wide Islay sky some of the older rocks on the earth's surface. They came into being 1,800 million years ago, a period of time which altogether defeats the imagination. The English Channel, for example, did not exist 8,000 years ago; England was then a part of France and the European mainland. The stone of the southern Rhinns coming into being is 225,000 times more ancient an event. Another way to put it is to imagine the earth's history as a 24-hour day. Human beings have evolved in the last 8 seconds of that day alone; even the dinosaurs didn't appear until 22:48 (and they lasted just 51 minutes). These rocks, by contrast, date back to shortly after lunch.

What are they? Dark green meta-gabbro and pink syenite, though weather and lichen combine to dull this potentially attractive colour combination. They formed far underneath the earth's surface, and the incomputable hazards of geological chance have brought them to the surface here. Don't go looking for fossils in the rocks on the

Portnahaven foreshore, though: not only did they form many miles beneath the earth's crust, but they predate life itself. The earth, then, was a purely mineral affair.

The northern Rhinns (the upper part of the witch's head) is old, too, though not as old as the ancient south. Most of its rocks are based on much crushed and deformed sea sediments, and include what is perhaps Islay's most beautiful rock, phyllite: a soft, finely foliated rock of grey or verdigris colour which glitters alluringly in sunlight. The etymology recalls leaves: think, too, of a mouthful of filo pastry. This mineral equivalent was created not by flour and brushed oil, but by mud and massive tectonic copulations.

The rest of the island – the witch's body – is younger still, though in terms of the history of the world we are still dealing with an old and tired land which has endured for 600 million years. As with the northern Rhinns, the minerals which form most of Islay began their existence on the bottom of an ocean, but disappeared later, crushed beneath a monstrous weight of newer rock. The crushing involved cooking: sand became . . . not glass, but not unglasslike either. It became quartzite (a quartz-rich sandstone). This tough rock makes most of the island. It is customary, indeed, to cap gateposts on the island with lumps of white quartz, which resemble mud-streaked gobbets of lard. On the south of the island, at the entrance to the Kidalton estate, an entire cottage has been made of quartz boulders. Just the place, you would say, for a witch to perfect reptilian recipes, though Quartz Cottage is, in fact, the home of an admired accountant. There is naturally much more than quartzite on the rest of Islay; you'll find further caresses of beautiful phyllite; nourishing limestone in the centre of the island; dull grey sandstone around Bowmore; outcrops of jolly slate and shale; sudden dykes and dramatic intrusions in the south. The fundamental geological fact, though, is that Islay is two islands glued together.

What did the gluing? Geologists define a 'fault' as a fracture along which two planes of rock bump and grind in a stressful embrace, and it is the Loch Gruinart Fault (a slice clean through the witch's neck) which brought the Rhinns into contact with the rest of the island. Islay's antique mineral constituents have, unsurprisingly, had a fidgety life. One theory holds that at the time when the sandy sea-bottom sediments which were later to form Islay's quartzite were quietly accumulating, the Rhinns itself was already part of the precursor continent which became South America, Africa and Australia (Gondwana). At the same moment, most of Northern Scotland was part of the precursor continent which eventually became North America (Laurentia) – and proto-Europe (Baltica) was tens of thousands of miles away from either. What a difference 600 million years of rock-shunting can make.

What does all of this mean for the landscape, the Islay that we know and can journey around today? To help lend the land a character palpable to those who might never have visited, I will divide the island up into seven landscape zones. That once-separate island of the Rhinns would be one, and the reeds and sands of the collapsed Fault another. The Heartland may deprive you of a sea view, but it is there you will find the grandest farming land (and, not coincidentally, most of the limestone). Mountain Islay is the fourth, largest and emptiest zone: a place of watchers and listeners, of eagles and deer, dominating the eastern half of the island. The boggy Moss lies adjacent to Mountain Islay, taking its water and letting it lie among the shy sundews, gentle milkworts and stoic sphagnums, composing peat. Finally come Islay's two last, contrasting landscape zones: the lonely, bleak, raven-haunted Oa, protruding like a high rock battleship into the Atlantic; and cosier, lichen-laden Kildalton, certainly the prettiest part of Islay. Let's begin in the west.

INTO THE OCEAN: THE RHINNS

Even those who know nothing of the geological history which I have outlined above might consider the Rhinns a world of its own, an island apart. Once you turn west out of Bridgend, the green and woody hamlet which lies at the head of Loch Indaal, you sense that something has changed. There soon begins to be a clearness and an openness about the landscape; you are leaving the brooding mass of upland Islay behind you. While summer clouds often cling to the mountains, the

Rhinns, and particularly its south-western tip, tends to bask in sunshine. If Islay could be said to have a corniche, then it is the road you find yourself on. The fifteen miles from Bridgend to Portnahaven cling as if infatuated to the sea loch. At first, and especially at low tide, the water will lie some distance from you, across marshy, tussocky flats where hundreds of barnacle geese endure cold, howling nights in winter, and over tidal sand bars where salt-hungry sheep and cows wander with the delicate amazement of urban picnickers come summer. You pass some of Islay's more picturesque cottages, and soon find yourself moving across a grassland which occasional gashes in the turf reveal to be former pebble beach towards the sea. There is livestock here at all seasons, and these sheep in particular seem unfazed by traffic, as if assured that speeding metal will always recognise the superior rights of hooves and wool. At night, with hundreds of quiet acres to choose for a few peaceful hours, a sizeable minority of ewes will perversely choose this road verge for their masticating doze between a late dinner and an early breakfast, as if soothed by the occasional rush of headlights and the rising drone of engines.

The road draws near to the water at a tragic spot called Blackrock (see page 166), then crests a headland and settles down for a long sinuous curve round a bright beach called Tràigh an Luig (Strand of the Hollow). This is a fine place to pull off the road and doze in the sunlight, for the turf on the foreshore is firm enough not to bog cars, even in wet weather. I have seen dogs walked in storms, here, their owners driving dryly behind them. At the back of the beach, there are low, shrub-capped cliffs over which hunting buzzards often hover; those cliffs are composed of the gravels and sand dumped by the icy glaciers which covered Islay for most of the last 80,000 years.

Bruichladdich is the first of the three major coastal settlements of the Rhinns; Port Charlotte and eventually Portnahaven with its little twin hamlet Port Wemyss follow. These are all places for those who love light, for there is nothing to clip or trim the huge sky above, while in front of you the widening sea loch busies itself about its reflective work at all moments. The result is an endless narrative of Hebridean changeability. Bruichladdich faces Bowmore across the loch, and on a squally day the two villages see each other then lose each other repeatedly. The view from the Bruichladdich distillery office resembles that from the bridge of a ship, though it is weather-fronts which provide the motion rather than a grinding ship's screw.

Port Charlotte looks out at Laggan Point, the witch's fists, and at the often-dark, shadowy mass of the Oa beyond: gold, silver and lead fill the early mornings as the sun climbs, now cloud-shrouded, now unveiled, spilling across the water. The hills of Antrim (Islay is closer to Ireland than to Glasgow) loom out of the sea on a breezy day, too. Port Charlotte is something of a cultural centre for Islay, in that it is home both to the excellent Museum of Islay Life, and to Islay's Wildlife Information Centre; the Port Charlotte Hotel (providing Islay's most comfortable accommodation and some of its best food and drink) and the Lochindaal Hotel (an intermittently rollicking pub with a great musical tradition) add to the sense of community there.

The road down to Portnahaven, despite its grand 'A' status billing, grows quickly slender after Port Charlotte and is often single-track; gloomy conifer plantations, planted for tax breaks rather than in anticipation of a timber return, occupy much of the gentle hill land above the road, while on the seaward side some moist fields of grazing roll swiftly down to the waves. Islay's most celebrated murder took place here at the Ellisters in 1698, when John McVeir and his confederates strangled a widow (for her money) and then pushed a witness into the sea (for her silence); McVeir was executed in Inveraray, and his severed right hand was returned to Islay for public display at the tollbooth at Kilarrow 'till it rot or wear away'. This was also the farming home of the brilliant Lincolnshire ornithologist Rod Dawson who, after his tragically early death in 1977 at just 34 years old, was buried near the summit of the Rhinns' highest peak, Beinn Tart a'Mhill. His widow Jane remained here and in Portnahaven, breeding wildfowl and raising ponies.

By the time you reach the tip of the Rhinns, you have wandered out into the ocean itself, and it is only by turning back you can recover the bulk of the island. There are two offshore islets at the tip of the Rhinns, Orsay (Oran's Farmstead) and Eilean Mhic Coinnich (Mackenzie's Island), with a narrow channel between them; the effect of the tide races is to make the level of the Atlantic beyond the islets seem several feet higher than the calmer water within this natural sea stockade, as if one was looking up and over a weir. It is on this corniche ride down the Rhinns that you pass two of Islay's six lighthouses, the stubby little Port Charlotte light, grafted on to the tough rocks of an igneous dyke, and at land's end the grander 29-metre-high Orsay light, which has flashed white every five seconds since being lit in 1825, and on foggy days emits three blasts every 90 seconds. It was sight of this light which initially gave hope but eventually spelled disaster to the ill-fated Captain Isaac Booth of the *Exmouth of Newcastle*, with his cargo of 230 human beings, as midnight drew near on Tuesday 27 April 1847 (see Chapter Seven).

Nowadays these three (or four) villages are struggling for year-round existence, since many of their pretty though tiny seaside cottages, built to lairdly decree for the evicted in the early nineteenth century, have become holiday homes. On a rain-lashed winter evening, Portnahaven and Port Wemyss can be lonely places, with more tearful yellow light out on the streets (and not much of that) than in the dark cottages. Summer is cheerier. You can sit on sun-warmed benches around the deep gash of its harbour, looking at the 1,800-million-year-old rocks which climb out of the water as the tide sinks. Then one of the rocks moves, with a flop or a roll. It proves to be a sunbathing, horse-faced grey seal; this is where Islay's major colony of this large and blubbery species is found. Suddenly you realise that there are ten or twelve of them, hauled on to those old rocks for a few idle hours between tides and fishing expeditions. Even at a winter high tide you may see a sleek head bobbing curiously out of the water, looking like a mad, pert swimmer in a bathing cap.

Portnahaven itself has a pretty pink-walled church divided into two halves, one for Portnahaven and one for Port Wemyss, while the village's other major attraction has until recently been a pub called An Tigh Seinse or 'House of Hospitality', run by Maureen MacKinnon. The home origins of every public house were never more evident than in this modest Gaelic example, where the bar was what separated Maureen's kitchen from her barely converted front room. The highly variable opening hours were generally handwritten on a piece of paper which was placed in the front window. Maureen seemed shy at first, yet she was an excellent cook and a surprising disciplinarian, chiding habitual drunkards with the stern words 'Don't come in here looking for drink!' Maureen, however, has just sold up – and the purchaser is Carl Reavey, formerly of the Port Charlotte Hotel, promising excellence of a different order.

It's hard to avoid the sense, as you head down for Portnahaven, that you are travelling a long pier into the wild Atlantic; the sea seems at all times to thump the exposed rocks here with needless viciousness, and much of the shoreline is covered in shoals of sea-crushed stone. Britain's first wave-power station lies here, concealed far more completely than any wind farm can ever hope to manage, cemented into an inlet just beyond the village's last houses. Visually concealed, anyway; on a wild night, the turbines in the rocks roar like a jet engine according to Jane Dawson, who lives just over the headland in Portnahaven. In a normal blow, they sound merely emphysematic. It was built by Wavegen of Inverness, who call it a 'Limpet': seven metres of crusading water sweep in under its concrete skirt to fumble with an oscillating water column inside the blockhouse; this feeds a pair of counter-rotating turbines, which in turn drive a generator.

From here northwards, the whole of the western Rhinns stretches away for twelve miles or more. Together with the Oa, this is Islay's most exposed stretch and the scene of its worst shipwrecks; most years bring screaming winds and 30-foot waves when atmospheric pressure drops away. Yet on an immaculate June night, as the sun slips gracefully into the sea, there is no sweeter spot on the island than the flower-strewn grasslands which lie above the cliffs, or the three softly sandy beaches which punctuate the coastline. The road north is a narrow and winding one, but full of surprises as the hills turn and dip, the ocean comes near to you and then retreats, and you meet family parties of cattle which demand a temporary halt to forward motion, and a sharing of the pleasure of island time. In lesser and narrower fissures than the main bays, the sea has pounded and sucked the rock into stone middens, caves and sculpture gardens.

Lossit Bay, Machir Bay and Saligo Bay are the names of the three silky beaches of this coastline. They bring nourishment to the acid land, since their sand is shell as much as silica, and the westerlies puff and blow this improving alkali inland. As you walk down to Lossit Bay, for example, you can see the pasture grow more sweetly floral with every step you take until it is snowy with daisies, to the obvious appreciation of hundreds of tumbling rabbits and contented, white-fleeced sheep. If you make an early summer visit, stroll over to the cliffs which lie south of the beach. You'll find them decked with fulmar nests, in each of which sits one or sometimes two contented chicks like holidaymakers on the balconies of seaside flats. These snub-nosed cacklers have not found the need to fear humans, and you can meet them as intimately as the cliffs allow without upset.

The road comes close to touching the water only once on this southern section, at the beautifully farmed, architectural bay of Kilchiaran. The farmhouse here has a rounded steading, its pregnant belly to the west: you can imagine the sense of comfort it would bring to wind-harried livestock in a rising winter gale at this exposed spot. Its roof is a masterpiece of chunky West Highland slatework. This is the point at which you realise that the Rhinns coast has genuine highlands of its own: the solid horseshoe of rock in front of you is made of crushed and compressed sea-sediments, marking the geological frontier between the old-rock southern Rhinns and the younger-rock northern Rhinns. This mass puts pedestrians at an advantage over car drivers, since with a nimble pair of legs you can be up and over the rock and down into big Machir Bay in under an hour, and with raptor-like views the while. The road route is far longer, taking you back to Port Charlotte and north again past Bruichladdich before dog-legging it back to the big beach.

The locals know this mass as 'Granny's Rock'; it's the site of an old radar station. Old? Well, the buildings are empty and abandoned, but there is a lot of gleaming new equipment installed on the well-maintained masts. In a gale such as that which sank the *Otranto* (see Chapter Seven), you wouldn't be able to stand up here but, hugging the ground, you could have seen the entire tragedy unfold; the scattered remains of this enormous ship lie below you, on the sea bottom. If, instead of taking the steep scramble down to Machir Bay, you make your way across the uplands to the cliff edge of Creagh Mhór (Great Rock), you will notice a small walled cemetery positioned serenely in the lush, shell-gorged grass which stretches away between you and the beach. There lie the remains of *Otranto*'s crew, including her captain Ernest Davidson and one of her cooks, Charles Hacking. On a warm afternoon in early July, as the growing fulmars begin to practise their spectacular gliding routines around the crags, it is a place of great peace. In winter, by contrast, choughs tumble on the buffets of wind, and the sea thunders.

You should, perhaps, also try to imagine the vast bay in front of you filled with scattered homes, for this place (which is called Kilchoman) was once one of the most prosperous and productive parishes on Islay. In 1844, for example, it was home to just under 5,000 people, and produced in that year 52 tonnes of barley, 61 tonnes of oats, 50,000 barrels of potatoes, 254 tonnes of rye grass hay, 76 tonnes of meadow hay and 2,540 tonnes of turnips, as well as being home to over 2,000 cows and 2,700 sheep. Rockside Farm which lies just inland from the bay has some of the best land on the island, but even so this level of productivity and human activity is hard to imagine today. The pitiful state into which the church has fallen underlines the decline; but the magnificent fifteenth-century ring-headed cross in the churchyard, and some of the proud recumbent slabs there, underline the wealth and populousness of the past. There is nowhere better on Islay to enjoy a summer sunset from than Machir Bay, though that was only coincidental to the fact that it was the venue of the wildest party Islay has ever known (see page 316).

Behind Machir Bay is Islay's largest inland loch, Loch Gorm. The break in the relief at Machir is caused by a small fault, and when sea levels were higher, Loch Gorm was in fact a sea loch. The fall in sea levels made it a lake – full of brown trout. The water itself and the intractable bogland around the lake made any island on it a place of relative safety, which is why the Lords of the Isles (who are said to have summered at Kilchoman) had on little Eilean Mór (whose name ironically means 'great island') a fort, of which only fragments remain.

North of Loch Gorm, the Rhinns grows wild. This headland with its cavernous gullies was where the *Exmouth of Newcastle* finally came to grief, and there are many other wrecks up here, too. The smashed driftwood and harvest of plastic bottles at Tràigh Bhàn (Fair Strand), which is only accessible by foot from the farm at Sanaigmore, bears witness to the pounding this morsel of Islay's coastline receives, and it is behind this often rubbish-strewn beach that 108 Irish bodies lie among the daisies, the buttercups and the thrift, most of them women and children, their resting place marked only by a single cairn and a simple slate memorial. Another way to measure the force of the wind and sea at this point is to clamber up to the Janus-like trig point at Cnoc Uamh am Fear (Hill of the Men's Cave). Its land face is smooth grey-brown, lichen-coated; its sea face, by contrast, is eroded, pitted, bleached and calcified. This stretch of the northern Rhinns is one of the places where you may come across the island's wild goats, shaggily leaping and bucking through the tussocky grass like Chinese dragons at a New Year festival. Ileachs quite accurately point out that you will usually smell them before you see them.

I have emphasised the wildness of the Rhinns, its westerly exposure to the biting Atlantic, and the sky-dazed corniche road of its underbelly, yet there is also a softer and quieter Rhinns, too. You can find this at Foreland, for long the home of the laird of this part of the island, where a huddle of trees hides a large house and a precious walled garden full of cheerful petunias and nodding lupins. Foreland sits on the northern edge of a ridge, a dump of glacial deposits, overlooking the lower lands of the Fault.

CLAMS IN THE SANDS: THE FAULT

Sea almost meets sea, here. To the south, Loch Indaal laps contentedly along the bright bay of Tràigh an Luig; to the north, the long tidal reach of Loch Gruinart comes flooding, moon-beckoned, over miles of sands to infiltrate the boggy flats of the island's northernmost RSPB bird reserve. The land which links these two inlets almost looks like flow country: sodden, reedy, pool-glittering.

Only one road threads this whole zone, turning off the main coastal road at a scruffy farm called Uiskentuie (which means 'water of the resting place' – it was where funeral processions stopped on the way to Kilchoman and Kilnave cemeteries). This road threads its way north past a physical embodiment of wind. A plantation of trees at a place called Coullabus has been sculpted, by the prevailing westerlies, into a smooth wedge of near-geometric perfection. There are several hill breaks of this sort on the island, but this is perhaps the most striking example of living sap and leaf obeying wind to within a foot or two. The trees at the back of the plantation are twice as tall as those at the front, which bear the full weight of the wind's body. Linger along the Gruinart flats in the winter to see the squadrons of barnacle geese, infiltrated by sociable greylags, come down at dusk; linger there at dawn in the summer to hear, from the nettley, grassy edges provided by the RSPB, the desperate, sex-hungry scrape of a lonely corncrake. It's not all birds, though; the Fault is productive, too. Gruinart is where Islay's bees meander home to make the waxy, honey-bleeding combs which can be bought in the bakery in Bowmore; and an astonishing range of herbs is grown on the flats, at Loch Gruinart House. Gruinart is also where you can acquire fresh, juicy oysters from Craigens Farm. If you have a rake, a bucket, some rubber boots, and the time to wait for low tide, you can scrape a handsome dinner of not-overly gritty clams out of the wild beds on the east of the loch at Carraig Dubh (Dark Sea-Rock). North of that, and the Fault is all sand. Carry on driving or cycling as far as the road takes you, then walk on further and you will, after stretched miles, reach a sand world. Not only does the tide make and unmake a huge bed of beach twice daily, but much of the long foreshore is a chaotic, bobbing sea of hot, snake-lively sandhills, anchored into place by wiry grass.

Across to the west, meanwhile, the road continues northwards from the RSPB Visitor Centre to Kilnave and Ardnave. The sandy theme of the Fault is echoed there – with added history and drama. Of the two great high crosses of Islay, the one which stands in Kilnave churchyard, next to the wistful and roofless little chapel, is the older of the two, and probably dates from 750 or so. It is damaged and heavily weathered, but because of this seems to wear its antiquity with more dignity than the improbably well-preserved Kidalton cross. The decorative motifs suggest its artist learned his skill in Ireland. Whisky enthusiasts will note the memorial tablet to a former Bowmore manager, John Baillie, set into the seaward wall of this same breezy, airy, sky-scoured cemetery.

Kilnave lies near the spot where, according to clan histories, the brutal Lachlan Mor Maclean met his end at the conclusion of the Battle of Tràigh Gruinart (Gruinart shore) in the warmth of an August day in 1598 (see pages 98–9). This was the climax to thirty years of bloody squabbling between the Macdonalds and the Macleans. No one really knows whether or not the 'Great Maclean' was killed with an arrow through the heart launched by a dwarfish archer from Jura called Dubh Sith or 'Black Fairy', hiding in a tree (of which there are few at Kilnave today); or whether the rest of the Maclean warriors, who took refuge in the chapel at Kilnave, had the key turned on them and were burned to death there. The cross, of course, saw all; but the cross isn't telling.

At Ardnave, finally, the grassed dunes taper away to the sea, while offshore lie the low yet protective Nave Island and some smaller rock fragments. There was, in the early twentieth century, a sizeable herring station here – before storms took the herring elsewhere, and over-fishing meant they never returned. We may be in the far north of the island, but the gentleness of this place, with its miniature, rock-broken, spring-watered beaches and its azure pools can seem (once again) almost Aegean on a warm summer day. The farm at Ardnave, its gloomy house in need of major restoration, overlooks a pretty loch on which I have seen scaup duck pootle, while chough follow the cattle on the headland in winter. The dead lie everywhere on Islay, and here is no exception: railings surround a tomb to one Duncan Campbell who lived at Ardnave and 'was interred in this spot by his own particular desire' in 1825. Some 48 years later, another coffin was lowered down to join his; this belonged to one Archibald McDonald, 'eldest son of the Honourable Archibald McDonald'. Why these two men, between whose clans there lies a long history of enmity, came to climb down into the earth together here is unexplained – like so many of the 'particular desires' human beings may cherish.

NOURISHING STONES: THE HEARTLAND

What, about the person of a hunched witch, might be construed as the Heartland? The answer is a big, broad band running from Laggan Point and Bowmore (her clenched fists) through low, leafy Bridgend (her leathery lungs) and across the island following the main road through the villages of Kilmeny, Ballygrant and Keills to Port Askaig (her sharp shoulder blades). There is much activity here. No zone of Islay is more populous, and Islay's geology grows unusually complex, too. The two have long been interlinked. Islay's two main rivers, moreover, make their way west to the sea through this zone, breaking up the landscape further.

Laggan Point and the Bowmore hinterland are dull and inaccessible. Most of this lumpy protrusion is a large bog, the source of Bowmore distillery's peat. The drive to the island rubbish tip lies to the north, while following the unmade road to the Big Strand to the south, just after the bridge over the river Laggan, is marginally more interesting, but only marginally: it bumps past plantations and down on to more sand-dune pasture before reaching the pounding sea.

Every visitor to the island, by contrast, knows the twisting road between Bowmore itself and Bridgend. The changing prospects and colours of Loch Indaal make, at all points and all times of the tide, a dangerous distraction. Bridgend Woods, with its paths which cross and recross the river Sorn, opens up the only truly leafy walk on the island. A still summer day there will bring you the scents of elder and rhododendron, the sound of trout flipping in the river, and the nodding of campions in the dappled light. The forgotten cemetery across the road, all that remains of the evicted village which became Bowmore (see page 128), is worth a ruminative visit. Islay House Square, once the heart of the Islay Estate Home Farm, is now home to the workshops of an observant batik artist called Liz Sykes, a skilled carpenter and furniture maker called Billy Muir, and textile restorer Sophie Younger; Islay's first microbrewery opened here on 17 April 2004. Islay House itself is screened from the road but can be seen from the back entrance to Islay House Square. It's a sizeable, rambling building whose appeal may lie inside but is hard to discern from the rear, the only view available to the public. It is no longer owned by the Morrison family of Islay Estates, who now use the former keeper's house of Eallabus as their Islay base. Instead, it is the home of Tom Friedrich, a Texan Vietnam air veteran and former US 'Top Gun'; it is a regular venue for classical music concerts on the island.

Then the road leads off over the hills; we enter slate and limestone country. The landscape is sometimes too rugged for cultivation, but where the contours soften, the limestone sweetens the fields to productive effect. Here is the place to come to smell the hay in summer. In former times, lime was kilned and carted elsewhere in the island from the Heartland; if you walk the mountains of the south or north, and find on their slopes green patches (often near to abandoned crofts) where the heather has kept its distance, thank lime. Its mineral seams were mined in former times, too, to provide lead, copper and silver. The Sorn is a smaller, shorter river than the languid Laggan to the south, but it is a more energetic one: the remarkable Islay Woollen Mill, with its heroically noisy Victorian machinery (including the only working Slubbing Billy in the world), once took advantage of the power of Sorn water as it tumbled down through slate. As in Islay House Square, the spirit of craftsmanship lives on in this sheltered wooded hollow of the Sorn valley: costumes for the film *Braveheart* were made here, and the Mill exports tweed jackets to New York.

Mining may have finished in the Heartland, but quarrying continues – at Ballygrant, where the Dunlossit laird Bruno Shroder continues to make a profit (to his own surprise) from turning the hard lime into road stone. Water, as everywhere on Islay, continues to lie in the lochs: the serene Loch Ballygrant and the smaller, prettier Lily Loch make the walk through the long strip of woodland which links the two an unusually soothing one; these lie in Dunlossit Estate, but pedestrians are welcome.

And, of course, there is watery Finlaggan. Chapter Two will tell you more about the importance to the Lords of the Isles of this reed-cut, water-filled hollow scooped in the low hills, but the standing stone above the loch and the Stone Age remains also found on its main island suggest that this was always a place of shelter, quiet and security. These are the physical lineaments, in other words, which generate a sense of the sacred, which was perhaps why the Irish missionary St Findlugan is held to have established a small community here, too, in the late sixth century, leaving his name to the place.

Take the road from here to Port Askaig on a clear, bright day; a day after cold rain; the morning, say, after a night when even Islay has felt frost, and when upland Argyll has taken a generous shake of snow, and you will be hypnotised with what you see before you: a pair of huge white breasts. These two rounded, gleaming mountains will seem so close in the spotless air that you are sure they must lie at the end of this road, though in fact they lie beyond the racing waters of the Sound of Islay. These are the Paps of Jura, giant quartzite nunataks which dominate the horizon wherever you are on the east of the island. (There are in fact three of them, the highest rising to 786 metres, though it is hard on Islay to find a spot from which two of them do not obscure the third.) To see them on an icy day is, in a way, appropriate: nunatak is an Eskimo word to describe bedrock which rises up through

glacier ice, and as this road tumbles down into the busy, sculpted hollow of Port Askaig it does so through a boulder bed whose rocks, when correlated with others around the world, suggest a vast global Ice Age of unthinkable (and, for human beings, unsurvivable) cold some 600 million years ago.

In addition to its two ferry services (one to Jura and one back to Kennacraig), Port Askaig has a shop, a snug little hotel and pub, and the Islay lifeboat, too. Is the only way back from Port Askaig to retrace your route along the main road through Central Islay? Not quite. There is an alternative: a tentative road approach to Mountain Islay.

Mountain Islay, as we are about to discover, has no roads of its own, but one fringes it here: this is called the Glen Road. It is a lonely loop which follows a parallel valley to that which I have just described, though by now the land is much higher and less fertile. This loop connects Ballygrant with Bridgend, crossing the river Laggan at Mulindry, just east of the gentle weir where the Bowmore distillery lade comes into being. The scenes which history has witnessed here, by contrast, have not always been gentle. A former Iron Age fort, now grassy and handsome, overlooks this stretch of the river, and it is idle to suppose it was not there for a reason; while Mulindry itself was, according to clan histories, the place at which a party of Macleans, taken hostage at the conclusion of a banquet welcoming them to their possessions on Islay, were murdered at the rate of two per day in 1586, during the long years of feuding with the Macdonalds (see pages 97–8).

The landscape to the east, meanwhile, has grown colder, darker and more brooding. Change is afoot. The enthusiastic Chloë Randall of Dunlossit Estate took me on an off-road ride here, past the former farmhouse (now perhaps the island's loneliest holiday cottage) at Kynagarry. This, by the way, was where the illicit still in the Museum of Rural Life came from; sure enough Kynagarry looks just the kind of place which Excisemen might find excuses not to visit. On, then, up to the Dunlossit rifle range beneath Loch Allallaidh where bullets streak over the little Killennan burn before stuffing a target; recruits to the Royal Marines come here to complete their basic survival course. It seems an appropriately empty shadowland under the peaks.

SKY BURIAL: MOUNTAIN ISLAY

Yes, Islay has mountains. It doesn't have anything to match the stark, mammary shock of Jura's thrusting Paps . . . or does it? Perhaps it is all a question of perspective. Visit, say, the island's seven distilleries, and only the views north from Bunnahabhain will give you a glimpse of just how rugged the island can be. The island's roads exist to connect farms, and farms, by definition, occupy the lowest, most fecund land. But take the ferry to Port Askaig on a stormy day and stare, from the pitching boat, at the prodigious gloom of McArthur's Head; or take the long and winding road along the south of the island to its terminus at Ardtalla Farmhouse, looking up as you do so at the great brown horse-shoe of Glen Leòra (Glen of the Muddy River) and cloud-scraping Beinn Bheigier to its right, and then you will realise that Islay, too, hides Highland grandeur in its cold, quartzite heart.

Mountain Islay means, in effect, the eastern portion of the island. The once-separate Rhinns does have a peak of its own, the 220-metre Beinn Tart a'Mhill (variously translated as Hartfell Mountain or Drought Mountain), but this tilted, igneous slab is oddly unimpressive when you are close to hand, perhaps because the view from the corniche road shows it draped in drab conifers almost to its summit. It looks more impressive in silhouette, as you head in or out of Bridgend.

The mountains of the east are a contrast in that they look, if anything, more grandly forbidding than their physical heights would suggest. At 491 metres, Islay's highest peak Beinn Bheigier (Mountain of the Vicar: the Ordnance Survey map's incorrect spelling should read Bheigeir) does not even come close to qualifying as what is known in Scotland as a Munro, a peak of over 3,000 feet, yet there are many Munroes which are easier to walk, and where the presence of nature is less harsh, less disconcerting, less kestrel-eyed.

Walking, it should be said, is the key which unlocks the door to Mountain Islay. There are no roads here. This is the empty quarter. What does the word 'stalker' mean to you? Stealthy and costly upland field sports, culminating in a bloody gralloch? The great 1979 film of Andrei Tarkovsky, plotting a journey into a forbidden zone of emptiness? Or merely the quiet, patient tracking of nature herself, which human activity is turning from a mother to a fugitive? Choose your meaning; all are appropriate.

'I do feel one of the great things about Islay is the fact that it is empty. But accessible. If you don't keep some empty spaces in the world, what will remain? So much of the world in my lifetime has been inundated and covered by little houses. Now one point of view is to say "Why shouldn't everybody have their little house and a piece of the shoreland?" They probably should. But should you not have some bits of shoreland where nobody is?' The highest portion of Islay belongs to the Mactaggart family; the speaker is Sandy Mactaggart who, as it happens, spent most of his working life in Canada, as a property developer who believed 'you have to be very careful not to over-develop'. At one stage, the Mactaggarts were going to put a road through to Proaig, the biggest bay in the empty quarter. This was at the same moment that the Schoders had put in the Glen Road; a grant for the road to Proaig had been applied for and obtained. 'But then my nephew John and I said, you know, this is one of the last places which is wild. You have to walk to get to it, it's not easy to get to; we *shouldn't* have a road in there.' There is, today, no road. Indeed nowadays there is barely a track, for no one lives at Proaig any more. The sheep are collected there a couple of times a year, and occasional walkers yomp in and out, but in the main this is a wilderness of bog and tussock.

There are, in fact, only two people who could truly be said to live in Mountain Islay, and their names are Howard and Suzanne Cobb. Mountain Islay divides into two sections: the large south-east of the island, shared between the Mactaggarts' Ardtalla estate and Bruno Schroder's Dunlossit estate, and the smaller north-east of the island, where Margadale Hill is found and which still belongs to Lord Margadale's Islay Estates. The Cobbs live at the north-eastern tip, in the old lighthouse buildings at Rhuvaal. They moved their furniture in using the former Jura ferry, and they get to and from the nearest roads at Bunnahabhain or Port Askaig by boat or by quad bike. The walk to Rhuvaal, consequently, is the easiest to make in Mountain Islay, since there is, unusually, a track of sorts to follow along the shelf between sky and sea. It takes you over the old herring-fisher's bay of Bachlaig and underneath a line of four peaks from which you will be monitored by cold-eyed red deer. Ravens slog the skies looking for dead creatures to clear up, and once you get to Rhuvaal you may find a line of preening shag waiting on the rocks for weary appetite to return. The view of the Sound of Islay and Jura's celebrated raised beaches will remain with you always, returning like a song every time you taste Bunnahabhain — for it is the distant sprawl of the distillery which beckons you home off this hill.

I asked Suzanne Cobb if she ever got lonely out at Rhuvaal. 'Lonely? No. I think you can be lonelier in a town. Even in the village I lived in before, I noticed it if I was on my own; you're different some-how from everybody around you – but I'm not aware of it here. You just get on with things. There's so much to look at and to see. Crystal days; incredible light; wonderful skies . . . then suddenly there's a deer looking at you over a wall, or a peregrine on a pinnacle of rock. No, I never feel lonely.'

It would take a fit walker, resident on the island, years to get to know Mountain Islay fully, since much of it can only be reached given a full day in summer light. Beinn Bheigier is one of the easier peaks to scale, starting from the field just north of the bridge over the Claggain river. On a bright June day, this is a jubilant climb. Swallows and stonechats dartingly encourage your start, then the sun-crazed larks take over, egging you up from their song-filled vaults in the air. Occasionally one will dart out from near your blundering feet, then explode melodiously upwards: an artful, nest-protecting distraction. You might flush a grunting grouse, too, or stumble across a dead sheep of which little, quickly, remains except skin, bone and horn; tens of thousands of bright yellow tormentil flowers will, though, mark its sky grave on these acid soils.

The apparent summit is deceptive, revealing a long ridge of frost-shattered quartzite to the real summit half a mile away. On the day my friends and I walked this way, we were kept company on this last section by a golden plover which refused to leave us. It haunted our sunlit stumble over the boulders with its mournful single-note peep, the saddest cry in the bird world. What tragedy befell this species to leave it lamenting like this for eternity?

Once on the summit you will, at long last, be able to see all three of Jura's Paps; here you can see the neighbours just down the sea roads, in Kintyre and Antrim; here you can see over to the Rhinns, past the bright blue splash of Loch Allallaidh and the deeper, distant gash of Loch Indaal. It is a great temptation to make your way down into graceful Proaig from here, once so busy with homes and livelihoods, now possessed by wind and bracken, and if you have the energy, do, though it's a rough walk for bipeds. McArthur's Head and three other big bays lie beyond, and still you wouldn't have reached Port Askaig. The empty quarter? Make that a generous half.

GLITTERING POOLS: THE MOSS

These form the witch's entrails. They are, if you like, the alter ego of Mountain Islay: low ground shadowing high ground, a place for water to gather in rather than a place from which water runs or tumbles. The hard quartzite of Mountain Islay, indeed, is waterless; the weight of blanket bogland, by contrast, is at least 85 per cent water.

There are, of course, bits of bogland all over Islay, as any enthusiastic walker knows. Follow a line beneath a hill, and you will come home with wet boots in even the driest season. On every walk there will be some stone; but there will be rather more deep, sucking mud. Firm, springy greensward, where the grass forms a thin skin over the rock, can at any moment give way to a patch of eerie trampoline, when a step forward sends a grassy ripple through what had seemed solid ground. The turf, then, is little other than a green crust on a kind of dark, hidden pond; you are, in effect, walking on water. The bogland, with time, becomes peat moss (Chapter Four describes this process in detail). Each of Islay's distilleries once owned their own portions of peat moss, and the fact that Ardbeg's lay within the present Ardtalla estate in the far south-east of the island, Bunnahabhain's was found on the lower slopes of Margadale Hill in the far north, and Bruichladdich's lay over near Loch Gruinart in the Fault shows that there are peat reserves more or less everywhere here, once you start looking for them.

There is, though, a gigantic Moss in the middle of Islay, of which the northern part is called Duich, the central part Glenegedale and the southern part Glenmachrie. It is this Moss which lies under the Mountains; it is this which separates Bowmore from Port Ellen; and it is this which, if you arrive by aeroplane, your wheels will first meet. It sounds an untrustworthy place to land, I know, but in the icier times which have dominated most of recent geological history on Islay, copious outwash gravels were deposited here by swift, chill rivers flowing off upland glaciers, and these gravels were quarried during the Second Word War to make sure that the airport had firm, concrete foundations.

The same cannot be said for the long, straight Low Road across the Bogland. This was originally begun as a job-creation scheme during Islay's nineteenth-century population explosion; the only prior alternative had been to plod a cart along the beach. Driving along the Low Road today is a vaguely maritime experience, as it rises and falls in soft waves, floating on the water. Its firmer predecessor was the High Road which connects Port Ellen directly with Bridgend, travelling as it does so over the mineral roots of Mountain Islay. This was originally all that was needed to link the central and southern population centres of the island, but when the laird decided to improve the splendour of his grounds at Bridgend by evicting those living in unsightly indigence there and re-establishing them at Bowmore in the 1760s, the need for the bog-crossing alternative became more pressing. The High Road, by the way, is the second means by which those unwilling or unable to walk the hills can make contact with Mountain Islay, especially if you take the fork which connects it with the Glen Road, running through the cold, shadowy plantations of Avenvogie, the frostiest part of lowland Islay. Other pleasures of the High Road include the dappled strip of ancient woodland beneath Cnoc Donn (Brown Hill), now classified as a Site of Special Scientific Interest (SSSI); the gentle watercourse which burbles amiably through it is, in fact, Bowmore's distillery lade on its long and winding way to the mash tun.

The Moss itself, of course, does not make for easy exploration, though parts are farmed; indeed the Leorin farmhouse to the south rivals Cladville on the Rhinns for the prominence and isolated majesty of its position. A journey along the Low Road reveals just how varied a landscape this is, though. Bog is never truly monotonous: cotton-spiked marsh replaces grassy gravel mounds, peat-stacks give way to glittering pools, while the reedy lochs which brim against the road from time to time gather down the sky. And it all ends, of course, in a five-mile beach.

This is Islay's 'Big Strand' (Tràigh Mhór). It begins in the north at the point where the meandering Laggan finally reaches the sea, giving its name to the whole broad bay, and it ends in the south where the great rock mass of the Oa comes thundering down out of Mountain Islay to push itself forcefully into the Atlantic. Between these two points the bog and standing waters gradually mingle with the sands, while a clutch of little streams, almost ebony with their burden of peat, leaves dark staining threads to show where sweet water finds salt. Islay's largest hotel, the Machrie, dominates the Big Strand from the south – not physically, since the scale of the Moss and its beach dwarfs all, but as a peg of light in the great darkness, and a place of warmth and food amid so much that seems cold, wet and lifeless. This hotel is run with singular humour and brisk panache on behalf of its owner by Ian Brown, a half-brother of the prolific British newspaper columnist Craig Brown. Behind the hotel lurks the Machrie links golf course (one of Britain's top 100), laid out amid the dunes and their ball-taunting winds. Walk down on to the beach from the golf course and you will find, down at the junction of the Oa and lying underneath Kintra Farm, one of the most beautiful of Islay's outcrops of phyllite, each mass softened and polished to a pastel patina by the abrasive caress of sand and wind. When it meets the sea, though, this gentle, sparkling verdigris grows black and pitted, like a mouthful of rotting teeth.

INTRACTABILITY: THE OA

Does the Oa belong to Islay? Glance at the map, and you might not be sure: it resembles a protruding growth, an excrescence, a bolus. From the sands of the Machrie or from the quayside at Port Ellen, too, it seems a place apart, a sheaf of distant hills striding into the sea, determined to slam the door on the rest of the island. It has but one spindly road to serve its entire mass. This little lifeline is obscurely accessed from either the Lagavulin-filled warehouses of Port Ellen, or from the muddy spur at the end of the long Low Road across the moss. As links go, it's tenuous.

All of this is deceptive. In geological terms, the Oa is very much a part of Islay; indeed its rocks (quartzite, slate and phyllite, with a bolt of hard limestone) are a succinct résumé of the Heartland and Mountain Islay. These rocks simply happen to be pushed skywards here with unusual vigour, lifting the mass high out of the sea.

The Oa, today, is sparsely populated. I have driven in a late November dusk back along the thread road from its tumbling terminus at Lower Killeyan, and the lights at the far-flung farm of Giol, or in the little sentinel cottage at Lenavore, seem brave almost to the point of folly. They spill a few yards on to the bog and the bracken, but then a vast pool of darkness swallows them up, and that black land is in turn swallowed by a greedy ocean beyond. The dwellings halfway across this lump of land at Risabus are the last which one might dignify with the description of a hamlet, and even then the shadows that fall about them, and the poignant dusk silhouette of the bell still fixed in the belfry above the ruined church, seem to mock any sense of lasting community.

It was not always thus. When laird John Ramsay was busy shepherding his tenants off to Canada in the mid-nineteenth century, and pushing the refusniks into a life of semi-unemployment in Port Ellen, the Oa was still one of the more thickly populated parts of the island. The gauntness of its tracts is thus newly acquired: Lower Killeyan must once, on a bright busy day, have been a gorgeously snug farming village with some of the sweetest grazing on the island; you can still see the outlines of extensive lazy-beds, once flecked with shy potato flowers, on the rolling hillside just across the gurgling water-course of Abhainn Ghil (the Gully river). Indeed the most majestic nineteenth-century photograph of Islay shows Lower Killeyan on just such a sparkling summer day, the washing laid out to dry on the grass, the hay neatly cut, with half-a-dozen tidy crofts piping industrious peat smoke up to the puffy cumulus overhead (see page 124). The awesomely dramatic Upper Killeyan, too, would have nourished half-a-dozen families on its extensive field systems and grazing grounds which loiter, Inca-like, over the crags and spires of rock and the thundering beach below.

Everywhere you look on the Oa, indeed, there are abandoned crofts and farmsteads, and old fields now cropped by the wild goats alone. Those which lie above the exquisite hanging valley lochs of Glenastle have long been abandoned, though their former owners would have watched, for some decades, the winking of the new Rhinns lighthouse punctuate their nights. The township of Tockmal is now vastly inaccessible, curtained from the rest of the Oa by gloomy plantations, yet it was once enough of a community to have its own church. Other dwellings have been given over to the birds and the sheep more recently. The long walk down from the road to Ballychatrigan and Stremnishmore, a bitter route of eviction for one Archibald Campbell (see pages 150–1), takes you along a track which remains well made today and past houses for which renovation is not yet risible. I have a sad wad of wallpapers, four of them pasted on top of each other and each pattern less cheerful than the last, lifted gently from the empty farmstead at Stremnishmore. The laird of the Oa, though, is now the RSPB. In the future it will be stonechats and whinchats, thus, who will cast proprietorial glances down to the sea from atop a foxglove stem, rather than human eyes from behind curtained windows.

You can almost feel this legacy of loss on the Oa, mingled with the bitterness of an intractable land. I met a farmer one November day at Upper Killeyan; he had just moved a flock of sheep in a break between showers. How long, I asked, had he worked this land? 'Too long,' he told me, looking about him, his weather-beaten face a work of geology in itself. Forty years he had spent on the Oa, he said; he now lived and farmed Kinnabus, over the hill eastwards. There were cattle gathered below us, mournfully chewing a dump of hay. He nodded at them. They were his daughter's, he said. It had been her partner who had looked after this farm for the RSPB until the summer just passed, when he had been killed riding down the road on his quad bike. 'A beast stepped into his way. He never saw it.' The daughter had wanted to keep the cattle, in memory of her lost man. The story was a tragic one, but the spectacularly gloomy surroundings made it seem a conspiracy of nature. I commiserated, in so far as a stranger was able. 'Ach, that's life,' sighed the farmer, looking down to the cattle. I had a sudden vision of clenched hands at the funeral, and inconsolable grief. We parted. Five minutes later, watching the chill sea slam an offshore stack, I was peppered with hail.

Topographically, the Oa seems corrugated; it advances towards the sea by a succession of hills and troughs, amply evident in the side valleys (like Glenastle) which lead off from the road. As in the Heartland, there is dolomitic limestone inlaid felicitously among the less nutritious rocks, hence the breaks of green grass which interrupt the moor land; hence, too, the beautiful garden at Upper Cragabus Farm (whose farm distillery produced, according to John Ramsay, the finest whisky ever made on Islay, one which he blended with Port Ellen to fulfil an order from Queen Victoria's Royal Household); and hence the rusting ploughshares which can be seen at both Lower Killeyan and at Lower Cragabus – the last will and testament of the lost farmers of the Oa. The chambered cairn at the latter farm is one of the most accessible Neolithic monuments on the whole island, telling us that it is at least 3,000 years of cultivation and habitation which seem to be drawing to a close.

The Oa's chief landmark, though, is the lonely, strange tower found at its prow-like south-western tip. This is known as the American monument. It was built of locally quarried stone in 1919, paid for by the American Red Cross, to commemorate the 550 or so American soldiers and sailors who were drowned or battered to death on Islay's rocks following the wrecking of the *Tuscania* and *Otranto* (see Chapter Seven). President Woodrow Wilson appended a perfunctory lozenge at its base, whose setting is beginning to crack and fissure.

There is a second, more personal message to be found on another Oa monument – the Carraig Fhada lighthouse which marks the entrance to Port Ellen's bay. This pretty, square-sided, cake-like erection was built in 1832 by the then laird of the island, Walter Frederick Campbell, as a monument to the memory of his first, insane wife – after whom the port itself is named. Did Walter Frederick write the sincere but McGonagallesque verses on the lighthouse, addressed to 'Ye who mid storms and tempests stray in danger's midnight hour'? Round the corner, meanwhile, is a pretty, vaguely monumental beach where the sands which carpet a rock grove are said to sing (it's another of the numerous Tràigh Bhàn or 'fair strands' on the island). I have never heard them do more than sigh conventionally under the sea's embrace, but perhaps I haven't been there when the wind is in the right direction. Or when summer mischief is in the air. Or after a dram or two.

STONE EELS: KIDALTON

Kidalton, the south-eastern strip of Islay which runs from the white sands and drifting peat smoke of Port Ellen all the way to the road's end at Ardtalla Farmhouse, makes a startling contrast to the rest of the island. The Oa's grandeur is austere; Mountain Islay scowls gloomily and smiles broadly by turns; the Moss broods; while the grass and stone catwalk of the Rhinns provides a bracing narrative of openness. Only Kidalton could be called exquisite. It is a landscape of prettiness and intricacy, a jewel box in which moss, grass, lichen and leaf lie teased together, dew-sodden or dripping with fresh rain, their tones incessantly filleted then filled by the milky blue felt of an invasive sea. To visit Islay and omit to explore Kidalton would be to defraud your memory bank. Calling in at Laphroaig, Lagavulin and Ardbeg will take you halfway into this intricate coveland and whet your appetite, but you must push on further by land to the Kidalton Cross, and by sea to the islands and skerries if possible, too (which it is: they are home to one of Britain's largest common seal colonies, and Gus Newman of Surnaig or Nicol MacKinnon of Seafari Islay will take you out on a watching brief). It never looks less than beautiful, but under the early or late sun of a long June day, this seems a masterpiece in which evolutionary chaos, geological history or an omnipotent creator have brought together every felicity of landscape in the repertoire.

Not only that, but Kidalton also seems to offer the rest of Scotland a distillery blueprint. If you cross to Islay by air, try to sit on the right-hand side of the plane. There are no guarantees (since wind direction and weather conditions vary), but the incoming Saab often makes its way along this coastline, giving passengers on the right-hand side a panorama of Kidalton. You will see the three grand distilleries reclining by their private bays, their names proudly painted in big black letters on white walls. You will note the quays and jetties where grain once arrived and barrels of whisky left; you will log their warehouses, and you can imagine the long winter nights of rain and wind which lash them.

Now look up to the hills behind, up to the brown heights, and there you will find the lochs which feed each distillery as neatly arranged in a line as bowls of water on a shelf. Read Hebridean history, trace the original eastward journey of whisky from Ireland to Scotland, and allow that in this climate working and suffering human beings need a dose of strong waters to keep their bodies and their souls warm; you will then inevitably conclude that these are the three distilleries above all their peers which had to exist. The landscape demanded it. If you are going to distil great malt whisky anywhere on the planet, this is the place.

So why, at Kidalton, does Islay suddenly turn so sweet? The answer lies in geology and topography. Imagine a shoal of stone eels invading the quartzite and phyllite heart of the island, swimming, leaping and wriggling up from Port Ellen towards the Sound of Islay. That is what you will see on a geological map. These stone eels racing through Kidalton are composed of intrusions called sills or dykes. They are made of tough, meta-igneous rocks (amphibolite, hornblende schist, metadolerite and metagabbro – all of them perfect for cutting human knees). Their arrival was a profoundly underground adventure which took place perhaps 550 million years ago. The vastness of time since has, eventually, heaved them up to the surface, where these stone eels have – and this is the crucial factor – proved far more durable and less prone to erosion than the mineral sea in which they swim. The eels remain upstanding. Hence Kidalton's distinctive landscape: a chaos of hillocks and hummocks, of wings and screens, of eruptions and interventions, of plunges and climbs, of breaks and lunges. The sills can be whale-sized or bigger, but they can also be no larger than a small, grassy cairn. It's a hard landscape to discipline proprietorily: drunken fences stagger in apparent aimlessness over grass-topped craglets. It's a seascape, too, for the stone eels swarm up out of a watery ocean as well as a mineral one, and as they do so they make an archipelago of islands and islets, skerries and rocks, pools and coves, beaches and bays. There could be no greater contrast to the plain gape of the Big Strand than this intricate and fragmented coastline, a kind of rock garden set in the sea.

And on top of all that, it lies in the Far South, and it lies beneath Mountain Islay. The mountains seduce clouds, and pull water out of the sky – to the profit of distillation, as we have seen, but to the profit of vegetation, too. When that water meets the nooks and crannies of this sculptor's landscape, and when it feels the warmth of a slow summer sun passing caressingly overhead, and when it notes the shelter from a water-hurling west wind and a piercing north wind, too, then the result is growth of unusual lusciousness. Long after most of Islay had lost the ubiquitous tree cover it won after the glacier ice receded some 8,000 years ago, this south-eastern tumble of stones remained the 'Forest of Nae'.

These are the reasons why Islay seems sweet in Kidalton, and why there is a sense of enchantment about the landscape there. The ancient woodland, in particular, is unique; nowhere else on Islay do old trees grow as statuesque, nor the ground beneath them turn as radiantly grassy or as sumptuously mossy. The woods around the ruined Kidalton House, underneath Cnoc Rhaonastil (Rowandale Hill), or near the now-unfindable remains of a burnt Iron Age fort at Trudernish must constitute some of the most graceful growing anywhere in the Hebrides. But there is everything here: stone headlands, sweet pasture, peat bog, hazel copses, blasted plantations (like the hillside trees on the tall road bank prior to Lagavulin), and great tracts of deep, silky brown deergrass, too. The bays are chiselled miniatures compared to the great storm-carved gashes on the west coast of the Rhinns, as those who have visited Lagavulin, dominated by the sea fort of the Lord of the Isles, will know. The bay which lies just east of Ardbeg, for example, filled by the gentle tidal loch An t-Sàilein (the Sea Arm), is almost cosy, a perfect place to watch common seals lounge and lollop. There is probably no more sheltered beach on Islay than the suntrap Loch a' Chnuic (Loch of the Hill), and Ardilistry just round the wooded headland, while more open, is no less peaceful. Aros Bay, though difficult to get to, is another spot where (as the Arctic terns wheel overhead) the binocular-clutching human, blundering out of the woodland and stumbling across the rocks, feels a trespasser in paradise. Claggain Bay further north marks a change of tone; by now the prettiness of Kidalton is beginning to fade from the scene, and we are moving into the grandeur of Mountain Islay. The swansong comes at the last little beach, immaculately sandy, of yet another Tràigh Bhàn, this one just a gentle stroll from Ardtalla Farmhouse (the Ardtalla Estate's most popular holiday cottage, partly because every dinner is candlelit: it has no electricity).

Needless to say, Kidalton offers fine farming and grazing ground, too, though in small parcels, cut and sliced thus by the sills; their main testament remains a handful of ruined crofting hamlets. Their inhabitants have only just passed out of living memory: Iain Maclean of Laphroaig, who died aged 90 in 2003, remembered when he was at school watching the children of the last crofters walk up home to the hills in the darkness. One of these villages, Solum above Ardbeg, became Islay's plague community; its story is similar to the celebrated history of Eyam in Derbyshire. A returning sailor walked up, fell sick; the inhabitants gravely conferred, and warned others to stay away. Food was left at the edge of the village for them – until the day when no one came to collect it any more.

There is, in sum, much more to Kidalton than its nine-foot-high Cross – which is not to lessen the astonishment that this piece of eighth-century stone carving, the only complete surviving Celtic high cross in Scotland, can provoke. It was chiselled locally by an artist from Iona, using the hard meta-igneous rock of the sills (called 'blue stone' on the plaque at the church), which goes some way towards explaining how it is still, twelve centuries of dreadful weather later, in such good condition. The scenes on its arms show a murder (Cain clubbing Abel to death) and a sacrifice (Abraham preparing to slit Isaac's throat): all most appropriate, given the horrors of Islay's Dark Age history. It is, nonetheless, a work of great beauty. In 1882, the cross was leaning badly so its foundations were restored, at which point human remains (of a man and a woman) were discovered beneath it. The man had, according to restorer Sir Arthur Mitchell, been 'blood eagled': put to death, in other words, by tearing the heart and lungs from the victim while still alive through the cracked back, an extravagant torture reserved for noble victims by the Scandinavian raiders who shattered the society of the Western Isles at this time. There is, perplexingly, another fine though unfinished later cross lying outside the cemetery, perhaps marking the final resting place of a distinguished reprobate (or suicide) forbidden entry to sacred ground. Some of the church's grave slabs are memorable, too, including that of Charles MacArthur of Proaig who wished, at the time of his death in 1696 and like many countrymen since, to be remembered by his long gun, his powder horn and his dog.

FIRST GLASS

Ardbeg

The island of rain —
is dry; cloudless. Pale sun rests
on the water's skin.

Is ARDBEG (pronounced as written) the last distillery on the island, or the first? If you drive off the CalMac ferry at Port Askaig, then Ardbeg will lie at the end of your road, 34 km away. As the eagle glides, though, it's the closest of the three Kidalton distilleries, a mere hill or two distant. Perhaps the best way to put it is this. If Bunnahabhain represents Islay's pale and intense northern extremity, then Ardbeg is the warm south. Ardbeg is fire; Ardbeg is depth; Ardbeg is nourishment and plenty.

There is no distillery on this island whose situation is anything but lovely, but even with competition of this order, Ardbeg can stop the breath. The only working view on the island to begin to match that from Caol Ila's stillroom is the one enjoyed by Ardbeg's mashmen as they dip their steel divers into the six Oregon pine washbacks. The workers gaze out over the 'foul waters' which Sunday sailors are cautioned by the Admiralty to avoid. Two dozen little rocks pierce the skin of the sea. In the days when every grain of barley arrived by boat, and when every drop of spirit left on the water too, this would have been the most hazardous of all the island approaches for puffer captains. Shortly before Christmas in 1925, the puffer *Serb* struck rocks off Ardbeg, eventually slipping below the waves and scattering her barley among the wrack and the stones. Other boats which have met misfortune here include the *Aurora* in 1866, the *Maythorn* in 1869, the *Ella* in 1890, the *John Strachan* in 1917 and the *Luneda* in 1937.

There is, though, one major difference between the Caol Ila stillroom and the view as you stand next to Ardbeg's washbacks. Caol Ila faces east, gazing across the Sound of Islay to stern Jura: while stirring, the view is often a cold and shadowy one. Ardbeg's fermentation room, by contrast, seems to gather sunlight and its attendant warmth, urging the yeasts to ever-greater ebullience. Perhaps my memory is playing tricks, but it seems to me that every time I have walked out of the stillroom next door I have been squinting, unable to see the water for the fiery silver which lifts from it.

MISSING SCENTS

Every time, that is, except once. This was my first visit to Ardbeg, back in March 1993. I was with Iain Henderson, at that time manager of both Laphroaig and Ardbeg. The former was busy, steamy, smoky, bustling, almost glowing in the moistly briny autumn air; Ardbeg, by contrast, was cold, quiet, gloomy and damp. It had been closed on 25 March 1981 and was to remain so, apart from a few months' occasional distilling just to satisfy blending orders. It was the scent, I remember, that was most plangently missing. Visit any working distillery, and you can never escape the smell of brewing and distillation, of hot-steeped grain and alcoholic fractions, darting about the distillery yard like June-crazed butterflies. At Ardbeg in 1993, there was none. There was only the memory of malt in the old grain stores, and nothing at all in the distillery save the moist, mute presence of the adjacent Irish Sea. Cold metal carries no scent. Iain pointed out all the work which needed doing, and which was not about to be done. 'My head told me,' he confided to me a decade later, 'we should bulldoze it; my heart told me we should resurrect it. Ardbeg's a superb spirit. A good businessman would not sell a competitor something that's going to bite him on the behind in ten years' time. It's already happening: Ardbeg is a big, big player. I want to see Laphroaig grow, and Ardbeg will be a fairly major barrier to that. I would have kept it and used the warehousing, and if the malts had come back to the extent that we could afford to run two on Islay, then fine. I would never ever have sold it. But I was a voice in the wilderness.'

The problem facing Allied-Domecq when the company sold Ardbeg was the same one which Jim Beam Brands faced when it found itself with both the Jura distillery and Bruichladdich, and which the Edrington group had to confront when circumstances made it the owner of Highland Park, the Macallan and Bunnahabhain. Where do you put your money: into distillery A or distillery B? Which do you promote? If you promote both, don't you end up competing with yourself? And if you run your distillery on a full-time basis, do you have blends in which you can stow all that malt until sales of the distillery product alone gather wind? For various reasons (not least among them, sheer lack of imagination), neither Edrington nor JBB nor Allied-Domecq found a solution to the conundrum, which was why Ardbeg was sold in 1997, Bruichladdich in 2000 and Bunnahabhain in 2003. Only the mighty Diageo has been able to keep and run two Islay distilleries, Lagavulin and Caol Ila, profitably. Even in this case, its forebear found it necessary to close Port Ellen, a decision now bitterly regretted.

Before we summarise the renaissance of Ardbeg under Glenmorangie and the talented Stuart and Jackie Thomson, let's look back over its earlier history. Like the two other Kidalton distilleries, Ardbeg has its origins in a farm. Indeed there is a farm here today, run by Charlie MacMillan, and allotted to his descendants for the next four generations. The neighbouring farm of Callumkill is run by Donnie MacNeill, whose mother Jean cheerfully cleans the offices and visitor centre at Ardbeg. Both farms are regular winners at the Islay Show. Even today, farming and distilling go hand in hand. The draff goes off to feed cattle, and a number of Islay Estates farms take the distillery waste to spread on their fields, thereby (I am told) remedying a copper deficiency. Ardbeg's waste, thus, is the only distillery residue on the island not to finish in the sea.

Ardbeg's distilling history is generally dated back to the tenancy of Ardbeg Farm by a family of MacDougalls from 1798, a time when most of the island was owned by the fecund Walter Campbell of Shawfield, father of ten. The previous tenant, Alexander Stewart, had been declared bankrupt and his land sequestrated in 1794; the MacDougalls took over the relay – including rudimentary distilling operations. The large buildings we see today, of course, bear no resemblance whatsoever to what the distillery must have looked like at the end of the eighteenth century. Back then, it would have been an affair of a few barrels, a worm in a tub, and a little pot still standing barely taller than a man, probably sharing shed space with cattle and horses. An intermittent, seasonal activity, in other words; something to do when the weather was too bad to do anything else.

Things were, though, soon to change. By 1835, around twenty years after a licence was first taken out, annual production had risen to 500 gallons (2,273 litres) a week and by the time the great Victorian distillery chronicler Alfred Barnard arrived in the mid-1880s, Ardbeg had become the most productive distillery on the island, with an annual production of 250,000 gallons per year. This equates to over 1.135 million litres a year, exceeding current levels of production. The industriousness was due in part to an enduring partnership between the MacDougalls and a Glasgow spirit merchant called Thomas Buchanan, who assumed the lease on the farm, and bought the distillery itself, in 1838. But it was also due to fresh blood.

THE KIDALTON ROAD INCIDENT

By 1850, a new name became connected with Ardbeg: Hay. The last male MacDougall, Alexander, suffered ill health, and he and his sister Margaret recruited the son of the Campbell laird's coachman, Colin Hay, to lend a hand. Things at this point were going very badly for the Campbells of Shawfield, and the Hays may have been glad of new work opportunities. The entire Campbell estate had been sequestered in 1847, at which point the laird's debts stood at the colossal sum of £815,000 (or £46.1 million in 1998 equivalence). Colin Hay proved a capable and effective manager, and eventually inherited the MacDougall's interest in Ardbeg.

The Hays, father and son, built Ardbeg into a powerful and productive distillery. There are a number of plans in the company records, one dating from 1840 and one from 1938. The 1840 plan shows a house and a small group of distillery buildings given a single outline. The 1938 plan has no fewer than 42 numbered buildings, including a 'chauffeur's house', substantial peat sheds and a peat store, and a tar pot. During the second half of the nineteenth century, there were some 200 people living at Ardbeg, allied both to the farm and the distillery: a sizeable, viable community with a football team and a Gaelic choir. Today there are just 22.

Ardbeg is unique on Islay in that it has copious distillery records dating back to this period, and even a cursory glance at these will reveal the thoroughness and fastidiousness with which the distillery was run in the Hay era. A number, indeed, have been laminated and used as tablemats in the Old Kiln Café, much to the delight of visitors and horror of professional archivists. One day I found myself eating pasta from a bowl placed on a laminated account of what must have been a messy incident on the Kidalton Road. The Commercial Union Assurance Company of Glasgow wrote to Colin E. Hay 'with reference to the claim made upon you by Mr John Currie for the loss of his cow'. The tragic event occurred toward the end of May 1920. 'From the particulars given on the claim form,' the canny insurer continued, 'it does not appear your chauffeur was at fault.' The Commercial Union heart was not entirely stony, though, and 'a sympathetic payment of, say, £10', was suggested, 'without any liability on the part of your chauffeur'. The reply from Ardbeg must have thrown the light of compassion, and perhaps guilt, on the incident. 'In view of what you say with regard to the question of liability,' reads another letter from the insurers dated 4 June 1920, 'and also the necessitous circumstances of the claimant, we are agreeable to pay the sum of £35. You will appreciate that our former attitude was based on the particulars supplied to us on the claim form.'

The efficiency of the Hays (Colin had two sons, Colin Elliot Hay following his father at Ardbeg while Walter became a doctor) was helped by the fact that the southerly, Kidalton part of the vast Islay estate passed in 1855 into the ownership of the most talented businessman ever to make a career and fortune from the island, John Ramsay (see pages 145–7). Ramsay's qualities were nurtured in the whisky business, and he was a distillery owner himself (of Port Ellen). The Hays would have had a landlord who may always have been keen to maximise his own revenues, but who would also have understood the economics and the mechanisms required to keep a flourishing distilling business going – as well as the community which depended for much of its livelihood on it. Times were not always easy; by the end of the 1880s, Colin Elliot Hay was writing to the Ramsay's factor complaining, 'in these times of diminished trade', about the cost of access rights to the Ardbeg pier. Throughout this period, the Buchanans remained as partners of the Hays.

And so things continued, through good times and bad. The Buchanan business was eventually absorbed into that of the Hays (which continued to trade, as it did until 1959, as Alexander MacDougall & Co Ltd). The Kidalton Estate, by contrast, faced problems which meant that by 1922 Colin Elliot Hay was finally able to become his own landlord, purchasing Ardbeg from John Ramsay's son Iain for £19,000. Hay died six years later, in 1928.

Accounts of Ardbeg's twentieth-century history, up until the time at which it was jointly acquired by DCL (a forerunner of Diageo) and Hiram Walkers & Sons Ltd (a forerunner of Allied-Domecq) in 1973, are surprisingly sparse. Like many distilleries, Ardbeg closed during the depressed years of 1932–35, a bleak period on the island remembered by few nowadays; it also closed during the two World Wars. Alexander MacDougall & Co continued to own Ardbeg until it was liquidated in 1959; between that date and 1973, the distillery was owned by a company called Ardbeg Distillery Ltd. Ardbeg's survival became threatened in 1978, which was the year in which Hiram Walker merged with Allied, putting Ardbeg into the same stable as the already well-established Laphroaig. The period between 1982 and 1997 was the most miserable in the distillery's existence: the north wind blew, and its very survival seemed uncertain. It was closed between 1981 and 1989, then opened for two months a year between 1989 and 1996, when it closed definitively again. Had no sale taken place within a year, the distillery would have been demolished. With the arrival of Glenmorangie, however, the wind swung round to the south.

A TEAR TO THE EYE

Glenmorangie's was not the only bid; indeed Bill Lumsden, the company's 'head of distilleries and maturation', says that the £7.1 million offered and accepted was not the highest bid. There were seven others, and they included a bid from a consortium headed by Mark Reynier, later to acquire Bruichladdich. Why did Allied accept an underbid? 'They looked favourably on us,' says Stuart Morrison, 'because we were going to invest a lot, and because we could guarantee 150,000 litres a year for their blends, Ballantynes and Teachers, for the foreseeable future.' Is the relationship still good? 'They seem happy with what they are receiving from us. Indeed they must be more than happy, because they've increased their order to 175,000 litres.'

Back in 1997, the buildings were broken and neglected, nibbled by the rain and the sea spray. Repairs had been improvisatory. 'It was held together by string and Sellotape and chewing gum,' remembers Bill Lumsden, who discovered an electrical junction on the wall covered only by an old shoebox. 'My first impressions?' said Stuart Thomson, trawling his memory. 'I remember getting to the top of the road and thinking "What the hell am I doing here?" I looked down at this place and it was pretty decrepit, to be honest with you.' Jackie Thomson admitted to a 'wee weep' when she first saw it. 'It wasn't the nicest day. It all looked so *sorry*. And the house . . . my God . . .' 'It helped,' added Stuart, 'that the company decided to develop the visitor centre. It gave Jackie and me the chance to do something together.' They used to dance beside the former malt steeps to keep their spirits up.

For the first six months, Edwin Dodson came over from Glen Moray to help with the renovation work. The old kiln – the building which now serves as the distillery shop and café – was the most dilapidated building on the entire site. 'All the moisture was coming out of the wall; there was hardly any paint on it at all. Warehouse number three was in a sorry state; there were holes in the roof. What is now the car park was just mud. You couldn't fill the heating tanks because they leaked so badly. All the steam pipework had to be replaced, as did the malt mill rollers. Electrically, the place was a shambles. There was a drainage problem at the back of the farmland which needed to be sorted, too.' All the renovation work was carried out by Islay builders Woodrow with the exception of the electrical work, contracted on the mainland. The dry spring and summer of 1997 helped keep renovation to schedule.

The stills first ran again on 28 June 1997. 'It was quite emotional,' recalls Stuart. 'When we saw that spirit trickling for the first time, it did bring a tear to the eye. This isn't just another distillery, remember; Ardbeg had acquired cult status over the years. Almost all of it went for blending purposes, with just a small amount of single malt. It was recognised as being very good, but nobody could get hold of it. So getting it going again was not only very good for the company, but it was also good for the industry as a whole, and for the island; most of the people standing round the still on that day had thought it would never run again. So when you're standing there with those people thinking those things, you can imagine . . .'

Ardbeg, though, was in such poor shape after the years of neglect under Allied that distilling could only continue for a couple of months in 1997 before technical problems meant another halt for further repairs between October 1997 and April 1998. A total of £3.5 million has been spent by Glenmorangie on the distillery at the time of writing; the visitor centre alone cost £750,000.

THE HILL

On Wednesday 12 February 2003, towards two in the afternoon, I set off with warehouseman Douglas Bowman to walk up via Loch Iarnan to Loch Uigeadail (pronounced *Oog*-a-dal), the finest and amplest water supply to any of Islay's distilleries. Southern Britain was uniformly icy, and partially snowy, on that day; on Islay, by contrast, there had been boisterous rain earlier in the week, but today was a typical Hebridean surprise: fine, sunny, still. As we walked up, we tugged off our hats, and later our jackets; it was bright on the open hill, and there was warmth in the sun. Instinctively I began to listen for lark song. It could, improbably, have been June.

We talked as we walked. Douglas had been in the Navy, patrolling Irish waters, but now he was married and had a family he was glad to be back on Islay. After crossing farmland, we walked through hazel woods. He gathered wood there, he said, to make walking sticks. A man came up annually for the same purpose from Surrey. Douglas gave him deer antler that he'd found on the hill to use for the handles, and in return, the man from Surrey gave Douglas tips on how to make fine sticks.

Within the distillery, Douglas's special task is to oversee the water supply, so he tries to walk up to Uigeadail once a month or so. This is seen as a chore by the other workers, but Douglas likes it; he has a taste for the open spaces, and on a wide day takes the upland route home, even though it adds an hour or two to the journey.

We reached Loch Iarnan, in effect the holding pool for Ardbeg (though there is another small pool at the end of the distillery drive, next to Ardbeg Farmhouse). The water surface, across which the wind must often tear like Velcro, was silky; the afternoon reached its glowing zenith. We walked on and through the ragged hill-line of tough rock sills which mark the Kidalton landscape, yomped across a stretch of flat boggy land, climbed the deer fence which marks the boundary between George Middleton's land and Sir John Mactaggart's beyond it, and pressed on across more bog making for a higher valley. Douglas showed me the place which, one hot July day in 2000, caused a major crisis. The stream banks had given way at a tender spot during a dry spell, and the water course had migrated aimlessly into the boggy ground. Gradually Loch Iarnan emptied, after which the holding pool at the distillery drained quickly. There is nothing worse for a distillery than losing its water supply, so when the problem became apparent Stuart faced a major emergency. Douglas went up the hill, then came back an hour or two later with the bad news. Stuart then conscripted a work party (including Douglas), and they struggled all day to make good the banks. 'It was a day I'll never forget,' Stuart told me. 'I got into the bath that night and picked forty-five leeches off my body.' Douglas thought the ticks were worse: harder to excavate. They bury themselves in human flesh like fish hooks in the tender mouths of carp.

I stared at the water unravelling in its dark brown furrow. That was the moment at which I realised how gratifyingly primitive a drink Islay malt whisky still is. This was, in truth, just a small burn; you'd leap it on a walk without giving it a second thought. This water had fallen from the sky in this empty place; it had lain amongst rotting grasses and heather; it had percolated past boulders of cold quartzite on long winter nights; from time to time, an antlered stag's head had loomed darkly up from out of the sky, and a warm tongue had been dipped into it. This fine coarse water off the hill was what gave the bulk to Ardbeg's beer, the beer which is distilled to make the spirit itself. When the distillery is mashing 12 times a week, it needs 700,000 litres of it (though most of this is for cooling purposes). Yes, it's peaty, though the colour is misleading: analytically there are no more than 0.1 parts per million phenols in the water, and no distiller will ever risk more than Bill Lumsden's 'possibly' when you ask if such water could affect the flavour. Perhaps a better question to ask, though, is what has been added to it or subtracted from it at the moment it is used. Nothing and nothing is the answer. This is water home from the hill.

It grew hot on the last steep climb, and we broke sweat. A small family of red deer watched us provide the afternoon's surreal entertainment; we were evidently fascinating, since fifteen minutes passed without their stirring. Eventually we reached the great scoop of Uigeadail, and Douglas celebrated with a cigarette while I fumbled in the water for a few handfuls to drink and a souvenir quartz pebble. The chill of the water was implacable; despite the afternoon, it could not have been much above zero. A distant eagle patrolled Beinn Uraraidh. Did she register our existence? I hope so, even though we evaded accidents and thus failed to provide her with a meal. Down below, the land dropped away to Kidalton's sea with its distinctive rock braids. It was a view which left me longing for wings and a tail of my own, and the chance to launch myself off the hill's lip and into the sky. At such moments it seems almost possible to salvage some faint memorial trace of the fit of an avian skeleton, the contentment of easing into a thermal, the exhilarating resolve of a stoop.

We took a different route back over the long ridge Douglas called the Mare's Nose. A misty cloud was, by now, rolling in from the west. As we crossed the ridge we came across three grazing stags, no more than 200 metres ahead, and exchanged frank glances, bolts in the fellowship of being, before they skipped nimbly away. The last of the sun tautened into silver on the black pools of the Sholum Lochs, Lagavulin's water source, 75 metres below us. By the time we passed the shepherd's houses near the abandoned plague village of Solam, the moment of fine weather had passed and there was water churning in the air again. As we came off the hill, in chatting to Douglas I discovered he was the great-nephew of Iain Maclean, the legendary nonagenarian of Laphroaig, who sadly died during the writing of this book. 'I've never known a man so set in his ways,' said Douglas. He described Iain's radical gastronomic conservatism: porridge, mince, potatoes, and little else. Someone once presented him with a packet of sausage rolls. 'What in heaven's name am I meant to do with them?' he cried, in distress. Douglas is now 33, but Iain still regarded him as dangerously young and 'not to be trusted with drink' – so at Hogmanay, a small glass of sherry was all he was offered.

WALKING ARDBEG

Stuart took me, first of all, to see the old malting floors, the last grain shovelled from there in 1980. No one uses these airy spaces at present except each summer's African visitors. 'They're lovely birds,' says Stuart of the swallows, 'but they do make a hell of a mess.' The Glenmorangie policy regarding its own malting facility is 'to look after it, just in case'; Stuart would love to see it re-used, but the financial burden would be too much for the company to shoulder at present. Restoration would cost at least £1.25 million, and malting is a labour-intensive business; the fact is, too, that commercial malt (from Port Ellen) is more consistent and less expensive than the artist's product produced by hand on malting floors, as at Laphroaig and Bowmore. Nonetheless, there may eventually be some practical encouragement for re-opening the maltings.

'Malt,' sighs Stuart, 'is by far and away our most expensive outlay. This year a tonne of malt for Ardbeg is £264. Glenmorangie, by contrast, would pay something like £205, so there's quite a difference over a production year.' (Indeed so. Ardbeg uses 45 tonnes a week, so over 12 months' production – Ardbeg being the only Islay distillery to distil without a break over the summer – that's getting on for £138,000 in additional costs.) Ardbeg does own a 3,500-acre parcel of peat moss in the Mactaggart family's Ardtulla estate at Kintour: the parcel, at present unused, lies just to the left of the Kidalton road after you enter Ardtalla, and was the historical source for Ardbeg throughout the distillery's history. Re-opening the maltings would mark a satisfying step backwards; why should we go forwards all the time?

I stepped gingerly into the old kiln, with its perforated floor and arthritic malt-paddles. It was cold, silent, dark. Even after twenty years, though, you could still smell the peat, worked into the blackened pores of the wood.

As we left the old floor maltings and walked across the car park to the former malt storage area, Stuart told me about the night death skimmed him. It was Boxing Day 1998; after a calm day, a ferocious storm blew up at the end of the afternoon, slicing the phone lines, stopping the electricity supply, and blowing in two windows at the distillery manager's house. During the night, the storm then tore the roof off the maltings, air-lifted it across the car park and sent it avalanching into the office and warehouse roof. As a result, all the fire alarms suddenly hammered into life. Stuart, Jackie and their eight-month-old son Robbie were the only ones on site, so Stuart set off into the storm to try to isolate them and turn them off. As he went through the gap between the café and the filling store, a huge sheet of flying asbestos spun overhead. He decided at that point that a noisy night alive was better than deathly quiet. When the wind eventually did fall, there was almost a quarter of a million pounds' worth of damage, and the site had to be closed to the public for six months.

The wooden malt bins are still in place, and are now (Stuart thinks) unique within the industry; fire regulations mean that they can no longer be used, so everyone else has knocked them down. You can still see bushel marks, crossed off in fives, chalked on to the wood by maltmen past; indeed the sweet, rooty smell of sprouting malt still lingers in the wood here, as the smell of peat does in the old kiln.

Ardbeg uses 45 tonnes of malt a week, ground into grist in a gracious old Boby mill (first installed in 1881), now painted the olive-grove green which Ardbeg has made its own. There is, though, one interesting modification from the old days which ensures, in a roundabout kind of way, that Islay's precious peat does not get burned in vain. 'Most of the phenol in peaty malt,' Stuart points out, 'lies in the husk.' The 50–54 ppm phenols which correspond to Ardbeg's malt spec would only result, in the normal way of things, in about 18 ppm in the spirit. A reverse jet aspirator was, thus, fitted to the mill in May 1998, and that whisks the husks (or coulms) which would otherwise be lost to the mash tun. This use of husks ups the final phenol content in the spirit to 23 or 24 ppm, Stuart thinks, and will provide a significant flavour modification for Ardbeg as it eventually makes its way into the spirit. (Bowmore does the same thing.)

Ardbeg has a tiny mash tun of 4.5 tonnes; it manages 10 mashes a week. Those visiting the distillery might think that the mash tun survived renovation after Glenmorangie took over, but don't be deceived: that 1961 date is merely cosmetic. It is in fact an entirely new stainless-steel mash tun around which the plates of the old cast-iron mash tun have been wrapped. The slotted plates at the bottom of the tun were from Glenmorangie, cut to size. It is a semi-Lauter tun, meaning that the rakes inside are not adjustable. There is, says Stuart, 'nothing special' about the temperatures of the three sluices of hot water run on to the ground malt to extract its sugars, and as usual the third water (the hottest, to extract the last of the sugars) becomes the first water for the next mash.

The six washbacks (or fermenters) are made of Oregon pine. 'The vast majority of malt distilleries nowadays have stainless-steel washbacks, but when you come to Islay it's only Laphroaig. Surprising, really.' But Stuart's happy enough: 'I'm a great fan of wooden washbacks. Wood helps give an estery, carbolic style to the wash which you just wouldn't get with stainless steel. We want to retain a high phenol content, but we also want to retain the sweetness and the fruitiness; we want the estery content especially to come through in the final spirit as well, since that adds to the balance and the complexity.' Bill Lumsden also speaks admiringly of the 'soapy, waxy, almost tart character' which comes from the wooden washbacks. Stuart would like to employ some fresh brewer's yeast as well as the cultured distiller's yeast Ardbeg uses exclusively at present because it draws out 'a sweet characteristic' in the 'jo' (the peaty beer) and eventually in the spirit itself. 'But to be honest, once you got the yeast out to the island you'd probably be down to thirty-five to forty per cent viability. With cultured distiller's yeast you get ninety-nine per cent viability, so it makes practical sense.' No one on Islay is contemplating a return to the days of fresh brewer's yeast; indeed the distillery on neighbouring Jura has already moved on to dried yeast.

Fermentations are relatively slow because the high phenol content inhibits the yeast, and they are deliberately slowed further at the weekend when the distillery doesn't operate. There are twenty wash-still runs per week, and the wash still itself is in its 29th year 'which shows you,' as Stuart says, 'the inactivity over the years. We expect another four or five years out of it at most.' Ardbeg's wash and spirit stills are the squattest on the island, according to the figures I have been given, though not the smallest in capacity. The wash still is of gently pinched lamp-glass design, with a gently rising lyne arm and an external condenser, giving plenty of opportunity for reflux.

The spirit still, too, is of lamp-glass design, with a more markedly pinched waist than the wash still. Again, the lyne arm rises, and the condenser is sited outside. The still when Glenmorangie bought Ardbeg in 1997 was retired in November 2001, having by then given an astonishing 52 years of service, something which was only possible because it had spent most of a decade cold and empty. (When the thickness of the copper, which begins at around 8mm, gets down to 2mm then it is time to order a new one.) You can now see this grand old industry warhorse at the entrance to the distillery car park.

The malt-whisky myth is that when a spirit still is due for retirement, every single dent and imperfection of the old still must be reproduced in the new still in order not to risk altering the character of the spirit in any way. According to Bill Lumsden, this was 'pure marketing bullshit'. Stuart is slightly more sympathetic, pointing out that in the days before anti-collapse valves and vents were routinely fitted to stills, pressure indentations would appear in them after little accidents. If a distillery was thought to be producing exceptionally good spirit from such a still, then it was not illogical to try to reproduce those indentations when the still was replaced.

In any case, the manufacturers of new stills (Forsyths of Rothes in this case) go to great lengths to reproduce the overall shape of the previous still as exactly as possible. The old still was measured in 85 to 90 places. 'I've got evidence from 1842,' says Stuart, 'and the dimensions of the still were exactly the same then as they are today.' Compare this with the dramatic changes in the shape of Bowmore's stills since the late nineteenth century.

The Ardbeg enigma, supposing there to be one, is that this is a very heavily peated malt (Scotland's peatiest, until Bruichladdich created Octomore), yet when you nose it and taste it, the spirit has none of the bluff ferocity of Laphroaig or even the carbolic unction of Lagavulin. Every taster comments on its balance, its harmony, its subtlety. Why? Where has the reek gone?

'If you're talking about Ardbeg,' said Stuart, pointing to a small, flask-like appendage hanging off the lyne arm of the spirit still like a ball of mistletoe hanging off the branch of an apple-tree, 'then I think that's the most important thing of all.' This appendage is called a purifier. There's a pipe with a U–bend underneath it which eventually drops back to the belly of the pot. It's also important to note that the lyne arm rises slightly as it makes its way towards the condensers, and that it is fitted with a non-return valve, too. So what's going on? I asked Stuart what we could see if all this equipment was made of glass, and if different alcohols could be visually distinguished.

'Pretty much for the first hour and a half of the run, it's very much the lighter spirit which is being removed. The heavier alcohols eventually make it to the top, but obviously if we just want to collect the lighter ones, we have to do something special. This is where the purifier comes into play. The lighter alcohols go along the top of the arm. The heavier, denser alcohols go along the bottom of the arm and are captured in the pot of the purifier. They're then fed all the way back down to the bottom of the still again.' Glenmorangie distillery itself is famous for having the industry's tallest stills. 'When you're talking about boiling alcohol, it is your initial light alcohols which are going to give you that sweet, fruity, fragrant effect. The taller the stills, the more the reflux. At Glenmorangie, because the stills are so tall, it is only the very light ones which can aspire. Continuous heat naturally breaks the heavier alcohols down into lighter ones the whole time. What happens here at Ardbeg is very similar to Glenmorangie, but using a different mechanism. The purifier provides an intense form of reflux. There is so much reflux, if you like, that you could say that Ardbeg is not just double distilled, but two-and-a-half-times distilled. We're halfway to triple distillation. It's that which explains the sweetness and the fruitiness.' And, Stuart might have added, what we might call the sublimation of the peat. If Laphroaig's peat is earthy and carnal, then Ardbeg's is cerebral and celestial. The purifier has done its work. 'Without it,' Bill Lumsden reckons, 'Ardbeg would be a lot more one-dimensional than it really is.' (It's also worth noting that Ardbeg's condensers, both of which contain 238 tubes, are copper-heavy, further accentuating lightness and finesse.)

No one, alas, has yet discovered when the purifier was first fitted and why, though author Neil Wilson (who has written Ardbeg's history) and Stuart have spent much time examining the distillery records to try to answer this question. The supposition is that it was a modification made in the early years of the twentieth century in order to tame what was perhaps a beastly spirit for new, refined Edwardian tastes and the scruples of the blenders. Glen Grant, Glenlossie, Strathmill and Glen Spey are examples of other distilleries whose stills have been fitted with a purifier.

Once distilled, the new-make Ardbeg, a pungent and hypnotic emulsion of soap and smoke, is used to fill top-quality bourbon barrels (mostly from Jack Daniels whose owner, Brown Forman, has a 10 per cent stake in Glenmorangie). The casks are half first-fill, half second-fill. There has been little sherry wood filled since 1997. 'Just the odd cask, to be honest with you,' says Stuart.

The spirit is stored in five dunnage warehouses illogically but typically numbered 3, 9, 10, 10X and 11, of which number 3 is the closest to the sea; the rest are near by. At present, every drop of Glenmorangie's Ardbeg has spent all of its life, up until vatting and bottling, on the island, but for the future Stuart will only say that every drop of new-make spirit will spend its first ten years on Islay. There is, though, room for further warehouses. 'I'm quite sure,' he says, 'that if you come back in ten or fifteen years, you'll see a new building or two.' There are no plans, however, to bottle on the island. Interestingly, Allied's sale contract with Glenmorangie stipulates that 11,000 casks of Laphroaig should be stored on the site.

How much, most malt enthusiasts will want to know, have Glenmorangie's practices since 1997 modified what went on at Ardbeg prior to that date? As far as the malt is concerned, Allied did not re-use husks as Glenmorangie does so, as we have seen, the same malt spec would have furnished a less peaty spirit than Ardbeg now produces. The wash stills, too, used to be filled more fully. 'I'm not being critical of Allied,' says Stuart, 'but because the plant didn't work most of the year, they obviously wanted to produce as much as they could in as short a time as possible. As they distilled, they would have the stills pretty much full to the neck, probably too full. That would lead to a lot of inconsistency, because the wash stills weren't in sync with the spirit stills.' The lack of reflux would also have meant a more robust, rustic style than present practices are designed to achieve. What about the spirit still? 'We run them much more slowly than Allied used to,' says Stuart, another strategy which should intensify the finesse of the spirit. He can't confirm for sure that the spirit cut itself is different because 'it was never measured' in Allied's day, but Stuart thinks that the cut was taken down below the 62.5 per cent abv at which the Ardbeg stillmen today now switch to feints, which again would have led to a gutsier, wilder style. Allied's wood policy for Ardbeg, finally, was (in Bill Lumsden's words) 'rather random'. The result of these changes should be that Ardbeg is slightly peatier yet slightly subtler, too, and a more consistent and carefully aged spirit than in the past.

Look back further into history, of course, and you will find more dramatic changes. The abandoning of on-site malting would have made an appreciable difference to the spirit, as would the post-war switch from direct coal-firing of the stills to oil-heated steam. Photographs from the early part of the twentieth century show rich, concentrated peat being cut from as deep as 15 feet; some commentators have suggested that using such peat to dry malt would have given a heavily phenolic character, but in fact it seems likely that the opposite is true (deep-cut, heavily decomposed peat produces more heat and less smoke than rougher, rootier surface-cut peat). Ardbeg, as already mentioned, would also have been a very different and much more savage spirit before the purifier was fitted to the spirit still. Nothing in this world is unchanging, and certainly not malt whisky distilleries, as we will discover even more conclusively in the Bowmore chapter. Indeed, further changes may be imminent for Ardbeg: at the time of writing, Glenmorangie's owners have just put the company up for sale.

What of the present-day blends themselves? Bearing in mind that everything in the malt whisky world requires a decade or more to elapse between creation and consumption, it will only be from 2007 onwards that Ardbeg under Glenmorangie stewardship can be fully appreciated. The Ardbeg on the market at present is Glenmorangie blended, but distilled and largely aged by Allied and its previous partners. It is hard to believe that it will not improve.

The stock inherited by Glenmorangie (all of it on Islay and purely Islay-aged) was troublesome in terms of its age profile. There was useful stock (some of it excellent) from between 1974 and 1980; this included stock of what was called 'Ardbeg-Kidalton', a virtually unpeated malt distilled between 1979 and 1980. There was then no stock at all from between 1980 and 1989; then ample stock distilled between 1989 and 1996 (including a huge stash distilled in 1990). Everything from 1990 and 1991 seemed to have been filled in second-fill casks, whereas from 1992 some top-quality first-fill casks had been used.

In 1997, therefore, the one thing which Glenmorangie could not do was blend a 'core expression' 10-year-old; that had to wait until the 1990 came on stream in 2000. The distillery relaunched itself, therefore, with a 17-year-old, drawing on that 1974–1980 parcel of stock (and therefore in general rather older than 17 years). There have also been other, rarer bottlings including a 1974 Provenance; a 1977; a

21-year-old (blended from five casks of 1979 and 5 casks of 1980); and various special bottlings for the 'Ardbeg Committee': an enthusiasts' club run from the distillery with 18,000 members worldwide. One of the latest of these, released in autumn 2003, is a blend of 'Very Young' Ardbeg, distilled in 1997 just after Glenmorangie took over – and labelled 'For Discussion'. The spirit (from first-fill bourbon) was promising, with the refined peat and wood combining to provide a warmly smoky flavour of great clarity and definition – though its youth meant a slightly dry, abrupt finish. The latest permanent additions to the range, meanwhile, are the 25-year-old Lord of the Isles and the younger, richly constituted Uigeadail. Most are bottled at 46 per cent (though the 17-year-old was bottled at 40 per cent 'to make it last longer', according to Bill Lumsden) and un-chill-filtered.

TASTING ARDBEG

What does Ardbeg taste like? Let's start with the new make spirit. It can be as difficult to discern mature characteristics in spirit freshly trickled from the still as it is to spy adult features in a week-old baby. Ardbeg's new make smells frankly phenolic, oily and carbolic. Mature Ardbeg is never quite as obviously peaty as this. Equally striking, though, is the fact that there is no spirit nip in the new make, no matter how aggressive one's sniff; it's smooth from the off. There are fruity notes there too, and a sweet cereal harmony. It reminds me of a powerful engine, quietly purring.

At the time of writing, the 10-year-old is in some ways a surprise: together with Bruichladdich, it is at present the palest of the island's seven 'core expressions'. This seems likely to change in the future as more and more first-fill bourbon begins to play its role; the Ardbeg 10-year-old is built on a core of second-fill at present. Look out, too, for lusher, richer peatiness as the use of the husks begins to feature from 2008 onwards. At present this is a subtle whisky, quietly outfitted: soft, rounded notes of oily peat, of warm spice and of pale lemon fall gently through its aromas and flavours like sunbeams through high windows.

The 17-year-old is more evidently beguiling, with its rich aromas of waffles and honey, and its dark, biscuit-like flavours. The peat, here, lies digested within the spirit, sweetly brocaded by wood and time. The blend at present is predominantly first-fill casks, and it contains a trace of the unpeated Ardbeg-Kidalton; it's a toothsome and teasing blend, though one which will be impossible to reproduce exactly in the years ahead. Supplies, as I write, are beginning to expire.

Uigeadail is a more exuberant and full-throated whisky, as one would expect from its relative youth (the launch blend in 2003 brought together casks from 1993 and 1990 with a smaller quantity of much older, sherry-aged stock). It's a full nut-gold, in contrast to the pale 10-year-old, with assertive and engaging scents of autumn leaves and bonfire-smoked toffee, and succulent, tasty flavours, powerful and multilayered. It would be a tragedy if Ardbeg was to abandon sherry-ageing altogether, as the gratifying richness of this sweetly autumnal dram underlines.

The Lord of the Isles is, for me, the most allusive and provocative of all the Ardbeg blends; one of the hallmarks of this malt's out-standing qualities is the fact that it can carry a quarter-century so lightly and nimbly on its strong, well-hewn frame. Raisins, toffee, marzipan, chocolate: all of these dart and flicker in the malt's scents. In the mouth, it is all sweet profundity, triggered depths, succulent power. Few malts on the island can match a fine cask of Ardbeg for sheer multidimensionality; few can bridle natural power so adeptly. When it was launched in November 2001 it was a blend of 1974, 1975 and 1976 distillate, including some sherry-aged spirit. The blend will presumably have to step into the shadows from 2005 onwards, when the lack of 1980–1989 stock will make itself felt. I hope its disappearance will only be temporary.

Ardbeg is a fine malt, too, with which to play the game of vintage-dated releases. The 1974 Provenance was almost Cognac-like, full of crystallised-violet refinement; the 1977 was a more evidently peaty dram, yet beautifully aged (partly in second-fill casks) to provide subtle liquorice-toffee notes and a glycerous mouthfeel. I've been lucky enough to taste my way around a few special casks in the warehouses, too, including one distilled on the first day of Glenmorangie's steward-ship (28 June 1997). Nothing, though, can for me quite match the quality of the 1975 spirit casked in a refill fino sherry hogshead. The smoky, dry, wine-like refinement of this malt showed Ardbeg with unparalleled finesse and elegance. I first tasted it at the 2002 Islay Festival, standing with twenty or so others in the cold and the damp of warehouse 3. Stuart Thomson drew off a generous sample jar full of this straw-yellow malt, and we passed it from mouth to mouth, sipping with a combination of respect for its age and its strength, yet barely concealed enthusiasm for its magnificent drinking qualities. Standing in the darkness, warmed by its fumes, lost in its thrall, I suddenly recalled the brightness outside. Here in a cask, forgotten for most of three decades, glowed the light of Islay's warm south.

Ardbeg DISTILLERY FACTFILE

Distillery operating hours	6 days/week @ 24 hours/day
Number of employees	13 full-time; 2 part-time; 8 seasonal
Water source	Loch Uigeadail
Water reserve	est. 55 million gallons
Water colour	brown
Peat content of water	trace
Malt source	Port Ellen
Own floor maltings?	no
Malt type	Optic
Malt specification phenols	average 54 ppm
Finished spirit phenols	average 23–24 ppm from May 1998; 16–17 ppm previously
Malt storage	70 tonnes
Mill type	Boby, installed 1881
Grist storage	5 tonnes
Mash tun construction	stainless steel, semi-Lauter
Mash size	4.5 tonnes
First water	17,500 litres at 64°C
Second water	8,000 litres at 82°C
Third water	17,500 litres at 90°C
Number of washbacks	6

Washback construction — *Oregon pine*

Washback charge — *23,500 litres*

Yeast — *Mauri cultured yeast*

Amount of yeast — *75 kg per washback*

Length of fermentation — *65–68 hours (shorts: week);*
96 hours (longs: weekend)

Initial fermentation temperature — *20°C (16°C on Fridays)*

Strength of wash — *8 per cent abv*

Number of wash stills — *1*

Wash still built — *1974*

Wash still capacity — *18,279 litres*

Wash still charge — *11,700 litres (64 per cent of capacity)*

Heat source — *steam coil with heating pans*

Wash still height — *12 feet 3 inches (3.73 m)*

Wash still shape — *lamp-glass*

Lyne arm — *very gently rising*

Length of low-wines run — *around 5 hours*

Low-wines collection range — *46 per cent abv – 1 per cent abv*

Number of spirit stills — *1*

Spirit still built — *2001*

Spirit still capacity — *16,957 litres*

Spirit still charge — *13,660 litres (81 per cent of capacity)*

Strength of spirit still charge — *25 per cent abv*

Heat source — *steam coil with heating pans*

Spirit still height — *12 feet (3.66 m)*

Spirit still shape — *lamp-glass*

Lyne arm — *gently rising*

Purifier? — *yes*

Condensers — *two, externally sited, containing 238*
tubes

Length of foreshot run — *around 10 minutes*

Length of spirit run — *around 5 hours 15 minutes*

Length of feints run — *around 3 hours 30 minutes*

Spirit cut — *73 per cent abv – 62.5 per cent abv*

Distilling strength — *69.5 per cent abv – 70.5 per cent abv*

Storage strength — *63.5 per cent abv*

Average spirit yield	–	*402.1 litres of pure alcohol per tonne of malt (2003)*
Disposal of pot ale and spent lees	–	*to local contractors for spreading on farmland*
Type of casks filled for branded malt	–	*50 per cent first-fill bourbon (chiefly ex-Jack Daniels, air-dried wood, barrels rather than hogsheads); 50 per cent second-fill bourbon (same origins); very little sherry; further finishes and experiments in hand*
Current annual output	–	*950,000 litres of pure alcohol*
Number of warehouses	–	*5 (numbered 3, 9, 10, 10X and 11)*
Type of warehouses	–	*dunnage (3,9,10X); racked (10,11)*
Storage capacity on Islay	–	*24,000 casks*
Percentage of branded malt entirely aged on Islay	–	*100 per cent at present. In future all branded malt will spend at least 10 years on Islay*
Vatting and bottling location	–	*Broxburn*
Distillery expressions	–	*10-year-old*
	–	*17-year-old*
	–	*Uigeadail*
	–	*Lord of the Isles (25-year-old)*
	–	*Vintage-dated bottlings*
	–	*Ardbeg committee bottlings*
Major blending roles	–	*Ballantyne's, Teacher's, Black Bottle*

CHAPTER TWO

Story of an island: early times

Sea-shuffled pebbles.
Then history: the hand held,
fire, thatch. And foes' eyes.

WHISKY AND JAZZ FESTIVALS, ceilidhs, agricultural shows and sports days, ferry timetables, school expeditions and congratulatory notices on graduation: these are the staple of Islay's local paper, the *Ileach*. It is a long time since the last beheading. None of the villages on the island has been pillaged within living memory, nor children massacred. Photographs of siege engines and field amputations do not feature much in the *Ileach*.

Islay, in truth, has known few quieter periods during its history than the present calm. Lairds such as the astute Bruno Schroder or the affable Sir John Mactaggart are unlikely to be murdered in their beds while their wives, children and grandchildren are put to the sword about their gashed corpses. Fit young men like David MacLellan at Bunnahabhain or Gus Newman at Surnaig will never be thrown into galleys and made to sail, march and eventually fight to the death on the wind-harried slopes of Mar for a rich man's quarrel of which they know nothing and care less. Starvation has probably stalked the Oa for the last time, and no one who is born on Islay today will ever be forced by eviction to spend two months below decks in humiliating confinement, the brig in which they find themselves groaning and creaking its way across a capricious Atlantic, before trying to make a weary new life in untilled Ontario.

It is, of course, hard to make generalisations about how the texture of life in the near or distant past was felt by those who were alive at the time. All perceived experience is relative. The twelfth-century crofter may well, after a leonine summer and with his wife safely delivered of healthy twins, feel a flooding joy at the sight of his five beasts grazing at sunset which no twenty-first century systems analyst, with a small bankful of money to his name, will ever know. Bloody events may not necessarily have been typical events; the passage of a dozen years between the terrible trauma of battles may look, to you or me, like ceaseless strife, but those for whom this period was a quarter of a lifetime, and for whom success in battle was the surest way to prosperity and elevation, may not have viewed the broil in that way. Nonetheless, any reading of Scottish Highland history between the Iron Age and the Battle of Culloden in 1746 cannot fail to reach one conclusion. Progress, at least here, exists. Things have got better. Life has improved. Human beings in this part of the world behave in a more generous, kindly and sociable way towards each other now than they did 1,000 years ago. There are injustices, difficulties and miseries on present-day Islay, as I will outline in Chapter Eight, but they are dwarfed by the nightmare shadows of the past. Highland history is often one of terrible deeds, often inflicted on close kinsmen by those they must have loved and trusted, or by those whose power over their victims was absolute. We know little of the miseries which such deeds branded into the psyches of the survivors: the mental wounds which would never heal, the annihilation of happiness, the way in which rancour might fuel a life. These wounds would dizzy modern therapists. We know little, too, of the terrible agricultural struggle implied by the repeated sacrifice of the strongest, youngest and fittest within society, and by their constant departure on campaigns of violence and loss. There are few women's tales from Scotland's dark ages, while the cattle have left us no account at all. But we can be certain that life on Islay today, for its community of the living, has rarely been safer or sweeter.

A WHISPER BEHIND THE BIRCHES

Islay's geological fascination has been mentioned in Chapter One. The seals at Portnahaven bask on some of the oldest rocks on the earth's surface, mineral combinations in existence for between 1,600 and 1,800 million years. To touch their jagged surfaces and feel their crystalline intractability is to marvel both at the possibility of physical endurance and the mystery of matter. What, though, of more recent time?

Ice. Little else. The land we know today was hidden, entombed beneath frozen water. When the sun shone, it shone on snow crystals, on wind-hollowed caverns and on mirrored, frost-slicked surfaces. The last two million years have seen at least 17 glaciations; were you to pick a year at random out of the last 75,000, the chances are around 4 to 1 that you would pick a year when most of Islay's topography was snuffed as absolutely as Greenland's contours are today.

The glaciers withdrew and returned repeatedly between 20,000 and 10,000 years ago, a period during which it was still possible to walk (as millions of creatures would have done) from the landmass we now call France to those now known as England and Scotland. As the sun lingered and the ice began to trickle, the trees of Europe's primeval forest crept northwards like soft green magma. Those out playing golf in the bright bareness of today's Machrie may find it hard to imagine, but Islay was, around 8,000 years ago, an island of trees: birch, oak, hazel. The earliest Ileachs lived in clearings in those forests. Down on the Rhinns, between Loch Gorm and the sea, recent archaeological research has revealed the messy but durable remains of Mesolithic (12,000–3,000 BCE) flint workshops. Every hundredth shard, we may take it, implies a dead deer, surprised at dawn by a whisper behind the birches. Every flake implies torn muscle sliced raggedly off the bone and consumed, half-raw in a blizzard, by a tense band of cold hunters tortured by worms and tooth decay. The sea helped feed these early Ileachs, too, as a midden of discarded shells found at Ardnave proves.

The climate worsened once again as the centuries and millennia succeeded each other. Ileachs no longer survived by grace of arrowheads alone; evidence for the island's first farms – fencelines and sheep bones — dates back to around 3,500 BCE. Their crop would have been the short-strawed, hardy ancestor of today's barley. The forests, by now, were retreating, partly due to human requirements of fuel, building wood and land, but partly, too, to miserable weather during the first phase of the Little Ice Age (3,300 BCE to 2,000 BCE). Those alive at the time may not have seen it that way, but standing water on cleared forest in the cold, storm-lashed north was useful in one respect: these conditions began to create the peat bogs which are now so precious for the island. Indeed when barley and peat joined Islay's air and water some 5,000 years ago, everything was in place for the birth of Islay's distinctive whisky . . . save understanding. That gestation took another 4,500 years.

BLOOD ON THE WATER

Fast forward to a cold, possibly moonlit night in early January 1156.

The Romans have been and gone. There is no evidence that any soldier in Roman uniform (almost all of them recruited locally) ever set foot on Islay, though that is not to say that the event never took place; Vespasian's conquering general Agricola considered an invasion of Ireland, having reached the Tay in AD 79, and any scouting activities may well have made use of the island. The Roman fort line retreated to Northumbria and Cumbria a decade later, leading to the building of Hadrian's Wall. A second advance into southern Scotland was marked by the construction of the Antonine Wall, a turf belt across Scotland's waist, in AD 142, once again putting Islay within Rome's grasp. Yet these frontier territories (and their atrocious weather) were always dispiritingly troublesome for the Romans, who once again fell back to Hadrian's Wall twenty years later. The renewed campaign in Britain led by the Emperor Septimius Severus at the beginning of the third century had little impact in Scotland. In effect, Scotland's Celtic tribes never tasted the material advances, nor suffered the injustices and humiliation, of the Roman conquest. When the conquering forces of an alien culture came, they arrived from a different direction altogether: the North.

First, though, a little background. In order to understand the texture and narrative logic of Islay life between earliest historical times and the Scottish ascent of the English throne in 1603, we need imagination and maps.

Relief maps, first of all, will show that the physical fabric of Scotland is utterly different to that of England, its southerly neighbour. Scotland is a nation of hills and mountains. Most of it, even today, provides a wholly inaccessible and wholly unwelcoming landscape for large-brained, comfort-loving, unfurred apes. For much of the year, Scotland is a sponge for rain, and a pan in which to gather darkness. Its steep slopes welcome the venturing human foot with expanses of bristling moorland and sucking bog. A gale can spatter into life at any moment of the year; when the air is briefly warm and the light lingers, so too do clouds of assiduous midges.

Now let's unsheathe our imaginations, and use them to achieve the near-impossible feat of eliminating every road in this nation, and uninventing the motor car. And what are we left with?

Sea water. On a good day, a flattish surface. With a well-made boat, a dry and comfortable place to sit. With a fair wind, the chance to travel on a vessel which requires nothing (no feed, no rest) in exchange for forward movement. Nothing, that is, save mastery of sail and skill with knots.

Back to our relief maps again, concentrating this time on the western half of Scotland. Few parts of Europe are as spiny and as intractable as Scotland's west coast. Even today, its 300 kilometres are incised by barely half-a-dozen major roads. The hills and mountains are invaded by the sea in this small, southerly echo of the fjordlands of Scandinavia. Rocky peninsula succeeds rocky peninsula: Kintyre, Knapdale, Morven, Ardnamurchan, Moidart, Morar, Knoydart, Applecross, Coigach, Assynt . . . every one a mass of rock heaved by fidgety tectonics to the sky and its rain. The fingertips of this austerely grandiose stoneland are broken and crumbled into islands: Islay, Mull, Skye, and then all of the smaller fragments, a hundred or more. To move about such a landscape, you need either a raven's wings – or a boat. Legs (two or four) are poor help, guaranteeing fatigue and delay. The motor car has made us forget the fact, but the natural roads of Western Scotland and Northern Ireland are sea roads.

The highland people the Romans failed to subdue were the Picts. Today's Scotland, however, is not called Pictland. Who were the Scots?

The Scots were Irish: Gaelic-speaking Ulstermen. The details are necessarily hazy, but it was the sea roads of the west which brought the Scots to Scotland – by waves and in waves, between the third and the eighth centuries. Their kingdom was called Dalriada (or Dál Riata). This name lives on in geological nomenclature if nowhere else, describing a series of ancient and gleaming rocks which compose most of northern and central Islay. Dalriada was a watery kingdom whose heart lay in the North Channel which divides today's Scotland from today's Ireland. Its lands and possessions lay to either side; its wagons were boats.

Eventually, in 843, the Scots and the Picts were united by Kenneth I, or Kenneth MacAlpin. MacAlpin was the paternal grandson of a Scot known as Eoachaid the Venomous and a Pictish heiress; MacAlpin is why we speak of Scotland and not Pictland. For the time being, however, his Gaelic-speaking kingdom was known as Alba.

And now back to our maps. Different maps, this time: maritime charts, paying particular attention to those sea-areas whose names will be so familiar to northern European radio listeners both on land and sea: Fair Isle, Viking, North Utsire, South Utsire. Norway's Bergen and Stavanger are closer to Shetland and the Orkneys, even Lewis, than are London, Bristol or Canterbury. Bearing in mind that (in fine weather) a seaway was the only equivalent our forebears had to the modern motorway, it was easier to reach most Scottish islands and coastal settlements from a southern Norwegian port than it would have been to reach those locations by an overland route from Glasgow or Edinburgh. All this, to explain why, in the late eighth century, using the very latest in modern technology and advanced warfare techniques, the Vikings arrived to rape, kill and plunder.

And, eventually, colonise. The sea roads gave the Norwegians a kind of raggle-taggle Southern Empire. The southern islands, down to the stronghold of Man, became the Sudreys; the northern islands became the Nordreys. Ireland did not escape: Dublin was, from 841, a Viking town. The Vikings brought terrible suffering, as all of the contemporary chroniclers describe through the teeth of their poignantly dispassionate narratives. Most of them, of course, were monks, and the Rome of this little world, the islet of Iona, was burnt to the ground in 795, and its abbot and monks murdered. This sacred spot just off the west of Mull, wide open to attack from the sea, was abandoned, and St Columba's bony relics transferred to Kells, north of Dublin. Both Scots and Picts were harried by the Vikings. Indeed the fact that the Picts were weakened more extensively than the Scots led to MacAlpin's unification of the two races against the common Nordic enemy. And, as if all these difficulties were not enough, Islay suffered a major earthquake in 740.

Rape, within a generation, can heal to love and marriage. Raiders become colonists; colonists become locals. The Irish-Gaelic society of Dalriada became, with this blond infusion, the Gaelic-Norse society of *Innse Gall* – the 'islands of the strangers'. This society, governed by the Lords of the Isles and generally called the Lordship, was distinct from Alba and later Scotland. It was, indeed, a feared rival to Scotland. Six centuries after the arrival of the Vikings, a Lord of the Isles was treating with Edward III of England on terms of at least local equality. John was *Dominus Insularum* (Lord of the Isles); Edward was *Dominus Hibernie* (Lord of Ireland). History generally accords this John the full name of Good John of Islay. Islay was, throughout the four or so centuries of the Lordship's existence, its capital. At no point since has it enjoyed even a fraction of the political significance it possessed then. It was the heart of a small and struggling nation.

With hindsight, it can be seen that these centuries of significance for Islay began on that cold, possibly moonlit and incontrovertibly violent January night in 1156. Who fought who? Why?

The Battle of the Epiphany brought the forces of a local warlord called Somerled, of mixed Gaelic-Norse ancestry, into combat with the heir to the kingdom of Man and the Isles, the Norseman Godred. They were brothers-in-law: Somerled had married Godred's sister (or, to be more accurate, half-sister: their father Olaf 'the Morsel' or 'the Red', unusually for the times, was a peaceful diplomat who preferred the pleasures of the bed to those of the battlefield). Olaf had been murdered by his nephews: a trio of ageing Dublin Norsemen who were claiming half his kingdom. This royal family was typically dys-functional: the regicidal trio's own father and Olaf's brother, Harald, had been blinded and emasculated by another brother, Lagman. Olaf's murder took place while Godred was in Norway paying homage to King Inge, overlord of this colonial region. Godred returned, duly murdered his three cousins, and assumed the crown of Man and the Isles in apparently tyrannical style.

Somerled was a fine warrior with a history of distinguished conduct in the field. He may well have fought among Scottish forces against the English at the Battle of the Standard in 1138, and one (admittedly unreliable) source has him beginning his military career by ripping the heart out of freshly slaughtered Danes with his bare hands on the hills of Morvern, 'because they were no Christians'. He would have been the natural focus of local resistance to colonial brutality, and perhaps a focus for Norse unease, too: a local Norse leader called Thorfinn Ottarson suggested that Somerled's son Dougall should replace the little-liked Godred. Somerled had the wherewithal to mount a challenge: eighty ships, apparently, implying a force of at least 4,000 fighting men, a greater number than all the adults and children living on Islay today. Godred had to address his challenge, and with superior force; he did so just after New Year. The night of the Epiphany falls between 5 and 6 January, but some think the battle may have been on 12 January: a full moon in that year.

No one knows exactly where; indeed almost everything about this battle is unsupported by historical record – save that it took place. Tradition and the Clan Donald record, though, have always held that axe blades met necks 'off the north coast of Islay'. The historian John Marsden, in *Somerled and the Emergence of Gaelic Scotland*, argues that the battle must have taken place in the northern part of the Sound of Islay, suggesting the narrows of Caol Ila. The tides here, however, are extremely strong, reaching seven knots, as anyone who has ever watched the Jura ferry cross the Sound to Islay will know (it sets a course substantially at variance with its target pier, and the fierce tide makes the necessary adjustment). Could the battle have been fought there? 'It's not possible,' says Islay boatbuilder and diver Gus Newman. 'The tides are wicked. You wouldn't get two boats alongside each other for long enough to fight.' Newman believes that, if the battle did indeed take place off the north coast of Islay, it would have unfolded near Loch Gruinart. 'That's my belief. It's what the locals say.'

Early Scandinavian sea battles were very different from the elaborate maritime ballet of Tudor or Napoleonic times. Norse galleys simply formed fighting platforms. These ships freighted with fear and aggression approached each other, and the warriors groaningly set to: letting arrows slip, hurling spears, and eventually hacking at each other with swords and axes. This was exactly what 8,000 or so men, the cream of Hebridean youth, did to each other on that cold January night, perhaps near the dunes of Killinallan, perhaps between Nave Island and Ardnave Point, or perhaps in the relatively sheltered waters of Bunnahabhain Bay. After night hours of mutilation, gashed arteries, blindings, amputations and death ('great slaughter of men on either side', according to the C13 *Chronicle of Man*) . . . no one had won. Politically, this meant a setback for Godred. 'And when day broke they made peace and they apportioned between them the kingdom of the Isles,' continues the *Chronicle*. Somerled took Mull, Jura and Islay; Godred had the rest, including Skye and Man. Godred's share was fatally divided, though, and two years later Somerled completely defeated him, becoming *rì Innse Gall* (King of the Islands of the Strangers) in his place. A further six years later, in 1164, Somerled led an even larger expedition of as many as 160 ships to sack Glasgow. Malcolm IV of Scotland had taken Galloway and was eyeing the Isles; he considered himself Somerled's overlord. Somerled disagreed. Glasgow was duly sacked. And Somerled was killed.

Somerled's lasting legacy, though, was genetic, not martial. He sired the Lords of the Isles, and his direct descendants founded Clan Donald, Clan Dougall, and (at a later date) Clan Ranald. Islay was his stronghold, and Islay remained a rival power-base, on occasion substantial, to Edinburgh and Glasgow for nearly 500 years. Not until 1615 was Islay's political importance finally blown to pieces, together with the walls of Dunyvaig Castle, by heavy artillery shipped over purposely from Ireland on the orders of James I of Great Britain. It was early February and, in the words of the professional soldier given the task, 'the worst of all possible weathers'. In three days of short-range cannon volleys, the ancient and majestic sea fort was a ruin (see pages 99–100). Within a year or two, the Macdonalds were gone; the Campbells had arrived.

We will return to the Campbells, a more successful though less popular clan than the Macdonalds, later. What, though, was Islay like as the Lordship flourished and challenged the rival Scottish nation?

TREACHERY AT FINLAGGAN

Finlaggan, today, is where you will find Islay's quiet soul. The loch, undrained by any distillery, seems lifted gently by the two low hills between which it sits, like a dark sacramental bowl. The sky settles on the water. At its south-western tip, the land drops away; the water forms a prow. Finlaggan might itself be a boat, moving through air and time, ballasted only with the weight of what its stones have seen and known. By and large, they are mute. The grasses move with the breeze; the reeds break the water as tenderly as bamboos cut sunlight. Even in pipeless silence, the music of loss seems to hang in the air.

What was Finlaggan? The city as an administrative centre was an alien concept to early Gaelic society, whose people lived as closely to nature as any curlew or dunlin. Nonetheless, at its greatest extent, the Lordship covered a vast area of the lands of the western sea roads from Lewis to the Glens of Antrim. Not only that, but the Macdonalds possessed Ross, too – that ferociously difficult tract of the Highlands which stretches inland from Skye and crosses the entire country, the landscape easing only when Easter Ross meets the Dornoch Firth at Tain, and when Wester Ross tapers into the fertile lands of the Black Isle just north of Inverness. The lands of the Lordship, in other words, bisected mainland Scotland. Agreed, 'possess' in the context of fourteenth- or fifteenth-century Scotland does not mean uniformed police, civil servants and a postal service; it means little other than a series of rough agreements and alliances. Each glen, in truth, was its own kingdom, and strong men would always have had their way. But the fact was that this enormous area was politically united at least from time to time under the Macdonalds, and its grand council met on Islay, at Finlaggan. The only surviving Gaelic Charter in either Scotland or Ireland, dated to 1408, concerns a grant of land on Islay and is signed by Islay men; there is even a wild and improbable story that Richard II, the deposed English king given (by Shakespeare) such magnificently poetic flights of self-pity, was to be found working in the kitchens of Finlaggan early in the 1400s, perhaps learning to bemoan his fate in entertainingly flawed Gaelic and boring anyone who would listen with tales of his escape from Pontefract Castle. The Lordship concluded at least one treaty with the English crown as if it were an independent state. The consequences of this 1462 Treaty of Westminster-Ardtornish were unfortunate, to put it mildly; the English reneged on the deal two years later; Ross, Kintyre and Knapdale were consequently forfeited; and the Lord who had negotiated it, John II, proved to be the last to hold this resonant title independently. (It is held today as a dignity by the heir to the throne of the United Kingdom, the Laphroaig-loving, field-sports enthusiast Charles Windsor.) The terms of the treaty would have been plotted and planned on Islay, though the place of signing, Ardtornish, is found just north of Mull on the Morvern peninsula.

Ardtornish was another Macdonald stronghold. Indeed the castle at Ardtornish was where John II's great-grandfather, John I or 'Good John of Islay', had died in 1387; his body was carried once again across the seas to Iona for burial. Finlaggan reached its apogee during Good John's long, 52-year reign, though archaeological research suggests it was already a place of substance in the twelfth century and the settlements on its islands date back to the pre-Christian era. There are two of these islets, originally connected to each other and to the loch edge by causeways, and the second of artificial con-struction. Let's imagine the scene in 1351 or so, some twelve months after Good John of Islay had sailed up the Clyde more peacefully than his ancestor Somerled – to contract his second, politically astute marriage to Margaret Stewart. She was the young daughter of the Scottish regent and the man who came to the Scottish throne himself as Robert II, thereby initiating the Stewart line which eventually acceded to the English throne, too.

There would be a large tented encampment around the edge of the Loch, and possibly some stone houses, too, to accommodate the 600 or so people living here temporarily. (Finlaggan has always been an attractive place to live on Islay. The standing stone visible as you drive towards today's Visitor Centre and its associated burial chambers testify to prehistoric settlement activity here, and across on the western side of the Loch are the remnants of a village called Sean-ghairt, where 17 families lived in 1841, cultivating the now-rough land.)

The larger of the two islets, Eilean Mor ('large island'), would have been fortified and palisaded. Inside, there were lines of crops grown on lazy-beds and as many as 20 buildings including a chapel and a great hall with kitchens and ovens alongside it. Great hall? On a Celtic scale, perhaps: 19 metres by nine. The savoury, nourishing warmth of peat smoke would have mingled with the visceral pull of roasting venison; human voices speaking soft Gaelic and the murmur of animals would have been punctuated by children's laughter, a creaking axle bumping down the main track to the settlements, and the slap of wet clothes on the shore. Between the buildings, most of them tiny, run alleyways. A steward stands in a doorway counting tubs of ale; in another building, a secretary smells parchment as he checks the small stock of sheets. Between clouds, the sun sweeps the loch and sets the smoke glowing.

On the smaller and further of the two islands, Eilean na Comhairle ('Council Island'), are three buildings. A guard lounges by the causeway, sharpening knives from a bundle. Inside a converted keep, John sits with a dozen other squat, bearded men; there are tatty documents by their side, and a smoky peat fire burning in one corner. This is the fifth year of imprisonment of Scotland's present King David II; a rheumy, red-eyed man describes the size of the ransom demanded by the English, and how it will continue to go unmet. This is Robert Stewart, later to be king; like his host and newly acquired son-in-law John (though the two men are about the same age), he is by nature a child-siring diplomat rather than a widow-making warrior. They understand each other, and on that understanding rests the relative peace and prosperity of Scotland's great tracts over the next 40 years. On this tiny island on Finlaggan, the strong men of Morar, Morvern and Ardnamurchan listen; they broadly like what they hear, as they show in the days of feasting which follow. Two hundred years later, the Dean of the Isles, Donald Monro, described (in his *Description of the Occidental i.e. Western Isles of Scotland*) a Finlaggan scene such as this. Monro specifies the 12 island nobles who sat down in the old keep on the Council Island 'and decernit, decreitit and gave suits furth upon all debaitable matters' with the Bishop and Abbot from Iona. 'In thair time,' the churchman summarises nostalgically, since matters were very different when he wrote in 1549, 'thair was great peace and welth in the Iles throw the ministration of justice.'

Finlaggan, over the following 150 years, knew some good moments but more bad. Would the Isles dominate Scotland? Would Scotland swallow the Isles? As long as there was some sort of balance and equilibrium between the two, all was well. The truth, though, was that that balance was quickly lost after John's death, and the squabbles, treachery and murder which typified Highland Clan society in all its gory ruthlessness took its place. Mafia morals chased away the 'ministration of justice'; 'peace and welth' ebbed away on tides of rapacity. The desire by Good John's descendants to maintain their hold on Ross, in particular, was an endless source of turmoil, all of which came to a head far from the tranquillity of Finlaggan and the lapping waters of Lagavulin Bay.

John's heir was the eldest son of his second marriage, Donald. (Controversially, the eldest son of his first marriage, Ranald, had agreed to give up his claim to the Lordship in return for extensive land grants on the mainland and in the northern Isles; he founded Clan Ranald.) Donald hoped to seal his hold on Ross by marriage to the Earl of Ross's sister; her own father, the Duke of Albany, wanted Ross for himself, and both ignored the claims of the true heiress, the Earl of Ross's disabled daughter Euphemia. Good John of Islay might have pursued the matter with diplomatic cunning; his son Donald sent a fiery cross through his lands to draw his fighters from the hills, assembled as many as 10,000, crossed the seas, marched the glens and then fought hard and implacably. At first, all went well. Dingwall was taken, then Inverness; the lands thereabout were plundered. Then Donald turned south, probably realising that a fresh challenge would be mounted from that direction. On 23 July 1411, the Macdonald Islemen camped near

Harlaw; their fires could be seen in the darkness from Aberdeen. The next day his adversary, the Earl of Mar, surprised Donald with a dawn advance, and the rest of the day saw such slaughter on both sides that the event has come to be known as 'Reid Harlaw' (Red Harlaw). The result of this extravagant human butchery was a stalemate. In the circumstances, this constituted a defeat for Donald, who fell back to Islay. Ross was lost, though Donald's son Alexander regained it briefly by the favour (short-lived) of James I. Nor was this Donald's only difficulty: he had earlier quarrelled with his own younger brother John, who as a result crossed the sea roads to Antrim where he married the heiress to the Glens and founded Clan Donald South. This brother John was eventually murdered, possibly because he had aligned himself locally against the unforgiving James I.

By the 1490s, under Donald's blundering grandson John II, things are going very badly indeed. Not only Ross but Knapdale and Kintyre have been lost; John has been forfeited once; and his bastard son Angus Og had deposed him, evicting him from Finlaggan and forcing him (one source has it) to spend the night sheltering, King-Lear-style, under the hull of an upturned boat. This family conflict later results in another gruesome sea battle, near Tobermory in Mull this time: the 1481 Battle of Bloody Bay. Angus Og wins; he then seizes lands in Skye, and goes off campaigning to regain Ross, but in the end is murdered himself, in distant Inverness – by his Irish harpist, Dairmaid O'Cairbre. Why? The motive is opaque. For this unmusical intervention, O'Cairbre was taken, tied between two horses, and pulled apart. Such were those times.

Little good does his son's death do John II; he is forfeited again in 1493. His nephew and heir Alexander of Lochalsh is murdered on the tiny island of Oronsay the following year; and his cousin, John of Dunyvaig, is captured with his son John Cathanach and taken to Edinburgh, where both are hung, thereby eliminating another two contenders for the Lordship. The pair was taken, treacherously, at Finlaggan. Meanwhile the main heir to the Lordship, Angus Og's son known as 'Dark Donald' (Donald Dubh), spent most of his life in prison, and eventually died of fever in Ireland. Finlaggan itself was abandoned in 1494 and left to the wind, the rain and the courting lapwing.

MURDER AT MULINDRY

The sixteenth century was known as *Linn nan Creach* in Gaelic, the Age of Forays, but it might equally well have been called the Age of Feuds. Despite its colossal inefficiency, the feud was a principal means for obtaining justice in Scotland until James VI signed 'An Act Anent Removing and Extinguishing Deadlie Feuds' in June 1598. This meant that murder was institutional, and treachery to be expected, especially from close family members; a violent and untimely death was almost routine for leading clansmen. Have you read or seen Shakespeare's *Macbeth*? If so, you may think the English playwright was letting his astonishing imagination off the leash to rummage among the myths of Scotland's distant and bloody past. The story he chose did indeed have distant, eleventh-century roots; but the psychological realities he depicted might almost have been front-line, contemporary reportage from Islay or Mull. The play was written some time between 1603 and 1606, and would have been highly topical: on 24 March 1603, James VI of Scotland had assumed the English throne from Elizabeth I to become James I of Great Britain and Ireland, and the Scottish house of Stuart replaced the English House of Tudor. Scotland was suddenly of interest and relevance to theatre-goers on London's Bankside. The historian Nicholas Maclean-Bristol has persuasively suggested that the murders of Duncan and Banquo in *Macbeth* were examples of 'Murder under Trust' – a statute passed in the first Act of Scotland's 1587 Parliament (Shakespeare's legal knowledge was first rate). What had inspired this statute? According to the seventeenth-century legal historian Sir George Mackenzie, it was none other than an event which took place on Islay the year before. Let's call it the Mulindry Affair.

In addition to its problems both with Clan Campbell and the Scottish crown, Clan Donald on Islay had also found itself fighting Clan Maclean over a number of issues, including cattle rustling and land on the Rhinns. The Macleans of Duart had originally been stewards to Clan Donald, but the two families had fallen out in 1545 when Hector Mor Maclean had deserted the unfortunate Dark Donald during a rebellion against the Scottish crown, establishing the grounds for a feud which subsequently cost many lives. This reached its zenith in the last two decades of the sixteenth century in the feuding between Hector's tall, handsome and ruthless grandson Lachlan (known as Lachlan Mor Maclean or 'the great Maclean') and the son of Dark Donald's successor: Angus Macdonald of Dunyvaig and the Glens of Antrim. Typically enough, the feuders were also closely related, in that Angus had married Lachlan's sister Fynguala. Lachlan was therefore Angus's brother-in-law.

The Maclean's claim to the Rhinns had, in fact, been renounced by Hector Mor back in 1546, but the Macleans continued to occupy this agriculturally fertile and strategically important peninsula of Islay (they had a castle on an island in Loch Gorm). From time to time, according to the ebb and flow of politics, the fire of the feud would abate a little; one such pause took place in 1586. The English crown had decided to legitimise Angus's administration of the Glens of Antrim, and the reassured Angus decided to do the same for the Macleans on the Rhinns, allowing them to stay – provided Lachlan recognised Angus as his feudal superior. To seal the deal, Angus and his young son James went to Lachlan's forbidding castle at Duart on Mull for a six-day blow-out – and Angus left James in Lachlan's care afterwards, as a goodwill gesture. He had, however, apparently been embittered by certain songs sung mocking the Macdonalds by Lachlan's bard during the 'gluttonie and drinking without all measure' which took place.

A return invitation was issued. Since Angus had trashed Lachlan's castle on Loch Gorm in the late 1570s, alternative guest arrangements were made at Mulindry. Nowadays, this is a quiet hamlet on the Glen Road, notable chiefly for its bridge over the Laggan, just downstream of which Bowmore's distillery lade comes into being. It was probably a quiet place in July 1586, too. What was certain was that it lay in Macdonald land, and was well away from the coast, too, where Lachlan's boats would have been beached. The Macleans were lodged in an outhouse which was used as a kiln, Lachlan taking the precaution of keeping Angus's son James with him at all times; Angus's brother Ranald was also kept on Mull as a hostage. After the first night's eating and drinking, the Macleans retired to bed – at which point Angus surrounded the outhouse with two hundred men. Angus then called Lachlan out for one more drink. Lachlan hoisted young James on to his shoulders and opened the door – to find Angus facing him with a sword. James's terrified cries saved Lachlan's life that night, but he was separated from his men. The next day, rumour having reached Islay that Ranald had been murdered on Mull, the Macdonalds began to kill the Macleans, two per day, in front of Lachlan: murder under trust. Lachlan himself was to have been murdered, but Angus fell off his horse on the way to watch his brother-in-law's execution and broke his leg, so the entertainment was postponed and Lachlan remained imprisoned. Following the king's angry intervention, Lachlan was released the following April. He subsequently attacked Angus in Kintyre, wasting his lands – though Angus himself managed to escape back on that occasion to Dunyvaig. Angus repaid Lachlan by burning his lands on fertile Tiree.

The feud, thus, endured. The climax came in August 1598, by which time the Macdonalds had also fallen out amongst themselves, James attempting to burn his father and mother to death at Askomel on Kintyre the previous winter. Some interpreted this would-be parricide as signifying that James and Lachlan intended to end the feud. Lachlan, too, seems to have thought that this was the way the wind was blowing, perhaps encouraged by the passing of the king's anti-feud act two months earlier. A meeting was arranged so that Lachlan and James could agree on the borders between their zones of administration on Islay, and particularly on the status of Port Askaig, which both wanted. Thus it was that the Great Maclean landed his boats and men on Nave Island on 5 August, then walked with a smaller number down the western shore of Loch Gruinart. It was a hot day. Lachlan, despite his long years' experience of murder and treachery, appears not to have realised that he was walking straight into a trap. He was wearing little or no armour, and was armed only with a rapier.

The Battle of Tràigh Gruinart (the battle of Gruinart shore) seems to have taken place somewhere near where the RSPB's bird hide lies today. Lachlan and his men were attacked by the Macdonalds, and at first had the better of this sudden fight, but then came a sinister surprise: the appearance over the low hills which overlook this spot of Irish reinforcements, probably led by James's elder bastard half-brother Archibald, indicating no little degree of premeditation. Lachlan was killed, more or less at the place where the geese of Greenland first land each October, legendarily by a dwarfish archer called Shaw from Jura whose services he had rejected with contempt a little earlier in the day. This little local mercenary is said to have hidden in a tree and sent an arrow through Lachlan's heart as he bent to have a drink at a well (one of three actions which an inevitable witch had previously warned him against). The Macleans who were with Lachlan were then chased up the shoreline to Kilnave, where they took shelter in the chapel only to have the Macdonalds set fire to it and burn them to death. Lachlan was buried at Kilchoman, and his corpse was accompanied there by a woman described as his foster-mother, who had her own son called Duncan with her. This Duncan, who was perhaps simple-minded, is said to have laughed at the sight of the Great Maclean's head and feet jolting on the makeshift hearse – so his mother murdered him at the place near Loch Gorm now called Carnduncan ('Duncan's Cairn').

This was hardly a promising start for King James's anti-feud policy, and his patience with the Macdonalds was rapidly running out. James sent professional soldier Sir Oliver Lambert to besiege and destroy Dunyvaig, the final symbol of Macdonald resistance, shortly before Christmas 1614. 'The Castle of Dunyveg,' wrote Lambert to James VI, 'is seated on high rocks, above the rocks but two stories high, reported to your Majesty to be infinite strong, the walls thirty foot thick. We found it otherwise; eight foot in some places, less in others . . . The greatest enemy opposed us was cold wet and perpetual storms.' Lambert and his men built a platform from which to fire at the castle (it is still there today; the former Lagavulin distillery manager's house is sited on it). As Lambert made his preparations, one of his captains was injured. 'In drawing the cannon, Captain Crayford, a painful, careful and a worthy captain, unfortunately received a shot that broke the small of his leg all to shivers. After five or six days he was dismembered, which he endured manfully, and died within two hours after.' Firing began at the beginning of February 1615. '[W]e spared no powder, and in a small time the places battered yielded such abundance of ruins and rubbish that the inward bawne, the well, and as high as the rock on which the bridge resteth that they must pass in and out of the castle was chocktt up.' The remaining Macdonalds escaped by the sea gates and were 'hunted about the island'. Lambert, who wrote with a soldier's plain brevity, was impressed by Islay, which he found 'large; good land; pretty fishings; salmon taken in many places; as requisite to be civilised, as commodious for good men to inhabit.' There was snow lying on the hills of Antrim, Kintyre and Jura, but none, he observed approvingly, on Islay. The Highlanders, though, impressed him rather less. 'They are obedient to no command, subject to no order; ravine and spoil all where they come.' He anticipated Royal reform. 'These Highlanders have good and able bodies; easily made soldiers in another government; as yet, more barbarous than the rudest I ever saw in Ireland. Men of good justice seated among them, idle dependency banished, reformation soon follows. Your Majesty's cannons have so well proclaimed your royal powers unto them, that they will hardly trust any stone walls again.'

Defeated by the Campbells and the Stewarts they may have been, but nobles the Macdonalds remained; they kept scattered lands and holdings, most notably Sleat on Skye and most tragically in Glencoe. The Campbells, though, replaced the Macdonalds in Argyll and on Islay – and with that regime change came the end of Islay's role as the capital of a nation of sorts.

MURRAIN AND MISERY

Two branches of Clan Campbell owned and dominated Islay for over 200 years, between 1615 and 1847. The island was not a possession of the main branch of the family, the Earls and later the Dukes of Argyll, but of younger brothers from the fourth and the ninth generation, male siblings being something the Campbells proved themselves adept at producing. Those two branches of the family were initially the Campbells of Cawdor (who owned most of Islay from 1615 to 1723), and subsequently the Campbells of Shawfield (whose ownership lasted until 1847).

Under the Cawdor Campbells, Islay suffered, for at least four reasons.

Initially, it suffered from the disruptions of a kind of civil war on the island, as the Macdonalds, very much the native stock, were driven out by the conquering Campbells. The 1615 date may seem a neat and convenient one, but it obscures many decades of warfare among different branches of Clan Donald itself, as well as the incessant struggle against those who crossed the seas to expel them from their home island and ancestral heartland.

Secondly, the weather was against the people, with many seasons of grain failure recorded in Scotland during the first half of the seventeenth and early eighteenth century (as the Little Ice Age drew on). Cattle plague (or murrain, locally called traik) periodically affected the island, too. There are no records of Ileachs dying of starvation at this time, but it is beyond certainty that many during the Campbell-of-Cawdor period had lives curtailed by malnourishment as well as disease, and that the short years they passed were marked by pitiful misery.

Thirdly, the Cawdor Campbells had acquired, by political and military means, far more land than their wealth enabled them to administer successfully. The family was continually in debt. This meant that they were unable to make the agricultural improvements which Islay desperately needed. Without such improvements, the islanders themselves fell more and more behind with the rents which the Campbells demanded of them, thereby in turn increasing the Campbells' own indebtedness.

Finally, the various members of the Cawdor Campbell family inheriting the island were not infrequently minors (which meant that the land was managed by salaried employees with no direct interest in it) or absentees (which meant much the same thing). When the Cawdor Campbells did take an interest, the island and islanders didn't necessarily benefit; indeed the second of the Cawdor Campbells (known as John the Fiar) brought in his own friends and family as tenants (or tacksmen) on the island, demoting existing landholders to sub-tenants. He was eventually declared insane, and his son predeceased him. The fourth Cawdor Campbell, Alexander, lived chiefly in London and Wales; and the fifth, John, having inherited the island at two years old, eventually proved to be a dismal businessman who concluded a poor deal over the island's sale. The exception to this generally sorry picture was the third of the Cawdor Campbells, Hugh, who took an interest in the management of his estate as well as its rents, and who began work on Islay House as an alternative to the now-demolished Dunyvaig. But with the magnificent Cawdor Castle to the family name, why worry about building much of a pile on Islay?

This period is noteworthy, though, for the fact that it gives us the first vividly written account of everyday life on the islands, Islay included: Martin Martin's *A Description of the Western Isles of Scotland*, published in 1703. Martin was a native Gaelic speaker from Skye.

The picture that emerges is of a deeply superstitious society living on intimate terms with a perfectly observed though imperfectly understood natural world. A man appealingly named John Fake on Harris, for example, was called the 'Rain Almanac', since he had sneezed for the last nine years whenever it was going to rain; women on Skye 'observe that their breasts contract to a lesser bulk when the wind blows from the north, and that then they yield less milk than when it blows from any other quarter'; on Canna, Martin discovers that the needle of a compass 'went often round with great swiftness, and instead of settling towards the north, as usual, it settled here due east.' Diseases are cured by a variety of techniques. Fanning the face of the patient with the pages of a bible is perhaps the least injurious of these; by contrast jaundice was cured on Lewis 'by taking the tongs, and making them red hot in the fire; then pulling the clothes from the patient's back . . . [and touching] the patient on the vertebrae upwards of the back, which makes him furiously run out of doors, still supposing the hot iron is on his back, until the pain be abated, which happens very speedily, and the patient is cured soon after.' A woman on Harris cured her deafness by stuffing her ear with tobacco, while a forester on the same island saw off colds by walking 'into the sea up to the middle with his clothes on, and immediately after goes to bed in his wet clothes, and then laying the bedclothes over him procures a sweat, which removes the distemper.' Jura seemed to Martin to be 'perhaps the wholesomest plot of ground either in the isles or continent of Scotland . . . to which the height of the hills is believed to contribute in a large measure, by the fresh breezes of wind that come from them to purify the air; whereas Islay and Gigha, on each side of this isle, are much lower, and are not so wholesome by far, being liable to several diseases that are not here.' One Jura resident had lived, Martin was told, to 180; 'Bailiff Campbell' had died three years earlier there at 106; and there was a 90-year-old alive there at the time of his visit.

Martin's account of Islay is not as fulsome as that of some other islands, though he does mention having an argument with a beggar woman there who insisted on walking round him three times after he gave her alms. He forbade boatmen taking him from Islay to Colonsay to indulge in this same 'superstitious custom' on the water; they did it anyway, so he was perversely pleased when poor weather forced them back. When exploring some of Islay's many caves, he was shown a well called Toubir in Knahar and told that it had originally been sited on Colonsay. When 'an imprudent woman' happened to wash her hands in it, the well took offence at 'being thus abused' and moved itself on the instant to Islay. Ever since, the well that jumped islands had been 'esteemed a catholicon for diseases by the natives and adjacent islanders; and the great resort to it is commonly every quarter day.'

Martin, too, provides useful detail on Hebridean drinking customs and habits of the time, significantly linking them (as those visiting Islay quickly learn to do) with the climate. 'The air,' he says of Lewis, 'is temperately cold and moist, and for a corrective the natives use a dose of *trestarig* or *usquebaugh*.' Both, he says, are made on Lewis of oats rather than barley (and as a Gaelic speaker this is not a detail he should have got wrong); they vary in strength. *Trestarig* he describes as 'aqua vitae, three times distilled, which is strong and hot; a third sort is four times distilled, and this by the natives is called *usquebaugh-baul*, id est, *usquebaugh*, which at first taste affects all the members of the body: two spoonfuls of this last liquor is a sufficient dose; and if any man exceed this, it would presently stop his breath, and endanger his life.' Cask strength, obviously. On Harris, by contrast, they drank brandy. They did, though, brew beer, which they flavoured with 'the seeds of the wild white carrot, instead of hops'. Brandy was drunk on Skye, too, in 'larger dose . . . than in the south of Scotland' since '[t]he air here is commonly moist and cold.' (Apparently three times the dose was required to keep the air at bay.) On Tiree, Martin was disappointed with his ale since it was 'too weak'. The innkeeper 'promised to make it better; for this end he took a hectic stone, and having made it red hot in the fire, he quenched it in the ale. The company and I were satisfied that the drink was a little more brisk, and I told him that if he could add some more life to our ale he would extremely oblige the company. This he frankly undertook, and to effect it toasted a barley cake, and having broken it in pieces he put it into the dish with the ale, and this experiment we found as effectual as the first.' These may seem odd practices (though the hot-stone trick lives on in the Rauchenfels 'stone beer' of Bavaria), but they do prove that brewing, distilling and the use of barley were commonplace throughout the islands at this time. The term 'dram', too, was already current. 'The air here,' said Martin once again when he reached Arran, 'is temperately cold and moist, which is in some measure qualified by the fresh breezes that blow from the hills, but the natives think a dram of strong waters is a good corrective.' Disappointingly, Martin does not make any reference to drink or drinking on Islay, though he does mention that barley was grown on the island.

What of drinking habits? 'The manner of drinking used by the chief men of the isles is called in their language *streah*, i.e. a "round"; for the company sat in a circle, the cup-bearer filled the drink round to them, and was all drunk out whatever the liquor was, whether strong or weak; they continued drinking sometimes twenty-four, sometimes forty-eight hours. It was reckoned a piece of manhood to drink until they became drunk, and there were two men with a barrow attending on such occasions. They stood at the door until some became drunk, and they carried them upon the barrow to bed, and returned again to their post as long as any continued fresh, and so carried off the whole company one by one as they became drunk.' This was the old way, and Martin was able to log a change for the better. 'Several of my acquaintance have been witnesses to this custom of drinking, but it is now abolished.'

On this not entirely convincing note, we will leave the story of the island to await resumption in Chapter Three. The eighteenth century, with all its intimations of encyclopedic knowledge and improving ways, has just opened; on Islay, though, it is no more than a distant glimmer in the dark. The last of the Campbells of Cawdor, John, is attempting to sort out his chaotic business affairs by letting the island, an arrangement which swiftly becomes a sale. For 'one who knows so little of busyness as I,' he wrote to the island's eventual purchaser, almost inviting a hard bargain, 'it is better to receive than to make proposals.' He had inherited the island when he was two years old, and it had been run by his uncle; just after John came of age in 1716, his island representatives were reporting 'the worst paid rent that has been in Islay these 100 years'. By May the following year, the murrain had plunged the island into crisis, with animal corpses littering the fields, basic foodstuffs in short supply, and overseas aid being solicited from Ireland to keep starvation at bay. Meanwhile the compasses were spinning on Canna, wells were flitting from island to island, and sick children were being fanned with the pages of family bibles. Enlightenment could not come soon enough.

SECOND GLASS

Bowmore

The loch a silver tongue.
Samples: drawn gold. Then snowflakes:
the sky-stepping geese.

A FEW FARM buildings, a sack or two of spare grain, the December rain drumming on to a roof of coarse slates and a blistered pot about which a man might throw his arm: those are the origins of most of Islay's distilleries. In the mid-eighteenth century, moreover, this was a scene you would find on almost all of Islay's tiny, scattered smallholdings, which was why traveller Thomas Pennant spoke of Islay as being cursed with 'a ruinous distillation' in 1772, and why the Kidalton minister, Archibald Robertson, could claim in the 1790s that the 'evil' of turning too much grain into whisky was the 'chief cause of our poverty'. Oddly enough, however, these scenes of happiness and squalor do not provide the origins of Islay's oldest surviving distillery: Bowmore (pronounced as written, though Ileachs tend to stress the second syllable).

Bowmore was never a sideline, a weakness or a poor antidote to mud and despair; it was a business from the off. It owes its origins to the desire of Islay's young laird, a cultured man in his twenties who had inherited the island from his vastly wealthy grandfather, to improve his own house and grounds at Bridgend. He was called Daniel Campbell 'the Younger', to differentiate him from his grandfather, 'Great' Daniel Campbell. He evicted an entire village, moving it off his doorstep (the place was previously called Kilarrow) and round the great bay of Loch Indaal to a suitable site called Bowmore. Young Daniel recalled the pretty Tuscan hilltop villages, built around prominent churches, which he had seen on his recent Grand Tour of Europe. On the Tour, he had met John, Lord Lorne, the son of the 4th Duke of Argyll, and so to sweeten the pill of eviction Daniel gave Bowmore a fine round church, built (according to its Latin inscription) 'with pious intent, and to promote truth and honour'; it was based on the discarded 1758 Inveraray designs drawn up for the 4th Duke by John Adam, and was completed in 1769. He also gave the pioneers of Bowmore more favourable tenure agreements (called feus) than those enjoyed else-where on the island. There was, in sum, a late eighteenth-century buzz about Bowmore, which may well have been why David Simpson (also spelled Simson) – merchant, farmer, distiller, house-builder, postmaster and mail-packet entrepreneur – undertook to create a distillery there.

We know little about the Simpsons; indeed even the founding date of 1779 is, according to the industry authorities John Hume and Michael Moss, conjectural. If true, it would make Bowmore the twelfth oldest legal distillery in Scotland, though quite why legality was necessary when there was no Excise Officer on the island and would not be for another twenty years is uncertain. Perhaps it was, precisely, due to the distillery's prominence in Islay's nascent 'business district'. Equally uncertain was the original water source for the new distillery, and even its exact position, since Simpson's original land grant was for land 'in Hill St and Shore St', whereas today's distillery is found across the main square in School Street. David Simpson seems to have been succeeded by John Simpson and Hector Simpson, while John Johnston of the nearby Tallant distillery (and the same family which founded both Laphroaig and Lagavulin) also figures in the records. Water, it would seem, was always something of a problem for Bowmore, since by 1825

Hector Simpson had taken a loan from the laird to build a 'Distillery Canal'; it was, however, only under the ownership of William and James Mutter, who took over in 1837, that the present-day distillery lade was completed. In 1833, Bowmore was one of twelve licensed distilleries on the island; in addition to adjacent Tallant, there were distilleries at Newton, Daill and Lossit on the road to Port Askaig, with two distilleries on the Rhinns (Octomore and Port Charlotte), and five in Kildalton (Ardbeg, a pair at Lagavulin, Laphroaig and Port Ellen).

WATER AND HARDSHIP

With the arrival of the Mutters, Bowmore grew. They were Glasgow merchants of German extraction, and had what appears to be considerable entrepreneurial flair: they expanded the distillery, ran their own steamship to and from Glasgow, and marketed and advertised Bowmore as a pioneer single malt whisky both at home and abroad. Increased production, of course, required a reliable and copious supply of water, and it was at this time that the complicated lade running off the river Laggan was constructed.

Though discreet, this meandering 14-kilometre channel is one of the most remarkable pieces of engineering on the island. The direct route between its beginning and end is barely half its actual length. The engineering challenge is the fact that it leaves the river (at the weir downstream of Mulindry Bridge) at a point just 30 metres higher than the distillery and has to circumnavigate numerous topographical obstacles on its journey. This is why it takes five kilometres to drop ten metres; when you walk it, indeed, there are points at which it seems to flow languidly uphill. Legend has it that its exact course was worked out by a patient Bowmore tailor, observing the movement of drops along lengths of waxed thread. The lade was created in the late 1840s, at a time of great hunger on the island due to potato blight, and when the colossally indebted final Campbell laird of the island had just agreed to sequestration. John Murdoch (see pages 136–41) was on Islay at the time working as an Exciseman, and he implies that the lade was created using 'Relief Committee' money which should have gone more directly to alleviate the suffering of the islanders. 'The inspector [from the Relief Committee],' Murdoch wrote, 'was a weak man and – he having at once fallen into the hands of the potent few – the work, the meal and the seed were largely thrown away. There was scope for the doing of much good in the way of extending tillage and in making drains on the farms held by the poorer husbandmen. But, so far as I remember, the works which would yield productive results were done for those who could afford to do them for themselves. One of these was the bringing of water to the distillery at Bowmore. Clearly, the proprietor or the distiller should have done the work required. But I remember speaking to Mr Stewart, the parish minister, when the Relief Committee inspector came along guarded by Webster, the factor, and James Mutter, the distiller. I just said, as they went away from the manse door: "That poor fellow has fallen already into the hands of the thieves." And events proved that I was correct.'

The Mutter family were still in charge when Alfred Barnard visited in the 1880s, by which time Bowmore was the second most productive distillery on the island after Ardbeg. The visiting Barnard's view of James Mutter contrasts starkly with resident John Murdoch's almost forty years earlier. Mutter was, Barnard assured his readers, a progressive farmer who grew Islay's first crop of clover, and as 'a benefactor to the poor and philanthropist, he was much beloved, and won the esteem of all classes'. One might assume that Barnard had been told as much by Mutter's own family, but they were absent when he visited; he was shown round by a (presumably loyal) manager.

Barnard was a maniac for measuring things, and he seems to have had a field day at Bowmore: his notes are more comprehensive than for any other of the island's distilleries. His book also provides a fascinating line illustration of Bowmore's still room, which annihilates the dogma that the shape of stills in a distillery is sacrosanct and unchanging: Bowmore's stills in 2003 look nothing whatsoever like they did when Barnard's book was published in 1887. Barnard says there were five stills (three wash and two spirit stills), though only four are shown in the drawing. Of the four, one is a bulbous lamp-glass in design, with an extraordinary lyne arm which leaves the still below its top and then rises very steeply, like a genuine swan's neck; another still (which Barnard confirms is a wash still) has almost no pot at all but a long,

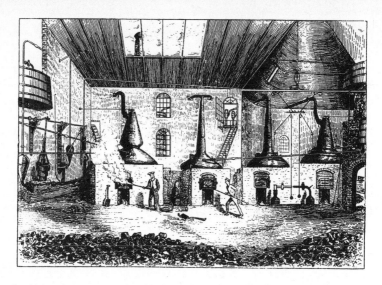

gradually narrowing neck which ends, astonishingly, in not one but two dipping lyne arms which are presumably condensed separately. The other two stills shown are variants of these, though the long thin one has just one lyne arm and the bulbous one is of plain rather than lamp-glass shape. Is there any resemblance between these and today's stills? None whatsoever. When you take into account that all malting was then done on site, and that all the stills were directly fired, we can safely say that the spirit which Barnard tasted would have been utterly different from today's Bowmore.

THE DEAD HOLE

For some reason, though no one knows why, the Mutters sold Bowmore in 1892 – to an outfit called the Bowmore Distillery Company; the scant distillery records say that Holmes was the name of the individual or individuals behind this company. The whisky writer and publisher Neil Wilson claims that this was 'a consortium from London' and that the sale 'was disputed' – which might explain why, during what was a boom time for whisky and when Glasgow blenders were finding it hard to source all the fillings they needed, Bowmore appears to have been idle. Testimony taken from Bowmore residents on 2 April 1894 for the Napier Commission (see page 149) paints a sorry picture. Duncan Campbell Macewan, an evidently bright Ileach who had spent 10 years running a large sheep station in Australia at the time of the goldrush in the 1850s, said that there was 'nothing doing' at the distillery.

'Is it permanently closed?' he was asked.

'Not permanently, it is open, but all they do in the twelvemonth could be done in a week.'

'Is the result of that that a number of people are thrown out of employment at present?'

'The fishermen and crofters, and others have nothing to do, and it is today the poorest parish in Islay.'

'Is it the case that a great number of people who used to find work at the distillery are at present out of employment?'

'Yes, that is the case; I estimate that at the very least £30 or £35 used to be earned in Bowmore, but now there is not £5 a week.'

'And so far as you know is there any prospect of the distillery being reopened or kept going at its full productive power as before?'

'Not the least, so far as I know.'

Macewan, it emerged, was a landlord in the village.

'You are a considerable proprietor of houses, are you not, in Bowmore?'

'Yes.'

'I see by the Valuation Roll that you have a good many?'

'But I am very sorry to say that I get no rent.'

'You find Bowmore is not prospering?'

'No, it is a dead hole altogether.'

'And you cannot get your rents in?'

'No, nor anything else, but I have to pay my taxes all the same.'

'But you are of the opinion that there would be prosperity if there was an additional quantity of land provided for the people?'

'By all means. The people would work instead of being idle and having to go to the poorhouse.'

'In fact, you would rather reduce the size of Bowmore itself and get the people out to the land, is that your cure?'

'Yes: they were forced into this little village when they were evicted from their farms, and here they are paupers.'

'Then there is no business of any kind carried on?'

'No business whatever.'

Another witness to the commission, Donald Magillivray, recalled that the Bowmore distillery manager under the Mutters used to pay the same sum mentioned by Macewan, £30 to £35, in wages each week, and confirmed that this income had now dried up; and steamboat agent Malcolm Macmillan pointed out that Bowmore still had no pier, so all the goods needed by the town (and whisky produced by the distillery) had to be ferried out into the loch before being transferred from one boat to another. Anyone who has ever set about rolling a full cask of whisky along solid ground can readily imagine the difficulties this must have presented.

Hard times for Bowmore, then. They continued through the Edwardian era and then the grim years of the First World War, when Bowmore's policeman had twice to abandon all his other duties and climb on his bicycle in appalling weather in order to log the tide of the dead washing up on the shores of Islay (see Chapter Seven). In 1925, finally, ownership changed again, to J.B. Sherriff (no longer family-owned but run by an entrepreneur from Skye called Duncan MacLeod). Like all the other distilleries on the island, it closed during the early 1930s and again during the Second World War; in 1950, it was sold to William Grigor and Son who ran the Glen Albyn distillery in Inverness (now demolished to make way for a shopping complex).

In 1963, the name Morrison first became associated with Bowmore, when whisky brokers Stanley P. Morrison bought the distillery from Jimmy Grigor's widow. In the same year, a young lad from the village, a lad who had often stopped off on the way to and from school to listen to the tales the maltmen told as they puffed on their pipes, took a job as a cooper at the distillery. He was called Jim McEwan, and he was eventually (in 1984) to become Bowmore's manager – and, more than that, the island's most celebrated advocate, a great storyteller and communicator of the Celtic spirit. Ownership changed once again in 1993 when the Morrison family sold out to the Japanese giant Suntory, which has (as with its ownership of the Bordeaux third-growth Château Lagrange and the fine German Rheingau estate Robert Weil) proved a supportive owner, and one with long-term commitment. With Suntory's backing and Jim McEwan's ambassadorial skills, Bowmore became the third of the island's malts, alongside Lagavulin and Laphroaig, to win a firm place in the world top ten: a striking contrast to the miserable situation prevailing just one hundred years earlier. Jim McEwan left to help revive Bruichladdich in 2000, inspired by the challenge of breathing new life into this great but neglected Rhinns distillery; since then Bowmore has continued to flourish under manager Ian McPherson, known to all as Percy, as well as the unforgettably forthright Christine Logan, who manages the visitor centre and worked at Jim McEwan's right hand for many years.

THE HILL

During the preparation of this book, I walked to each of the distillery water sources with the manager or one of the distillery workers, and it was a moist, heavy day of hanging clouds when, on 18 July 2003, Percy and I set off after lunch to trace the route taken by Bowmore's distillery water. Or, at any rate, the lower, unitary part of it, for it rises via a dozen or more scattered burns and brooks in the hills of Bruno Schroder's Dunlossit Estate. Two of the larger of these streams, Barr and Cattadale, come together to form the river Lossit, and it is just down-stream of Mulindry Bridge, next to a little weir, that the inconspicuous Bowmore distillery lade sets off on its long dither to the mash tun, marching with Lord Margadale's Islay Estates and crossing the Jennings family's Laggan Estate as it does so. The water is peaty, though perhaps less so than that of the Kidalton distilleries.

On the map, this is the easiest of the seven Islay water walks. In reality, it is by far the most testing and the least gratifying. There is no chance to set out and stride the high hill, to surprise stags, to watch the sea recede and fall until it becomes a coastline. Instead, this is the nearest Islay can provide to a jungle-trekking experience. Percy battled through clawing brambles, ankle-twisting grasses, sucking bog rushes, an infuriation of tussocks, thick grey willow copses and sickly-sweet bracken banks, struggling at all moments to keep the tenuous lade in sight. I followed, marvelling at his patience with the cloud of fat-bodied brown cattle flies which worried at our heads; it was only by swatting them away with the map that I was able to keep my sanity.

Later in the walk, they were joined by clegs: soft, stupid grey flies which settle on you, then swiftly slide a lazy needle under your skin. Inevitably you whack them as they do this, and they make no attempt to escape, but just fall, dead, to the ground. After a while I learned to blow them off, appalled at my own gratuitous killing.

At several points we were independently felled by terrain of malicious clumpiness, yet Percy's composure remained intact. The most beautiful point of the walk is where it passes through the strip of ancient woodland just north of Loch Tallant, yet even here the chest-high vegetation, a mist of silky grass and layered bracken, made the going hard, while the attentions of the flies made stopping to admire the writhing, moss-laden branches (and their tumbling ticks) inadvisable. For lengths of the lade, especially where it has been mechanically widened, you would not dream that it was possible to run a thirsty distillery on the miserable trickle of water lying stationary in pools and puddles there – nor would it be, were the water not gathered at the distillery holding pool, just to the east of the main road into Bowmore. Jim McEwan remembered how the workers were always sent out in the summer silent season to clean the lade; in good weather, it was an enjoyable job that they would make last as long as possible. Percy recalled it, too, remembering how they used to take a football with them to play in the fields (once cut for hay, but now in many cases gone under rushes) at lunchtime. 'It was a great summer job. But then one manager said it was a waste of time, so he brought in diggers. The lade used to be just two or three feet wide, and it ran. But once the diggers had been in it went up to six or eight feet wide, so it slows right down. And the broader it is, the more the weeds grow, because the sun gets down into it.'

WALKING BOWMORE

If you are visiting Islay and do not have time to tour all the distilleries, then Bowmore and Laphroaig are the two you should choose first. Why? These are the two distilleries which still make a proportion of their own malt; it is therefore possible to see the entire whisky-making process, from harvested grain to finished glass, unfold before your eyes. Bowmore malts about 40 per cent of its needs, which is a higher proportion than Laphroaig. The raw barley comes from the Scottish borders; Bowmore, Percy told me, has contracts with 16 lowland farmers who grow Optic specifically for the distillery, meaning that the grain can be traced from a particular field through to a finished cask of whisky if need be. The peat, meanwhile, comes from the Gartbreck Moss just south-west of Bowmore itself, and is mechanically cut for the distillery by Alec MacIntosh. Good stuff? 'Everyone argues about that one,' says Percy. 'I don't think there's any difference whatsoever, to be truthful, but if you argue with folk, everyone says something different. It's nice fibrous peat, at any rate; not the black stuff. You want smoke; you don't want heat.'

The barley is steeped in water from the lade to take it from its natural 12 per cent moisture up to around 45 per cent; it is then laid out on one of the three malting floors for seven days in winter and six days in summer, getting turned (night and day) every four hours. This was, once, heavy and intense work, which the burly Percy still recalls. 'There were six of us in the old days; now there is just one. Each malt floor took us an hour and a half. It was back-breaking work, but you got used to it; you can train your back, just like you can train everything else. The old fellows, though, had to have their pipe in the morning before they'd start. As a young seventeen-year-old, I used to say 'Come on, let's get started.' But no, the pipe had to be smoked first.' A turning machine and an electric shovel to move the malt into the kiln (which dries 21 tonnes at a time, making it twice as big as Laphroaig's) were 'the best equipment we ever put in. Can you imagine shovelling twenty-one tonnes?' As at Laphroaig, the drying of the malt is done in two stages: peat smoke first at a relatively low temperature for 18 hours to flavour the malt, and then later a stream of hot air for 42 hours, to finish the drying. The other portion of this wholly traceable malt passes through the hands of Port Ellen and other maltsters, and malt from the various sources is mixed to ensure complete uniformity.

Malting, of course, requires heat – and Bowmore is, thanks to the ingenuity of a former distillery engineer called Harry Cockburn, a model of parsimoniousness. Each distilling season begins with a tankful of cold water which is heated in the still condensers. That heated water then sets off on a closed-circuit, hot-cold journey which sees it providing hot air to finish the malting; preheating the mashing water, the wash and the low wines; as well as heating the reception centre and the Bowmore swimming pool next door (which I have often swum in and which, believe me, is kept at Caribbean temperatures). This innovative heat recovery system was first installed in 1982 and has been much imitated in other distilleries since.

What of the peating levels? Bowmore is Islay's distillery of the golden mean: at 25 ppm in the malt, it lies perfectly pitched between the peatier, heavier spirits (like Ardbeg, Caol Ila, Lagavulin, Laphroaig, Bruichladdich's Port Charlotte and Octomore, and Bunnahabhain's new and as yet unnamed alternative spirit) and the less peaty, smoother spirits (such as classic Bruichladdich and Bunnahabhain and Caol Ila Highland). This level of peat in the malt results in 8–10 ppm in the new make spirit (measured by HPLC), and in principle both the Bowmore-smoked and the purchased malt should give identical results, though Percy admits that 'our own malt seems smokier as you smell it'. When one tastes just how well this works for Bowmore in terms of balance, elegance and finesse, it is remarkable that none of the other Islay distilleries has adopted mid-level peating.

Since Bowmore gets more visitors than any other distillery on the island (around 10,000 a year), all of the equipment is made to look as sweet as possible – which was one reason why the old copper water tanks next to the copper-covered mash tun (originally from Jura distillery) have been retained. Each mash is 8 tonnes in size, a fair island average, but look closely as you walk through to the fermenting room; you will pass what appear to be washbacks numbered 7A, 8A and 9A. The wooden cladding on these is there for cosmetic reasons, as Percy explains. 'In fact they're tanks for effluent, cold water and hot water, but they look terrible and they're on the main tourist route, so we had to dress them up a bit.' The real Oregon pine washbacks, six in number, lie next door.

Interestingly, Bowmore is the only distillery on the island to have switched from wooden washbacks to stainless steel ones – and then back to wood again, in 1990. 'Taste reasons, they said.' Does that phrasing mean that Percy isn't convinced? 'No, I'm not convinced. I don't think it makes any difference.' We have already seen (in Glass One) that Stuart

Thomson and Bill Lumsden of Ardbeg do think it makes a difference; Jim McEwan, too, used to claim that the floral notes found in Bowmore were attributable to fermentation in wooden rather than steel washbacks. The Diageo view, by contrast, chimes with Percy's. It is, in sum, a question about which everyone has a different opinion, as we will further discover in the other whisky chapters which follow. What is certain is that Bowmore's fermentations (48 hours during the week and 62 hours at the weekend) are relatively brisk and warm, and that its wash is fermented to one of the lowest strengths (7 per cent) on the island. These factors will lend a vivacity and a boisterousness to its spirit compared, for example, to the cool, tapered purity provided by Caol Ila's or Bunnahabhain's long fermentations and higher-strength washes.

There are two wash stills and two spirit stills, all plain in shape. The wash stills have big, roomy pots; relatively wide, squat necks, and horizontal lyne arms, whereas the spirit stills have squatter pots and more slender necks with gently rising lyne arms. Three of the condensers are sited inside; the fourth (the second spirit-still condenser) is sited outside the stillhouse, since there is no room for it inside. Internally, these condensers are unique, since they are divided into two halves and provide two different recovery temperatures, one warmer than the other. The reason for this design is to enable the condensers to form part of the overall heat recovery system. The charges in the still, meanwhile, are relatively full, especially for the spirit still (over 90 per cent capacity); and the spirit cut is a broad one (from about 74 per cent abv down to about 61.5 per cent). What does all this tell us about the character of Bowmore's spirit?

TASTING BOWMORE

The fundamental character of a new-make spirit is conditioned by its malt specification; that is a whisky's genetic inheritance, if you like. However, the way in which it is fermented and distilled can alter that genotype dramatically, as we will discover when we come to compare Caol Ila with Lagavulin. (Both of these whiskies are based on the same malt spec yet, once distilled, they produce very different spirits.) Fermentation and distillation is, to pursue the analogy, akin to the upbringing an individual might receive. Tall stills with a relatively low percentage charge, steeply rising lyne arms, a purifier on the lyne arm (as at Ardbeg), a narrow spirit cut and condensers packed with a high number of narrow copper tubes working at a warm recovery temperature: all of these factors will maximise the contact the alcohol makes with copper, producing a fine-grained, ethereal spirit. Reverse all of these factors, and you will have a big, pungent, gutsy spirit. There is no doubt that Bowmore's distillations lie (like Laphroaig's) towards the pungent, gutsy end of the spectrum, though this may not be so obvious since its malt spec is less peaty than Laphroaig's. When you nose the new make, indeed, it does not seem notably peaty; what you notice is its bright exuberance, its sense of washday freshness, its breezy yelp.

The spirit, as we already know, will have altered hugely since Alfred Barnard's late-nineteenth-century visit, but there have been major changes in the twentieth century, too, such as the change from direct firing of the stills to gas firing in 1963. Percy has been at the distillery long enough to remember the last days of coal firing. 'Don't talk to me about that – I nearly gave up on distilleries there and then. It was a terrible job. You put on a fire, then it ran too fast so you pulled some of the fire out and threw it on the floor – then it ran too slowly so you threw some of the fire back on again, then it would begin to go too fast again so you pulled it off . . . I remember doing all that. Not for long; just two months, but even that was horrendous. If you think of the Health and Safety Regulations nowadays – we're not even allowed to take a candle in here. While back then we would be throwing burning coals on the floor, and the man standing at the spirit safe would be smoking a pipe, and then you'd be taking drams at night, sometimes a full bottleful for two on an eight-hour shift . . . how we weren't blown up I don't know. We should be in heaven by now. When we switched to gas all the old boys said the spirit changed, and it probably did.'

Everything we have said about the spirit character so far relates to its 'new make', the transparent firewater which runs out of the stills, but the ageing of the spirit, of course, modifies its genotype enormously too. Like the island's other strikingly pungent and exuberant spirit, Laphroaig, Bowmore is aged only in first-fill recipients; together with Bunnahabhain and Bruichladdich, meanwhile, it is one of only three distilleries on the island still to be using a sizeable minority (here around 14 per cent) of sherry casks. This relatively assertive wood regime means that the spirit can be ready for market sooner than most – Bowmore Legend doesn't carry an age statement, but is around eight years old. Aged stocks are good, too (there are 27,000 casks in Bowmore's three warehouses), which is one of the reasons why the Bowmore range of core expressions is the biggest on the island. Another reason is that this whisky seems to have mimetic, chameleon tendencies, quickly empathising with whatever character a particular cask might lend it. (In this respect it is very different to Laphroaig.) I have had the chance to nose and taste a wide range of casks in Bowmore's beautiful number 1 cellars (dunnage vaults which are lit, uniquely on the island, with all the drama of a Bordeaux château's barrel room) both with Jim McEwan and more recently with Percy, and the differences between these casks are as striking as I have ever come across. Three magnificent 1964s, for example, were each vastly different: a second-fill sherry cask (almost the only second-fill recipient on the site, according to Percy) was creamy, perfumed, almondy and marzipan-like, whereas a contrasting '64 Oloroso sherry hogshead was dark and Madeira-like, with fresh tangy apple notes joining salt, smoke, black raisins and black treacle. A '64 first-fill bourbon cask, by contrast, managed show-stopping aromas of peach, honeysuckle and Indian balsam, reminiscent of white wines based on the Viognier grape variety, with almost minty, liqueur-like flavours. This began life as peaty beer? It seemed hardly possible.

Legend, the youngster, stresses Bowmore's marine side, with its seaweedy, foreshore scents and smoky, kelpy flavours. One hop, and you could be over the white distillery wall and whistling your way along the beach. (Surf is another junior sold in duty-free outlets.) The 12-year-old marks a measured retreat from this seahorse charm: it's a darker, more sober, more raisiny dram, marked by a slight adolescent uncertainty about what it wants to be, or might be, or truly is. With the 15-year-old (christened Mariner), the assurance is returning: there are earthy, chocolate hints and a light nuttiness stealing into the aromas, while on the tongue the malt has more body and weight. The seaweed and salt is still present, but growing more sinewy with each month which passes. The 17-year-old sees this slow transformation completed: the dram's nutty, cask aromas and rich, chewy, complex flavours contrive to mark a decided step back from the beach and into the calm and darkness of the warehouse. With the 25-year-old and the 30-year-old we are into other experiences altogether. Old Cognac is marked by its floral notes, the result of prolonged yet controlled cask oxidation, and Bowmore's chameleon nature manages to evoke something of the same: the 25-year-old can suggest roses, violets and creamy mint, while the 30-year-old adds heather and meadow flowers to the mix; both are venerable, multilayered yet finally gentle drams which are best without water. In general, indeed, Bowmore seems to need watering rather less than most of its Islay cousins (all of the whiskies above are bottled at either 40 per cent abv or 43 per cent abv). Collectors will know that there have also been releases at 21 Years Old, 22 Years Old and even 40 Years Old (a stolen decanter of which was once held to ransom in Canada).

Bowmore Darkest (also 43 per cent) is a sherry-aged style which comes leaping out of the bottle with rich smoky-toffee scents and an insistent, toothsomely raisiny flavour; this is one of the few expressions in the range to suggest something dense, oily and Lagavulin-like. It is given 12 years in bourbon casks, then finishes in sherry for a further two, and was created following the success of the legendary 'Black Bowmore' (see below). Darkest makes a fascinating contrast with the port-casked Bowmore Dawn (51.5 per cent) and the Bordeaux-casked Bowmore Dusk (50 per cent). Dawn, unsurprisingly, is a little sweeter than Dusk, with a smooth, winey style and an elderflower grace to it; Dusk is denser, perhaps subtler, the more assertive wood notes pressing complexity into the spirit. There is, finally, a Cask Strength (56 per cent) of relative youth and pronounced bourbon-wood character; behind the exuberant vanilla you'll find a good slap of seaweed and a lungful of sea air, making it very much the big brother of feisty little Legend.

Finally? Not really: Bowmore has a long tradition of special releases dating back to that charismatic 'Black Bowmore': a 1964 release of Joycean allusiveness which still makes the knees of those who have tasted it knock in recollection, and which commands astonishing auction prices whenever a bottle comes up. (It had 20 years in a first-fill Oloroso hogshead – which then began to leak, so it was serendipitously racked for another two decades into a first-fill bourbon hogshead.) Recently the distillery has revisited the same rich seam with a further trilogy of 1964 releases, drawn from Fino, Oloroso and bourbon casks. There is, though, nothing intrinsically special about 1964, other than that the distillery managed not to lose its star casks in the anonymity of the blender's vat. It was a lesson well learned. We can, in other words, look forward to other fine single-cask releases as the cellars lying between the young voices of School Street and the soft, watery slap of Loch Indaal slowly surrender their treasures.

Bowmore   DISTILLERY FACTFILE

Distillery operating hours	*5¹/₂ days a week @ 24 hours a day*
Number of employees	*18*
Water source	*River Laggan*
Water reserve	*variable*
Water colour	*brown*
Peat content of water	*trace*
Malt source	*around 40 per cent own malt (1,700 tonnes in 2003), with balance from other maltsters including Port Ellen*
Own floor maltings?	*yes*
Malt type	*Optic*
Malt specification phenols	*average 25 ppm*
Finished spirit phenols	*average 8–10 ppm*
Malt storage	*180 tonnes*
Mill type	*Porteus, installed 1960s*
Grist storage	*8 tonnes*
Mash tun construction	*stainless steel, semi-Lauter*
Mash size	*8 tonnes*
First water	*27,000 litres at 84°C*
Second water	*13,000 litres at 90°C*
Third water	*27,000 litres at 100°C*

Number of washbacks	–	6
Washback construction	–	*Oregon pine*
Washback charge	–	*40,000 litres*
Yeast	–	*Mauri and Quest cultured yeasts (75/25)*
Amount of yeast	–	*100 kg per washback*
Length of fermentation	–	*48 hours (shorts: week);*
		62 hours (longs: weekend)
Initial fermentation temperature	–	*19°C*
Strength of wash	–	*7 per cent abv*
Number of wash stills	–	*2*
Wash stills built	–	*not known*
Wash still capacity	–	*30,940 litres*
Wash still charge	–	*20,000 litres (65 per cent of capacity)*
Heat source	–	*steam coils and pans*
Wash still height	–	*20 feet 8 inches (6.3 m)*
Wash still shape	–	*plain*
Lyne arm	–	*straight*
Length of low-wines run	–	*c. 8 hours*
Low-wines collection range	–	*46 per cent abv – 1 per cent abv*
Number of spirit stills	–	*2*
Spirit stills built	–	*no 1: 1986; no 2: not known*
Spirit still capacity	–	*no 1: 14,750 litres; no 2: 14,637 litres*
Spirit still charge	–	*c. 13,500 litres (92 per cent of capacity)*
Strength of spirit still charge	–	*c. 27 per cent abv*
Heat source	–	*steam coils and pans*
Spirit still height	–	*19 feet (5.8 m)*
Spirit still shape	–	*plain*
Lyne arm	–	*no 1: rises about 10°; no 2: rises*
		about 5°
Purifier?	–	*no*
Condensers	–	*three internally sited, one externally sited;*
		length 15 feet 1inch (4.6 m) to 16 feet
		5 inches (5 m), containing between 176
		and 218 1¼ inch (32 mm) copper
		tubes; all condensers bipartite (one half
		cool, one half hot)

Length of foreshot run — *15 minutes*

Length of spirit run — *2.5 to 3 hours*

Length of feints run — *3.5 to 4 hours*

Spirit cut — *74 per cent abv – 61.5 per cent abv*

Distilling strength — *68.8 per cent abv average*

Storage strength — *63.5 per cent abv*

Average spirit yield — *408 litres of pure alcohol per tonne of malt (2003)*

Disposal of pot ale and spent lees — *pot ale to Caol Ila, then dispersed in Sound of Islay; spent lees to sewer*

Type of casks filled for branded malt — *71 per cent first-fill American oak barrels; 15 per cent first-fill American oak remade hogsheads; 14 per cent first-fill sherry butts and puncheons*

Current annual output — *1.7 million litres of pure alcohol*

Number of warehouses — *1 at distillery (numbered 1); 2 outside town on Low Road (numbered 5 and 6)*

Type of warehouses — *dunnage (1 and 5); racked (6)*

Storage capacity on Islay — *27,000 casks*

Percentage of branded malt entirely aged on Islay — *100 per cent*

Vatting and bottling location — *Springburn (Glasgow)*

Distillery expressions — *Legend (no age stated; circa 8 years old)*
— *Cask Strength (no age stated)*
— *12-year-old*
— *Mariner (15-year-old)*
— *17-year-old*
— *Aged 24 Years*
— *Aged 30 Years*
— *Darkest (sherry-casked)*
— *Dawn (port-casked)*
— *Dusk (Bordeaux-casked)*
— *plus Surf (duty-free) and special vintage-dated releases*

Major blending roles — *Black Bottle, Rob Roy, Islay Hallmark*

CHAPTER THREE

Story of an island: recent times

The walls stand, roofless;
beasts still, under moss; birds flown.
Not so the hard tales.

AND THUS IT WAS THAT, in the autumn of 1723, the new Campbell laird purchased Islay, two farms excepted, for just over £12,000 (the 1998 equivalent of more than £1.5 million).

The world had turned. The old Campbells of Cawdor were late medieval Scottish aristocrats, which is to say the descendants of warlords who had acquired their land by force of arms and the political arrangements which perfume these, rendering them permanent. They presided (from afar) over a little Islay world of misery, mud and magic. A clutter of relatives, administrators and hangers-on devoured their inadequate rents – often quite literally, since a substantial proportion was paid in kind: in fowl, eggs, butter and grain.

Daniel Campbell of Shawfield, by contrast, was a figure much more familiar to us today: entrepreneur, financier, and a politician whose contacts and activities brought him considerable personal advantage. To be sure, his businesses (which included the slave trade, ship-owning, tobacco, iron ore and Customs collection) had a chancer's heterogeneity which is unusual today. Just how powerful a member of the ruling establishment he was can be gauged by the fact that, two years after purchasing Islay (and part of Jura at the same time), he managed to get the Glasgow city fathers to disburse to him three-quarters of the very sum he paid for these vast tracts, some £9,000, in mere compensation for having his own palatial Glasgow residence damaged by a mob. (The mob, eleven of whom were killed, was angry that he had voted in favour of Scotland adopting the 1725 malt tax, an unwelcome English import certain to raise the price of beer and encourage consumption of imported wine and brandy. Campbell suspected there might be trouble, and had already moved valuables from his home.)

He was 56 by the time he bought Islay, a Whig politician well known and liked at Westminster (he had voted for the Act of Union in 1707) and an intimate of the nimble East Anglian Sir Robert Walpole; he already owned two Lanarkshire estates, at Shawfield and at Woodhall. Since his physical size matched his political clout as well as the lavish wealth which his acquisitive canniness had brought him, he was known as 'Great Daniel'. He tasted personal grief, though: he was widowed once, and all three of his sons predeceased him. On his own death (in 1753) Islay passed to his grandson, Daniel the Younger, whom we have already met in connection with Bowmore.

'. . . LEAN, WITHERED, DUSKY AND SMOKE-DRIED'

The administration of Islay, as might be expected, grew a great deal more businesslike under 'Great Daniel'. Leases were shortened and fixed at 19 years; rents were payable in money alone; and since the laird himself was now a man of unimaginable wealth, he enjoyed absolute invulnerability in holding for himself and his family very nearly the entire island. In particular, this meant that the tacksmen, the farming middlemen who may have hoped to acquire land in their own name under a heavily indebted and distantly related laird, saw their chances of a modest landholding evaporate. One such, Lauchlin Campbell of Leorin (the hill land above Port Ellen) took 31 families off to New York in 1738, and encouraged more to make the move over the next two years. Emigration from Islay had begun.

Another example of the new, brisk and calculating mood abroad on the island was marked by the arrival of cartographer Stephen MacDougall on the island in the late 1740s. His work, the first accurate mapping of Islay, was penned to help no one steer their way from Ardbeg to Ardnave, but rather as a vital tool in putting order into the teeming agricultural holdings of the island and the many oral agreements and understandings on which these were based. And from that, of course, to maximise rents. 'By the mid-eighteenth century,' as Robert Dodgshon has written, 'the cartographic survey had become an essential part of estate management.' It was boom time for map-makers; every Scottish laird suddenly required their services. Islay was already populous, though within 70 years it was to become still more so; the simplified map of Islay assembled on the basis of MacDougall's smaller and more detailed plans shows around 170 separate townships and few parts of the island unproductive. No matter, in other words, how bleak the view eastwards seems today on a November drive up the lonely, rough road along the island's spine from Avenvogie to Ballygrant; no matter how empty the bracken-brown hills below look as the Glasgow plane takes a turn over the high lochs which supply the Kidalton distilleries; no matter how desolate and sinister the empty passes and crags seem from the ferry as it nears McArthur's Head: back in 1750, there were men and women making a life from the land, and raising children, in those places. Smoke from their fires would have braided the hills; their voices would have peopled the mist. Indeed within 20 years of MacDougall putting his cartographer's pen to paper, another artist, Joseph Banks, was sketching the two scenes which, later engraved and published in Thomas Pennant's *A Tour In Scotland and Voyage to the Hebrides, 1772*, provide the closest we can come to a view of what eighteenth-century life was like for most Ileachs. One shows a stone-walled cottage, the upper parts of its gables turf-topped, and with a thatched roof in a state of some disrepair, lashed down against the wind by a swarm of heather ropes. An old woman hobbles with a walking stick in front of it, while a man has gathered together a bundle of faggots. The second shows the interior of such a cottage: dark and smoky, since its fire sits in a central hearth, while three generations stare forlornly into the low flames. Such 'habitations', declared Pennant, were 'scenes of misery . . . without chimnies, without doors, excepting the faggot opposed to the wind at one or other of the apperters, permitting the smoke to escape through the other, in order to prevent the pains of suffocation. The furniture perfectly corresponds: a pot hook hangs from the middle of the roof, with a pot pendent over a grateless fire, filled with fare that may rather be called a permission to exist, than a support of vigorous life: the inmates, as may be expected, lean, withered, dusky and smoke-dried.' There are dogs on the floor in the illustration; cattle also shared the living space. Despite the arrival of the potato on the island around 1750 (Pennant himself enjoyed 'some excellent new potatoes . . . served up at dinner' when staying with Campbell of Ballinaby), famine was stalking the island during the summer when he visited, averted only by the arrival of a ship containing £1,000's worth of meal. Pennant was in no doubt where the blame lay: 'a ruinous distillation prevails here,' he wrote, noting that more barley 'is drank in form of whisky, than eaten in the shape of bannocks'.

Great Daniel died in 1753. His eldest son John had died six years earlier, in 1746, so it was John's eldest son (by a second marriage, his first wife having gone childless to her grave) who inherited the magnificent estates. This was Daniel the Younger, a well-educated 16-year-old. He was cultured, enthusiastic and stylish; he travelled; he lavished money on books, clothes, wine and musical instruments. While the grandfather had been interested in improving the island as the shortest way to improving his rents, the grandson took the more compassionate view which occasionally surfaces in generations born to great wealth. Improvement did not yet principally mean eviction. Daniel the Younger, indeed, even encouraged immigration on to Islay for those able to fish proficiently and professionally, and thus able to teach the Ileachs a trick or two. 'The Inhabitants,' Daniel the Younger wrote in 1766, 'know no Art of Fishing but by the hand line and rod;

wherewith they take Cod, Haddock, Whiting, Flounder; and a great Variety of other kinds particularly a Delicious Fish which they call the Merry Fish . . . But for want of method no great quantities are Caught.' He offered three acres, peat rights and a rent holiday of seven years to experienced cod and herring fishermen willing to settle the island. There were eight mines open around Ballygrant and near Finlaggan, taking lead, copper and silver from seams in the deposits of limestone and diamictite in the central part of the island (Glasgow Museums possess a handsome goblet made of Islay silver in the late eighteenth century). Experienced mineworkers, too, came on to the island from mainland mining districts. Flax growing and linen manufacture, a particular obsession of Daniel the Younger, set looms spinning; turnips, potatoes, wheat, barley, oats, beans and peas nourished themselves on summer light and the improving lime. By the end of the century, some 2,000 cattle were leaving the island yearly, taken across on the ferry to Jura and from there ferried again to the mainland. Kelp or 'sea ware', used for hundreds of years as fertiliser on the island, was burned to provide an alkali useful in glass-manufacture, and this became a secondary export until the end of the Napoleonic wars.

Daniel the Younger's main physical testament, though, is Bowmore itself, which he had planned and laid out; building commenced during the 1760s. The aim behind the creation of this village was the usual lairdly mix of self-interest top-dressed as social benefit. Daniel the Younger passed summer and autumn on Islay, and was keen to improve and expand Islay House. In order to do this, he needed to clear the inconvenient settlement at Kilarrow, which was in his way and spoiled the plans for the park. Killarow is not a name you will find on any present-day map of Islay, since Daniel the Younger pushed the villagers round Loch Indaal to Bowmore. All that remains of it is a little cemetery tucked away to the south of Islay House, full of the surprisingly elaborate tombs of well-to-door farmers and factors from Central Islay, many of them called Campbell. This communal eviction is why Bowmore's celebrated round church does not belong to a parish called Bowmore. It is, rather, the parish church of Kilarrow. Bowmore was also useful for soaking up those moved off the land as the laird went about his work of improvement and reorganisation: those settled in Bowmore were thus given a small tenancy. If Bowmore is Islay's oldest surviving distillery, this is not unconnected with the fact that Daniel Campbell the Younger threw up a small town around it.

'. . . UNWONTED ACTIVITY AND BENEFICENCE'

Daniel the Younger died in 1777, a 40-year-old childless bachelor. As a laird, he had been a well-meaning spendthrift. His younger brother John, also a bachelor, had died a year earlier in 1776; so Islay passed quite unexpectedly into the hands of the next brother, a lawyer called Walter Campbell, together with a jaw-dropping debt of £90,000. Walter was 36 at the time.

Great Daniel had acquired Islay, and turned it from a little Celtic kingdom into a business; Daniel the Younger, by contrast, had set about improving and modernising the island with a reformer's enthusiasm and an aesthete's prodigality. Walter Campbell combined both approaches, and did so with what seems to have been considerable success, especially considering the dreadful summers the island saw during this period. He bought back one of the estates which Great Daniel had not been able to acquire initially (Sunderland on the Rhinns, which included the fishing village of Portnahaven); he produced copious children (10 by the first marriage alone); and the island and its swelling population achieved remarkable agricultural diversity under his lairdship. James Macdonald visited the island in 1808 as part of the research for his *General View of the Agriculture of the Hebrides*, and on the basis of what he saw he declared Walter Campbell 'the first of the Hebridean improvers', a man who worked for those living under his stewardship with 'unwonted activity and beneficence'. According to Macdonald, Walter Campbell had managed to triple his rents since taking over the estate from his brother, and ensure that they were in the main paid without arrears. What better proof could there be of his beneficence? Why, he even 'resides in that island for three or four months of the year'. To be fair, Macdonald claimed that Walter Campbell spent 'a large proportion' of his Islay rents on improving the island further, for which reason the tenantry 'love and respect him'.

The stability and relative prosperity of his tenure of the island are perhaps indicated by the fact that its darkest incidents were odd maritime hazards, while local controversies were often amusingly trivial. In 1778, for example, the American War of Independence was briefly waged in the Sound of Islay – by a Scotsman. John Paul Jones was a lad from Kirkcudbright who, by the succession of strange chances a life at sea can throw up, found himself successively a seaman in the slave trade, a murderer on the run and then an American naval hero and the scourge of British naval frigates in the North Atlantic. He was given command by Congress of the newly built *Ranger* and, much to the satisfaction of both the American and French authorities, caused havoc in a swashbuckling run through St George's Channel and the Irish Sea between 1777 and 1778. Most notably for our story, he captured the Islay ferry on its way to Port Askaig and robbed the passengers. On board was a military member of the Campbell family returning to Islay after a profitable career in India, his fortune, alas, all too portable and present, in the form of gold bars and other valuables, on that occasion. 'As he was about to land on his native Island,' according to the Ileach writer William MacDonald, 'the whole of his wealth was seized by Jones, and the Major, who a few hours before was vastly rich, landed penny-less.'

Even more distress was caused when an American privateer called *The True Blooded Yankee* sailed into Loch Indaal towards dusk on 4 October 1813 and dropped anchor at Port Charlotte. She had 260 men aboard under the command of Captain Duplait, and her 26 guns left the 25 or so other merchant ships anchored in the Loch highly vulnerable to her attentions. Duplait and his men raided every one, then set them all on fire or stranded them, lighting the autumn night with a horrible, water-glittering brightness. The losses sustained amounted to £600,000 (around £22 million in 1998 figures), a colossal sum and well in excess of what the whole island changed hands for some 40 years later.

If affairs on the water were lawless, on land they were much less so. Islay, indeed, had a kind of parliament during these years, composed of 'Gentlemen, Fewers, Heretors, Tacksmen' – in other words, of the posher and more well-to-do sections of island society; it met twice a year. The meetings were, it would seem, kept well-refreshed: in 1778, for example, the dinner bill included 110 bottles of punch; 9 bottles of port wine; 44 bottles of porter; an unspecified number of 'cold drams' – and 10 broken glasses at sixpence each. By 1806, the 'Bill of Entertainment' had grown so enormous that in future it was decided that each gentleman attending should be limited to a half-bottle of wine and a bottle of punch each, with a bottle of brandy to be shared between all; only small beer was available in unlimited quantities. The gentlemen's servants, meanwhile, 'shall be Limited to a half mutskin of Whisky'. Gentlemen, in other words, drank punch, wine and brandy; whisky was for menials.

In 1793, Islay's dog crisis headed the agenda. 'The Meeting considering that the number of useless Dogs in this Country are a great grievance, and that for many obvious reasons their number should be diminished, and it also being represented that a number of Half Greyhounds very destructive to Hares are kept by Many – This Meeting recommends to the Gentlemen of the different quarters of Islay to Intimate to the people of their neighbourhood that all useless and superfluous Dogs are to be killed . . . the Meeting also recommend that no dog be seen at Church or other publick Meetings.' By 1804, pigs were the problem. 'It has now been represented to the Meeting that the Town of Bowmore is very much annoy'd by a destructive Crowd of Pigs running up and down the Streets, and that many of the Inhabitants, regardless of Property, keep their Dunghills upon the Streets. The Meeting consider themselves Authorised to order a better Police . . .'

The assembled worthies also, naturally enough, had to consider the problems caused to the island by whisky distilling. Let's examine the background to this.

'ETERNAL DRAM DRINKING . . .'

The first Scottish record of the use of malt for making whisky is a celebrated entry of 1494 in the Scottish Exchequer Rolls: Friar John Cor of Lindores Abbey in Fife was given eight bolls of malt 'wherewith to make aqua vitae'. It was for King James IV of Scotland's use. Not necessarily recreational: James himself was a modestly skilled doctor and surgeon, and an amateur chemist, too. By 1505, the Guild of Surgeon Barbers in Edinburgh had managed to get a monopoly on whisky manufacture, which suggests that it was still considered primarily medicinal. As the sixteenth century drew on, though, whisky-drinking quickly became social. In 1579, some 200 years before the 'Gentlemen, Fewers, Heretors, Tacksmen' of Islay sat down to consider the matter, it was on record that malt was being used throughout Scotland on a farm basis to make whisky to such an extent that grain for food use was in short supply. (It was because of an anticipated short harvest that a Scottish Parliamentary Act in that year limited distilling to 'Earls, Lords, Barons and Gentlemen for their own use'.) Duty on spirit in Scotland was first levied in 1644 though it subsequently lapsed; the Union with England in 1707 brought uniform duty rates. The Malt Tax which had led to the sacking of Great Daniel's Glasgow home had, perversely, led to a boom in Lowland whisky distillation at beer's expense, since whisky could still be distilled from a mixture of malt and unmalted grains (we call it grain whisky today) whereas beer at the time was a pure malt drink. The Gin Act of 1736 also stimulated whisky production, which officially peaked in 1752 at over 500,000 gallons (2.27 million litres). Unofficial production would have been vastly greater than that. Much of it, too, would have been a drink which few present-day readers of this book would recognise. The use of wild yeasts and small-scale distilling apparatus, combined with grain of varying quality and rudimentary hygiene at all times, would have produced often unpalatable and sometimes dangerous spirits whose flavour required disguise. When Pennant had visited the Western Isles in the 1770s, he noted the tradition of using 'thyme, mint, anise, and other fragrant herbs' in distillation; by that point, the term 'usquebaugh' was used to refer to compounded (flavoured) spirits, while 'aqua vitae' described a pure malt spirit.

In 1757 the British government unwittingly gave a great boost to illegal distilling – by banning legal distilling. It did this because of a disastrous crop failure in 1756, and the ban was renewed every year until 1760 (and again on subsequent occasions during this century of poor weather). Legal distillers went out of business; illegal ones flourished; and throughout the 1760s the quantity of whisky distilled illegally exceeded the legal total tenfold. By 1777, Edinburgh had eight licensed distillers – and over 400 illegal stills, and most contemporary accounts of the times concur in noting that the late eighteenth century was a very drunken time indeed in Scotland. Whisky drinking, according to Elizabeth Grant's *Memoirs of a Highland Lady 1797–1830*, 'was and is the bane of the country; from early morning until late at night eternal dram drinking was ever going on.' Drunken – but often starving, too: the use of grain for distilling after years of crop failure, as in 1783 and 1784, caused hundreds of miserable Highland deaths.

Islay, of course, was no exception, as Thomas Pennant had already observed. 'Considering,' declared the 'Gentlemen, Fewers, Heretors, Tacksmen' of Islay in 1794, 'the great Exertions of the Legislature in Surpressing the Distilling of Spirits & the great revenue given up by Ministry for the purpose of providing a sufficiency of Grain for the use of the nation, which in many parts is threaten'd with a Famine, and Considering that great Exertions have already been made in surpressing the Distilling in this Island, This Meeting unanimously Resolve Individually and Collectively to exert themselves in putting a total stop to the said Illegal Practices.' Behind the harrumphing, there was obviously a human cost, best illustrated by quoting the Reverend Archibald Robertson, Minister of Kidalton, from the *Statistical Account of Islay 1791–9*. 'This island hath the liberty of brewing whisky, without being under the necessity of paying the usual excise duty to government. We have not an excise officer in the whole island. The quantity therefore of whisky made here is very great; and the evil, that follows drinking to excess of this liquor, is very visible on the island. This is one chief cause of our poverty . . . When a brewer knows that a poor man is at a loss for money, he advances him a trifle, on condition that he makes sure of his barley at the above price [17 shillings the boll]; and it is often bought by the brewers at an even lower rate; while those who are not obliged to ask money until they deliver their barley, receive 20 shillings or more for it. This evil, of distilling as much barley as might maintain many families, it is hoped, by some means or another, will soon be abolished. It may take some time, however, to prevent the people from drinking to excess; for bad habits are not easily overcome: but there would surely be some hopes of a gradual reformation, if spiritous liquors were not so abundant, and so easily purchased.'

With the Excise Act of 1801, the authorities began to revise their approach. The Islay Parliament foresaw possible grain shortages that year (there was miserable spring and summer weather throughout the Highlands in 1801, '02, '07, '08 and '09) and resolved 'to use their utmost exertions for preventing any of the Grain of the Island being destroy'd by Illegal Distillers'. An Excise officer arrived on the island at the turn of the century, and the result was a huge swoop which netted no fewer than 233 convictions from illicit distillers scattered all over the island – including members of the founding families of Laphroaig, Bowmore and Lagavulin distilleries, as well as those bearing the same surnames as the present-day Ileach managers or directors of Bowmore (a John McPherson of Carrabus), Bruichladdich (Mary McEwen of Ardnish and William McEwen of Storakaig) and Bunnahabhain (Donald McLellan of Ranach and John McLellan of Kilnave). But it was only by instituting a licence fee of £10 and halving rates of duty in 1823 (after dramatically increasing the penalties for illegal distillation in 1822) that legal distilling became more attractive than its illegal counterpart. The last conviction for illegal distilling on Islay came in 1850 when Excisemen caught three distillers working in a cave on the Oa, at Lower Killeyan, though the practice certainly continued among the unconvicted for the best part of another century. W.N. Blair, an Ileach who emigrated to New Zealand in the 1860s, remembered (as he wrote his memoirs 30 years later) seeing malting for illicit distillation taking place in a cave at Proaig, and he also personally recalled the celebrated Islay smuggler and illicit distiller known as Baldy Mhurachaidh, about whom stories continue to circulate to this day. The late Dougie MacDougall, the father of Christine Logan of Bowmore, knew the lonely eastern side of Islay intimately; he claimed that Baldy's croft was at Rubh' a' Chladaich, and that the bay to its south was known as Baldy's Bay. Its isolation, the peat banks which lay behind the old croft house, and the two streams that ran down into the bay made it the perfect spot for 'the small still'. Baldy was considered the master among Islay's illicit distillers. Dougie MacDougall also remembered that his two maternal uncles came across distilling apparatus and illicit spirit when they were exploring caves on a poaching expedition along the west coast of Islay, a memory which takes the practice into the twentieth century. The illicit still on display at the Museum of Rural Life in Islay came from Kynagarry, while the museum also displays a photograph of a jaunty illicit distiller with his 'black pot' out on the hillside. This distiller is said to be a man called Alex MacKay who lived and distilled, uncaught, at Kintail until 1943.

'. . . SO MANY PASSIVE CREATURES'

'The first of the Hebridean improvers', Walter Campbell, died at Islay House in October 1816, his reign over the island having been a long one: 39 years. His eldest son Jack had (as was by now customary in the family) died before his father – but not before siring an heir (one of nine children) of his own. This was Walter Frederick, who duly succeeded to his grandfather's estates – or most of them. Old Walter's surviving sons (thus Walter Frederick's uncles) acquired a smaller estate each: Walter the younger bought Sunderland on Islay from his father (and later built and planted the secluded Foreland House there), while Robert acquired Skipness and Colin Ardpatrick. Walter Frederick was 18 when Islay became his to own and administer. It was, in the end, a tragic legacy. Walter Frederick died, a ruined and broken man, in Avranches in Normandy, within sight of Mont St Michel, in 1855. What happened?

Walter Frederick was laird of Islay in its most populous days. At no point before or since has the island's population ever matched that of 1830 or so, when there were some 15,000 souls who called Islay home. The vast majority of these people were busy on the hills, struggling to grow enough potatoes, oats and turnips on the lazy-bed rigs of their split tenancies to keep the teeming children fed, and living with but one ambition: the ownership of a cow, and with it milk and the chance of a calf or two per year. The weather in these years continued to dash the ripening grain and the spirits of those who had planted it, with at least one major harvest failure per decade as the nineteenth century opened. The end of the Napoleonic Wars brought a collapse in the kelp market; cattle prices, too, halved between 1810 and 1830. The consequence barely needs iteration: unpaid rents.

Worse was to come. It was in August 1845, in a field just outside Port Ellen, that the symptoms of *Phytophthora infestans* were first noted in an Islay crop of potatoes. By the end of the following year, this fungal disease had buried its spores deep into the precarious agricultural balance of the island – as it was doing to still more devastating effect in that larger adjacent island of Ireland, where a million were to die prematurely, starving and sick, over the next decade. According to Kilmeny's clergyman, Donald Macdonald, Islay smallholders were forced to sell the grain which could have assuaged their hunger to the distilleries – in order to pay their unpaid rents. More than a third of those living on the island were facing 'want, and extreme destitution, and starvation'. The laird, of course, did not face starvation, but by April 1847 he was contemplating his impending ruin and bankruptcy. According to Joseph Mitchell, a travelling engineer to the Fishery Board Commissioners, the 'poor laird' was 'despondent beyond measure. We attributed this to the dreadful potato blight, so disastrous to the country and his people; but he was depressed by what was to him a more serious calamity. Owing to the general distress, the rents were not forthcoming, and the holders of bills and bonds were not paid their interest. The banks also became alarmed, and stopped further advances . . .' Walter Frederick's health was giving way under the strain, and he was advised by his son John Francis Campbell and the canny John Ramsay (of whom more later) to leave the island, which he did, in October. 'I remember,' wrote the émigré W.N. Blair, 'the dark day when a yacht came to Lochindaal and carried him to voluntary exile in Normandy.' In November, he wrote from his new French home to agree ('though it is a bitter Pang') to sequestration, which duly took place on 2 December 1847. There was a house-shaking thunderstorm on Islay on the night before sequestration took place.

What kind of a laird had the last of the Campbells been? It is notable that even as savage a critic of the system of land ownership in Scotland as the land-reform radical John Murdoch, working on Islay at that time as an Exciseman, was ready to describe the island's owner as being one of a 'nobleminded and generous hearted family'. (Perhaps his customary rigour was mollified by the fact that his own father, also called John Murdoch, had worked as a gamekeeper for Walter

Frederick, and had been given a farming tenancy in the pretty spot of Claggan, on the edge of the woods that surround the Sorn at Bridgend.) 'For all his extravagance and passionateness,' 'Murdoch of the Kilt' remembered, 'he possessed all the natural elements of popularity. He was a fine-looking man with a ruddy complexion and brown hair. He was strong and active, too, and took much delight in promoting manly sport. To the folly of shooting and game preservation, however, he was devoted to an excessive degree. He carried this craze so far that there was no offence so great, in his eyes, as to meddle with game and salmon.' Murdoch was later to found the Land Restoration League, the *Highlander* newspaper, and chair the first meeting of the Scottish Labour Party, and he was well aware of what had happened over the last 30 years in Sutherland, where crofters had been cleared from the land with shocking ruthlessness and savagery by Patrick Sellar, James Loch and other agents of Lord Stafford and his wife, the Countess of Sutherland. No road on Islay, though, had ever taken the pounding of soldier's boots; no glen had echoed to the crack of musket fire; no aged Ileachs had been burnt out of their homes and left to die on the frost-laced hillside.

Walter Frederick had been as full of schemes and endeavours as his grandfather, and the architectural legacy of his lairdship still stamps the island today. He founded Port Ellen (initially named Port Ellenor or Ellinor after his first wife, who suffered from mental illness and died early – her memorial can be read with some difficulty on the 1832 Carraig Fhada lighthouse across Kilnaughton Bay) and Port Charlotte (named after his mother, a society beauty who was widowed at 34 with nine children, and later became a minor novelist). His uncle, meanwhile, built Portnahaven and, a little later, Port Wemyss, in which Walter Frederick perhaps had a hand, too, since its name commemorates the fact that his first wife was a daughter of the earl of Wemyss. The Islay, Jura and Colonsay Agricultural Association came into being in 1838 under the patronage of Walter Frederick and his two uncles, and both Walter Frederick's Home Farm and his uncle's Sunderland estate on the Rhinns were used for improving experiments. Walter Frederick's personal generosity was unquestioned, and was even noted locally towards the end of his days when he was living in relative indigence in France. 'A fixed rent day,' recalled W.N. Blair, 'was unknown in Islay – when the tenants had money they paid the rent, and when times were hard and crops bad, the Laird did without it.' This was an accurate recollection: rent arrears at the moment of sequestration stood at £32,095 (the 1998 equivalent of about £1.8 million). Walter Frederick's 'chief luxury', his son later remembered, 'was to give pleasure to others'.

Yet clearances there were, still remembered with some bitterness 50 years later, as we will see a little later in this account. John Murdoch himself, as a young man growing up on Islay, witnessed a catastrophic eviction at Kilchiaran on the Rhinns carried out in 1829 by Walter Frederick, which he later wrote about at length. A farmer called White from Fife, 'supposed to be wealthy', persuaded the laird to let him have the land of this fertile spot, evicting the six farmers and 19 cotter families which had previously lived off it. 'Some of the old tenants went to law with the landlord and were ruined. Some went to America. One man . . . is a miserable pauper in the country. And one, in his extremity, stole a few turnips from a field belonging to the proprietor, was imprisoned for the felony, and died of disgrace and a broken heart.' Walter Frederick had to build a new house and outbuildings for Farmer White, who immediately laid out the farm based on Lowland principles, taking no account of Islay weather conditions. He failed, and left again four years later, leaving the laird several thousands of pounds worse off.

The contrast in 'lifestyle' between that enjoyed by the laird and that endured by the islanders, moreover, is still striking to modern eyes. In addition to Islay, Walter Frederick kept up an estate on the mainland and a London residence, too (he represented Argyll in parliament for 19 years, and was a member of the original committee of the Reform Club). Islay House grew in splendour under Walter Frederick. 'This magnificent mansion,' wrote William MacDonald, '. . . is surrounded by far spreading plantations; and the pleasure grounds, private drives and walks, around and connected with it, are extensive and varied, and laid out with much taste and judgement, suitable in all respects, both for convenience and recreation. The gardens, hot-houses and fountains, are superior to any private gardens in the West of Scotland; so charming that they remind the visitor of the enchanting grounds and fairy scenery mentioned in Eastern story, than of a reality. The extensive offices, and other vast accommodation, embrace everything requisite for a princely proprietor . . .' In the Islay Museum of Rural Life, you can see 'equine carpet slippers' which the horses had to wear when they walked over the lawns.

Compare MacDonald's account with what Lord Teignmouth (Charles Shore) saw when he visited 'an extensive hamlet' on Islay in the early 1830s 'consisting of hovels, or rather shapeless tumuli of sod and stone. They contain a single apartment furnished with a door on each side . . . to allow of ingress and egress on the side not exposed to the wind: with a hole in the roof, which, in several, served for window, as well as chimney, whilst others were furnished with a single pane in a side-aperture. To some was attached a rudely constructed byre: but most of them shared their dwellings with their cattle, separated by no other partition than by some stone flags.' 'Smoking dunghills' was another brief description of ordinary Islay homes. John Murdoch remembered the cotters of the day: 'a stock of people that can hardly be equalled anywhere. They were all on one social level and lived in a rough sort of way – many of them having the cattle going in the same door as themselves, the fire on the floor, and the hens roosting overhead. But some of them,' he continued, 'had money in banks before there was a branch on the island; and numbers were creditors of the laird when he came to grief.' Even the polite MacDonald, in his short 1850 *Descriptive and Historical Sketches of Islay*, referred to 'rackrenting and no corresponding advantages given to the Tenants, [which] has reduced the natives in every point of view.' He noted in concluding his history that he had written almost entirely about 'the deeds of the great, the people being lost sight of almost entirely, excepting as so many passive creatures, fit for war or fit for the payment of rent, and responsible to no authority but that of the owners of the soil. As the Island passed from one Lord to another, it did so with its unwilling complement of serfs, called tenants, almost completely and virtually as a South Carolina plantation does with a pack of Negro "servants". The apologists of British slavery may say that Tenants are at liberty to leave their country, whereas American slaves are not. True; and they are also at liberty to perish for want of food while the land lays waste, because they cannot pay exorbitant prices for liberty to till God's earth at home!' Matters were not, alas, about to get better.

'. . . NUISANCES AND BURDENS TO SOCIETY'

Between 1848 and 1853, Islay was in administration, taken in hand by an Edinburgh accountant, James Brown. Walter Frederick's much disliked estate factor, William Webster of Daill Farm just east of Bridgend, used this period to feather his own nest. 'The laird was now away,' noted John Murdoch, recently installed on the island as an Exciseman. 'The trustees were in Edinburgh. And Webster was more master in the island than ever. . . . The case as between himself and the laird was remarkable in that the master went bankrupt – while the servant had nearly all the best land in the island in his hands. He had got himself planted in the best house in the island when he came at first. And now that things were getting into a state of dissolution he was taking farms in every direction – until I remember old Sandy Campbell and myself making up one day that he had farms which had been held by nearly 37 substantial farmers in former times.' Murdoch couldn't help but contrast the scene in 1850 with his memories of 'all that populous country' a quarter of a century earlier. 'All these places and objects possessed a beauty at that time which no longer exists. Hillside and hollow, and even hilltop, were alive with groups of people moving north or south. The ridges in the landscape were everywhere occupied with houses. Whichever way we looked from Claggan, we saw houses so situated – although, since then, numbers of them have fallen and the materials are in the stone fences of the larger farms.'

The estate, meanwhile, was dangled under the noses of Britain's richest men for £540,000 (the Campbell debts in the end came to a jaw-dropping £815,000, or about £46.1 million in 1998 equivalence). The energetic and optimistic John Murdoch had a better idea for the island than its unitary sale to yet another moneyed grandee, which he outlined in a pamphlet published in 1850 with MacDonald's *Sketches* called '*A new and ready way of disposing of that interesting island which would pay the debt, restore the late proprietor, and give the best return to large and small capitalists'*. Murdoch criticised Brown and the creditors for refusing to contemplate the piecemeal sale of the estate; his own idea, based on Chartist ideals, was that it should be split up into 3,000 different farms or properties (which he estimated would raise a total of £703,000 rather than the asking price of £540,000). The benefits would be manifold: the creditors would receive all of their jeopardised money with £100,000 left over for Walter Frederick (the full extent of the debt being incorrectly computed at that time), the land would be much improved, and above all the islanders would benefit. 'As proprietors,' he wrote, they would be 'in a position far superior to that which they occupied as tenants, even supposing the land no more productive than before, when they had to support a costly aristocratic establishment, wasting their strength, employing their skill, and pinching themselves . . . to enrich (the laird's) factors, to polish his flunkies, to trim his ornamental attendants, to supply many of them with the means of besotting themselves and becoming nuisances and burdens to society; and what went to feed the dogs, game, horses and a thousand other expensive trifles, can be applied to their own comfort, refinement and gratification, and to the bringing up and educating of their own families.' Needless to say, Murdoch's prescient if sketchy ideas impressed only the paper on which they were printed, plus a few of his like-minded friends.

So what happened? The rumour that Queen Victoria wanted to buy the island proved unfounded, and in August 1853 it was sold (at the reduced price of £451,000) to the man known to his contemporaries as the 'Napoleon of shopkeepers'. His name was James Morrison, and he stayed for a little under a week with his family at the Bridgend Hotel during bad weather in July 1849 – and never visited the island again. He died on 30 October 1857. He was a self-educated innkeeper's son from Middle Wallop in Hampshire who, in 1814, had married Mary Ann Todd, the daughter of a London wholesale haberdasher called Joseph Todd with whom James subsequently went into business. Despite these modest origins, he was a man of prodigious commercial intelligence, one of those rare entrepreneurs whose grasp of opportunities was so energetic, so swift yet so sure that he found it hard to fail. And, very early in his career, he realised as much. 'I will make your fortune for you,' he told his first collaborators confidently, 'if you will undertake not to interfere.'

In addition to acquiring vast personal wealth, he was also a man of limitless curiosity and – initially at any rate – no little social conscience. He was a friend of Jeremy Bentham and a co-founder of University College, London; he entered parliament as a radical in 1830, albeit a radical who had purchased his St Ives parliamentary seat (he later won Ipswich by more conventional democratic means); he served as a magistrate; he taught himself foreign languages, and travelled widely and lengthily in Europe. He struck up conversations with strangers wherever he went, and advised his eleven children to do the same, telling them that 'Everybody knows more about at least one subject than you do'. One of the problems he faced throughout his career was a shortage of suitable investments in which to put his vast engine of wealth to work – and so, interesting himself in both architecture and agriculture, he began to acquire land and country estates all over England with some ardour. His main residential estates were at Fonthill in Wiltshire – still owned by his direct descendant Lord Margadale – and at Basildon in Berkshire, now a National Trust property; he also acquired Hole Park in Kent, Malham Tarn in the Yorkshire Dales and Hillesden in Buckinghamshire (originally part of the Stowe estate). Islay was, for the now-elderly and corpulent James Morrison, no more and no less than an agricultural investment (the sales particulars 'safely' averred that 'an Estate superior to Islay has seldom, if ever, been offered for sale'). He had been a fellow Reform Club founding committee member with Walter Frederick and may have liked what he heard of the place around the polished oak dining tables in Pall Mall, but the fact that he took four years over the purchase and struck a hard bargain suggests that there was little sentiment involved.

Curiosity, moreover, abated with purchase. Morrison 'does not now wish,' his son Charles wrote in the year he bought the island, '. . . to be troubled by anything being said about it . . . and only looks at his investment ledger to see how much of his capital he has spent on it.' How John Murdoch must have fumed at these fat-cat absentees.

Charles declared himself 'an unmitigated Cockney' and tried to get his brother Alfred to look after the island, though without success. There was no question of the Morrisons actually living in Islay House, with its 'old, faded, unfashionable, shabby' furnishings; 'we must make all arrangements as if we were never going to visit the island except in flying visits and at long intervals,' he wrote in 1854. Which, sure enough, was exactly what happened, at least until the moment when Charles's heir, Alfred's son Hugh, married in the early 1890s. His bride was Lady Mary Leveson-Gower – who, tellingly, was one of Walter Frederick's many grandchildren. (Less comfortingly, Leveson-Gower was the family name of Lord Stafford, the infamous 'improver' of Sutherland, from whose lands the most brutal evictions of all took place.) Perhaps, however, this maternal link with a family that had genuinely loved the island and its people mollified the rigorously businesslike approach of the Morrisons, since from that time on they did begin to spend more time there. Hugh inherited the estate in 1909, when the unmarried and colossally wealthy Charles finally died.

Charles Morrison had, from the outset, urged his factors to take a strict line on rent arrears, yet he quickly learned 'the illusory character' of the income promised to the new proprietor in the point-of-sale particulars. The family could, of course, afford a loss, yet was congenitally keen to minimise it – so this became the point at which the sole lairdship of the entire island ended. The Morrisons had bought the entire island save for Sunderland (sold by the Campbell family in 1846 to one Alexander McEwan from Glasgow) and Ballinaby, which were relatively small and scattered holdings on the Rhinns. Within eight years, Charles Morrison had sold off all of the island south of a line running (approximately) from Laggan Point to Port Askaig. The Morrisons were still the largest landowners on the island, as they remain today, but Islay was no longer a little kingdom, and the lairds in Islay House (or, rather, in the Reform Club, and in the comfort of their fashionable English addresses) were no longer the only men of substance in the land registry. They were joined by others.

Sadly, one of these others was not, as he had often hoped, the son of Walter Frederick, the man known on the island as Iain Og Ile. He had been christened (in 1821) John Francis Campbell, and his upbringing was a testament to his parents' lack of *hauteur*. 'As soon,' he recalled later, 'as I was out of the hands of nursemaids I was handed over to the care of a piper. His name was the same as mine, John Campbell, and from him I learned a good many useful arts. I learned to be hardy and healthy, and I learned Gaelic; I learned to swim and take care of myself; and to talk to everybody who chose to talk to me. My kilted nurse and I were always walking about in foul weather or fair, and every man, woman and child in the place had something to say to us. Thus I made early acquaintance with a blind fiddler who could recite stories. I worked with the carpenters; I played shinty with all the boys about the farm; and so I got to know a good deal about the ways of the Highlanders by growing up as a Highlander myself.' As John Murdoch put it, 'this part of John Francis Campbell's education formed his great inheritance when he came to man's estate.'

His life was an extraordinary one. He was taken away from his shinty-playing Islay friends (one of whom had been John Murdoch) and sent to Eton, and from there to study law at Edinburgh University (accompanied by the Ballygrant schoolmaster Hector MacLean, a man only three years older than Campbell and his friend and intellectual equal). He practised very briefly at the bar, but didn't enjoy it, and was soon appointed Private Secretary to the Duke of Argyll (who was then Lord Privy Seal). This led to work for successive Royal Commissions, which enabled him to throw himself into the scientific and engineering tasks he relished; at the same time, he set about (with Hector MacLean and others) tramping the Hebrides to collect the Gaelic folk tales which he assembled into four volumes, and for which he remains well-known today. He was a polyglot, speaking 12 languages, and an inveterate and fearless foot-traveller, writing up his often exotic journeys in his *Circular Notes* and illustrating them with sketches and watercolours of more than ordinary competence. He worked for a while as Groom-in-Waiting to Queen Victoria, at all times wearing (as she requested) highland dress; he explained geology to her (he published two volumes on the formation of the earth's crust); he invented the prototype of the sunshine recorder used at Greenwich Observatory until the Second World War; and he was a pioneer of photography. He also threw his not inconsiderable weight (and magnificent beard) into the establishment of a Celtic Chair at Edinburgh University in order to further Gaelic Studies in Scotland, and was said to be dismayed when neither he nor Hector MacLean was its first occupant. Like his father, he died in France – at Cannes, in 1885. He had been responsible (with John Ramsay) for his father's affairs at the time of sequestration, and had struggled hard, though without success, to salvage a portion of the island for the family. The fact that he was much liked and admired on the island is testified not only by his Gaelic soubriquet ('John of Islay'), but also by the monument to his memory erected two years after his death on a prominent, gorse-covered hill on the Bridgend-Bowmore road. It stands there to this day, surveying the industrious tides as they work their way up and down Loch Indaal, commemorating the greatest laird Islay never had.

No: the coming man, in 1850, was John Ramsay. Ramsay was the future: he was a self-made man, and one whose fortune had, moreover, been largely raised on the island during difficult years. He was, in his way, every bit as remarkable an individual as John Francis Campbell, though their characters were continents apart. In place of Campbell's shaggy multitude of talents, Ramsay had but one: business acuity. He left home to seek his fortune at 12, and at the age of 13 was working as a cotton mill clerk, paying for his lodgings (though they were with an aunt), buying all his own provisions, and entering every item of expenditure in a neatly written account book. He underwrote his own education (taking Latin lessons and paying reading-club and library subscriptions); at 14, he noted a loan of £5 to his own father Robert, and made him a gift of £1. 15s for a purchase of clothes the following year (also entered in the accounts book). This pecuniary acuity seems to have been something of a Ramsay family tradition; John banked his savings with his eldest sister, and took 4 per cent interest from his cousin on a loaned lump sum of £26 given to him by his eldest brother Thomas, who was working in Canada. The world, for the Ramsays, was a gigantic business opportunity: John's father also emigrated to Canada to establish a saddlery business, while his uncle James was a successful merchant in New Orleans. John was considering job offers in South Africa and India when another uncle, Ebenezer, asked him to go to Islay in 1833. Ebenezer was Procurator Fiscal of Clackmannanshire and had an interest in Port Ellen distillery, built in 1825 and managed by a cousin – badly. Ebenezer's own son Eben had gone there to discover what was going wrong, but had failed to report back.

John Ramsay's first landing on the island had, according to Freda Ramsay (his grandson's widow) a semi-mythical, Dick-Whittington-like quality. His boat, fighting contrary winds, found it impossible to get up the Sound of Islay to Port Askaig, so dropped him in Baldy's Bay (Gleann Choireadail), just north of the brooding McArthur's Head. Perhaps there were a few crofters around to tell him the footpaths he needed to take, but the journey from there to Port Ellen across the wild, quartzite heart of Islay is, even for a fit young teenager, the hardest walk on the island. Ramsay was not dissuaded. He reached Port Ellen (Eben had already left); he furnished his uncle with the necessary analysis of its problems; and, after having studied distilling for a short time on the mainland, he became Port Ellen's manager. The unbusinesslike Walter Frederick quickly spotted his talents, and in 1840 helped John Ramsay acquire both Port Ellen distillery and the nearby farms of Cornabus and Kilnaughton. Ramsay was still only 25.

He made a great success of both. He reinvested money inherited from his five aunts and uncles with great canniness, building up a profitable import and export business in Glasgow. He perfected (with James Stein, his factor and distillery manager) the spirit safe which is still to be found in almost every malt whisky distillery (though under current Excise rules its use is purely decorative), and pioneered the system of duty-free warehousing. He became a close friend and advisor to Walter Frederick, though his beady accounting eye served only to underline how desperate the family's financial position had become. The two bought a steamer together, the *Modern Athens*, to serve the needs of the island. When sequestration came, he acted as a trustee for Walter Frederick. When the absentee James Morrison made his purchase, Ramsay was ready and, astonishingly, able to purchase Kidalton from him. (Indeed both Freda Ramsay and Morrison's biographer Richard Gatty claimed the two had agreed this sale in advance, which makes one wonder how effective a trustee he could have been for the ever-innocent Walter Frederick.) He extended his purchases on to the Oa in 1858, and then bought most of the present-day Laggan estate in 1861, which took his now-vast landholding all the way up to Laggan Point, near Bowmore (his total outlay for these purchases was £125,265 or just under £8 million in 1998 equivalence – a difficult sum for a self-made distiller on Islay to accrue today). The year before, meanwhile, the Morrison family had sold (for £53,960) what is now the Dunlossit estate to a banker called Smith Child, who had married a Jura Campbell and was looking for land locally. John Ramsay persuaded Charles Morrison to co-fund a cargo service between Glasgow, Port Ellen and Ardbeg (the *City of Worcester*) just as he had coordinated provision of the steam packet *Islay* which replaced the *Modern Athens*; he was elected MP for a mainland constituency (the Sterling Boroughs); he contributed articles on agriculture to the *Glasgow Herald* under the pseudonym 'Scottish Farmer'. As well as being a much-emulated model distiller, he built roads, churches and schools, and fathered three childen with his young second wife (his first having died of appendicitis in 1864, seven years after they married). Ramsay himself died on Islay in 1892. He was certainly the most influential figure on Islay in the nineteenth century; indeed this incomer was perhaps the most successful and important islander since Good John of Islay in the fourteenth century.

'. . . A VERY QUIET INOFFENSIVE RACE'

How widely admired was he, though, as a laird? Like Walter Frederick, he was held by those who knew him to be a man of compassion, though in Ramsay's case that compassion was tempered with a scalpel-keen sense for profit and loss. He had arrived on the island at its most populous moment; he had seen the ravages of the potato famine and the perpetual misery in which many Ileachs lived; when he bought the southern portion of the island from James Morrison, he bought areas (in particular the Oa) which remained, at mid-century, thick with impoverished crofters. And he did everything he could to move them off the land.

He did not want them, as Walter Frederick and his grandfather had, fishing from the villages; he wanted them away to Canada. A short period of lairdship 'much modified the opinion which I at one time entertained, as to the powers which [land ownership] confers on the holder to do good to the population.' Despite his educational and agricultural improvements, he wrote to a friend in 1860, 'I am sorry to say I cannot discern much improvement among the people. The villagers were very poor when I got the property and some of them are now deeper in debt than they were five years ago. I really do not know what to do with them as they are helpless when the land is taken from them and merely sink till they get on the Poor Roll . . .' The year before, his ever-sharp pencil had calculated that Islay had one pauper for every sixteen 'self-supporting members of Society' compared to a national average of one per 23. They were 'a very quiet inoffensive race' held in check by 'excessive dependence . . . on the produce of the soil' and the lack 'of the blessings of a sound English education'. In order to help them leave, he was prepared to cancel their rent arrears, buy up their stock and pay for their passage; he persuaded Charles Morrison and Smith Child to adopt the same approach. So concerned was he for their welfare that he went to Canada himself in 1870, to see how the emigrants were getting on, and his account of the sometimes arduous journey undertaken by this 55-year-old is both punctilious and readable. Ramsay recounted how those émigré Ileachs he spoke to stressed that they were far more prosperous in Canada than they would ever have been had they stayed on the island. This is beyond doubt; indeed it is still recognised by Ileachs today. 'Best thing that ever happened to them,' farmer James Brown of Port Charlotte (who has relations in Canada) told me when I discussed the evictions with him. Yet their going was intensely painful. The emigrant W.N. Blair had witnessed evictions on Islay. 'No matter,' he wrote, 'how gently the operation was performed, the result was all the same – "a dividing of bone and marrow".' The fact was that those who had belonged to this land set in the wild sea for generations, who had worked it, cropped it, loved it, detested it, and eventually nourished it with their own flesh and bones, who had lived exclusively from it and given everything they had to it, were taken from it against their will by a small class of men whose only claim on it was administrative, springing from their own recent wealth. An old tale.

It had, finally, its telling. When the Royal Commission under Lord

Napier was belatedly set up in 1883, spurred by a rent strike at Braes on Skye, to examine the injustices of a century of Highland clearance, it came to Islay (albeit eleven years later), and it discovered there, as it did elsewhere, this tragic legacy of dispossession and loss. The local commission, under the chairmanship of the sympathetic MP Angus Sutherland, sat at Port Ellen on 28 March 1894, at Port Charlotte on 2 April and Bridgend on 9 April. The testimonies it heard, mainly from elderly Ileachs, paint a remarkable picture, not least because so many of those appearing before the commission remained shyly deferential to their landowning superiors, even when natural justice was transparently on their side. (John Murdoch deplored this 'craven, cowed, snivelling' attitude: 'There is one great, dark cloud hanging over them in which there seem to be the terrible form of devouring landlords, tormenting factors and ubiquitous ground-officers.')

Most were examined in Gaelic, and the minuted English translations of what they said have a hauntingly simple poetry to them. John Campbell of Giol on the Oa spoke of his lost land, now 'gone under rushes' for want of cultivation. Archibald Campbell, when asked how long he worked his former holding at Lurabus on the Oa, replied simply, 'My people were there for generations untold.' Duncan Campbell Macewan of Bowmore was asked how long his feu (tenancy) had to run, and replied 'Life – while water runs and grass grows'. Donald Orr could name twenty-six families evicted from Avenvogie and Killinan by Smith Child: 'Some of them are away to America, and others are dead.' The land at Killinan, meanwhile, 'is going under fog and water'.

A number of testimonies show that the generally charitable accounts of the behaviour of Walter Frederick Campbell, Charles Morrison and John Ramsay were not always accurate – or, perhaps, that their factors did not always behave as the laird might have wished. Here is what Duncan Macindeor had to say. 'I am seventy-five years of age, and reside at Kilmeny . . . I never lived out of the island. My family carried on farming in the island for generations: my great-grandfather, grandfather, my father and myself all had farms in Islay, and always were able to pay our way honestly. I was a farmer and carried on farming in Airidh-Ghuairidh successfully for twenty-three and twenty-four years. I was always able to pay my rent, as my receipts will show. Mr Webster, the under-factor at this time, had put out a lot of small farmers and had taken the land into his own hands. He wanted my farm as well at this time, promising me another if I would give it up quietly. I refused to do so, and then he noticed me out of the farm. Nevertheless I had paid my rent, I protested against such unjust actions. He compelled me to leave my farm. I next wrote to Mr Dickson, and laid my case before him, but was too late in taking steps in this line of action. Mr Webster had so falsified matters to Mr Dickson that before he knew the truth of the whole case the lease had been signed and Webster got the farm. Notwithstanding his fair promises about giving me another farm when he got possession of mine, I could not get another worth anything under him. Moreover, after my corn was sown and was just coming through the ground, he sowed rye grass seed, and in harrowing it spoiled my own corn crop, and I could not get compensation from him for it. There were many others as well as myself put out or deprived of their farms about this time to make way for Webster. Four tenants got notice to leave Airidh-Ghuairidh; six or seven got notice to leave Strongaig. At or about that time, Rostern contained four who had to be moved from their holdings. Nosebridge had eight tenants who were also moved; Conegarry also contained eight tenants; Benveridle also contained seven tenants; and four farmers got notice to quit Kilbranan and three to quit Dranich; in other words, no less than forty-four or forty-five had to leave their holdings to give scope to Webster and sheep.'

Archibald Campbell was a 60-year-old, working as a carter in Port Ellen who, 23 years earlier, had finally been thrown off his land at Lurabost on the Oa (under John Ramsay's lairdship) and moved to the adjacent Ballychatrigan.

'Did you get as good a holding there as you had at Lurabost?'
'Yes, it was as good.'
'Then why did you leave Ballychatrigan?'
'We had to make room for sheep, and go to strange places.'
'You did not go of your own free will?'
'We had to go.'
'Where did you go to?'

'Strimnish.'

'And how long were you there?'

'Four years.'

'And why did you leave Strimnish?'

'We were not allowed to stop.'

'Why?'

'They wanted the land for sheep.'

'And when you were put out of Strimnish where did you go?'

'We came to Port Ellen.'

'There was no provision made for you when you were put out of Strimnish?'

'I had nothing; I had to go to some place.'

'Did you get any compensation for any improvements you had made on the holdings you had in any of the places?'

'We got nothing as compensation.'

'You got nothing for the houses?'

'We got nothing for the houses.'

'Who put up the houses you had in Lurabost?'

'My forefathers.'

Campbell confirmed to the Commissioners that he had never been in arrears with his rents. A fellow Port Ellen carter of the same age, Angus Macnab, had been evicted from his family holding in Cragabus 30 years earlier when his father died and 'Mr Ramsay, the proprietor, would not allow the son to succeed the father in the holding.' When Ramsay's Kidalton factor, Peter Reid, was interviewed, he flatly denied that any tenants were forcibly evicted. 'I might read extracts to show that the great majority of those who left the Oa went entirely of their own free will; and Mr Ramsay himself told me that he had a good cry over the head of a number of them going [to Canada] . . . He stated that he did not wish them to go.'

'Are you aware of any steps he took to induce them to stay?'

'No.'

'How could the tears be very genuine then?'

'I don't think that is very relevant to your enquiry . . . I don't think it is very generous, at all events towards a person who is dead, to discuss such a matter.'

(Ramsay himself, in a letter written in May 1872, claimed that all the 'removals were entirely voluntary'.)

Perhaps the most damning testimony of all came from an outside observer, a man who had no personal interest in owning, factoring or crofting. This was a 47-year-old called James Nicholls. He had arrived on the island 18 years earlier, and was working as a mines manager at Rebolls (called Robolls on present-day maps; the mine manager's house is said to be today's Ballygrant Inn). 'During that time,' Nicholls said, 'I have, of course, been situated right in the middle of the agricultural districts in connection with our works, and my experience has been that during that period farming carried on under the present system of large sheep farms has proved rather disastrous than otherwise to the interests of the island as well as perhaps to the interest of the community at large. I may state that the gentleman who owned the farms on which our works are situated (the combined farms of Finlaggan and Rebolls), stated to me that after fifteen years farming upon the large sheep farm principle he had not made "a brown penny". These were his own words on the occasion of his sale when he sold out at Finlaggan. At that particular time there were some cottars living in close proximity to our own works; these, I think, applied to the present factor, Mr Ballingall, and obtained a park of about 13 acres in extent. At the time they got this park it was overgrown with rushes, heather, and rough grass, with a good deal of lime rock jutting here and there. These men at that time were kindly granted the park, and by their industry and cultivation of the land they have made a splendid park out of it . . . [In] travelling over the island otherwise, I look around me and see the ruins and the great havoc that have been made by evictions in the past (I am not prepared to say whether justifiable or otherwise), and I see the amount of arable land now under large sheep farms, and so many people in our midst hungering and thirsting as it were for the land that they to-day are not in possession of, but which their forefathers held, and held advantageously and beneficially for themselves and their country. These men reared up big families and sent them out into the world, and today they fill all sorts of professions and occupations, noble and hardy and strong men. I should really like very much to see these farms broken up once more and placed in the hands of the people, who would utilise the land and obtain from it a much larger product than it yields today. Today our importation is very great, consequently impoverishing our island. We have to pay for imported feeding stuff when we should really be drawing money for exports from such a beautiful and lovely island as Islay. I am fully persuaded that if the land was once more handed back to the people it would benefit the community at large, and I am convinced that the only royal route to agricultural prosperity is the breaking up of the land.'

Nicholls pointed out that the average weight of a sheep on Islay tended to fall from 65lbs when they were moved on to recently crofted land down to 45lbs when the land had returned to its naturally rough state, and that the large sheep farmers were consequently demanding reduced rents from the lairds. Estate owners, meanwhile, were turning more and more towards 'sport' as a way of raising revenue.

'Is it a common thing to see it stated in advertisements for the sale of estates that there are new crofters or no crofters on them, as the case may be?'

'It is quite a common thing: you can scarcely look into a paper without seeing such an advertisement, "without cottars" or "without crofters", as if they were a great pest.'

'Does that suggest to your mind that the proprietors are desirous generally of turning their lands into sporting grounds?'

'It certainly does.'

Nicholls also pointed out that, despite the reduced population and the amalgamated farms, there was still hardship on Islay, with milk being costly and scarce at that time. Matters were made worse when a terrible storm in November 1893 wrecked no fewer than 38 fishing boats. The population may have fallen threefold (to around 5,000) by the turn of the nineteenth century, then, but the ordinary Ileach did not necessarily have any easier a life.

'. . . THEY WOULD ALWAYS FIND FAULT WITH YOU'

Islay's dramas in the nineteenth century were largely internal, and centred around the question of the land itself. Who owned it? Who lived on it? To what use should it be put? To whom should profit from the land accrue? In times of hardship, who should assure the well-being of those living on the island? The Lordship of the Isles may have come to an end 300 years earlier, but Islay in the era of omnipotent lairdship was not so different. The island was still, more or less, a little kingdom.

The twentieth century quickly proved a total contrast. The dramas were external, not internal: Islay increasingly suffered, and profited, from events unfolding far away from Bowmore and Port Ellen. Within two decades, it was not a new life in Canada which took fit young Islaymen from their homes, but Lord Kitchener's finger; it was not a log cabin in virgin forest which awaited them, but a squalid, muddy death in the trenches of northern France. Within the same two decades, those on the island were no longer taking shoals of silver herring from the seas, but shoals of dead Americans, their bodies battered beyond recognition (see pages 301–14). If the distilling business suffered, it was because an American president amended his country's constitution to institute Prohibition in 1919, because the gold standard collapsed in the 1930s, because authoritarian, fascist solutions to complex economic problems had led to a strong nation invading a weak one in Central Europe, or because drinkers in the bars of Hong Kong, Tokyo or Los Angeles began to prefer 'light' white spirits in their drinks to 'heavy' darker ones. Farmers on Islay, too, were less and less concerned with feeding a local population, and more and more concerned with finding a mainland market. The little kingdom became part of a large nation, and part of a wide and often troubled world.

Islay lost 181 men in the First World War, many of them serving with the Argyll and Sutherland Highlanders, a regiment which saw no fewer than 6,900 of its soldiers slaughtered during the conflict. John Ramsay's son Iain, who had inherited the Kidalton estate and Port Ellen distillery on his mother's death in 1905, joined up – and was lucky enough to return home again afterwards, as an invalid captain (his trainee distiller was killed, as was the only son of the local Church of Scotland minister). What had happened to the Campbells of Cawdor and then the Campbells of Shawcross now happened to the Ramsays, the only difference being that it happened more quickly: the wealth and possessions created by the first generation slid away from its successors. After the First World War, Iain Ramsay was forced to sell the entire Kidalton Estate and its distilleries (each of which was purchased by its existing tenants). The sales particulars (prepared by Knight, Frank and Rutley of Hanover Square, London) make mouth-watering reading, and the photographs show just how immaculately the estate, which occupies by far the prettiest part of the island, had been maintained. Some 54,000 acres (134,670 ha) were offered, including the still-beautiful Kidalton Mansion built by John Ramsay (a ruin today), the White Heart and Islay Hotels, the Machrie Hotel and its golf course, the fine Cairnmore House (or dower house) outside Port Ellen, as well as a number of farmhouses and workers' cottages. The 'average game bag for the last seven seasons' was said to include 150 blackcock and 800 grouse, as well as 600 woodcock and 350 snipe; 60–70 salmon were taken from the Laggan; and 36–40 stags were killed annually.

The purchaser, in 1922, was the most extraordinary laird Islay has ever known: Talbot Clifton. He had been born in 1868, and at 16 (while at Eton) had inherited vast, ancestral estates in the Fylde, the great low lobe of Lancashire which lies between the Wyre and Ribble estuaries. The family seat was at Lytham St Anne's; manor courts had been held on the estate, presided over by successive Cliftons, for six hundred years. Despite the extravagance of his material good fortune, Clifton had not been happy at home as a child. According to his wife Violet, who wrote and published a lengthy yet partial account of her husband's life and travels in the early 1930s called *The Book of Talbot*, 'he suckled his mother so fiercely that she had a wound in her breast.' A poor start, obviously, to this key relationship – and, according to Violet, it was downhill all the way after that. Dysfunctionality was something of a Clifton family tradition, since Talbot's father Harry had also been maltreated by his own mother (who had in turn been forced against her will to marry his grandfather John). 'At Lytham I was not happy as a boy excepting when once I was ill and left in the house alone with my nurse Patch,' Talbot recalled. He was a taciturn man.

It is not easy to pick out the thread of fact in *The Book of Talbot*, partly because its widowed author nurtured almost hagiographic feelings for her dead husband; partly because she has a wild, untidy and emotional way with a story; and partly because (either wittingly or not: Violet was, after all, born in Rome, schooled in Brussels, and spent her adolescence in Peru) the book's style is odd. 'Talbot was so othergates than still people' is a typical Violet Clifton phrase. She refers to herself in the third person throughout ('It seemed a mock to Violet that insects should outbuild the men,' she writes on seeing an anthill taller than the huts in a Senegalese village), and for several chapters she switches entirely if mysteriously into a shapeless and baggy blank verse. However the tale she tells, and the lost world she evokes, is so astonishing that the book's faults can easily be forgiven. How, moreover, can one not warm to an Islay resident who feels moved to summarise autumn on the island as 'Fire and blood, anger and desire'? The book was admired in its day, winning the James Tate Black Prize for biography in 1932. A press cutting sandwiched in my 1933 (American) edition reveals that it was still being urged on readers of the *New York Times Book Review* as 'one of the curiosities of modern literature' in 1944. Indeed.

Talbot Clifton was a moneyed, amateur explorer of northern Canada; of Siberia; of Burma, Malaya and Indonesia (with Violet in search of orchids); of Tibet; and of East and Central Africa. 'Because,' as Violet put it, 'in his loveless home his worth had been questioned, he had gone into the wilds to prove himself to himself. Hammered on the anvils of hardship he had proved his power.' England for Talbot is summarised (by Violet) as 'experiment and overindulgence . . . the harass, the overspending'; travel for Talbot meant 'great simplicity and hardness of life . . . asceticism and escape'.

'Placing myself in voluntary exile,' wrote Talbot in one of his diaries, 'gave me that peace which civilization and its currencies do not hold for me.' A fellow Old Etonian, Sir John Stirling Maxwell, remembered Talbot's 'extraordinary determination and utter contempt for danger' which made him 'altogether unlike the ordinary type of rather smug Eton boy'.

Unfortunately he was neither a good speaker (the 'slowness of his speech, counter-battering the quickness of his thoughts, fretted him') nor a man much given to writing up his exploits. 'My only regret about him,' recalled the Reverend J.M. McWilliam, an ornithologist who enjoyed his hospitality at Kidalton, 'was that he never wrote his travels, and never would have done so if he had lived to be a hundred. He was almost secretive about what he had done.' Had he been able to do either, his name might well be a familiar one to us today. Violet's accounts, pieced together from his laconic diary entries, from letters and from their conversations together, are never less than astonishing.

Talbot rarely bothered much with preparation, only seemed to tackle journeys where privation would be extreme and survival uncertain, and then spent much of his time on these battles of the will over circumstances dangerously ill. His considerable hunting abilities frequently saved him and his (usually native) companions from starvation; indeed by shooting anything which aroused his curiosity he ended up by having several new species named after him. One such was the wild Siberian ram *Ovis cliftoni*; another was a previously unknown species of marmot (shot while hibernating) called *Arctomys cliftoni*. The skins of both were given to the Natural History Museum. He also shot a large Siberian bear in dramatic circumstances (it eventually fetched up, stuffed, in Arundel Castle) as well as an albino reindeer; the whole purpose of his Canadian expedition was to shoot a musk-ox, which he eventually did – using, on his return journey, its severed head as a pillow. On Christmas Day 1901 in Siberia he organised perhaps the most extraordinary Christmas feast known either to exploration or to gastronomy. It began with a soup made from the bear he had shot, and was followed by its jellied paws. Next came roasted *Ovis cliftoni* (no sooner discovered than eaten), and then a dish of mammoth, courtesy of a German professor called Hertz who had recently excavated it from the permafrost. ('They ate it thoughtfully, for was it not about eight thousand years old?') The last pangs of appetite were satisfied with Siberian capercaillie, and finally a plum pudding 'of Talbot's own making, and from a receipt he but half remembered'.

Violet was living in Lima in 1906, looking after her manic depressive father (a diplomat called Nelthorpe Beauclerk), when she met Talbot, who was 15 years her senior. He was in Ecuador at the time, trying to put together an expedition to Isla del Coco and the Galapagos to search for buried pirate treasure (an expedition seemingly mounted on the throwaway suggestion of Charles Berry of the celebrated St James's wine merchants Berry Bros and Rudd). Talbot could not get official permission to sail for the islands, and instead watches a revolution in progress ('I took photos of one or two dead men'), experiences an earthquake, catches fever, explores the mountain jungle, goes to a bullfight ('as barbaric as it could be') – and then hears about a young Englishwoman in neighbouring Peru 'who had shot the horse she had ridden, because she could not have faced seeing anyone else riding it.' Talbot liked the sound of Violet, in other words, and went to meet her in the Andes. Their relationship, fanned by the wings of condors, deepens swiftly (she is prepared to jump off moving Peruvian trains at a word from Talbot), and they sail back to England to marry.

Talbot never liked living at Lytham Hall (which, in addition to all its emotional defects, lay five feet below sea level), so they rent houses in Scotland (his breast-wounded mother was a Scot), live on a racing yacht called *Maoona*, and travel lavishly. When they are at Lytham, they look after the orchids they have brought back from Asia, while Talbot builds an organ (he was an accomplished musician who never travelled without his silver flute). Violet attempts to buy two pygmies ('It would be wonderful to have some to study, and we could make them happy') but is stymied by pedestrian English law, so Talbot buys her a small Icelandic pony instead, which is led into the dining room each night to take dinner with them. The couple find time to produce five children, only four of which Violet ever troubles to name in *The Book of Talbot*; even then she gives little idea of their relative ages or personalities. Harry was the eldest son, and Michael a second; Aurea was the eldest daughter, and Easter a second (or Muriel Easter Daffodil Therese, to give her full name). 'Even the children of Violet may have felt sometimes forlorn,' Violet tellingly writes, 'for she did not weigh them against her husband and would, at any time, leave them to follow him.' The children must have been more familiar with their paid household staff than with their parents. On those rare occasions when the parents were at home, their childhood was still a singular one: 'to make them hardy, Violet would whisper to her sons when as each slept: "Your body must be the slave of your will – your body must be the slave of your will."'

At the outbreak of the First World War, Talbot and Violet raced off towards the action in northern France, where he drove the important and the injured around in the latest in a series of large cars he had bought, while she did translation work. Then the Admiralty asked him to take his yacht the *White Eagle* up to Stornoway for coast-watching duties; later in the War he exchanged the *White Eagle* for a larger yacht called the *Cabar Feid*, and patrolled the Connemara coast. The place pleased him, so he bought an estate at Kylemore ('its price was a jest,' recalled Violet) which, oddly enough, was near a town called Clifden; the family stayed on, in so far as it stayed anywhere, after the War. In 1921, though, during the turbulence which led to the founding of the Irish Free State, Talbot fell out with a local Sinn Fein group after it commandeered his best car, a Lanchester. (He offered them a Ford instead, and was outraged when they insisted on the Lanchester.) This squabble led, eventually, to Talbot shooting and gravely injuring Captain Eugene Gilan of the Irish Republican Army, which in turn led to a hurried exit from Ireland for the wealthy Cliftons. They returned to Lancashire, but still felt threatened even there, and were under police guard for a year. 'A man is coming for the Squire of Lytham', was the word from Liverpool. Later, when the Free State was established, the local IRA men invited them back to Connemara and even returned the Lanchester, albeit in a bloodied and battered state. By then, though, Iain Ramsay had put the Kidalton Estate on the market, and Talbot snapped it up; he already co-owned land and water for summer fishing on Lewis. The family moved to Islay.

Islay, according to Violet, was the only 'home' Talbot ever felt truly happy in. His Islay years 'crowned his desires. A strong sense of possession joyed him; his eyes rested thankfully on the hills that were his. Never before had he possessed hill country; his eyes swept gratefully over the sea coast, his own – over the islands and the Skerries.' He shot and gralloched copiously; at night, Kidalton Mansion echoed with the toast 'Blood, more blood, coupled with the name of [whoever had killed the stag in question]. Standing, the guests repeated: "More blood", and would say the name of the killer of the stag.' The finest stag killed in Scotland in 1926 was 'grassed' by Talbot at Proaig, and it was the roar of the rut, and the crimson and gold of the heather and hill grasses, which led Violet to characterise autumn on Islay as 'Fire and blood, anger and desire'. In quieter moments (such as 'a sunlit Good Friday'), Talbot played his golden flute to the seals which throng the Kidalton skerries. 'The seals, tired of fighting and of thrashing each other, came up near the rock where he was – with black heads thrust out of water, they listened to the music that told of the joy of all creatures redeemed.' This pastime has become something of a Kidalton tradition (see page 264). Violet brewed ale, and together they bottled Burgundy and Spanish wine which Talbot had shipped up in cask. They also made a kind of vatted malt of their own for guests: 'Felicity, to fill for guests a great barrel of blended spirits, the whiskies of Islay, made on the island because of the sweetness of the water which carried the flavour of the peat, and of the bog-myrtle.' Daily Mass was said in the small chapel on the estate.

Talbot, of course, continued to travel. 'I am going to Baghdad to see Gertrude Bell, and on into Persia. Will you come?' Talbot asked Violet one morning, much as a holidaymaker in one of the Ardtalla Estate cottages might today ask his wife if she'll pop down to the Co-op in Port Ellen with him. The children, of course, were left behind. This journey later led to the Sheikh of Bahrain, his brother, and two of their eight wives coming to stay at Kidalton, where they enjoyed watching the wild rabbits but were terrified by having a fire lit in their bedrooms. During a journey he undertook alone across Central Africa in 1926, Talbot acquired a black servant from Chad called Mohamed Noa whom he took back with him to Islay. He was more ill than usual during this typical calvary of a trip. 'Am better but very weak,' reads a typical diary entry, written between Lake Chad and the Sudan. 'Managed to sit my horse for two and a half hours. When we come to the six hours' trek without water I shall collapse. My horse stumbles every step. Damn. Rather interesting country. I vomit all the time.'

Despite these difficulties, and despite the forebodings of catastrophe which Violet experienced at Kidalton on New Year's Eve 1927, the pair of them, accompanied by the faithful Mohamed Noa, left Islay for Timbuktu early in 1928. 'For the approaching journey to Timbuktu Talbot made almost no preparations.' As their boat lay in the Gironde estuary downstream from Bordeaux, delayed from leaving for

Dakar by 'a mutiny of the ship's firemen', Talbot was 'shivering with ague'. He was iller still in Dakar, but insisted on pressing on for Bamako. Eventually they arrived. 'It was a stage set for their much suffering,' wrote Violet. After a day or two, even the iron-willed Talbot realised he could go no further, and they took the train back to Dakar. (During its 50-hour journey up to Bamako, one of the passengers had died of the heat; his corpse was removed as Talbot's half-dead body was carried on for the return leg.) After a day in the French Military Hospital there, Talbot commenced his final journey: a rough, three-day passage to Santa Cruz de Tenerife in the Canaries. X-rays taken at Santa Cruz revealed that Talbot had advanced lung cancer (the only item he had taken with him on every journey, apart from his flute and his copy of Shakespeare, was his pipe). Three weeks later, aged 60, he was dead. Violet travelled (on a neat, brisk Norwegian fruit boat) with her now-embalmed husband back to London; thence to Islay. The mourners took six days to assemble; Violet slept by the coffin at night. Twelve Islay men carried Talbot to Cnoc Rhaonastil, the steep hill on the Kidalton Estate beneath which he was buried, and where he still lies today; Violet calls it Green Hill. (The locals call it Knock Hill, while its Gaelic name means Rowandale Hill; the Middletons, who live at Kidalton today, call it Fairy Hill.) She threw a single wild violet and a bunch of orchids on his coffin, and never wore her jewels again. 'Slowly, like a coral island, the ages had built up that form of a man. Nearly a thousand years of privileged beings lay behind it. Good-bye to the efflorescence of a line that had spent itself in blood, and sacrifice, and wealth.'

Violet's words were premonitory. Talbot himself seems to have been popular on the island: 'I'm missing my good master up and down the paths,' an unnamed gardener apparently told Violet, 'for I have seen lairds very plenty, but never such a one – he was a most decent gentleman . . . Ah, that he might be back here in his splendour.' The Clifton succession, though, proved to be no happier than the Ramsay succession had been, and the estate was at first neglected and then sold off in several portions by Harry Clifton, the eldest son of Talbot and Violet. He disliked Islay just as his father had disliked Lytham; but while his father took refuge from childhood grief in the rigours of exploration, Harry seems to have preferred the fast life in London (where he is said to have kept rooms at both the Ritz and the Dorchester) and America. He became internationally celebrated for losing £30,000 in a 15-minute game of stud poker in the Villa Riviera Hotel in Los Angeles, and for giving 600 diamonds fashioned into the form of a gardenia to a Hollywood mystic called Violet Greener, self-styled 'Priestess' of the Agabec Occult Temple. He married an American called Lillian Griswold in 1937; 'after the marriage,' a local paper reported, 'Mrs Clifton developed a distressing nervous malady.' She eventually broke her back after falling out of a window under obscure circumstances at Lytham; they divorced in 1943. He also squabbled very publicly in 1944 with Rudolf Palumbo over the sale of the Lytham Estate, and the dispute ended in the courts – where Harry was described (by the *Lytham St Anne's Express*) as 'lacking in business capacity and experience and stability of purpose. Some of his answers to questions were very inconsequent [sic] and rather silly.'

Harry's younger brother Michael lived at Kidalton for a while and, perhaps remembering with affection the Iceland pony who took dinner with the family at Lytham, was renowned for allowing assorted animals and poultry the run of the house – as Sandy Mactaggart, uncle of Sir John Mactaggart, personally remembers. 'Michael had bought chickens and turkeys and pigs, but he hadn't given the pigs anything to eat, so they ate the daffodil bulbs and rooted up the lawn. The house had been in good shape and well furnished, but he had all the windows open and the chickens and the turkeys were sitting on the chairs. They were up and down the stairs and crapping on everything. He used the place as a barn.' Unsurprisingly, it gradually declined towards its present-day ruinous state. Sadly, Violet never joined Clifton in death; perhaps this was Harry's decision. According to Fiona Middleton, Harry left the last remnants of the Clifton millions 'to the fortune teller at the end of Blackpool pier'.

The bulk of the old Kidalton estate became the Mactaggart family's Ardtalla estate, while the magnificent woodlands, deer park and former ornamental gardens which surrounded Kidalton Mansion, semi-ruined when Harry Clifton finally relinquished them, were acquired by George Middleton and are now owned by an intricate network of companies and charities controlled by various Middleton family members. The Laggan portion of the old Ramsay estate has been through many changes of ownership, the most recent being that of the Jennings family from Ulster; while the largest landowner on the Oa is now the RSPB. The Dunlossit Estate has been owned since 1937 by the Schroder family; and Islay Estates, though reduced in size, is still the property of the Morrison family. Islay Estates (55,000 acres/22,259 ha), Dunlossit (18,500 acres/7,487 ha) and Ardtalla (14,800 acres/5,990 ha) are the three largest estates on the island, between them accounting for some 63 per cent of the island's total landmass (140,000 acres/56,568 ha). The only part of the island which has managed to achieve any sizeable measure of owner-occupation by its farming and crofting community is the Rhinns, thanks largely to the fact that Rod Dawson's widow Jane was able to sell the Ellister Estate's tenant farms to the tenants in 1978, and due to the partial break-up of the Foreland Estate when it passed out of the ownership of the Doyle family.

During the middle part of the twentieth century, the Morrison family of Islay Estates was intimately involved in Conservative party politics; John Morrison, the great-grandson of the once-radical MP James Morrison, acted as chairman of the 1922 Committee (which oversees the election of Conservative party leaders) for nine years, a period during which Sir Anthony Eden, Harold Macmillan and Sir Alec Douglas-Home served successively as party leaders (and Prime Ministers). In return for these labours, he was given one of the last hereditary peerages ever awarded in Britain, choosing the title 'Lord Margadale' in part so that he would not be obliged to alter his initials, though his grandson Alastair (the present Lord Margadale) says it was also because he considered Islay 'his spiritual home'. Two of his sons (though not the eldest, James, the second Lord Margadale) followed their father into national politics, Charles becoming Conservative MP for Devizes and Peter for Chester. Through these connections, Alec Douglas-Home, Ted Heath and Margaret Thatcher all came to stay at Islay House, with Mrs Thatcher staying several times (Peter Morrison was a close political ally of hers). Victor MacLellan at Bunnahabhain recalls that a visit Ted Heath made to the distillery was viewed unenthusiastically by the workers. 'Ted Heath was here one day,' he told me. 'We were all working away, but when we saw him we just disappeared. We all hid in the lower tun room. Waited till he'd gone.' Mrs Thatcher, according to the present (third) Lord Margadale, enjoyed her stays – except for losing to more adroit juniors while playing Islay House after-dinner games. Eventually she abandoned such frivolities and worked at her papers until bedtime instead. Perhaps it was on Islay, though, that she acquired her celebrated taste for an evening dram.

The island's population has continued to fall throughout the twentieth century, dipping below 5,000 after the Second World War (it was 3,457 in the 2001 census, a decline of just 81 people since the previous census in 1991). The first telephone links came on 19 September 1935, while electricity (called 'the hydro' on the island) arrived sporadically via private generators; a diesel generator was installed at Bowmore in 1949, and the island was finally connected to the national grid in 1962. What was life on the island like before the arrival of electricity? 'Oh dear, that was grim,' ex-Laphroaig worker Iain Maclean told me when I asked him how he passed the winter nights. Maclean had been born in 1913, lived almost all his life on the island, worked his entire career for Laphroaig, and finally died in 2003. 'Paraffin lamps, that was all we had. And the newspaper: *The Daily Record* or *The Daily Express*. That was your lot. We didn't even have a wireless in those days.' During the Depression, all the distilleries shut (as they also did during the two major wars). 'I was on the dole for the first time of my life in 1933. Wait till I tell you this. I had 12 shillings and 6 pence a week to live on to start with, but then they reduced it to 2 shillings and 6. Can you believe that anybody was expected to live on that? It was under a Tory government, of course. I would never vote Tory; I've always kept that at the back of my mind. I could never forgive them that. I wondered at the time how my mother fed us. There were five of us in the family, and my father was unemployed as well; the total amount we had coming in to the house was less than a pound a week. A pound a week! I'm a strong socialist, and that's what did it.'

Maclean, like many others, resorted to poaching. 'I poached rabbits. I was quite a good poacher. I went out on moonlit nights, Saturday nights, to set the snares. And I'd go up on a Sunday morning early and walk through the snares and get the rabbits and that would be it for the week. You were terrified in case you'd be seen. They'd have you in court for poaching rabbits. You couldn't walk through anybody's land in those days.' Fish was another way of supplementing a meagre diet, and Maclean used to go out 'splashing' (catching salmon with nets near the mouths of the island's rivers). 'I did it at night, like everybody else. I wasn't the only one at that caper; there were quite a few of us at it. What's the harm in putting a net out in an open bay? I can't see it. Yet they found fault with you; they would always find fault with you.' Lily MacDougall, the mother of Christine Logan of Bowmore, remembers doing the same. 'I always maintain it's the Queen's fish,' she says. 'What laird would claim that he owns the Queen's fish?'

The Second World War on Islay was not, as the First World War had been, marked by maritime disasters (described in Chapter Seven); instead it was air accidents which underscored the difficulty of the days. On 12 September 1943, indeed, there were no fewer than three plane crashes on the island between three and eight in the morning. One Bristol Beaufighter Mk X crashed into the moss near the airport just after take-off at five to four in the morning, due to unconfident piloting (both crewmen were killed); another Beaufighter then crashed up in the hills above the moss while distracted by the flames from the first crash. A third crashed while attempting to land just after seven in the morning; not a good four hours for the RAF. Another two Beau-fighters were lost the following January, one crashing on Sunderland Hill on the Rhinns on New Year's Day, killing the pilot, and another near the airport on 9 January, once again killing the pilot. A Short Stirling Mk III crashed in February 1944 close to the airport, killing six crewmen, and there was a 'secret' crash just after the War, when a De Havilland Mosquito B Mk IV, having (probably) just dropped a trial anti-shipping bouncing bomb into the water from 30 feet, was caught by the splash and lost its wing before diving into the sea.

The worst air accident of all, though, occurred on 24 January 1943 at Blackrock, a little group of houses on the road which runs around Loch Indaal, sited about halfway between Bridgend and Bruich-laddich. A large rock called Carraig Dubh (Black Sea-Rock) lies just offshore there; in certain lights, it looks like a shipwreck. Loch Indaal during the Second World War was briefly home to a squadron of Short Sunderland flying boats (Squadron 246, operational for four months only – and then broken up, precisely because the weather conditions were too difficult). It was a wild night, and the Sunderland in question had been patrolling the North Atlantic for almost 13 hours, and was very low in fuel. Because of the gale, it had been instructed to land at Oban, but couldn't establish radio contact there so pressed on back home to Islay. The landing proved difficult since, in order to provide a little shelter, the flare path guiding the plane down had been positioned closer than usual to the shore; it had been aborted a number of times. On the final approach the Sunderland's own lights seemed to give out at the critical moment. The result was that it crash-landed short of the water's edge, taking the roof off the joiner's workshop at Blackrock.

All was well – almost. There was a crew of 12 on board. The injured pilot and two others got away down to the sea shore, while eight other crewmen ran up to the road. At that point, the eight realised that one man, the rear gunner, was trapped on board. They ran back to help him. As they were doing so, the depth charges stored on board the Sunderland exploded, killing all nine instantly. Some idea of the strength of this blast can be gauged from the fact that it blew in the doors of Kilmeny Church in the centre of the island (where evening service was in progress), and remodelled the landscape at Blackrock itself. The residents of Bowmore, directly across the loch, couldn't fail to realise what had happened – and they included wives and girlfriends of those on board. It was an international tragedy: the captain ('Soapy' Lever) was a South African and his co-pilot (Wally Johnson) a Canadian, while two of the crew (Ernest Palmer and Roy Jabour) were Australians. There is today a beautifully crafted wooden memorial on the seaward side of the road at Blackrock in memory of another of the crewmen, Sergeant Navigator Walter Heath, placed there in recent times by 'Margaret'.

Just under three months later, meanwhile, it was the turn of an Islayman to lose his life far from home – on 17 April, in Tunisia. This was a young man from Avenvogie: the dark, quiet place where the forestry plantations are to be found on the back road between Bridgend and Port Ellen. His name was Alisdair Williamson, and he was a corporal with the Argyll and Sutherland Highlanders. In such times, there was nothing remarkable about his death. After it, though, his family received a letter which he had prepared (as many soldiers did) for such an eventuality. It was written with such simple dignity and such certain sense of purpose, though, that the family could never lay it to rest with his other effects. It found its way to the Museum of Islay Life where, once displayed, it proved so affecting to visitors that a ready supply of photocopies is required. It is with this letter (whose grammar and punctuation I have left unchanged) that this final chapter of Islay's history ends, an account of recent times being found in Chapter Eight. Under Somerled and the Lords of the Isles, young Islaymen had to leave home to fight distant battles; they were still doing it one thousand years later. The reasons Alisdair Williamson was prepared to make this sacrifice would have been recognised by his forebears. The fact that few have had to emulate him since, and the way in which the 'Islay way of life' survives (despite all the challenges of changed circumstances), puts us all in his debt.

Dear Father and Mother

I had hopes never to have to write in this strain I did not expect to die in this war no one does. At first when I knew I was in danger I thought a lot about it. I worried frantically at the thought of all the happiness I would miss and of you dear Mum's who loved me so wonderful, & built your lives around my health and happiness so successfully. I am deeply conscious of what I am fighting for & would not sit at home during this war. What I am fighting for is not any abstraction to me. It is not any vague ideal of freedom or democracy. I reduce it to the most elemental of emotions, that of man's instinctive dominating intense desire to protect those individuals whom he holds dearest. So the fact that I may die while I am protecting you does not appal me in the least, if I do so I shall be happy to have done what I have to preserve your lives and way of life. Do not grieve for me do not be bitter, remember me as the lovable cheerful boy, that loved you all, and was always content. I go to meet my maker fearless undaunted and glorious, and I will meet you all some day live

out your lives to the fullest without loneliness or pain where ever
I am I will be at peace I have a clear conscience and a clean soul.

> *Farewell Father*
> *Farewell Mother*
> *Farewell Sisters and Brothers*
> *Alisdair*

THIRD GLASS

Bruichladdich

Low tide. Wrack. Cooled stills.
From under the sea's eyelids —
leaps dolphin spirit.

BRUICHLADDICH (pronounced Bruch-*laddy*, with a susurrant 'ch' as in 'loch') is a loner. By dint of geography, first of all. The three southerly Kidalton distilleries are evident siblings, while Caol Ila and Bunnahabhain watch more distantly but no less solicitously over each other on the east coast. Grandfather Bowmore has the island's largest community gathered around it, but Bruichladdich . . . Bruichladdich lies way out west; Bruichladdich is the distillery of the Rhinns, once a separate island to Islay and still prone to no little independence of spirit; Bruichladdich watches over the gates to the Atlantic. This was so even before 2000; now that the distillery chooses to call itself 'the only independent Islay distillery' and 'the distillery with attitude', claiming to be the 'independent Scottish company owned by real people NOT anonymous corporate conglomerates', it has become even more true. Bruichladdich may, by the time this book is published, be a little less lonesome: when Kilchoman's farm-scale distillery becomes operational at Rockside, there will be two distilleries on the Rhinns for the first time since illegal distillation ceased, and Bruichladdich will no longer be Islay's most westerly distillery. (Talisker on Skye is a little further west than either.) But Bruichladdich, by dint of its fierce and feisty independence, seems likely to continue to ginger the rest of the Scotch whisky industry in the future just as it has done (generating enthusiasm and irritation in equal measure) over the last four years.

The distillery was born in the best of times and the worst of times. It was the worst of times far from Islay, in the vineyards of France: the phylloxera pest – a tiny, root-feeding insect of American origin – was devastating wine production and with it, of course, the French brandy industry. The International Phylloxera Congress was held in Bordeaux in 1881, at the height of the crisis, to try to fix on a solution; French wine production was in the middle of a freefall tumble from 84.5 million hectolitres in 1875 to 23.4 million hl in 1889. The solution (grafting native European vines on to American vine rootstocks) had been suggested as early as 1869, but it remained controversial, because of its immense practical difficulties and the fear that it might affect quality; it was not universally accepted until the late 1880s. This Gallic catastrophe, naturally, made it the best of times for Scotch whisky distillers, who were faced not only with rising domestic demand during the heavy-drinking 1870s but also with the realistic possibility that they might inherit the world brandy market within the coming decade. It was into this climate of optimism, in the same year as the grim-faced vine experts met around a table in Bordeaux, that both Bruichladdich and Bunnahabhain were born.

Bruichladdich's founders were members of a powerful Glasgow distilling family, the Harveys; their Dundashill (or Port Dundas) distillery in Glasgow was, by the mid-1880s, a 35-washback monster with three continuous stills and five pot stills; while their equally venerable Yoker distillery (both were thought to have been established around 1770) on the outskirts of town had switched to grain-whisky production alone. The Harveys' choice of Islay was prompted by the fact that blenders were thirsty for flavourful malts which could 'cover' high percentages of grain whisky and lend it some character. According to Bruichladdich's present-day CEO Mark Reynier, the original site for the distillery was to have been at Kilchoman itself, 'on the outflow of Loch Gorm, but at the last minute they realised that landing and off-loading casks from the highly exposed beach on that side of the Rhinns would be too risky – so it was built in its current location.' It was not as large or ambitious a project as Bunnahabhain (which was producing over twice as much malt as Bruichladdich by the time Alfred Barnard called in the mid-1880s), but it was modern. So modern, indeed, that it was made from an entirely new building substance on which the Glasgow contractor (John MacDonald) held a patent: concrete. The entire project was completed with remarkable Victorian expedition between May and December 1881. Barnard was impressed with the distillery's unity and harmony of construction, such a contrast to the higgledy-piggledy, 'organic' development of distilleries like Lagavulin; its design of separate buildings around a central courtyard was in part prompted by fire fears (every whisky distillery and its warehouses are a kind of communal petrol bomb, just waiting for an opportunity to explode). It is this design which makes the distillery such a pleasure to visit today – and never more so than on the customarily sunny 'Bruichladdich day' during the Islay whisky festival, when the courtyard becomes a theatre of music and dance.

THE UNLOVED DISTILLERY

As is customary in the whisky business, the optimism of Bruichladdich's founding didn't take long to dissipate and, with time, this was to prove the most repeatedly traded of all of Islay's distilleries. By the turn of the century, after the reverberative collapse of Pattisons of Leith and with depression setting in, the mighty Dundashill had closed, Yoker had been sold and the Distillers Company had taken over J & R Harvey & Co. All that the family managed to keep was the Islay minnow. Barnett Harvey, the builder of Bruichladdich, died in 1897, and the distillery was run by his nephew William (the fourth of that name). It pootled on until the next depression, then closed for seven years, between 1929 and 1936, when William Harvey died. Two years later, this great distilling family sold Bruichladdich and quit the business altogether.

The new owner was briefly a Scottish businessman who had made (and lost) money in Canada called Joseph Hobbs; but later that year Bruichladdich became the first of Islay's distilleries to be American owned, by National Distillers of America (via a Scottish subsidiary called Train & McIntyre Ltd). It was silent again during the Second World War, then resumed work afterwards. Ownership changed again in 1952, when it was bought by brokers Ross & Coulter; in 1960 it changed hands yet again, the new owner being A.B. Grant, a company which had already bought Bladnoch distillery in Galloway from Ross & Coulter. Grant in turn sold it on to Invergordon Distillers in 1968, thereby once again making Bruichladdich a malt in a grain whisky family; it was joined within Invergordon by fellow malt distilleries Deanston and Tullibardine in 1972, and by Jura in 1985; Tamnavulin was built by Invergordon in 1965–6. Bruichladdich had made good progress in the swell days of the 1960s and 1970s (Scotch whisky exports tripled between 1960 and 1971), and two new stills were added in 1975. However the purchase of the Jura distillery in 1985 was eventually to pose renewed problems, as did the slump of the 1980s; by 1984 the distillery was only working one day a week. Blenders Whyte & Mackay (a subsidiary of the American company renamed Jim Beam Brands in 1995) bought Invergordon in 1993. With the return of the Americans, Bruichladdich's gates were closed once again; Jim Beam didn't see the need for two island distilleries in its portfolio, and Jura, being a singleton on its own island, took precedence.

The unloved Bruichladdich was, yet again, up for sale, but this time the story took a different twist. London wine merchant Mark Reynier, having established a whisky bottling company called Murray McDavid in 1996, had been keen to acquire Ardbeg during its own years of silence in the early 1990s when, as a stablemate to Laphroaig, it was proving surplus to Allied Distillers' requirements. He coordinated a bid (audaciously: London wine merchants don't normally do that kind of thing); but was unsuccessful. Sir John Mactaggart of Ardtalla estate, one of the three main lairds on Islay and a potential investor in the Ardbeg bid as well as a property developer by profession, remembers the Reynier approach. 'Mark Reynier rang me up one day and said, "I hear you are interested in whisky and you live on Islay." I said "Yes and yes." He then said, in his usual direct way, "I want to buy Ardbeg; would you like to be involved? I want you to be chairman." I said "Look, Mark; we'd better meet before you come to that conclusion." We did meet, and we got on; I was touched by his enthusiasm, as most people are. We put together a consortium and made a bid for Ardbeg, but we didn't get it. We were the underbidders by a million. Anyway, Mark went away and hid in his burrow for a bit, but not for long, because as usual he was up to something. He dug out Bruichladdich, and this time it got serious and real; broadly speaking I raised something like thirty-five per cent of the equity. Again he invited me to be chairman, and again I said no, because I felt that this was not a business I knew well enough to feel comfortable with that responsibility. I was also highly conscious of the fact that, even if I was looking after the money I had brought to the table, I also had a responsibility to Islay, which has always been very important to me.' Discussions with Jim Beam Brands about the purchase began in January 2000, and the deal was finally struck on 19 December; the purchase price, including all the stocks, was £7.5 million (according to Mark Reynier there were 35 rival bids). Also among the shareholders was Bruno Schroder of Dunlossit Estate. 'I've always thought that Bruichladdich whisky was the best one of the lot on Islay because it's a light malt,' he says, 'so when I heard that somebody enterprising was involved I thought "Oh well, I'll take a chunk for fun – but it really is just for fun."' Lord Margadale of Islay Estates is the only one of the three major landholders on the island not to be involved in Bruichladdich.

The purchase, though, provided only half of the drama. The balance was made up by the fact that Jim McEwan left Bowmore to act as Production Director and get Bruichladdich back on its feet, together with Reynier and his two Murray McDavid collaborators (long-term partner and former school friend Simon Coughlin, and Gordon Wright of the family which owns Springbank in Campbeltown). McEwan – known to the world as Jim, but known to his friends and family on Islay as James – is the most charismatic distiller of his generation, not just on Islay but throughout the whole of the Scotch whisky industry; his abilities as a Celtic storyteller and showman combine with a thorough knowledge of the business (he began as a cooper) and well-honed nosing and tasting abilities to powerfully communicative effect. Throughout his career, though, his name had been synonymous with Bowmore, so the shock of his leaving School Street ('without,' it was rumoured on the island, 'so much as a fish supper') was total. McEwan quickly got an enthusiastic and energetic team in place around him led by Duncan McGillivray, who had first worked at Bruichladdich back in 1974 as stillman, later becoming engineer and brewer. After five months of frantic renovation, distilling began again on 29 May 2001 at precisely 8.26 in the morning. It was a great day for the village, as well as for those in the distillery. 'A number of times,' remembered Jim McEwan, 'I came down to open the distillery and found a wee plate of scones on the doorstep. No note; no anything. But it was just the villagers' way of saying "We know what you're doing; we're right behind you."'

THE HILL

Bruichladdich means 'slope of the shore'. There are no steep hills or high lochs hereabouts; and the water source for mashing is a reservoir built less than a mile back from and about 55 feet (16.76 metres) above the distillery in 1881. It lies just south of the farm called Gartacharra whose owner, Donald McGregor, worked at the distillery at the end of the Harvey era in 1936; he remembers unloading a cargo of barley from a sailing ship, the *Asta*, and winching it up to the barley loft using his horse. He also remembers growing barley for the distillery, in a hillside field poignantly called Canada.

It was a windy, dark day in November when I visited the reservoir with Duncan McGillivray; the peaty water slapped against the grassy banks and tumbled down the overflow as if it was a mill race. The reservoir is fed from a mass of drains leaching from the main watershed of the Rhinns. This rumpled shoulder of high land slopes gently and boggily down towards Bruichladdich; it drops much more suddenly and steeply down on to Rockside and Kilchoman, by contrast, beyond the mass of little peaks which divide the two sides, where no road and few tracks will take you. The water reaches the distillery from the reservoir via a short lade, a tumble through bushes and some long stretches of pipework, plus holding pools just above the distillery. This loch reservoir is not Bruichladdich's only water source, though we need not address the second one until the bottles beckon. The cooling water, meanwhile, comes from Bruichladdich burn, which runs down to the sea on the west side of the distillery.

WALKING BRUICHLADDICH

As I walked the distillery with Duncan, I asked what Bruichladdich had been like when the gates swung open again just before Christmas 2000. 'The place looked terrible. In the first few months, we got through two and a half thousand litres of masonry paint. The stills were okay, though we had to renew one condenser, which cost us twenty thousand pounds alone. We had to rewire the mashhouse and the tun room completely, and we're still working on the stillhouse.'

'It was an amazing moment, walking through those gates on January seventh,' remembers Jim McEwan. 'It was a real dreich [dreary] day. I thought, "My God, what have you got yourself into, Jimbo?" John Rennie and Duncan MacFadyen were there – and within five minutes, I knew we could do it. The passion in their eyes . . . it was like a blind man seeing again.'

Between 1994 and 2001, Bruichladdich had only ever worked for six weeks in 1998, when Jim Beam Brands brought the distilling team over from Jura. Interestingly, it was not classic, barely peated Bruichladdich (3 ppm) that was distilled then, but between 100,000 and 120,000 litres of a peaty spirit (at about 38 ppm), which was filled into good casks, including some sherry butts. (When nosed in 2001 from a second-fill sherry butt which had been subsequently transferred to a first-fill Manzanilla butt, this spirit was shaping up beautifully: a teasing combination of marzipan, toffee and aromatic pipe tobacco.) There were also around 10,000 casks of older Bruichladdich, and since then, Duncan McGillivray says, the company has bought up a further 2,000 to 3,000 filled casks from blenders, so as to have plenty of stocks to sell. Selling whisky has been vital for Bruichladdich, since it has no giant parent company to provide working capital, 'and it takes a lot of money to make a place like this chug on. Malt is about eight thousand pounds a load, and we're using a couple of loads a week . . .' The cost may rise, too: in March 2004, Bruichladdich distilled its first run based on organic Scottish barley, and there are plans to use biodynamically grown malt, too, as well as Islay-grown malt. (Biodynamics is a radical form of organic cultivation which uses composts and field treatments based on the 1924 agricultural lectures of Rudolf Steiner, the founder of the anthroposophical movement.)

Limited resources were part of the reason why the old equipment at Bruichladdich has been kept and lovingly renovated, though only part: the new team also has a reverence for the old ways (gallons, inches and degrees Fahrenheit are all still used here). The original Robert Boby mill, by way of example, was lovingly restored by a Yorkshire craftsman called Peter Steggles, and its flywheels and drive belts now purr away as smoothly as ever they did in 1881. The mash tun, too, dates back to 1881 – though it initially belonged to Bunnahabhain, and was acquired by Bruichladdich in 1900. It is cast-iron and open-topped, with old-fashioned iron rakes, meaning that mashing takes about twice as long as it would do with a modern Lauter tun; it also requires four additions of hot water rather than three. Perhaps this slowness, and the gentle oxidation the wort receives, has flavour implications; Duncan is unsure.

There are six Oregon pine washbacks, though the oldest one of all (which Duncan thinks was made by his mother's uncle, a cooper, back in 1881) is currently unused and due for replacement. The six look as if they are different sizes, but this is deceptive; the squatter ones have a larger diameter. Jim McEwan is keen on wood rather than steel for fermentation, claiming that it adds flowery notes to the final spirit, though Duncan envies the longevity of steel, and the ease with which it can be cleaned. Fermentation begins at a relatively warm 21°C, and there is a big contrast in fermentation times between the short weekday fermentations of 60 hours and the much longer weekend fermentations of 106.5 hours. Overall, though, this is a relatively slow fermentation regime with, Duncan says, excellent attenuation of the sugars, setting the scene for an elegant, polished spirit.

The wash stills are unexceptional: plain in design, with a relatively wide neck tapering up toward the lyne arm, which dips slightly. The charge is about 68.5 per cent of their filled capacity, and they are run slowly, with what Jim McEwan calls 'trickle distillation': again, all of this will help to create finesse and breed in the spirit, and keep pungent, robust characters at bay.

The spirit stills, though, are unusual. Why? Because they have necks as long and slender as those of any of the thousands of geese which patrol the skies above the distillery every dawn and dusk during winter. In overall terms, these spirit stills are not unusually tall, but their thin necks occupy a disproportionate percentage of that overall length (some two-thirds of the overall still height). The effect of these long, tall necks, according to Duncan, is to 'slow the vapour up'. They are also filled to just 58 per cent of capacity and run very gently, once again providing lots of copper contact for the nascent spirit and helping to create the fine-grained, creamy elegance which provides Bruichladdich's hallmark. 'We tend to err on the side of caution,' says Duncan. 'If the low wines look as if they are not that clear, we just cut back until they are. The same thing goes for the spirit. If we're not happy, we just carry on a bit longer on foreshots, and the foreshot run is very long here anyway – around forty minutes. We constantly monitor everything. Even when the spirit runs absolutely clear [when mixed with 50 per cent water, the standard practical test], even then we sometimes give it another five minutes before we go on, just to be sure. The worst that can happen is that you redistill, which only costs you a bit more money. Because we're going for single malts only, we need to have the best. And we're not chill-filtering. We can't mask anything; we can't lose anything in a big blend. That's why we have to get it absolutely right at the beginning.'

Jim McEwan vividly remembers the early morning of 29 May 2001, when the stills ran again for the first time since their brief flurry in 1998. 'I'd never worked on the Bruichladdich spirit stills, so I didn't know where the middle cut was. We took samples; we nosed; we tested the break point with water; you have to stay with it all the time. I've seen my two daughters born, and that was extremely emotional, but this . . . We had webcams running, but we couldn't find it; it just wasn't happening. I went to wash my face at the sink, and offered up a prayer, a big deal to the big man. Then, about ten minutes later, boom! I handed the sample to Duncan; we all looked at it; we all nosed it. It was crystal clear, as clear as a burn on Thursday morning. None of us spoke. To speak would have been to cry. We all found a hole in the floor to look at. The distillery had come back to life again; we had found its pulse. Along with building my first whisky barrel, that was the professional high of my lifetime.'

The condensers at Bruichladdich are all sited inside (they were outside until 1975), and are relatively large: 3.4 metres long, weighing about two tonnes each, and containing 210 thin half-inch copper tubes. This gives plenty of copper contact for efficient condensation, which once again mothers the intrinsically creamy finesse of Bruichladdich. Unusually, though, the company fills its casks at still strength rather than the standard 63.5 per cent abv. 'Basically,' says Duncan, 'we are a small company, and we can't afford to be storing water. But we do also feel that it ages better at that strength. There's another reason, too. When you store whisky filled at 63.5 per cent for forty years, it can end up under strength [i.e. below the 40 per cent minimum at which Scotch whisky must be sold]. In forty years' time, the stuff we're filling will, hopefully, be sitting at forty-two to forty-three per cent.' The company fills a huge variety of sizes and origins of cask, but Duncan says that in general it works out at about 60 to 65 per cent bourbon, 25 per cent sherry, and the remainder 'wine and other things'. 'Our range,' he added, 'is expanding rapidly.'

Indeed. Perhaps this is the point to begin to track a little of the new Bruichladdich's prodigiously creative spirit. As I have already mentioned, 'classic' Bruichladdich – which means in effect everything which has been sold in the new livery since 2000 – is a legacy of the distillations of the 1960s, 1970s and 1980s. Like all Islay distilleries, Bruichladdich originally produced peaty spirit; its peat was cut from the nearby 'pipers' village' of Conisby until 1944, and then from peat moss near Loch Gorm. In the 1960s, though, Bruichladdich switched to producing the unpeated malt which the light blends of the time required and which the American market preferred; the old malting kiln was dismantled, and the peat level in the spirit from then on was fixed at just 3–5 ppm. There was a sense, when the new regime began distilling again in 2001, that this peatlessness undermined the malt's Islay credentials, so Jim McEwan put it up to 10 ppm for the 2001 season, 'just to give it an Islay mark', as he told me at the time. Yet what happened? The blends which Jim had put together of the unpeated malt began to win prizes and friends around the world; the soft, 'cream-of-the-barley' style proved very popular with customers. For 2003 and subsequently, therefore, 'classic' Bruichladdich moved back to 3–4 ppm.

If malt drinkers wanted a peaty alternative from this distillery, the reasoning ran, then it should be something altogether different. It was, in fact, this peaty spirit which first trickled from the stills on start-up day in May 2001 (lightly peated Bruichladdich didn't run until 19 September that year). The malt used had a spec of 40 ppm, and was subsequently christened Port Charlotte – in memory of the lost distillery in the village of the same name, some of whose warehouses Bruichladdich now uses. This, in turn, led to a fancy to create 'the world's peatiest spirit' – with a malt specification of over 60 ppm. Port Ellen (the supplier of the malt for Port Charlotte) was asked if it could match this. Sometimes, came the answer; one load might be at 65 ppm, but the next might only make it to 58 ppm. Bairds of Inverness, the supplier of the malt for Bruichladdich, reckoned that it had the means to guarantee a peating level of over 60 ppm on all occasions – so Jim and his team asked the company to send over the peatiest malt it could manage. Bruichladdich announced to the world that this malt measured 80.5 ppm, putting the full analysis up on the website. The whisky was christened Octomore, after another lost distillery sited above Port Charlotte; it was first distilled on 16 October 2002.

This third spirit has proved controversial on the island, with some of the other distillers pointing out that the peating in malted barley is usually measured colorimetrically rather than by high pressure liquid chromatography or HPLC, which tends to give higher readings than colorimetric analysis. (See Chapter Four for a further discussion of this issue.) The rumour was that Bruichladdich had used HPLC for its Octomore readings, 'inflating' the levels by comparison with other distilleries' colorimetric analysis for their malts. When I put this to Jim McEwan and Mark Reynier, they decided to clear the matter up by getting the malt analysed by both methods – and the results are astonishing. The 2002 contract with Bairds specified phenols 'to be greater than 50 ppm on delivered malted barley'. Bairds own colorimetric analysis gave a figure of 68.2 ppm, but when analytical chemists Tatlock & Thomson put it through HPLC, the reading was indeed 80.5. For the 2003 Octomore contract, by contrast, the spec was 'to be 80ppm minimum on delivered malted barley'. This time, Bairds (which had redesigned and enlarged its kiln) hit the jackpot – though the company didn't at first realise as much. Its own colorimetric analysis read 76.5 ppm, but when Tatlock & Thomson put it through HPLC they discovered it measured no less than 300.5 ppm. T & T then rechecked the colorimetric figure, coming up with an eventual corrected reading of 129 ppm. However you measure it, then, the 2003 run of Octomore seems likely to represent an altogether new level of peatiness for modern malt whisky. Naturally, most of these phenols are lost in brewing and distillation: the final levels in the new make are 29.6 ppm in the 2002 run (a 36.8 per cent recovery rate), and 46.4 ppm in the 2003 run (a 15.4 per cent recovery rate). Even so, drinkers will need to take a deep breath when these prodigiously smoky distillates eventually reach the market. Not only will it be interesting to compare the different levels of peatiness in Port Charlotte and Octomore, but it will also be fascinating to see if the Islay peat for Port Charlotte gives a different character to the mainland peat used for Octomore. In principle, the comparison will be all the more valid since the three spirits are distilled in the same way; the only difference is that the more heavily peated malts tend to produce slightly less strong beer and therefore a smaller quantity of spirit than the lightly peated version.

Bruichladdich is filling a greater variety of wooden casks than any other distillery on the island at present. Most are first-fill bourbon barrels and sherry hogsheads, but the distillery is also filling rum casks and a wide variety of ex-wine casks from France, including some from Château d'Yquem (the greatest of all Sauternes properties), from Chambertin (Charles Rousseau) and from Le Musigny (Christophe Roumier). Unusually, too, on Islay, Bruichladdich has ample warehouse space, with eight warehouses at the distillery itself, plus another four (classed as one) in Port Charlotte, giving space for about 35,000 casks. In addition to its own stocks (about half that total), Bruichladdich is able to make a little extra revenue by storing blending stocks for Whyte and Mackay from other Islay distilleries like Ardbeg, Laphroaig and

Bowmore, and the Isle of Jura distillery, too. Unsurprisingly, everyone at the distillery expresses absolute conviction in the importance of ageing the spirit from the day of its distillation until the day of its bottling in the moist, maritime conditions of Islay. Others, as we will see in later distillery chapters, disagree.

On 25 May 2003, Bruichladdich achieved another first, becoming the only Islay distillery to bottle all its own stocks on the island (and giving work to some of Islay's disabled residents as it did so). This was a decision partly forced on the company by the shoddy treatment it received in autumn 2002 at the hands of independent bottling companies on the mainland, but it also sprang out of the company desire to do everything itself, to bring as much employment as possible to the island, and to imbue its spirit with as much Islay character as possible. The water used to bring the spirit down from its storage strength to the strength at which it goes to market (which in Bruichladdich's case is never less than 46 per cent) does not come from the reservoir, but from a spring sited on Port Charlotte farmer James Brown's land. This water is crystal clear and totally unpeated, just like the water from Margadale spring used by Bunnahabhain. The spring itself is sited just to the north of the little road which runs from Port Charlotte up to Kilchiaran (its ON map reference is NR 239583). In return for the use of the water, the legendarily good-natured and sociable James Brown has been given the honorific title of 'Entertainments Officer' at the distillery, as well as the first filled cask of Octomore (and the only one to be privately owned). The former Octomore distillery building lies next to his own house, and he has converted it into a light, bright holiday cottage with a commanding view of Loch Indaal.

Bruichladdich, moreover, is now one of only three distilleries in the Scotch whisky industry to have its own cooperage. In May 2004 the island's first apprentice cooper since 1966, Peter Mactaggart, signed his four-year indenture papers and was presented with the tools of his trade. Mactaggart is to be trained by Master Cooper John Rennie; Jim McEwan, too, initially trained at Bowmore as a cooper and will be keeping a close eye on the young trainee's progress.

Nor does the creativity stop there. Jim McEwan's dream for a 'Single Malt Academy' on the island is now underway, with the first students spending a week on Islay learning the arts of malt distillation with Jim, Duncan and the team in May 2004. Other plans for the future include a library devoted to whisky and Celtic culture, and an 80-seater restaurant 'to feature the best of Islay food: oysters, scallops, crab, lobster, venison, beef, lamb . . .' Bruichladdich is a busy place, in sum, and the world is watching. The distillery achieved sudden notoriety in September 2003 when surveillance experts from the American Defence Threat Reduction Agency in Fort Beaver, Virginia, idly searching for Iraq's illusory 'weapons of mass destruction', found enough time on their hands to inform Jim and his team that their distillery webcam wasn't working properly.

TASTING BRUICHLADDICH

The idea that a particular distillery produces whisky of a single, distinctive and unchanging flavour is beginning to look dated. All over Scotland, in particular whenever a distillery passes out of the ownership of a large corporation and resumes independence, malt whisky distillers are asking themselves why they should spend all year, every year, producing just one type of whisky when only a lack of imagination stops them from distilling softly peaty spirit, vigorously peaty spirit, robust spirit, spicy spirit or elegant spirit, all of it variously caressed and shaded by time spent in a huge spectrum of casks of different origins and characteristics. The Bruichladdich team deserve much of the credit for this mental liberation and the stimulating and deliciously complicated future it promises. But it does, of course, mean that we can no longer speak of 'the taste' of Bruichladdich, but rather the tastes.

New makes, first. When it runs fresh and colourless from the still, Bruichladdich itself is perhaps the most charming spirit on the island: sweet, elegant and marzipan-like, with little soapiness and no rough spirit nip. The 2001 season Bruichladdich spirit (with the malt at 10 ppm rather than 2 ppm) was a little darker and more adolescent in character, not exactly peaty but with its natural sweetness lying in shadowy abeyance, qualified by sinew and seriousness. Well-aged casks of this run will make interesting collectors' items in the years ahead.

Port Charlotte's new make is, evidently, more smoky, though somehow it is not classic peat reek which lifts from the sample glass, but something more akin to tobacco, wood smoke, woodland twigs or old furniture – a legacy, surely, of the finesse of its distilling regime. After those phenol-derived notes comes, tentatively, the sweetness of oats.

The 2002 run of Octomore betrays its weight of phenols with an oily, leggy texture, an earthiness, a fattiness. Initially its aromatic notes are rustic; later, after the spirit finds the air, it suggests treacle and toffee – astonishingly, bearing in mind that it has not even been within a blown kiss of a cask at this stage. But those who were expecting 'the peatiest whisky in the world' to be a bruiser; a heavyweight; a kind of hairy, eye-rolling, dirk-hurling cousin to Laphroaig – prepare for disappointment. It is very much a member of the Bruichladdich family, and Bruichladdich means polish and refinement. I suspect that this will be the case even for the 2003 run, which is peatier still.

And that, of course, is more or less all we have to go on for Port Charlotte and Octomore at this stage. In order to help raise working capital, the distillery has been selling casks of Bruichladdich and Port Charlotte new make (though not of Octomore); in November 2001, I bought one of the ex-Yquem casks of Port Charlotte, and at the same moment my brother Steve bought one of the ex-Yquem casks of the Bruichladdich. Almost exactly two years later, Steve's Bruichladdich (cask number 747) was ageing superbly, with the ghost of Yquem's botrytis and succulent, glycerol-laden sweetness beginning to float through the rich grain; my Port Charlotte version (cask number 842), by contrast, was somewhat shyer and terser, throwing up a heavy screen of sulphur when watered. Early days, though.

There is no doubt that the whisky world has been astonished by the quality of the classic Bruichladdich bottlings which have been released since 2000. The malt's prize-winning performances in blind tastings (including 'best whisky in the world' for a 1970 in bourbon wood from America's *Malt Advocate*), plus the awarding of the 'Distillery of the Year' accolade to Bruichladdich twice in three years by the *Malt Advocate*, backs up this public enthusiasm. Some of the credit should go to Jim McEwan's cask-picking and marrying skills, yet Jim would be the first to redirect the praise elsewhere – to former Bruichladdich distillers like Ruiradh MacLeod (who still lives in Port Charlotte, listening to Gaelic radio and chatting on the phone to his son in New Zealand in Gaelic), Neil MacTaggart and Duncan McGillivray himself, and to former managers like Sandy Raitt, Peter Logie and Ian Allan. The influential decision to bottle uncoloured and without chill filtering has also played its part, adding breadth, fatness and creaminess to the expressions. The astonishing fact, though, is that all of these whiskies were lying in the warehouses unsung and unchampioned throughout Jim Beam Brands' ownership of Bruichladdich. Why did the company not know? Because the company didn't want to know. Bruichladdich didn't suit its brand marketing strategy, even though its malt had more intrinsic quality and interest than the placid spirit of the Isle of Jura. What is right for shareholders and company balance sheets does not always benefit consumers. Brand marketing is primarily a vehicle to drive profits rather than to create and disseminate quality (though it may coincidentally do these things once the profits are assured).

Classic Bruichladdich is unpeaty, but it is a remarkable whisky nonetheless. The current 12-year-old, for example, which is a blend of 50 per cent second-fill sherry and 50 per cent second-fill bourbon, has scents of remarkable refinement and perfume for its age, full of nuances and touches: mint, apple, peach, pollen, meadowflowers. No other Islay malt has the soft, glycerous, toothsome appeal of Bruichladdich, both nourishing and complex. A dash of water reveals lemon peel and mown grass within the softly whipped cream. The profile deepens with age; I will never forget a bottle of the sustaining 15-year-old, an entrancing combination of barley and orange and a dram as closely woven as any plaid, drunk at one sitting between three of us in the cottage of Octomore itself as the shadows lengthened on Midsummer's Day 2003. (One of the drinkers was the colossus of Port Charlotte, farmer James Brown, which admittedly makes a difference . . .)

By autumn 2003, the penetrating yet spring-like 20-year-old had disappeared. It was another lovely malt: sweet-tempered and (in its pure-bourbon first edition guise) a less assertive malt than the 15-year-old (whose first edition included 20 per cent from sherry casks). What is the stock profile like, I wondered, and will the almost total absence of spirit from between 1994 and 2000 pose future difficulties? 'If we had massive sales, there would be a problem,' says Duncan. 'But Bruichladdich is high-quality, niche-market stuff. We've introduced the twelve-year-old to meet the coming problem with the ten-year-old. We're going to have to roll back a bit. But we've got enough stock overall; it's just getting stock of the right years in place. The twenty-year-old, for example, will be back in about eighteen months, though it won't be the same; it will be a different edition. There'll be individual bottles to carry us through as well; the warehouses are full of all sorts of goodies.'

They certainly are. I can remember some wonderful casks: a gingery, spicy 1990 refill sherry hogshead and a much paler, dryer, more wine-like sherry butt (perhaps Manzanilla?) from the same year, as well as a dark, burnt, raisiny, almost Christmas-pudding-like Oloroso cask filled in 1986. It is casks like this which provided the inspiration for the Valinch series, only available to personal callers at Bruichladdich. The system is simple: the cask stands in the shop, you are given a bottle, and you fill it yourself. When one cask is finished, it is replaced by another. Not since the days of farm distilling and 'the black pot' has whisky purchase been so artless and informal. (The word 'valinch', by the way, refers to the long copper pipette used for takings samples from whisky casks.) A second, similar series christened 'Babe' celebrates the pig festivals organised on Islay by Chloë Randall, Dunlossit's pig-loving estate administrator (see Chapter Eight).

There are also two other series of vintage-dated releases available to those unable to get to Islay. The first of these is the vintage range, available in brown tins rather than the customary blue and cream; Legacy, finally, is the series name for the oldest vintage releases. At present, the vintage range includes a succulent, almost buttery 1973, reinforced on the palate with an impressively spicy backbone; while the second release in the Legacy series is the 1965, a dram of magnificent harmony, crystallised flower perfumes and liqueur-like refinement and depth.

No description of Bruichladdich would be complete without an account of how 'the distillery with attitude' presents itself to the world. The tins all contain descriptions of the whisky in question . . . or rather a pile of exuberant and sometimes puzzling adjectives and nouns in several languages, dialects and argots (look out for the 'bonzer' 17-year-old, the 'favoloso' 15-year-old and the 'gallous' 10-year-old – which according to my dictionary means that 'it contains gallium in the divalent state', which I rather doubt). The little yacht pictured on the tin moves further westwards past the distillery with each increment of age, and there is a distillery motto in Gaelic, too: *Clachan a Choin*. How can I, for non-British readers, put this delicately? I can't. 'The dog's bollocks' is a popular phrase used to identify the real and genuine article in a world swimming with imitative dross ('bollocks' being a slang word, I'm afraid, for testicles); this is a Gaelic rendering of the phrase. The more delicate and poetic Gael, though, uses the word *clachan*, meaning 'stones'. According to Duncan McGillivray and Mary McGregor (the daughter of farmer Donald at Gartacharra), both of them Gaelic speakers, the rendition is incorrect; it should either be *clachan a chu* (the dog's stones) or *clachan na choin* (the dogs' stones). Will we see a future correction? Either way, the implication is the same: this is a distillery which doesn't take itself too seriously, and which never forgets that even the greatest whisky should be fun, too. Bruichladdich may be a loner, but it is an exceptionally good-humoured one.

Bruichladdich DISTILLERY FACTFILE

Distillery operating hours — *5 days a week @ 24 hours a day;*
bottling hall 7 days a week

Number of employees — *24 (including part-time employees)*

Water source — *Bruichladdich reservoir (brewing water);*
Bruichladdich burn (cooling water);
James Brown's spring (dilution water)

Water reserve — *est. 9 million gallons*

Water colour — *brown (Bruichladdich reservoir);*
clear (James Brown's spring)

Peat content of water — *trace (Bruichladdich reservoir);*
zero (James Brown's spring)

Malt source — *Bairds of Inverness (Bruichladdich,*
Octomore); Port Ellen (Port Charlotte)

Own floor maltings? — *none*

Malt type — *Optic and organic Chalice*

Malt specification phenols — *Bruichladdich: 3–4 ppm (8–10 ppm in*
2001)
— *Port Charlotte: 40 ppm*
— *Octomore: 68.2 ppm (2002);*
129 ppm (2003)

Finished spirit phenols — *Bruichladdich: trace*
— *Port Charlotte: 20–25 ppm (estimate)*
— *Octomore: 29.6 ppm (2002); 46.4 ppm*
(2003)

Malt storage — *180 tonnes*

Mill type — *Boby, installed 1881*

Grist storage — *14 tonnes*

Mash tun construction — *cast-iron; rake and plough*

Mash size — *7 tonnes*

First water — *24,230 litres at 65°C*

Second water — *12,488 litres at 86°C*

Third water — *16,775 litres at 88°C*

Fourth water — *16,775 litres at 93°C*

Number of washbacks – *6 (5 operational in 2003)*

Washback construction – *Oregon pine*

Washback charge – *36,000 litres*

Yeast – *Quest cultured yeast to start fermentation;*
Mauri cultured yeast to finish
fermentation

Amount of yeast – *150 kg per washback*

Length of fermentation – *60 hours (shorts: week);*
106.5 hours (longs: weekend)

Initial fermentation – *temperature 21°C*

Strength of wash – *6–7 per cent abv*

Number of wash stills – *2*

Wash stills built – *1: base original; rest restored; 2: 1975*

Wash still capacity – *17,275 litres each*

Wash still charge – *12,000 litres (69 per cent of capacity)*

Heat source – *pans and single steam coil*

Wash still height – *c. 21 feet 6 inches (6.55 m)*

Wash still shape – *plain*

Lyne arm – *gently descending*

Length of low-wines run – *4$^1\!/_2$ – 5 hours*

Low-wines collection range – *average 22.5 per cent*

Number of spirit stills – *2*

Spirit stills built – *1: late 1940s; 2: 1975*

Spirit still capacity – *12,274 litres each*

Spirit still charge – *7,100 litres (58 per cent of capacity)*

Strength of spirit still charge – *27 per cent abv*

Heat source – *pans and two steam coils in each*

Spirit still height – *c. 20 feet 6 inches (6.25 m)*

Spirit still shape – *plain (goose-necked)*

Lyne arm – *gently descending*

Purifier? – *no*

Condensers – *four, internally sited: length 11 feet*
2 inches (3.41 m), containing 210 half-
inch (1.25cm) copper tubes

Length of foreshot run – *about 40 minutes*

Length of spirit run – *about 3 hours*

Length of feints run	– *about 3 hours 10 minutes*
Spirit cut	– *varies: on to spirit at between 76 per cent abv and 71 per cent abv; off at 64 per cent abv*
Distilling strength	– *Bruichladdich 72 per cent*
	– *Port Charlotte 71 per cent*
	– *Octomore 69–70 per cent*
Storage strength	– *stored at distilling strengths*
Average spirit yield	– *401 litres of pure alcohol per tonne of malt (2003)*
Disposal of pot ale and spent lees	– *taken to Caol Ila and piped into Sound of Islay*
Type of casks filled for branded malt	– *about 65 per cent first-fill bourbon barrels; about 25 per cent first-fill sherry hogsheads; remainder rum and wine casks*
Current annual output	– *320,000 litres of pure alcohol*
Number of warehouses	– *8 (numbered 2, 5, 6, 10, 11, 12, 13, 14) plus 4 at Port Charlotte (as single unit)*
Type of warehouses	– *dunnage (most) and racking (2)*
Storage capacity on Islay	– *35,000 casks*
Percentage of branded malt entirely aged on Islay	– *100 per cent*
Vatting and bottling location	– *Bruichladdich, Islay*
Distillery expressions	– *10-year-old*
	– *12-year-old*
	– *Links (14-year-old)*
	– *15-year-old*
	– *17-year-old*
	– *20-year-old*
	– *Vintage range*
	– *Legacy range*
	– *Valinch bottlings*
	– *Babe bottlings*
Major blending roles	– *Black Bottle*

CHAPTER FOUR

Peat

A dark, living clock
of rain-gorged plants, burned – for what?
To drink wilderness.

THIS WAS a strange collision of lives. A blustery day in late May, and a gaggle of prosperous French, Scandinavian, American and Canadian whisky enthusiasts stood, wind-ruffled and rain-spattered, up on the bogland above Islay airport at Glenegedale Lots. Bowmore's show, it was: a plucky little green-and-white-striped tent had been incongruously erected on the desolate moss; from inside, drams were being dispensed to keep the inadequately dressed (which meant almost all of us) warm. From time to time the wind would promise to puff the tent away over the mountains, only to relent at the last minute and give the struggling pegs a little respite. The 2002 Feis Ile (or Islay Festival of Music and Malt) was underway, and Norrie Kimble's hour of glory had come. He was showing the world – or at least the small, self-selecting representatives of all the earth's nations to bring themselves to this spot – how peat was traditionally cut on Islay.

Norrie has the most famous face on the island. Whenever photo libraries are plundered for pictures of 'the real Islay', it is usually Norrie who emerges to take his place on the glossy sheets, doing his bit for labouring humankind between the hollow advertisements for perfume, Swiss watches and fast cars – snapped on a sunny day, of course, his silver hair blown back in the wind like a Celtic Ulysses, the lines on his face telling their own tale of elemental struggle, and with his chin jutting forward all the more prominently for the lack of teeth in the mouth above it. The photographer has usually prostrated himself in front of Norrie so as to capture the gleaming brown of the freshly cut peats; Norrie has stuck his fork into one, and his shoulders have got the heave of it; he's ready to toss it into a rough heap before stacking and drying.

I hung around on that occasion after everyone else had gone. Norrie's croft was half a mile across the moss, but there was a prefabricated cabin by the access track; we went inside out of the wind for a chat.

'Were you born here, Norrie?'

'I don't know. If I was to say yes, I might be telling you a lie; if I was to say no, I might be telling you a lie. I'm the tenant on the ground.'

'How old were you when you cut your first peat?'

'I was twelve years old. With my uncle, John Campbell. He cut peat all his life. I've been cutting it for forty-four years.'

'What's the life like?'

'Good. I would think so.'

'Even in a howling wind?'

'Aye, well, you just retire that day. Go and meet your friends in the pub. Mmm. Well, it's been known, anyway.'

'Who else cuts?'

'Very few now. Very few, aye.'

'There's Iain Brown cuts for Laphroaig.'

'I'm not sure he cuts any more. I think he's got a bad back.'

'How's your back, Norrie?'

'Mine's fine.'

'It must be important to a cutter.'

'I would think so. The younger you start, the more mature your back will be. Whereas somebody coming into it new, they might not stand it.'

'When do you start each year?'

'I would take the turf off at the end of March.' Norrie pronounced the month 'Marchhhhh', and I could hear the wind rushing through it. 'And I would think of cutting in April. If it was for a distillery, you'd think of cutting as much as possible, maybe into August, because they're not particular how dry they'll be. But if it's for your own house, you'll want them right dry. And ideally you'd like to be a year ahead of yourself.'

'What do you do in the winter?'

'I'm capable of building dry stone dykes. That again, it's similar to the peats; it's a dying art. The farmers are putting up fences instead of attending to their dykes.'

'You do that during the winter?'

'If there's anything available like that.'

'Have you never been tempted to leave the island?'

'I have. I went to London. And it was as busy in London at half-past-five in the morning as it is in Glasgow at dinner time. And that was enough for me. I fled. I ran home. Well, I got a train, I think. I never stuck it. There were three of us. We were cutting peats for a distillery and we made quite good money. So we wanted to see a wee bit of life, to experience it. We had a few quid about us. I think we stayed three days. But I wouldn't do it again.'

'You didn't fancy the social life?'

'I used to run a discotheque at one time. The Revolving Disco. So that got me out and about. Although my name's Norman Campbell, I changed it to Norrie Kimble. Similar to *The Fugitive* who was on the run in those days.' (Norrie's reference was to a 1960s cult television series.) 'Norrie Kimble looked better up in the lights than Norman Campbell. That was the story there.'

'How long did you run the disco?'

'Must have been twenty years. It was the first one on the island. It was a success. I done plenty talking. I used to travel the island. I had fifty-pound shirts, and a Stetson hat. Some of the halls aren't even standing now; they got knocked down or blown down.'

'And you kept the name?'

'And why not?'

Norrie and I looked through his collection of old 45s, unplayed for years, piled into a black bag in the corner. 'Itchycoo Park' by the Small Faces; 'Neanderthal Man' by Hotlegs; 'Breaking Up Is Hard To Do' by Neil Sedaka.

'What do you think of pop music today?'

'Rotten. It's rubbish. It's all right for the young ones, because they were brought up with it. But the majority of folk think that the music of the 60s was better.' I nodded in sage agreement.

'How do you like my view?' Norrie asked. I told him I thought it was fine. The wind was moaning around the cabin.

'Does the wind ever drop up here?'

'Aye, it does, but then you get the midges. In the morning, if it's damp at all. Until the sun gets up.'

So what are they exactly, these dark sods which Norrie has been cutting for 44 years, and his uncle John Campbell cut for a lifetime before that, and which Islay's farmers have been cutting to keep themselves warm and cook food with for the last 5,000 years?

Dead plants. Not just any plants, though; these are the plants of an irredeemably wet place, a place from which the water cannot drain. Visitors to Islay are sometimes surprised to hear its peat bogs described as 'moss'. Surprised – because the intractable, unwalkable, boot-filling bogs don't look at all like the vivid green carpets and soft poufs of woodland moss you can find on a forest stroll. True; but examine those bogs more closely, and you will see that much of their mass is made up of coralline *Sphagnum capillifolium* and its many relatives: a strange, rootless community of plants commonly called bog moss. Sphagnum is sponge-like; its tiny, orange-yellow 'leaves' are in fact nothing but water flasks. The chlorophyll in them is squeezed into slender strands between rain-gorged cells. This is why sphagnum can absorb eight times its own weight in water; this is why a blanket bog itself is not *terra firma* at all, but a kind of soup. During the First World War, dried sphagnum moss was used as a dressing for wounds: in addition to its remarkable absorbent capacities, it is also a deodorant and anti-putrescent. Were one sphagnum plant to grow in isolation, it would rapidly collapse under the weight of the water it absorbs. Instead, it grows as a mass, a mat, a community, fighting every other plant for life, but supporting every other plant as it does so. Remind you of anything?

Perhaps, though, I opened the previous paragraph erroneously. Sphagnum is deathless – as only a rootless plant can be. Together with its kind, it just keeps climbing, growing from its bud tip, lifting the whole bog by a whisper more than a millimetre a year. There are dormant but living buds beneath it for 20 centimetres or so; after that, the dormancy becomes permanent and irreversible. Even then, decomposition is difficult, since there is no air (just water), making for an acidic medium devoid of nutrients. Accumulation occurs. Peat forms. This process has been underway in Scotland for about 7,000 years, since the warm, dry, tree-growing weather which followed the last Ice Age gave out; banks of peat up to 10 metres deep are found on Islay.

Of course sphagnum is by no means the only plant group found in a bog moss: silky, brush-like bog cotton bobs cheerfully in summer breezes; there are grasping rushes and sedges in profusion; bog myrtle draws scent from the water-locked substrate; bogbean, heathers and heaths provide flowering colour; and carnivorous sundews give the wee beasties their comeuppance. In winter sunlight, the russet deergrass makes the moss glow like children's eyes. Some of these plants (and there are hundreds of others) have developed special survival strategies to cope with the wet austerities of their surroundings: bog myrtle furnishes its own nitrogen using bacteria in its roots, while bog cotton creates air-filled spaces in its roots and leaf bases (and tiny, brightly coloured jewel beetles then use these spaces as apartments).

Peat bogs are divided into two unequal sections. The upper part, about 30 cm deep, is called the acrotelm: that is where you find the living plant material. Underneath that is the much thicker catotelm, where the plant matter (and particularly the fragile sphagnum) has broken down to form a shapeless, dark brown colloidal mass. Water can move swiftly through the acrotelm, but much more slowly through the catotelm; remember that the water for all of the Islay distilleries except Bunnahabhain comes tumbling out of the sky into a mass of plants of this sort, and then spends weeks, years or decades lying locked up in this vegetative tangle before finally emerging into the lochs, reservoirs

or rivers. The transition between the two sections of peat, of course, is gradual; if you watch Norrie Kimble cutting a peat bank, you will see that the rougher, hairier acrotelm gradually modulates into the smooth, dark catotelm. By the time Norrie has sliced down a metre or so using his peat spade (tipped with cow horn), the peat resembles bricks of chocolate ice-cream. Distilleries want the hairy stuff from the acrotelm, since it burns much more smokily; dark bricks of catotelm are preferred for domestic fires on the island, since they provide more warmth and less smoke.

Once cut, the peats have to be stacked and dried over the summer: they need a good drying wind for about three weeks, which will enable them to lose 75 per cent of their water content and shrink by 25 per cent or so. Not every summer provides perfect drying conditions. Port Ellen maltings was using peat from the Scottish mainland during 2003 because the summer of 2002 on Islay (with a particularly sodden June) meant that it was not possible to get enough peat cut and dried.

Those maltings, of course, are the main consumer of peat on the island; they use around 2,000 tonnes a year. At present, this is being cut from Castlehill Moss which lies just to the south-east of Glenegedale and Glenegedalemoor, north of the Leorin Lochs (which once provided the Port Ellen distillery's peaty water source, and which now provide the peaty water used for steeping the barley). Alec MacIntosh, known as Tosh, is the main contractor used for 'winning' the peats for both Port Ellen and Bowmore (Iain Brown wins Laphroaig's peat), and he does it with what is called on the island 'the sausage machine'. This is a tractor with six rear wheels, three on each side, and a peat extruder fitted behind it. The extruder is dragged through the peat, excreting the long sausages behind it. Scary work, according to Ian McPherson from Bowmore. 'It's crazy. The whole lot's floating up there: you can see the wave move down the bog in front of the tractor. Somebody's going to go out of sight up there one day; somebody's just going to disappear. There's nothing below but peat, peat, peat.' I watched the process in action one afternoon with Jim McEwan, and it is indeed a kind of slow-motion cross between ploughing and surfing, though those six big tyres spread the load as well as providing the necessary traction. Castlehill was opened up as the main peat-extraction moss on Islay after the 'Battle of Duich Moss': the major environmental confrontation in Islay's history, which took place in August 1985 (see pages 353–4). Prior to the Duich Moss squabble, the peat used to be taken from a number of different locations on the island, including near Loch Gorm on the Rhinns.

Peat extraction, as Duich indicated, had become a controversial matter by the late twentieth century. Peat is a finite resource which renews itself only very slowly; peat bogs are also a precious habitat for rare plants and birds. Environmental organisations such as Friends of the Earth and Greenpeace have mounted successful campaigns against the use of peat in horticulture. Can we say that its use to flavour the malt for whisky production on Islay is a dangerous prodigality?

On balance, probably not. Diageo's Kay Fleming estimates that there are about 5,000 years' worth of peat left on Islay at present rates of extraction, though not all of this would be economic to cut. Some renewal would take place during that time; nonetheless extraction rates on Islay cannot truly be regarded as sustainable. Present global extraction rates, by contrast, are sustainable: around 100 million cubic metres of peat are deposited annually, and around the same amount extracted.

Globally, two-thirds of peat is burnt as fuel (especially in Eastern Europe and Scandinavia), and around a third used for horticulture; its use in whisky production is statistically insignificant. The UK has 1.9 million hectares of peatland, the world's tenth largest reserve; its reserves are exceeded by those of Belarus, Canada (whose 11.1 million ha make it top peat nation), Finland, Indonesia, Malaysia, Norway, the Russian Federation, Sweden and the USA. Few countries have no peat reserves at all; even such unlikely spots as Algeria have 22,000 ha of peatland, while countries such as Iraq and Uganda have almost as much as the UK. Nonetheless, 90 per cent of the world's peat lies in the temperate and cold belts of the Northern Hemisphere. Some 40 per cent of all the peat used in the UK is home-produced, with most imports coming from Ireland (whose total land mass is 16.2 per cent peat bog, though some of this counts as UK reserves as it lies in Northern Ireland). Over half the peat bogs in the European Community remain pristine, as do almost all of those found in Canada and Siberia. There is, in sum, plenty of lonely, cold, wet and desolate peat bog left on Planet Earth.

A more provoking question is exactly what distinguishes Islay's peat from that found elsewhere. Obviously the range of plants found in Islay's peat will be very different from that in Malaysia's; it will also differ, though, from that found in peat in Caithness or Donegal. In times of shortage, both Scottish mainland peat and Irish peat has been burned at Port Ellen and has proved less phenolic than Islay's own; according to Kay Fleming, Islay's peat even has 'a seaweediness and a saltiness' which you don't find in other peat sources. John Thomson, who manages the Port Ellen maltings, says that Diageo doesn't analyse its peat for seaweediness or saltiness; 'salt (as in sodium chloride) would not transfer directly via peat smoke to the malt anyway. The flavour characteristics of some of the relevant components of peat are such that they are reminiscent of seaside smells, but this can be true even of peat that has not been anywhere near the sea. The chemistry and organoleptics of this whole area is a bit of a minefield. We have carried out some trials recently with mainland peat. We found that, in like-for-like situations, Islay peat gave slightly higher phenol concentrations in the final malt than mainland peat. Not huge, but a useful difference.'

If Islay's peat is unique, of course, this would constitute one of the rare elements of *terroir* (characteristics attributable to place of origin) in its whiskies. Indeed for Diageo, this would be the only one, since the company disputes the influence of Islay's water sources on whisky character and Islay's air on whisky maturation.

'Islay' has, in the past, spent millions of years underwater, but not since its present peat bogs were deposited, so if there is indeed 'a seaweediness and a saltiness' in Islay's peat, then it must be wind-borne. And if the wind is capable of infusing a peat bog with those characteristics, then why should it not also infuse whisky in the same way, stored as it is in a far-from-airtight cask which is never topped up?

The one Islay whisky which demonstrates more than any other those notes of seaweed and salt is Laphroaig, though no one is sure why. Manager Robin Shields posited that the difference may be its own peat source, used for around one-third of its supplies; Laphroaig's own peat is indeed cut from nearer to the sea than Castlehill, to the west side of the Low Road running past the airport. Yet when in August 2003 a batch of Laphroaig was made using this peat alone, Allied master blender Robert Hicks declared that the 'iodine' note was missing from the new make. If it comes from anywhere, therefore, it must be the Port Ellen malt – in which case the 'iodine' should also be present in the island's other peaty whiskies, all of them supplied by Port Ellen. It isn't. Conclusion? Oddly enough, it would be that this maritime note is derived in some way from Laphroaig's brewing and distilling practices.

Port Ellen makes malt for eight distilleries at present: the Islay seven, plus Jura, too. Boats arrive with between 750 and 1,200 tonnes of barley every 12 days or so: Scottish barley is used first, then English barley when Scottish is unavailable, and finally imported barley if neither is on offer. Up to 650 tonnes can be stored on the very visible pier silo, with a further 2,040 tonnes at the maltings. The high-yielding, easy-malting Optic is, at present, the preferred variety, though eventually this modern strain will lose its fungal resistance, drop its agronomic yields, and another variety will then have to take its place.

The malt is steeped with peaty water from the two Leorin Lochs and the moisture level in the grains rises from under 15 per cent to 45 per cent. Does the use of peaty water flavour the malt? 'We have analysed Leorin water,' says John Thomson, 'but the humic acids which come off the peat do not contain any significant levels of the phenols that are used to signpost smokiness. Peat has to be burned to create these phenols. So even if water does contain high levels of 'peat', this water does not reach high enough temperatures in the distillery process to generate these signpost phenols.' The flavour, in other words, is vegetal rather than smoky at this stage.

There are eight steel steeps holding 25 tonnes (and 30,000 litres of loch water) each; when I toured the maltings, an inverted pair of Wellington boots protruded, with dark humour, from one full steep. After just under four days of alternate wetting and draining (called an 'air rest'), the now-growing grain is transferred to one of Port Ellen's seven cog-rimmed steel Boby drums, the largest malting drums in Britain; each holds 65 tonnes of moistened barley. In the low light and the gentle moisture-laden fog of the plant, these giant, toothy, gross-bellied beasts look sombre, almost sinister. The drums rotate every eight hours while humidified air is blown through them, and the malting process continues for around five days, until each grain has produced a mass of curly roots and the beginnings of a shoot within the grain (called the acrospire: it should be more than half the length of the grain when malting is complete).

The would-be plants are then transferred to one of Port Ellen's three kilns, where their hopes for growth and life are shattered by hot air (from computer-controlled oil-fuelled burners) and peat smoke. The peat smoke comes first, since it is most easily absorbed by the malt when it is wet; it continues until the point known as the 'break' is reached, which is when all the surface water has dried off from the grains of malt. The kilning requires skill, and there is a strong sense of rivalry between the seven kiln operators, each of whom has a unique way of banking and tending his fire so as to get the most smoke and the least heat out of it. This, too, is another evocatively industrial scene, unfolding in peat-scented, faintly smoky gloom to the roar of a giant fan: not exactly the fires of hell, but delicately infernal nonetheless.

I watched kiln operator Willie Johnston as he hosed down a slag-like mound of peat. The smoke poured from it, and it was slurped up into the kilns like a Dali-esque, anti-gravitational stream of water. Six tonnes of peat are needed in order to give 30 to 40 ppm phenols to a wet load of 65 tonnes of barley; this will result in 50 finished tonnes of malt at 4–6 per cent moisture – and copious peat smoke blowing over the village of Port Ellen itself, perfuming the washing on the lines. The peat, both whole sausages and the fragments and dust called 'caff', is loaded into the kiln by machine, but Willie said he had to tidy and sort out the ashes, and work with the kiln doors to perfect the draught. Kilning a batch is a multi-shift job, taking 30 hours to complete. Peat ash, incidentally, is white, light and astonishingly odourless, as those who have burned peat in Islay's holiday cottages will know; all of its vital essence leaves in the smoke.

Tiny birds were flitting to and fro in the air, braving this nether region of gloom and danger in order to feed on the spilled grains. Nor are they the only creatures to dine out on malting leftovers: after the malt is finished, a machine called a dresser removes all the rootlets. These rootlets are mixed with dust from the incoming barley, dampened with water and then pressed into cattle-feed pellets. Cattle on Islay don't mind the reek, but if the pellets are destined for mainland beasts they have to have five per cent molasses added to sweeten the peaty pill.

Kilning is not an exact science – and nor, just yet, is the measurement of 'peatiness' in malt. The 'ppm' or parts per million phenols quoted by Port Ellen in its malts is always an approximate figure: precise, consistent levels are impossible to achieve, since the peat itself varies, burning more smokily on some occasions than on others. Port Ellen measures the ppm in its highly peated malts colori-metrically; this measurement is taken by using colouring agents to bind with the phenols. These assume vivid colours which are then measured using a light meter. The ppm in new-make spirit, by contrast, is generally measured by HPLC or high pressure liquid chromatography: a more precise system, which tends to give higher readings. Indeed we have already seen from the analysis of Bruichladdich's Octomore malt described on pages 179–80 that colorimetric results can differ according to who is doing the analysis: Bairds' 76.5 ppm on Octomore 2003 malt was eventually corrected by Tatlock & Thomson to 129 ppm. This is not as surprising as it might look: there are no less than seven different methods for arriving at a colorimetric analysis figure. More striking still was the fact that the HPLC equivalent figure was an astonishing 300.5 ppm: at higher levels of peatiness, the two systems give wildly different results.

Even with HPLC, uncertainties remain. HPLC analysis is based on readings for a wide range of chemical compounds; the final analysis figure is based on the seven most prominent spikes shown in the read-out. The Octomore HPLC figure, for example, is based on phenol, guiacol, m/p-cresol, o-cresol, 4-methyl guaiacol, 4-ethyl phenol and 4-ethyl guiacol. It may well be, though, that one of the chemical substances present in lesser quantities, with a smaller spike, may be organoleptically more powerful than those substances present in larger quantities; we may, in other words, not necessarily be measuring the same things that our noses and our taste buds are measuring. Another interesting element is the fact that proportions of these compounds vary at different peating levels. The proportion of guiacol is most significant, for example, at low peating levels, whereas phenol and o-cresol are proportionately more important at higher peating levels. This fascinating area will certainly be more thoroughly researched in the years to come, and may tell us not only how Islay's peat differs from mainland or foreign peat, but exactly where that famous 'seaweediness' and 'saltiness' come from.

Bunnahabhain

Icicles at dawn
on bracken's brown lace. Higher:
breath, curling through horn.

THE WORD may look tongue-tangling, but its pronunciation is simple enough: Boo-na-*ha*-venn. 'The foot of the river' is the Gaelic meaning. This is Islay's most northerly distillery. It is the loneliest, too.

Those who sleep at Bunnahabhain (as you might: the distillery offers four holiday cottages for rent) know that they are nightly surrounded by little, out in the roaring darkness, other than sea and rock. A deep elemental sleep is possible here, particularly if you have walked the track which leads over the tussocky, deer-grazed hills between these terminal buildings and the island's wild northern tip at Rhuvaal the day before. A thread-like lane winds from the Port Askaig road further south up to the distillery, rising and falling with the wooded ridges and outcrops which dominate the eastern side of the island, and giving acrobatic views down over the scurrying waters of the

Sound of Islay. That meandering tarmac is the only contact Bunnahabhain has with the human world of books, butter and nail-varnish remover. All goods and all human souls pass up and down it. Barley and fuel oil travel north along it; filled casks, crabs and lobsters travel south. Bunnahabhain is Islay whisky's last outpost.

Like Bruichladdich and Ardbeg, it is a distillery in transition. When I began work on this book in 2002, it was the saddest of the seven. It's a big distillery, capable of producing over 2 million litres of pure alcohol a year. Production then, though, was just 750,000 litres; indeed when I visited in mid-December 2002 the distillery had been silent since 28 October, when the iron paddles on the mash tun (by far the island's biggest) had caught on the worn, slotted, gun-metal bottom and, with a metallic groan, ripped it up, damaging 40 of the plates. They were lying forlornly in the yard, with the new stainless-steel ones (which had to be made to measure, at a cost of £55,000) not due for delivery until late January 2003. This accident should have been avoided by loving maintenance – but the distillery was up for sale, and loving maintenance was not a priority.

Its former owner, the Edrington Group, also owned the Macallan and Highland Park, and felt that one great Speyside malt and one great Island malt was as much as the company (a charitable foundation of no little commercial shrewdness) could cope with. Bunnahabhain was, in effect, a competitor to Highland Park, and in such a struggle, Orkney's great malt became overlord. Bunnahabhain was just one of an Islay gaggle of seven; Highland Park was very nearly a singleton on Orkney. Highland Park still malted; Bunnahabhain did so no longer. And Highland Park had for many years been crafted as a complex, stand-alone dram, whereas Bunnahabhain had, since its creation, been a quiet blender's malt which had suddenly felt a spotlight swung on to it as the world's whisky drinkers became fascinated with Islay. It was, in truth, not always wholly comfortable in the role: unpeated, and given cask supplies of variable quality. This was nothing that imagination, invest-ment, and ten years of maturation couldn't fix: as anyone who has tasted the best casks in the warehouse will attest, Bunnahabhain can be an intense, sinewy dram of arresting beauty, and the planned return to its original peaty character seems likely to lend layers to its fascination.

(Indeed, great limited-edition bottlings of Bunnahabhain, like the 1968, have beaten both Highland Park and the Macallan in open competition.) Imagination, investment and ten years' grace, though, were not what Edrington had in mind.

So Islay's north pole grew colder. Visually, moreover, there is something forbidding about Bunnahabhain. It is the one distillery on Islay which looks as if it could readily double as a prison camp; all that is missing is the barbed wire and a watchtower or two. The fact that Islay's most visible shipwreck lay just around the corner from Bunnahabhain Bay added to the sense of mischance which hung over the place in the 1990s. So, too, does the fact that 13 of the houses at Bunnahabhain are empty and derelict. The distillery's facial severity had been intensified when the whitewash which formerly covered it was replaced by a dour grey pebbledash in the 1960s; you could almost hear Soviet-era martial music drifting on the wind as you took your souvenir photograph down on the pier. Will brave Gaelic whitewash once again find its way along the thread-like road? I hope so, and soon.

The new owners are Burn Stewart Distillers, part of a newborn conglomerate called CL World Brands; the sale took place on 10 April 2003. This means that Bunnahabhain now shares a bed with Angostura Bitters, Poland's Belvedere vodka and the sublime Cognacs of Thomas Hine, as well as Burn Stewart's other distilleries: Tobermory (on the island of Mull) and Deanston. The sale price was around £10 million pounds, valuing Bunnahabhain more highly in 2003 than either Bruichladdich in 2000 (sold for £7.5 million) or Ardbeg in 1997 (sold for £7.1 million). This price, though, included the Black Bottle blended whisky brand as well as the large Bunnahabhain site itself, and the option to buy any of the stocks (which Edrington retained). Bunnahabhain has a five-year rolling contract to continue supplying Cutty Sark with a sizeable percentage of its blending malt, too.

Bunnahabhain is, at least until the planned farm-scale operation at Kilchoman fires up, one of the two youngest distilleries on the island. Whisky distilling has always been a business of fluctuation: the need for most of a decade's maturity before sale constantly provides mismatches between supply and demand, which is why so many of the former distilleries of Islay have not survived. Bunnahabhain's first good fortune was to be built at the beginning of one of the nineteenth century's boom periods. The figures '18' are found on one of the distillery's giant gateposts; with neat numerical symmetry, '81' is painted on the other. Yes, Bunnahabhain and Bruichladdich came into the world in the same year.

Bunnahabhain was the creation of an enterprise called The Islay Distillery Company, whose four directors were William Robertson, John Marshall, James Ford and James Greenlees. Nothing is known about Marshall and Ford, while Greenlees was a member of Campbeltown's leading distilling family and an associate of the enterprising blender and salesman James Buchanan, later Lord Woolavington. Robertson's was the key name, though: he was the leading light in the Glasgow blending company Robertson & Baxter (established in 1857). Robertson & Baxter worked closely at the time with Bulloch Lade, the owners of Caol Ila; the canny Glaswegians were enormously enthusiastic about this (then relatively small) distillery's blend-friendly malt. Bunnahabhain may not have been intended to duplicate Caol Ila in the way that Peter Mackie's Malt Mill was intended to be a clone of Laphroaig, but it was certainly an attempt to build further on what Caol Ila has already achieved.

It's hard to imagine what the setting for Bunnahabhain must have looked like on 6 May 1881, the day when the steam puffer *Islay* unloaded the first wood for the workmen's huts on to the pebble beach of this lonely bay. Perhaps the best way to recover that moment is to walk, at the opposite end of the island, from Ardtalla Farmhouse over the headland to Proaig Bay. Both Bunnahabhain and Proaig would once have been thriving farm townships, before the inhabitants were shuffled off them earlier in the century to make way for braying sheep. By the time 50 men began digging foundations and quarrying stones with which to build the distillery, the Margadale valley which runs down to Bunnahabhain would have been empty apart from shepherds' shielings (temporary summer huts) and fanks (sheepfolds). All the original farming community had left by the 1861 census, though one Catherine McDonald and her family were recorded as living at Margadale just ten years earlier. Bunnahabhain, in other words, would have looked much like today's Proaig: a lonely, quiet and empty place. The only cheery sounds would have been the manic piping of the oystercatchers. The sudden gloom thrown by shadows as racing clouds interrupted the bright May sunshine would have given the landscape its movement, together with the bending and nodding of the grasses in the wind.

THE HILL

In earlier times, by contrast, the scene would have been a busier one, particularly further up the valley at the point at which the Margadale spring rises. Margadale itself means 'Dale of the Marketplace': there was a thriving community here whose ruins still stand, including lazy-bed cultivation rigs and a house with a corn-drying kiln. Regular market fairs were held among its buildings and spaces. Present-day Bunnahabhain manager John MacLellan walked me up there, on a sunlit July evening, with his wife Lindy, son Sandy and their two stupendously energetic Jack Russell terriers Honey and Fraoch (which means 'heather' in Gaelic). As we looked across the hillside to the old settlement area, John pointed out how green patches marked out the former fields, once set to potatoes, oats and barley and improved with lime (hence dissuasive to modern-day heather). The quartzite which composes so much of mountainous Islay temporarily gives way here, in any case, to the limestones found in the island's central valley (dolo-stone, a magnesium-rich form of limestone, at this precise point); it is possible, indeed, that lime workings in this area were exploited as early as Viking times. There was no road up from Port Askaig at the time these half-hundred men began their work in 1881, but one of the oldest tracks on the island (now fallen almost entirely beneath rushes and moss) runs over to Bunnahabhain via Margadale from Killinallan and Gortantaoid on the eastern side of Loch Gruinart.

The prosperity and ambition of the founding partners is testified by the scale of the Bunnahabhain site. The purchase of the land from the laird, Charles Morrison, cost £2,000 (equivalent to around £129,000 in 1998 prices), but the buildings themselves, on which 100 workmen were eventually employed, cost £30,000 (or £1,931,000). A box of blackened and mouldering human bones was found buried on the beach by one of the workmen; whose bones they were, or how they had come there, was never explained. The autumn of 1881 brought the usual storms, and at one point two large boilers were blown off the beach where they were waiting for installation and bobbed chaotically across the Sound of Islay to Jura. The building work was eventually completed in 1882, and the first spirit ran from the stills in January 1883. That solid Victorian Alfred Barnard, who arrived on his regal progress around the island halfway through the distillery's first decade of work, was deeply impressed with the 'life-like and civilised colony' he found here in a 'portion of the island' previously 'bare and uninhabited'. (Barnard was no social historian.) Houses, a school for the distillery workers' 18 children, and a shop eventually grew up around the distillery. Barnard praised 'the commodious and handsome pier' which, alone, had cost £3,500. (This wood-and-metal pier was replaced with the present concrete one in 1951.) The barley arrived, and the whisky left, courtesy of the trusty, deep-bellied puffers which made Scotland's west coast a trading artery in the pre-motor age. Water and peat, meanwhile, came off the hill – Margadale Hill. 'Nothing but peat,' wrote Barnard, 'is used in the kilns which is dug in the district and is of exceptionally fine quality.' The initial water source, meanwhile, was the burn tumbling down from the peaty Loch Staoisha, sited to the south of the distillery in the valley which separates the hills above the Sound from the rugged central heights in this empty quarter of the island. At some point (there is no record of this), however, the water from Loch Staoisha became used for cooling alone, while that used for brewing became the unpeated, crystalline water of the Margadale Spring north-west of the distillery, for the use of which payment has traditionally been made to Islay Estates in whisky.

Bunnahabhain's original whisky, as the foregoing account suggests, was utterly different to that produced during the second half of the twentieth century: it was robustly peaty, and it remained so until the early 1960s. Between then and 2003 it was unpeated, apart from one or two experimental runs using peat in the latter years of the Edrington regime (there was a run at 28 ppm in 1991 and another at 38 ppm in 1997). Like all the surviving distilleries on the island, Bunnahabhain went through periods of closure – during the two World Wars, during the Depression of the 1930s (it closed between 1932 and 1936), and during the whisky recession of the 1980s (it closed between 1982 and 1984). There were buoyant periods, too: output was doubled in 1963, as sales surged of its main blending expression, Cutty Sark, though it was the requirements of this pale, light blend which meant a switch of character away from peat. Ownership throughout remained relatively constant. By 1887, Bunnahabhain had amalgamated with William Grant and Co (owner of Glen Rothes, and an entirely different company to the William Grant which built Glenfiddich in that very year) to form Highland Distillers, Robertson & Baxter remaining its agent. And there, in the heart of Highland, it remained until 1999, at which point the publicly quoted Highland was taken back into private ownership by its part-owner the Edrington group, which had joined forces for this purpose with William Grant and Sons of Glenfiddich fame. A change of ownership? Not really: the official name of the new Edrington/Grant company (the shareholding was 70/30) was 'The 1887 Group' – that name alluding to the moment when Highland Distillers came into being. The descendants of founder William Robertson, moreover, are still involved in The 1887 Group. You could convincingly argue, therefore, that CL World Brands is only the second owner of Bunnahabhain since its creation, which would make it the least-traded of all Islay distilleries.

A NICE QUIET NIGHT

There are no memories of past peaty periods at Bunnahabhain among the present-day workers; the doyen, Victor MacLellan (who, despite the same surname, is no relation of manager John MacLellan), began in 1969. Victor is an Ileach whose family has been on the island 'for as long as anyone can remember'; he joined the distillery after having been a farm-hand, a fisherman and a forestry worker. At that point, the distillery was working 'flat out', seven days a week, with over 30 on the staff roll; all the malt came in by boat, and all the whisky left by boat, too. The malt, Victor remembers, came from Ireland. 'Very good, it was. We were getting great results with it; we were always top of the league.' Working conditions were harder – six days a week were expected, and 12-hour days were not uncommon. The consolation, if consolation it was, was that the dramming tradition was still in place. 'That was what kept you going. You had one first thing in the morning; one at lunchtime; one at five-o-clock, and one at about eight-o-clock at night. It depended what sort of mood the brewer was in. The brewer at the time hadn't got much of a clue; if you had an argument with him, that was how he settled it. "You'll be needing a dram" – and that was it, settled. Lots of the boys would start an argument just to settle it like that.' Victor also remembers that it wasn't just the distillery workers who would put in an appearance at the dramming shed. 'They'd be coming from all over the island for drams. There'd be a dozen shepherds working in the fank up on the hill there, and they'd be in the queue, too.' Look-outs were posted to keep an eye out for the resident Exciseman.

The dramming tradition came to an end in the 1970s, under an ex-Army distillery manager called Bob Gordon. 'It became half-a-bottle a week, then a bottle a month; then eight bottles every six months. Now they give you vouchers.' Gordon was a fierce taskmaster and an unpopular manager. 'He was a beast. I think he still thought he was in the Army. He'd have you with a paintbrush in one hand, and you still had to do the stilling as well. While he was here, in the '70s, it was just bulk, bulk, bulk. Steam everywhere. I think that's why there's still so much from the 1970s in the warehouses. We notice that it's a lot of the newer stuff that's gone away.'

Victor was one of those on duty in the still room on the night the *Wyre Majestic* was wrecked, 18 October 1974. This Fleetwood trawler bottomed on to rocks at 19.40, just past the southern end of Bunnahabhain Bay; it had been following its sister ship, the *Wyre Defence*, through the Sound of Islay. The wreck is easily visible to anyone who chooses to scramble around the boulders of Rubha a'Mhill (the Rough Promontory) – hence it is much photographed. The Hebridean winters, though, are taking their toll, and the remains of the trawler have recently begun to break up; the bow came off in January 2001.

'It was a nice quiet night,' remembers Victor; as wreckings go, it all passed off in a most orderly manner, albeit lavishly seasoned with choice Lancashire expletives. Present-day manager John MacLellan had been due to go to a dance that night (it was a Friday), but when the coastguard call came through he came up with his friends and they spent most of the night there. 'The boat had been into Oban to discharge her catch and get it off to market. The mate was at the wheel,

and he'd been told to wake the skipper when they got to the north end of the Sound here. But it was a nice calm night, so the mate thought he'd carry on. He took her into the bay to avoid the tide a little bit, but as he came back out the boat got caught on the rocks. Unfortunately it was the top of the tide at the time, and every day afterwards the tide got lower, so it jammed on.' Port Ellen shopkeeper and local historian James Macaulay formed part of the lifeboat team that night. 'There wasn't much we could do,' he remembers. 'We stood by until high water the next morning and passed a wire rope between the *Majestic* and the *Defence* – but no chance. It broke several times. She was stuck fast.' Oddly enough, Victor MacLellan remembers, another member of the *Wyre* family went aground to the other side of Port Askaig almost a year to the day afterwards, but was floated off successfully on that occasion. Islay must be Fleetwood's least popular Scottish island.

WALKING BUNNAHABHAIN

Any true distillery walk must begin at the water source which, in Bunnahabhain's case, is found high up among the rushy grasses of Margadale Hill. Bunnahabhain's water is doubly unique: it is the only brewing water on the island which comes from a spring rather than a river or loch; and it is the only water which is crystal clear. Like the waters of Bruichladdich and Caol Ila, it doesn't see the light of day in its journey from spring to distillery, moving instead through pipes and a 30,000-gallon covered holding tank. While this ensures that the dead sheep which I saw decomposing in the water courses of two of Islay's other distilleries can never find their way into Bunnahabhain's wash, it does not mean that it is entirely wildlife-free. On one occasion, Bunnahabhain's water supply stopped suddenly and completely (a serious emergency for any distillery). The eventual cause of the blockage was found to be an adventurous otter which had got wedged, with fatal security, in one of the stretches of water pipe.

Does Bunnahabhain's crystal water affect the flavour of its spirit? Industry experts invariably suggest that the peatiness or otherwise of the water is almost irrelevant compared to the peat specification in the malt itself. The idea that water affects flavour was described as 'baloney' by Mike Nicolson, who managed both Lagavulin and Caol Ila; according to Diageo's Douglas Murray, the notion that water affects the taste of whisky is 'the biggest myth that we, as an industry, have perpetrated'. Islay distilleries may use nature's open-air supplies, but other distilleries (including those that produce much admired malts like Oban) rely on municipal water supplies. The experts may be right – yet . . . I can't help rejoicing, in my secret ignorance, in the fact that Bunnahabhain's water trickles directly into the mash tun from the vast, intestinal masses of quartzite, dolostone and diamictite which compose Islay's northern hump. Would the whisky be the same if the water was exactly the same stuff that flows out of the taps in Birmingham? I don't believe so. All that manager John MacLellan will say on the matter is that the water is exceptionally good for distilling.

The mash tun is the biggest on the island. It normally mashes 12.6 tonnes of milled malt, and occasionally is filled to over 13 tonnes 'when we start up again after the silent season or after Christmas'. In the past, mashes were as big as 15 tonnes, John MacLellan says; he likes to point out malt's loss in value after the whisky brewer has used it. 'The malt comes in the door at two hundred and fifty pounds a tonne. We use it for twelve hours in the mash tun and it goes out of the door at five pounds a tonne.' (Each mash does, of course, produce around 16 butts of malt whisky – whose eventual value is considerably more than the £3,150 the malt has cost.) The spent malt is called draff, and is used for animal feed. 'Draff is very strange stuff. If all the distilleries on Islay are working, then draff is more or less worthless. The farmers don't even want it; they're doing us a favour by taking it. When draff is scarce, though, those guys will kill for it. What you need to sell draff is wind and rain. As soon as it starts getting stormy, that's when they want draff.' Big, generously built Bunnahabhain is lucky in that it has ample draff storage – enough for four mashes. 'The lorries can come and take away twenty-five tonnes at a time. Some of the other distilleries don't have this, and lorries have to be ready to pick up at three a.m.'

Since the mid-1960s, the peat specification in Bunnahabhain's malt has been minute – less than 2 ppm, translating into impalpable traces in the finished spirit (less than 0.5 ppm in the finished spirit cannot be detected by humans, no matter how acute their faculties). All of that changed on 17 November 2003, when the spirit from a 250-tonne batch of peaty malt (38 ppm) began to trickle through Bunnahabhain's stately stills. (There is no name yet assigned to this peaty alternative, though Margadale, Rhuvaal and Ardnahoe are all possibilities.) Highland's previous experiments with a peatier style at Bunnahabhain date to the period during which John MacLellan's predecessor, Hamish Proctor, was manager back in 1991 and 1997, with two different peat specifications (28 ppm and 38 ppm). 'The whisky was really good,' remembers John, though Victor MacLellan disagrees, saying he found it 'a wee bit sickly'; the only problem, according to John, 'was that it took seven or eight weeks to get rid of it afterwards. All of that semi-peaty spirit had to go for blending, and Highland took the view that it was too long a spell to have to put up with it.' The experiments were thus ended. The plan now, by contrast, is to distil the peatier spirit on a regular basis.

Like all the distilleries on the island, Bunnahabhain used to do its own malting; the last grain was raked up from the three malting floors in 1963. The barley loft and the malting floors still exist, though, so if CL World Brands ever wants to return to malting, it would be possible; production, at about 40 tonnes a week, would be similar to that of Laphroaig. Some 90 per cent of Bunnahabhain's malt comes from Simpson's Berwick maltings on the Scottish mainland at present, with the ten per cent balance being supplied by Port Ellen. Once again, Bunnahabhain has ample malt storage space, enough for 900 tonnes. 'Macallan would die for storage space like we've got. It goes back to the days of the ships, when we used to bring a boatload in every five weeks.

We were still doing that up to about a decade or so ago.' If the distillery were ever to go back to malting, though, it would have to build new kilns, since the old ones were converted into malt bins in 1964.

The mashing cycle at Bunnahabhain is relatively long (about 12 hours from start to finish) because of the amount of malt involved; this, too, is the reason why the grain is washed with four waters rather than three (the last two waters become the first water of the next cycle). Bunnahabhain's traditionally raked mash tun, moreover, slows the process; a lauter or semi-lauter tun would be quicker. After mashing, the wort passes through an underback to clarify to the maximum extent: 'What we want to have,' says John, 'is clear wort.' Why? Distilleries producing a light, pure style of new make, as Bunnahabhain has been doing for the last forty years, prefer a very clear wort; slightly cloudy or opaque worts are preferred at distilleries (like Inchgower or Blair Atholl) where the desired new-make spirit is nutty or spicy.

Everything at Bunnahabhain is large in scale, and the six Oregon pine washbacks are no exception: each is charged with 66,500 litres of wort (the result of a single mash), which makes them almost three times the size of the washbacks at Lagavulin or Ardbeg. Again, a light and pure spirit requires a relatively slow fermentation; the longer the wort takes to ferment, the more acidic the consequent wash will be, and an acidic wash which has been through copper distillation produces (as every Cognac distiller will confirm) a very fine spirit. Bunnahabhain's fermentation times have been extended from the 48 to 63 hours used in the hurried old 'bulk' days to a more gradual 60 to 80 hours today. A mixture of Quest M and Quest MX yeasts are used, and the fermentation temperature begins at between 18°C and 20°C, rising to 34°C at the height of yeast activity.

There have, since 1963, been two wash stills and two spirit stills at Bunnahabhain (prior to that there were one of each). One washback provides enough wash (or beer) to run both of them twice each. Each has a calibrated capacity of 35,356 litres, but as usual this is a meaningless figure: what matters is the charge of wash, which is about 16,625 litres here, a quarter of each mash. The charge, in other words, is just 47 per cent of the capacity of the still. Compare this with Ardbeg's or Bowmore's wash still, where the charge is almost 65 per cent; filling a lower charge in the stills is another technique by which one can accentuate lightness and finesse in a distillate. A third means of achieving the same end is by running the stills slowly, giving the wash more time to interact with the copper itself, which will claw out impurities as the spirit vapour passes, with ghostly passion, over it. The wash stills are a very flat onion shape and relatively tall, with straight lyne arms, and the wash takes about five hours to run through them, the low wines being initially collected at around 48 per cent abv and then running down to under 1 per cent abv.

The shape of the two spirits stills is a contrast to that of the wash stills: they are more of a rounded pot shape, with a relatively high belly giving plenty of boil and reflux. Again, the lyne arms are straight. The calibrated spirit-still capacity is 15,546 litres, and each is charged with between 9,000 and 9,500 litres, or around 60 per cent capacity; compare this once again with Bowmore, where the spirit still charge is 92 per cent of capacity. Again, lightness rather than pungency is the aim. At present, the foreshot run is about ten minutes, the stillman cutting to spirit at 72 per cent abv. The spirit run itself lasts just under three hours, until the spirit drops to 64 per cent abv, when the run is switched to feints, which take another three hours to pass through the stills. These cuts give an average spirit strength of 68.5 per cent abv, diluted to the usual 63.5 per cent when the casks are filled. In its distillation regime, then, Bunnahabhain is run as a middling distillery between the extreme lightness of Caol Ila (with its very slow fermentations, very narrow cuts and high distilling strength) and the more pungent and gutsy approach taken at Laphroaig or Bowmore. Will this be modified for the peaty version of Bunnahabhain? In principle not, though the spirit is being cut off to feints at a slightly lower strength of 61.5 per cent rather than 64 per cent according to John MacLellan, since 'the phenols tend to run through at the bottom end of the spirit run.' There is one interior and one exterior condenser for the wash stills, and the same pattern for the spirit stills. Bunnahabhain's unpeated new make is very clean and fresh, its natural polish meaning there is less spirit nip to it when sniffed than for some of its island peers; the peated new make, by contrast, is much more forthright, with curls of soapy smoke lifting alluringly from it.

Bunnahabhain's seven warehouses, giving storage space for 21,000 casks, is adequate to ensure that every drop of spirit going into distillery bottlings is aged on the island. Indeed under Highland and Edrington experiments were carried out to see if 'Islay ageing' could genuinely alter the character of *any* whisky stored on the island: in the late 1980s, casks of spirit from other distilleries (such as Glen Rothes) were sent over for storage on Islay. The results, though, were never made public, and the warehousemen say that most of the experimental casks have now been removed. 'If someone sets up an experiment like that,' comments John MacLellan, 'they're either dead or retired by the time the result's known.' The most 'marine' of the warehouses would be number 7, a single-storey warehouse containing up to 700 casks sited on the bay-side of the main distillery thoroughfare; least exposed to maritime influences would be number 8, a racked warehouse containing 6,000 casks sited up the hill. Bunnahabhain's site, though apparently exposed to the battering of sea winds from the Sound of Islay, is in reality one of the more sheltered ones on the island. This is because the prevailing wind on Islay is from the west, and Bunnahabhain faces east; the lie of the land, too, means that the distillery shelters under rugged hills which lift that prevailing wind and carry it across the Sound to Jura. Both sherry and bourbon casks are used for Bunnahabhain fillings, in contrast to most of the other distilleries on the island which now use bourbon alone.

TASTING BUNNAHABHAIN

I have, for consolation and companionship, a glass of Bunnahabhain 10-year-old on the desk in front of me as I write this. It was poured from a squat bottle, out of the label of which peers a bearded Scots seaman stationed behind an extremely large wooden ship's wheel. He wears a tam-o'-shanter; the stiff sea breeze blows his scarf; and he shades his eyes, the better to make out his sea route back to the bay – since this image is captioned 'Westering Home'. It's a local song, two verses of which are printed on the back label, which commemorates the joy felt by Ileach seafarers as they near their own front doors after journeying to 'the Orient gay' and experiencing 'the riches and joys o' Cathay'. (It also contains the phrase '. . . and it's goodbye to care' used for Islay's promotional car stickers.) Brilliant packaging, in my opinion, since it simultaneously evokes the sea, Islay's seafaring distinction, the island's musical traditions, the return home after chancing it among life's hazards, and rest and recuperation in general. (I like it so much that a change is doubtless imminent.)

The whisky declares itself 'aged 12 years', though it's an open secret that the average age of Bunnahabhain has actually been rather more than that of late. You can tell, visually, that sherry wood plays a role in its ageing by its colour, which is a rich orange gold (and deeper in colour at present than the Ardbeg and Bruichladdich 10-year-olds, and the Caol Ila 12-year-old). No peat, of course; in its place some heather, marzipan, honey, hessian and leather. Perhaps it's autosuggestion, but a sense of brininess hangs over the dram, too, a hint of that rain-laden sea breeze tugging at the homebound sailor's scarf. Despite the full colour and the heather and honey notes, it's a relatively crisp dram, a ginger-snap, a tonic, a bracer. It doesn't have the sappy, creamy, grassy notes of its other Islay unpeated rival, Bruichladdich; it's less immediate, less sensual, more meditative, more masculine. A fine dry dram, in other words, for those moments when you might want a break from the peat.

But it's also a work in progress. As I have already mentioned, the change of ownership means that we will, over the next decade, make the acquaintanceship of different styles of Bunnahabhain. The potential of this under-rated distillery, though, is exciting, as those who have tried some of the special bottlings released from time to time (under names such as The Family Silver and Auld Acquaintance) will know. The greatest whiskies I have tasted from Bunnahabhain have all been from casks, in the number 5 warehouse in early December 2002. A 1981 from refill sherry hogsheads had the pale, winking green-gold colour of Chablis; it was a malt of sappy, sinewy refinement, its rolled-marzipan notes giving way to a finish of close-knit saltiness. A 1970 from a first-fill bourbon hogshead was prettier, softer, creamier, yet the hallmark Bunnahabhain tautness kept everything neat and shipshape. Best of all was a 1963 from a sherry hogshead of remarkable, almost donnish dryness, mouthcoating yet crisp, too, hinting at herbs, finishing on a note of burnt currant, and extraordinarily drinkable for such a venerable spirit (age, remember, always turns into enmity; the only question is when). In July 2003, after walking to Margadale spring with John, Lindy and Sandy MacLellan, I tasted the bottled blend which had been composed of seven 1963 sherry hogsheads (hand-filled by night at the distillery: an island first); again, its herbal, fern-like style, its hints of grass and mint and bog myrtle, almost suggested a monastic liqueur. The Family Silver bottling of the 1968 (tasted in November 2003), with its scents of pine and fern, its fresh-air complexity and delicate, subtle arrangement of creamy orange struck many of the same plain-song notes. A taut style, a dry finish and a grand refinement are all somewhere near the heart of Bunnahabhain's character, and probably always will be.

Bunnahabhain   DISTILLERY FACTFILE

Distillery operating hours	*5½ days a week @ 24 hours a day*
Number of employees	*11*
Water source	*Margadale Spring (whisky water); Loch Staoisha (cooling water)*
Water reserve	*not known*
Water colour	*clear*
Peat content of water	*zero*
Malt source	*Simpson's (Berwick) 90 per cent; Port Ellen 10 per cent*
Own floor maltings?	*unused*
Malt type	*Optic*
Malt specification phenols	*Bunnahabhain: less than 2 ppm; new peaty spirit: 38 ppm*
Finished spirit phenols	*Bunnahabhain: trace; new peaty spirit: not yet analysed*
Malt storage	*900 tonnes*
Mill type	*Porteus, installed 1964*
Grist storage	*30 tonnes*
Mash tun construction	*stainless steel: rake and plough*

Mash size   –   *12.5–13 tonnes*

First water   –   *43,000 litres at 82°C plus 7–8,000 litres*
of cold water to achieve first-water
temperature of 64°C

Second water   –   *24,000 litres at 80°C*

Third water   –   *20,000 litres at 90°C*

Fourth Water   –   *23,000 litres at 90°C*

Number of washbacks   –   *6*

Washback construction   –   *Oregon pine*

Washback charge   –   *66,500 litres*

Yeast   –   *Quest cultured yeast*

Amount of yeast   –   *250 kg per washback*

Length of fermentation   –   *63 hours (shorts: week);*
80 hours (longs: weekend)

Initial fermentation temperature   –   *20°C (weekdays); 18°C (weekends)*

Strength of wash   –   *6.5 per cent – 8.5 per cent abv*

Number of wash stills   –   *2*

Wash stills built   –   *1: 1989; 2: 1963*

Wash still capacity   –   *35,356 litres*

Wash still charge   –   *16,625 litres (47 per cent of capacity)*

Heat source   –   *steam pans*

Wash still height   –   *25 feet 10 inches (7.87 m)*

Wash still shape   –   *plain*

Length of low-wines run   –   *c. 5 hours*

Low-wines collection range   –   *46 per cent abv – 0.5 per cent abv*

Number of spirit stills   –   *2*

Spirit stills built   –   *1: not known (pre-1963); 2: 1963*

Spirit still capacity   –   *15,546 litres*

Spirit still charge   –   *9,000–9,600 litres (around 60 per cent*
capacity)

Strength of spirit still charge   –   *26 per cent abv*

Heat source   –   *steam pans*

Spirit still height   –   *20 feet 10 inches (6.35 m)*

Spirit still shape   –   *plain*

Lyne arm   –   *straight*

Purifier?   –   *no*

Condensers	– *Two wash-still condensers, each 14 feet 4 inches (4.37 m) long, one sited internally and one externally, tube width $^7/_8$ inch (2.2 cm), number of tubes: information not available. Two spirit-still condensers, each 13 feet 9 inches (4.19 m) long, one sited internally and one externally, tube width $^7/_8$ inch (2.2 cm), number of tubes: information not available*
Length of foreshot run	– *about 10 minutes*
Length of spirit run	– *2–3 hours*
Length of feints run	– *about 3 hours*
Spirit cut	– *Bunnahabhain: 72 per cent abv – 64 per cent abv; new peaty spirit: 72 per cent abv to 61.5 per cent abv*
Distilling strength	– *68.5 per cent abv average*
Storage strength	– *63.5 per cent abv*
Average spirit yield	– *409.5 litres of pure alcohol per tonne of malt (2003)*
Disposal of pot ale and spent lees	– *piped into Sound of Islay*
Type of casks filled for branded malt	– *90 per cent first-fill bourbon hogsheads; 10 per cent first-fill and second-fill sherry casks of various sizes*
Current annual output	– *1,000,000 litres of pure alcohol (2003)*
Number of warehouses	– *7 (numbered 2, 3, 4, 5, 6, 7, 8)*
Type of warehouses	– *dunnage and racking*
Storage capacity on Islay	– *21,000 casks*
Percentage of branded malt entirely aged on Islay	– *100 per cent*
Vatting and bottling location	– *East Kilbride*
Distillery expressions	– *12-year-old*
	– *Vintage-dated special releases*
Major blending roles	– *Cutty Sark, Black Bottle, Famous Grouse, Scottish Leader*

CHAPTER FIVE

Weather

The sky a blue forest
where rain panthers come padding
– to rip the land's flesh.

ISLAY'S WEATHER is an adventure. Endured or enjoyed?

For the island's beasts, this adventure has to be experienced in the open, whatever may fall or befall, with the serene stoicism which provokes such wonder in humans. Farm beasts included: 'outwintering' is an island speciality – to benefit, as we will discover in Chapter Six, the precious choughs. The auctioneer at an Islay cattle auction I once attended pattered repeatedly that the nimble, disconcerted youngsters he was about to hammer down had 'never seen the inside of a barn'. Geese, otters, buzzards: the rest of the island's wild population has to take whatever the west (for it is usually the west) brings. The owls must feed well when they can, for there will be many nights every year when the rain and the wind robs them of their faculties, and their rodent prey can scuttle among the long grasses in storm-secured safety.

The adventure can also be lived as most humans do, hurrying from shelter to shelter when the rain drums, yet lingering in the warmth and the light when the sky's mood changes. It could be observed from a wheelchair, on the dry side of a window pane, with no less interest. Adventure implies a narrative of change, moments of drama, adversity endured or overcome. There are few days when the view from an Islay window doesn't change, sometimes hourly, along these lines. If you like weather, Islay is the place. There's masses of it.

This crumb of rock lies to one side of the broad avenue of the Atlantic. There are many such crumbs: Lanzarote, Belle Ile, Lundy, St Kilda, the Faeroes. Islay, of course, lies closer to the icebergs of the Greenland Sea than it does to the hotels of Lanzarote. The North Atlantic is brooding, moody and uterine, swept by an unfolding crisis of fronts and depressions. Islay harvests these.

This short chapter is one of lived experience, not statistical distillation. All the same, there are useful weather statistics on the island. Perhaps because unpredictable and often extreme weather is a feature of Islay life, those living here have often wanted to track the course of meteorological events, and both Islay Estates and the golf links at the Machrie Hotel have extensive weather records (the Machrie pins recent weather figures to the notice board just inside its porch). Islay estate records reveal that the wettest year on Islay since the mid-nineteenth century, for example, was 1923, when 75.82 inches (1,925.8 mm) of rain fell, which is over three times London's average annual rainfall of 23.35 inches (593 mm). Two notably dry years on Islay were 1887 (with 38.78 inches or 985 mm) and, driest of all, the war year of 1941, when just 37.59 inches (954.8 mm) fell, though this was still a lot more rain than would have dampened the bomb-harried dome of St Paul's; in general, recent years have been towards the dry end of the range (2000 produced 39.80 inches or 1,010.9 mm, while 2001 was only a little wetter at 42.81 inches or 1,087.4 mm).

As elsewhere in Scotland, May, June and September enjoy a good reputation as fair-weather months to visit Islay, yet the great Atlantic roulette wheel means that you might plan visits in these months and struggle with facefuls of rain while a canny goose-loving acquaintance booked much cheaper visits in November and February and enjoyed improbably bright skies. Take 2002, for example. The two driest months were August and December, while February, June, October and November were all extremely wet. There were only six days in June, indeed, when it didn't rain, and the monthly total of 6.13 inches (155.7 mm) was a disaster in peat-drying terms, meaning that Port Ellen Maltings had to order supplies from mainland Scotland later in the year. In general, of course, copious rainfall is taken for granted on Islay, so when rainfall is lower than normal for a month or two, the opposite problem presents itself. In the late summer of 1997, for example, four months passed with little rain. Most of the distilleries had to stop production until their water sources were replenished in late autumn.

Temperatures are, in general, steadier and more predictable than rainfall, and will strike the reader living in Minneapolis or Moscow as being startlingly moderate. Let's take the example of 2002 once again. January days oscillated between 2°C and 8°C and June days between 9°C and 18°C. It was never colder at night than -4°C (and that frost came in the early hours of April 14th; January itself was frost-free), while the hottest day was 1 August when the temperature reached a torrid 22.7°C. What every visitor to Islay notices, though, is that the wind rarely drops. That wind makes summer temperatures feel rather cooler than the figures would suggest, and winter temperatures often feel much colder. Even at the height of summer, sunbathing on Islay's many beautiful and unpeopled beaches is at best an occasional activity, and candlelit dinners on linen-covered tables outside followed by cigars among the fireflies rarer still. I have swum in Loch Indaal on a bright August day, but those are four minutes of my life I am not in any hurry to repeat. It was a pleasant enough evening to begin with outside the Port Charlotte Hotel on 25 May 2002 when the Bruichladdich crowd (whose guests included leading Alsace winemaker Olivier Humbrecht, his wife Margaret and two of their friends) sat down to a seafood barbecue: bright but blowy, with white crests on the waves out in the loch and a foamy stir as they broke over the shore rocks. As the evening drew on, though, the wind got colder and colder; I shiveringly retreated to the hotel conservatory to enjoy a glass of the Zind-Humbrecht 1989 Rangen de Thann Pinot Gris, marvelling at the resilience of those (including the Humbrecht quartet) still sitting at the table outside in what seemed to me to be a rising gale. Everyone enjoyed this magnificent sipping wine – but in truth is was an evening for gulping. And, eventually, for drams.

Yes: the wind, of course, can rise. Islay's storms are noteworthy. We have already heard how a 1998 Boxing Day storm nearly decapitated Ardbeg's manager Stuart Thomson and closed the distillery to visitors for six months; the account of Islay's most tragic shipwrecks in Chapter Seven is, not unnaturally, also an account of serial meteorological violence. One of the twentieth century's most timely storms is remember by Dunlossit laird Bruno Schroder. His father Helmut Schroder had bought Dunlossit in 1937, and as war threatened he assembled his own children on Islay plus those of a number of acquaintances. 'We ended up with thirteen children there and five nannies, and we all had great fun. I have a vivid memory of seeing the convoy ships going up and down the Sound of Islay, American four-stackers, old destroyers which Churchill had got sent over. The day war broke out, my mother and my sister and myself were visiting the farms. It was a lovely sunny day – until Chamberlain made his broadcast at eleven o'clock. Immediately after the broadcast, the heavens opened; it was the worst storm anyone could remember – the wrath of God. All the bridges over the Laggan were destroyed.' A similarly programmatic storm seems to have marked the end of Campbell ownership of Islay in October 1847, as Walter Frederick sailed away on his yacht to a life of indigence in Normandy.

My own initial attempt to reach Islay was defeated by a storm. I had first set eyes on the island six months earlier, when a happy conjunction of circumstances (never, alas, repeated) had deposited me by helicopter on the neighbouring island of Jura. I walked, that immaculate evening in May 1993, down through woods filled with wild garlic, bluebells and scampering rabbits to a beach of white sand. Islay's northerly latitude means long, luminous dusks as midsummer's day draws near, and the sky was still glowing; the sea was taut silk. I looked across to the lighthouse at McArthur's Head, and its white-painted buildings and walls suddenly resembled (again the Aegean kinship) a Greek island monastery. The peace of the scene was impeccable: the wind had dropped; no engine broke the silence; even the rabbits seemed unfrenzied, stunned by the sweetness of the world around them into taking an unusually languid supper. I knew, then, that I wanted to visit Islay as soon as I could.

The moment finally came on 29 November that year, when I climbed on board a Shorts SD3-60 at Glasgow airport. The construction of this workaday, shack-like aeroplane meant that I was looking, from my seat, up into the strut-supported armpit of the wing; it was a wild night. We skidded and lurched down the runway and clambered up into the air; during the journey what had begun as a white murk slowly thickened into a blue murk, the pathetic wing beams shining a few hopeless feet ahead. Despite the lurching and the swaying, all on board seemed phlegmatic: I remembered an elderly man in tweeds with a hearing aid sitting mutely (perhaps it was turned off), and two dark-haired girls with black gloves and neat eyes sitting in equally silent aplomb. The pilot told us the wind was 'well over 60 knots' on Islay and we would therefore have to return to Glasgow – which we did, the plane coming in to land crab-style and bumping its way back up the runway. When we disembarked after our ride into the storm, the air smelled of oysters. Even in Glasgow, the sea seemed to be invading the land.

The storm had blown itself out by the following morning, and when I eventually reached the island Iain Henderson at Laphroaig told me that his team had been picking seaweed out of the gutters. (I was never quite sure when Iain was teasing.) The photographs I took that day glow with the brilliant clarity of light which follows a storm's scouring. The low winter sun shone on to the white-painted walls of the maltings with tempered extravagance, while the dark roofline above the walls and the brown, sea-gnawed rocks below cut the brightness precisely. It didn't last; it rarely does on Islay. By the time we got over to sad, cold Ardbeg (idle and unused just then) in the afternoon, the darkening grey clouds had returned, and they blackened as dusk drew on, though this grumpy ceiling held itself just high enough to permit a bright orange-gold bar to irradiate the horizon prior to sunset.

In truth, despite loitering hopefully on the island more often during the darkest winter months than during exquisite (but expensive) summer, I've never yet experienced a genuinely implacable Islay storm, the kind of storms which John Edwards and Mark French, both of whom farm on the west coast of the Rhinns, have told me about. The animals seem to disappear into the pile of the land, according to John, though it's hard to tell where or how they have found shelter; opening a tractor door on the windward side, Mark reminded me, is impossible, as is remaining vertical in the wind without support from behind. Chloë Randall, estate manager of Dunlossit, recalls seeing the slates on her roof move up and down like piano keys. Being out in such weather is akin to wing-walking. If there's rain, it will sting your face. Conversation is impossible above nature's roar.

I have, though, fretted through some passingly wild nights in various cottages on Islay. As the wind rises, every house acquires a new character, one which you had no idea it possessed before: its Aeolian personality. They all sing. (Do Islay architects and builders plan for this? Do they bang tuning forks to find the pitch for a house corner, or fine tune a line of guttering in a force seven wind?) On Christmas Eve 2002, as I lay in bed in Port Charlotte with piercing back pain acquired by dancing with misguided exuberance at the Bruichladdich Ceilidh, I picked out three strands to the long cadenza: a timpani of buffeting, syncopated over a high screech and a lower, more genuinely musical whistle. The latter two varied in pitch and intensity but remained constant, whereas the buffeting was genuinely random and it was that unpredictability (in addition to the back pain) which kept me awake. From time to time a squally front of rain would pass up Loch Indaal; I could tell because a madman seemed to be hurling rice at the window panes. On other occasions, in other cottages, I have enjoyed other tunes: the wind is capable of making bathroom extractor fans sound like idling jet engines, and any chimney can produce a rumble like distant thunder. Every wire on the island will whistle and screech. The nagging wind, in sum, gives the island its voice, and too much (if you're on your own) can leave you slightly unhinged. The islanders are inured to it, taming it with whisky and understatement, but even they must buckle in private moments and give way with an expletive, a cackle or a sob.

That Islay is dull in winter is a myth. Even if you miss the season's wildest storm, you will be treated to a huge repertoire of meteorological nuances during the admittedly short days, and the combination of low, reticent sunlight and constantly rain-washed air is capable of generating and refracting colours of striking radiance. Summer has no equivalent, but if it did you would have to be up at dawn or out at ten at night to find it. Perhaps the most implausibly beautiful sight I have ever seen on Islay took place at a time and in a place where few humans, and certainly no tourist, should have been, namely lonely Glen Golach on the Oa as dusk approached one November afternoon in 2003. In this narrow, hanging valley lie the two Glenastle lochs. Once you get down to the head of the first loch, the valley tapers away before you, so that only a thin braid of land at its distant tip seems to separate the water from the great sky above (and under brighter circumstances the wide sea beyond). To each side, the hills formed black silhouettes, massive yet graceful. The cloud-strewn sky was, at that moment, a great causeway of dappled white, grey and pewter, shot from the west with the urgent intensity of a distant and invisible setting sun. Invisible, that was, but for the salmon pink the dying sunlight had airbrushed on to the western edges of these gunmetal clouds. The seamless water mirrored every note of this sky, leaving the onlooker feeling suddenly projected upwards into a ruffled, metallic midheaven. I was briefly angelic.

On another occasion, visiting Bunnahabhain in early December 2002, I was lucky enough to meet Islay in one of its rare frosty moods. I woke, at the Bridgend Hotel, to find a rose light in the northern half of the sky and four or five squadrons of geese already on the move, anxious to locate their breakfast chlorophyll. The river Laggan was full and coolly brisk, tugging brownly at its banks; bare tree branches leaned over the water, the profuse lichen hanging off them like tufts of pale green wool. John MacLellan came to pick me up, and we set off towards Port Askaig, the winter mist lingering in the dips and hollows, while the low sun crept hydraulically up over the hill tops. As it crested them, everything suddenly seemed to catch fire. I was dazzled; how could John keep the car on the road? The sunlight seemed to explode in every ice-encrusted grass stem, each rime-heavy rowan twig, among all the frost-sharpened bramble thorns and through every glittering bracken shambles. At the darkest time of the year, we were driving through a carnival of light.

A stroll in winter sunlight, if you can find firm enough ground, will reveal how busy the god of small things can be on this island. Walking from Bunnahabhain to Rhuvaal, as I did on a sunny morning in November 2003 while the rest of the nation watched a famous rugby match, was a good choice, since the quad bike tracks of Howard and Suzanne Cobb (see pages 46–7) provided reliable footing. This walk was continually interrupted, however, as I marvelled at the way the sun was tangling with patches of moss to create a foam of transcendent green at a moment when growth was supposed to be in abeyance. Occasional burns interrupt the track, and the sunlight on the peat-stained quartzite pebbles which line them, caressed by brown water of hypnotic limpidity, provided slashes of dark brilliance across the exhausted pale brown of the late autumn hill.

More often, of course, the winter visitor to Islay will feast on both light and its antithesis, gathered into one single sky. I have written in 'Landfall' about Upper Killeyan on the Oa, where a chance meeting preceded hail and a tragic story. The two photographs I took on that occasion seem to brim with moving darkness and light. In one, the sheep of good fortune are just crossing a grassy flank which the sun has made emerald, while the rough hill land behind them drains and steams briefly; in the other, the sheep of ill fortune retreat from the cliff's edge into a dark, cold shadow-pasture of iron green, while the final few rays of light just burnish the tops of their fleeces. Beyond the darkness of the land, though, the bowl of the sea is obliterated with white brightness; the cliffs look as if they fringe a giant crater of light. Apocalypse can often appear imminent on Islay.

On a bad day, by contrast, the gloom can be absolute. My first view of Islay showed me McArthur's Head in the sweetness of May from a garlic-scented beach of white sand on Jura. The ferry provided exactly the same view as it laboured towards Port Askaig on 20 December 2002. Gone, now, was the Greek serenity; instead the black rocks plunged into a still sea of dark jade, while lithium clouds suffocated the peaks. A little paler light cascaded down Gleann Choireadail, but it only served to emphasis the clots and skirls of gathering darkness. The lighthouse had shed its monastic radiance and looked frail, vulnerable and lost as the weather and the night closed in about it. Our boat, indeed, seemed sturdier; the seamen stood outside, washing the windows with mops. As we made our way up the racing Sound of Islay, the sea surface grew troubled with eddies and foam. Suddenly, a broad glassy disc would drift by; then we would pass what seemed a mill race, where the water tumbled over a non-existent lip. It was impossible to read the great fists of water beneath, and the gigantic rock claws of the bottom, yet everything on the water's surface told the observer of how eventful matters were down there.

The weather can help the sea tell tales. On a sweet, still winter's day along the Kidalton coastline, all seems perfection, and each tiny morsel of rock part of an immaculate sea garden. The idea that anyone might bury hull-ripping rocks just beneath the surface seems impertinent. Wait, though, until the barometer drops and the clouds begin to trot; wait until the wind sets the trees bending. The skerries then come alive with waves and foam and, one by one, all the hidden rocks betray their presence – when the great waves rolling in from Antrim suddenly explode into the air for no reason, like geysers whose hour has come.

Winter can surprise at any time with light; spring can surprise with both light and warmth. I have already described that February day when, walking with Ardbeg's Douglas Bowman up to Loch Uigeadail, it grew so sunny and warm that I couldn't understand why the sky was not woven with larksong. By March, under clear skies, the light can grow extravagantly bright – and the Caol Ila daffodils, specimens as healthy and juicy as you are ever likely to see, seem almost delirious in their swaying, be-bop fits of yellow heroics. It was in March that Lagavulin's Donald Renwick had taken me up across the rangy grasses which lead to the Sholum Lochs and we found, in among their pale, weather-bleached scarecrow hair, a new seethe of green stems on the move. Exploring the high hills above Kintra on the northern hinge of the Oa on that same visit, I found I could lie down in a bed of bracken to rest for 20 minutes as warmly and comfortably as a dozing cat. Yet the very same morning, getting out of bed and opening the curtains at the Machrie Hotel, Islay had been immobile, held in a vice of steely winter mist. Expect anything, at any time.

Summer's long hours of daylight, of course, provide maximum opportunity to watch four seasons unfold in a day. If it's raining, know that the rain will stop; cloudless blue sky will rarely remain uncovered for long. Long, muggy, soupy hours can give way to a drench which dissolves in turn into a stealthy mist; a distant break in brooding clouds can create on the instant a sea of herringscale silver; and summer can blow, too, with uncomfortable penetration under a grey sky or with buffeting coruscation under a clearer one. But when the summer sun does command Islay, moments of glory follow. The soaring clarity and sparkle of the air is as intoxicating as any ten-year-old cask-strength malt; the seas are cobalt, dusted with solar glitter or licked white by a freshening breeze. In June you can step outside at midnight and still see a glow in the sky which, three hours later, will begin to surge again to the chatter of small birds. In summer, there is always time. Even the beasts know it. I drove back along the High Road late one evening in early July, and passed a field in which the silage had been freshly cut; a maternity unit of cows and their offspring was freshly installed there. In the low dusk light, the pale green felled meadow grass glowed like luminous paint. It was quarter to eleven at night, yet two calves were chasing each other friskily around the field. For joy; why else?

Caol Ila

In the hill's pocket
glow six copper acorns. Food
for wind-harried souls.

IF ANY ISLAY distillery can be said to occupy a secret location, it is Caol Ila (pronounced Coll Eela). An unguided explorer, landing on a primeval, virgin Islay with no maps to guide him and no roads to ease his path, would take months to find the beach beneath the steep, wooded cliffs which provides the distillery's site. The tumbling quartzite and sandstone, wiry with heather, has nowadays been tamed by lawns and shrubs; come spring, the daffodils braiding the road explode into light. The setting, though, remains that of a lip or a shelf set between a rugged open hill and a treacherous sea race, with the fierce, rangy emptiness of Jura beyond.

When Alfred Barnard visited in the bustling 1880s, all he could see of it as he was driven off the Port Askaig road was 'a stump of a tree on a rock' – which turned out to be the top of the distillery chimney. He, of course, was travelling by horse-drawn trap, and the route down to the distillery was 'so steep, and our nerves none of the best, that we insist[ed] on doing the remainder of the descent on foot, much to the disgust of the driver, who muttered strange words in Gaelic.' The setting, claimed Barnard, was 'the wildest and most picturesque locality we have seen . . . on the very verge of the sea, in a deep recess of the mountain, mostly cut out of the solid rock. The coast hereabouts is wild and broken, and detached pieces of rock lie here and there of such size that they form small islands.'

Even today, it lies at the end of a road which leads nowhere else. The exact route of the road down into the distillery has been altered since Barnard's day (there was a fatal lorry accident here in the late 1950s), yet the final approach still takes you on a steeply dropping ski-turn around the distillery buildings. When you get to the bottom, the sea water almost splashes the warehouse walls. As snug and secret as a nightjar's nest: that's Caol Ila. No wonder Diageo chose it as the first in its range of 'Hidden Malts'.

There is, of course, an irony in this. In terms of production, Caol Ila is Islay's elephant. No distillery on the island gushes like this one. You will find Caol Ila in more whisky blends than any of its fellow islanders, and if you come across a bottle of single malt claiming to come from Islay but without revealing its distillery of origin – from an independent bottler, for example, marketed under a fantasy name – then the chances are that its contents cascaded through the spirit safe at Caol Ila.

The single quayside warehouse, as it happens, is gradually filling up with whisky from its sister distillery, Lagavulin. Even if it contained nothing but Caol Ila, there would only be room for three months' production there. Every drop of spirit distilled at Caol Ila is now trucked off the island in bulk, and doesn't meet wood until it settles down on the Scottish mainland. Caol Ila, if you like, is Islay's flag carrier among the great gunships of the Scotch whisky industry. It's the antithesis of Bruichladdich.

It was founded in 1846 by Hector Henderson, a Glasgow businessman with extensive distillery interests; he had just, as it happens, withdrawn from Littlemill. The previous decade had seen a recession in the early Scotch whisky industry, with 61 of the newly licensed distilleries closing between 1835 and 1844. Things initially seemed to go well for Henderson: he bought Camlachie in Glasgow in 1847, and part-acquired the Lochindaal Distillery over at Port Charlotte in 1850. Two years later, though, his company was forced into receivership, and Norman Buchanan took over, acquiring the Isle of Jura distillery at around the same time. The Buchanan reign lasted eleven years before he, too, was sequestered. As so often, the blenders and merchants seemed better able to keep to their course through financial squalls than the distillers themselves, and it was blenders Bulloch Lade (the Bullochs had been in charge at Camlachie since 1856) who replaced Buchanan in 1863. The timing was right, since the boom of the heavy-drinking 1870s and the phylloxera-stoked 1880s was just around the corner. Bulloch Lade's stewardship lasted almost 70 years, and was initially a great success. Caol Ila was first marketed as a single malt under their early ownership, while Barnard claimed that during the 1880s it was on allocation only, 'such is the demand for this favourite Whisky'. The thirst for Caol Ila and other Islay classics (five per cent of which in a blend was said to 'cover' 95 per cent of bland grain whisky) inspired the creation of its northern neighbour Bunnahabhain.

The problems caused for the blended whisky market by the First World War and American Prohibition saw Bulloch Lade go into liquidation in 1920. The distillery then swiftly passed through the hands of failing Dallas Dhu owner J.P. O'Brien and on to a consortium called Caol Ila Distillery Ltd in which whisky blender Robertson and Baxter played a leading role. By 1927, though, after seven difficult post-Prohibition years, the mighty DCL (Distillers Company Limited) had won control, and in DCL's variously gloved hands it has remained ever since. Diageo is, of course, the latest multinational name for what was once DCL.

Caol Ila endured a longer closure than most during the Depression of the 1930s (1930–37), and another three years of silence fell during World War Two (1942–45). After that, all was steam and plenty until the early 1970s, when it was decided to rebuild the entire distillery. Process operator Neil MacLean (since retired) was the oldest distillery worker when I visited; he remembered the friendly, intimate atmosphere of Caol Ila before the rebuild, when the floor maltings were still operational and there were only two stills. There were 34 staff year-round then; Dutch barges brought in the grain, and the company's own puffer, the *Pibroch*, supplied the coal and took away the spirit. During the two years in which the distillery was rebuilt, Neil had to work on the roads, and when he came back 'it seemed like a different distillery. It was more like a factory. We all felt a bit sad about it.' The six new stills, though, had been closely modelled on the existing two, and Neil recalled how the new make seemed much the same to the workers as the older version, which was a tribute to the workmanship of those in charge of the rebuild. The modern feel of Caol Ila, too, was not inappropriate, since this had always been a distillery ahead of its time, as former general manager Grant Carmichael points out. 'Caol Ila had condensers, horizontal ones, when everyone else on the island had worm tubs for condensing. And it always had steam firing for its spirit stills, even when the others were directly fired.'

Caol Ila had a difficult patch in the 1980s. 'Things were very low here,' remembers present-day manager Billy Stitchell. 'There was actually a time when we were laid off for thirteen weeks, plus there were four-day weeks when we were just ticking over at five mashes a week, which was nothing for a place this size. If we hadn't had friends in high places, I think we would probably have been shut totally.' Times, happily, are more promising now, and Caol Ila purrs away, producing between 3.2 and 3.5 million litres of pure alcohol a year. Not all to the same peat specification, of course: more of this later.

The earliest existing photograph of Caol Ila dates from around 1870, and was published in a pamphlet to mark the distillery's 150th anniversary in 1996. The scene it shows is a lively one, with at least four sizeable sailing ships moored to the quay, seven visible distillery buildings, and more humans scuttling around them than you will ever see at Caol Ila today save during Islay's whisky festival. The photographer even managed to site a decorative family group on rocks in the foreground. The photograph was taken from the southern end of the bay, more or less at the place where a cottage of simple, Ionian perfection now stands. This is Yellow Rock Cottage, the home of Lily MacDougall, the mother of Christine Logan of Bowmore.

Caol Ila means 'Sound of Islay'; the view here is haunting. It does not have the soft dreaminess that you find on a calm summer day down at the Kidalton distilleries, nor the savage howl of a westerly gale beating down on Bruichladdich or Bowmore, nor even the cool, polar perfection of still winter weather a little way north up the Sound at Bunnahabhain. What it does have is drama. The view of the Paps of Jura (two, as usual, obscuring the third) is never better than from here, and it is here, too, that you can watch the illogical eddies and sinister, oily curls of the seven-knot tide race between the two islands. Observing the flotilla brought by the Classic Malts cruise lunging and swerving out of the flow for the safety of Caol Ila's moorings each summer makes for pulse-quickening entertainment. The panorama through the clear plate glass of the stillroom is so mesmerising that you wonder how the stillmen manage to concentrate on their work; the same goes for the prospect from the distillery manager's terraced office, which seems to hang over the water like a kingfisher's perch.

Behind the distillery itself is a waterfall. Its proximity to the alcoholic fumes of the place is testified by the fact that the trunks and branches of the trees and bushes from which the water cascades are black. No, not the scars of a former fire, but a coating of the minute *Torula* fungus which survives on alcohol vapour, and which renders spirit warehouses black not only on Islay but in Bristol, Cognac and Armagnac, too.

If there has been activity in the hidden cove of Caol Ila for centuries, it is because of that waterfall and the easy power and cleaning source which it provided; indeed there was a waterwheel on the fall which powered everything in the distillery via a series of drive belts

prior to electricity arriving on the island in the late 1940s. Islay's lead and silver mining area lies some way inland from Caol Ila at Mulreesh and Robolls, near Finlaggan, but smelting took place at Caol Ila, as author Thomas Pennant observed in 1772. Manager Billy Stitchell's grandfather and great-grandfather both worked here, and he remembers stories of those earlier times. 'The area around Finlaggan was full of mines: lead, silver, other metals as well. Ballygrant Inn was the mine manager's house, and in Ballygrant there was a row of houses called Miners' Row, and it was full of Welshmen and Cornishmen who came up to do the mining. I had an uncle called Edwards: I think that was a Welsh name. There were buildings at Caol Ila that were part of the mining industry at one stage. There was huge mobility of people, then; it was the same with the herring fishing. There used to be a herring station up at Bachlaig, just to the north of Bunnahabhain; you can still see the slips if you go up there. The herring fishers used to come in and dry their clothes at the kilns and things like that, and they'd swap fish for drams. The women who did the gutting and filled the barrels were from the East Coast – Aberdeen and round that way. The herring fishing used to be very big on Islay. But my grandfather told me that one winter there was a huge storm and the herring never came back. Just disappeared.'

It seems barely credible nowadays, but the little beaches which lie just north of Caol Ila were also, once, an address of sorts. There are two or three collapsing shacks on them today, but Billy remembers the names of the families who owned them. 'The McIndeors lived in the first one, and then the one where all the tin has collapsed down the way, that belonged to the Buies. I'm told that when it was Glasgow Fair time in the summer, everything would shut up in Glasgow and all the family would come home, so you'd get anything up to fifty or sixty people living in these shanties. The last one to be used was the furthest one along; that belonged to Neil MacTaggart, a stillman at Caol Ila. He used to stay in it sometimes in the summer time; just an odd night.' Meanwhile, one of the prettiest and easiest of all Islay's off-road walks is to take the old path which leads from the south of the distillery (it begins under the former distillery manager's house, which now belongs permanently to Billy Stitchell) over the hills to Port Askaig. 'That was called the Burma Road,' says Billy; the name was a World War Two joke. 'There were no cars here in the old days, so that was the path. Everybody walked.' At a sharp, sunny moment like the March afternoon on which I walked these gentle crags, the views from the Burma Road of the CalMac ferry arriving at and leaving Port Askaig were almost aerial, buzzard-clear. New grass shoots were pushing up from between the fawn bones of the dry bracken, while the painfully cheerful gorse flowers swarmed like bees on their bushes. The Sound of Islay was unusually still, its surface merely feather-flicked by the tidal agitation beneath, while the sunlight invading it all the way to its pale bottom turned the water an improbable turquoise. Port Askaig, from the cliffs above, looked like a model village, dappled by the sunlight falling through the bare trees which shelter the drive up to Bruno Schroder's Dunlossit House. The walk seemed a privilege.

THE HILL

As at Bunnahabhain, peat was cut locally, part of it from Islay Estate land at Ardnahoe and further up the coast at Rhuvaal, and part of it on Jura. The process water, meanwhile, comes from Loch Nam Ban, which Alfred Barnard described as 'a lovely lake called Torrabus'. Warehouseman Donald Morrison took me up to see it: it lies just up the track which begins opposite Torrabus Farm on the road to Bunnahabhain. Since it is a relatively short distance down to the distillery, it is piped all the way. For such a busy distillery (Billy reckons he must use around two million litres a week when in full production), the loch seems surprisingly petite, and the source of its water is also something of a mystery. 'It's quite high up,' says Billy, 'so it actually has quite a small catchment area. There's no hills to speak of around it; no rivers and no burns. I guess there must be a lot of drains on the far side which keep it fed, plus the rainfall. It's quite shallow at the dam end.' I suspect Barnard never visited his 'lovely' Lake Torrabus, since he claimed (in a suspiciously purple patch) it was 'nestling among the mountains, over which ever and anon the fragrant breeze from the myrtle and the blooming heather is wafted'. In fact, it's a high pool in a bare scene. It is certainly peaty, though it seemed (to my crudely calibrated eye) less so than the three Kidalton water sources, especially Laphroaig's Loch na Beinn Brice. Thirsty Caol Ila, fed by this smallish loch, is vulnerable to dry spells: the distillery shut for a full seven weeks because of the 1997 drought. It's unique on the island, though, in using sea water to cool its fresh water during the summer, pumping in 150,000 litres an hour to run through a massive heat exchanger.

The malt all comes from Port Ellen, and for Caol Ila itself the peat spec is 35 ppm. This is identical to Lagavulin – yet the finished spirit contains only 12–13 ppm, in contrast to Lagavulin's 16–18 ppm. Why the difference? We'll discover a little later, when Billy talks us through the Caol Ila distilling process. 'It's been thirty-five ppm consistently for the last ten years,' he confirms, 'though we did do some low-phenol trials in the nineteen-eighties. I don't exactly know what the figures were, but I think it was around ten ppm.'

It may happen, though, that you pay a visit to Caol Ila and fail to smell peat at all. If so, that is because the distillery will be distilling what is called Caol Ila Highland, an entirely unpeated spirit used for blending only. (All distillery-bottled Caol Ila is the classic peated spirit, based on a 35 ppm malt spec.) More of this, too, below. The reason, by the way, that Caol Ila and Lagavulin have the same peat spec, according to former general manager Grant Carmichael, was simply convenience; Port Ellen, when it worked as a distillery, had a spec of 35 ppm too. All the malt being puffered or barged out by DCL to its three Islay distilleries was thus interchangeable.

WALKING CAOL ILA

Unlike the distillery itself, the mash tun is not the largest on the island (Bunnahabhain's is bigger); it's been a full Lauter version since 1989, which has halved the mashing time. It is, though, one of two cast-iron mash tuns on the island, the other being at Bunnahabhain. There are eight Oregon pine washbacks, and Billy smilingly tells me he isn't able to plunge into the controversy about whether or not this has any sort of effect on flavour, since he has never worked with stainless-steel versions. He does admit that the wooden ones 'form a slight crust on them, which you don't really want to clean off'. That would not be true of stainless steel.

What certainly matters at Caol Ila is the temperature at which the wash goes into the washbacks. 'The temperature is critical. We're lower than most – at around sixteen degrees Centigrade. What we want is a clean, green, grassy spirit. If the wort is too warm and fermentations are too quick, we run the risk of creating a nutty spirit, which is wrong for Caol Ila. Our short fermentations [during the week] are a minimum of eighty hours, and our long fermentations [over the weekend] are around one hundred and twenty hours. We do eight of each for the peated spirit per week, and eight long and just four short for the unpeated spirit.' Compare these long, leisurely, relatively cool fermentations with the warmer, brisker ones at Lagavulin to see the first of the major flavour-creating differences between these two distilleries which, despite using identical malt, send such different spirit to market.

The unpeated Caol Ila Highland is, according to Billy, harder to produce than the peaty Caol Ila itself; not only does it have to be fermented more slowly but it also has to be distilled more slowly, too. 'There's lots of subtle things you've got to do to get the results you want; it's certainly not as easy as making peated spirit. The guys have got to work a lot harder.' An example? 'In the midweek break, we open up all the doors to expose the copper to oxygen to regenerate the copperwork inside. Getting the spirit vapour to run over clean copper inside the still helps give you the lighter spirit we are looking for. It's a whole lot of wee bits and pieces.' On the day I walked the distillery with Billy, 27 March 2003, it was Caol Ila Highland and not Caol Ila running from the stills, and the smell was that of sweet, oven-toasted cereals, not the wilder, smokier whiff of peaty spirit. Billy confirms that the Highland spirit is very popular with blenders. 'There's a market out there which can take everything we produce. It's always been the case here that we can produce large volumes of consistent spirit, and that's what blenders want. They want to know that if you put a certain new make into a cask, then in ten or twelve years they'll get exactly the spirit they want.'

After those dawdling fermentations, it is of course time for distillation. Another way in which to create Caol Ila's nuanced, elegant, light-bodied style is not to fill the stills too full; the charge for both wash stills and spirit stills is just a whisper over half their total contents. This gives the wash and the low wines plenty of chance to 'chat' with the microfilaments of the copper as they bubble and vaporise in the still.

Caol Ila's three identical wash stills and three identical spirit stills are all tall, and plain in design rather than ball or lamp-glass; the wash-still pots are slightly squatter than those of the spirit stills, which are more gently contoured. The lyne arms for the spirit stills slope down very gently (about 5°), though in the distillery itself they can look from certain viewpoints almost horizontal; those running off the wash stills have a more pronounced downward slope (about 10°), though less so than at Lagavulin. These six seem the most handsome stills on the island, though the cool north-easterly light which cascades through the tall stillhouse windows, burnishing their copper, may have something to do with this, as may the great sliding, churning mass of the Sound of Islay beyond. There is plenty of opportunity for reflux within the bellies of these great, airy beasts.

Perhaps the most important of all the differences between Caol Ila and Lagavulin, though, is the fact that Caol Ila's cuts are much smaller than Lagavulin's. The wash-still collection range begins at just 42 per cent rather than 50 per cent at Lagavulin, running down to 1 per cent over around four hours to give (once the feints have been added) a low wines strength of around 28 per cent. When it comes to the spirit run, Caol Ila comes on at 75 per cent and is taken off around two-and-a-half hours later at around 65 per cent, whereas Lagavulin comes on at 72 per cent and is taken off at 59 per cent. This gives Lagavulin an average spirit collection strength of 68.5 per cent, whereas Caol Ila's is closer to 71 per cent; both, of course, are reduced to 63.5 per cent for filling (though that reduction will be made by mainland water at Cambus for Caol Ila, whereas Lagavulin is cut with water from Islay's Loch Sholum). The search at Caol Ila, in other words, is for the lighter, finer, higher alcohols rather than the more rumbustious, gustier, more phenolic alcohols gathered up at Lagavulin (and to a still greater extent at Laphroaig).

What about Caol Ila Highland? The main difference in the way the stills are run, according to Billy, is that both wash and low wines begin at lower temperatures and are brought up to evaporation points more slowly for the Highland spirit, so the distillation cycle takes longer. The cuts are identical.

The brewing and distilling refinement of the peat character in Caol Ila is evident from the start, in its new make, which is much less earthy and smoky than at Lagavulin or Laphroaig, and more hospital-like (there's an antiseptic, TCP note, and a clear resemblance to coal-tar soap). There is also a floral hint, and a touch of vellum and musk. Caol Ila Highland's new make is, of course, a very different style of spirit: much fresher and creamier.

And that is the point at which the spirit says farewell to its island home. The plain fact is that the contents of every bottle of Caol Ila has spent little more than a week or two on the island, with all its long years of maturation passed elsewhere. The casks (second-fill and third-fill American ex-bourbon hogsheads and barrels) are filled on the Scottish mainland at Cambus, Blythswood, Bonnybridge or Auchroisk, then stored at Cambus itself, Blackgrange, Carsebridge, Menstrie or Leven. Caol Ila is bottled at Leven.

Given this, to what extent can we consider Caol Ila a genuine Islay malt? This question is discussed at length in the Lagavulin chapter, since most Lagavulin, too, is aged away from Islay. The official Diageo line is that (to use the word chosen by distilling expert Douglas Murray) it is 'irrelevant' whether Lagavulin or Caol Ila are aged on Islay or in Central Scotland. Billy Stitchell points out that Caol Ila has never traditionally been aged on the island, since there is so little storage space at the distillery; even in the days when the former Lochindaal warehouses were used for Caol Ila, much of it used to leave the island on the *Pibroch*.

My own view is that this is indeed irrelevant for the bulk of production from Caol Ila, since all of this spirit will eventually be 'lost' in blends. Hidden away inside a bottle of Johnnie Walker, Teacher's or Famous Grouse, who cares? The consistency and quality of the blend is all that interests drinkers. But for the two per cent of those 3.5 million litres which does go to market as Caol Ila branded single malt (approximately 70,000 litres), the place and circumstances of its ageing matter enormously. Caol Ila's packaging makes great play of the fact that this 'hidden malt' is an 'Islay single malt whisky' and that it is 'highly prized among devotees of the Islay style'. It does not seem fair to market a spirit in this way which has only ever spent a fortnight on Islay. It would certainly not be beyond the resources of the mighty Diageo to build enough warehousing locally in which to store the relatively small amounts of Caol Ila it is likely to sell under the distillery name. This is simply a question of honesty, regardless of whether or not passing 18 years on Islay would produce a different result than passing 18 years near Alloa.

Size aside, big Caol Ila is the most important distillery on the island in another way, too. The process of distilling produces enormous quantities of liquid waste. When you look at the fermenting wash in a washback, it's important to remember that most of it will eventually be thrown away – a combination of the pot ale which is left behind in the wash still, and the spent lees which are left behind in the spirit still. Water used for washing vessels, too, has to be disposed of responsibly. Caol Ila disposes not only of its own liquid waste, but also of that from Bruichladdich, Bowmore, Lagavulin and the distillery on the Isle of Jura. Laphroaig has a long enough pipe to dispose of its own waste out beyond the confines of its little bay, while that from Ardbeg is taken by Islay Estates to spread on its land. Bunnahabhain, meanwhile, is in the same lucky position as Caol Ila, that good fortune being to have a seven-knot tide race at the bottom of the pier.

'It's all part of the European Waste Water Directive,' smiles Billy, 'designed to clean up the Rhine – but it's had a huge effect on Islay. We can have up to eighty tankers a week taking the road up to Caol Ila.' Indeed; the small road has had to be resurfaced to cope with the strain, and since Islay road fuel is among the most expensive in Europe, this directive will have put pennies on every case of Islay malt. Fortunately, the lorries don't go all the way down to the distillery; there are two big collecting tanks up on the hillside above Caol Ila. Each contains 30,000 litres of waste; and it's pumped out at ten litres per second, night and day, to a point 100 feet out, where the marine express-train passing through the Sound scours its way along a 90-foot trench. 'The authorities wanted 1000:1 dilution, but the tide race means we give them a lot more than that.' Was it really necessary? 'I think some things could be a bit more flexible. Distillery waste, remember, isn't toxic; it's just part of the food chain. We've been pumping for two years now, and

I've never seen so many fish in the bay as there are now. There was even a basking shark last summer.'

TASTING CAOL ILA

Caol Ila is the elephant of Islay, and 3.5 million litres of spirit fills a lot of bottles. Why am I repeating myself? Simply to point out that it is very easy to acquire Caol Ila on the open market. The consequence is that most independent bottlers will be able to offer individual casks of Caol Ila. The standard of these independent bottlings varies a great deal as always; this will remain the case so long as the Scotch whisky industry relies on second-hand casks in which to age its spirit for decade after decade. None of it, moreover, will have been aged on Islay. If you want to try Caol Ila, I would urge you to acquire one of the three 'Hidden Malts' distillery bottlings. Not only is there a chance that a tiny percentage of the spirit will have been aged on Islay, but more practically no bottler will have a greater range of casks of Caol Ila to chose from than its owner, and only the best will be used. So what are these three malts like?

The 12-year-old is a dram of pale refinement. You can still detect the hospital wards so typical of the infant spirit on the nose, though the subtle oaking (and all that clean Firth of Forth air) has given it some lift and fill, some light cream and fat, a faint hint of pears and honey. After a while, it remembers its malt origins with the crisp cereal notes familiar to anyone who has ever crunched a mouthful of malted barley (or sat down to a bowlful of wholegrain breakfast cereals); leave it a little longer again, and something resembling sizzling bacon fat shows up. Neat, it's sinewy, leanly smoky and mouth-wateringly clean to finish; add a dash of water and you have a very pure, catwalk-elegant dram in which the long-legged 'cratur' strides out across the mouth with an alluring flourish of smoky lemon.

The cask-strength version (a slightly younger spirit, though bottled without an indication of age) is every bit as pale, and seems to need a splash of water, or some very brisk aeration, to begin to detonate its aromas. These are a little dryer and greener than for the 12-year-old, with lots of hay and sweet-flower scents, like the memory of the flower-strewn grasslands up near the shoreline at Ardnave or Kilchoman on a hot, lark-loud June day. You know the peat's there, but once you've made the acquaintance of the dram, it's easy to forget it, lost in all that bright, clean air. In the mouth, there's a pale fire licking gently, and a wonderfully appetising, sappy, almost shocking quality to it, like the teasing flick of a wet towel just when you least expect it. The shy weal on your soft tongue then subsides, very creamily. Agreed, I could add more water, but nothing quite this well bred ever resorts to true violence. (Talisker it isn't.)

The 18-year-old, finally, is deeper in colour, though we're still only addressing a light, green-tinged gold. The scents are extraordinary, particularly when first poured. Is it back to hospital, with those hints of lint and linseed, of antiseptic cream and talc? Or are we in a vegetable rather than a flower garden, slicing courgettes from their stalks, pruning trees and cutting dry grass? Taken neat, this is a solid, surprisingly chewy dram with honeyed, herbal edges; add water, and you'll bring out the sweetness, spreading honey over the oily lemon. I suppose it's an accident that the two most elegant whiskies on Islay come from close northern neighbours Caol Ila and Bunnahabhain. It can't be the air; it can't be the light; it can't be the water – but it's true for all that.

Caol Ila　　DISTILLERY FACTFILE

Distillery operating hours	*5 days a week @ 24 hours a day*
Number of employees	*11 full-time; 1 seasonal*
Water source	*Loch Nam Ban*
Water reserve	*not known*
Water colour	*brown*
Peat content of water	*trace*
Malt source	*Port Ellen*
Own floor maltings?	*no*
Malt type	*Optic*
Malt specification phenols	*average 35 ppm (Caol Ila); 0 ppm (Caol Ila Highland)*

Finished spirit phenols	–	*average 12–13 ppm (Caol Ila); 0 ppm (Caol Ila Highland)*
Malt storage	–	*250 tonnes*
Mill type	–	*Porteus, installed late 1950s*
Grist storage	–	*23 tonnes*
Mash tun construction	–	*cast iron, steel bottom, copper top, Lauter*
Mash size	–	*11.5 tonnes*
First water	–	*42,000 litres at 68.5°C*
Second water	–	*13,500 litres at 76°C*
Third water	–	*44,000 litres at 79°C*
Number of washbacks	–	*8*
Washback construction	–	*Oregon pine*
Washback charge	–	*54,000 litres*
Yeast	–	*Mauri cultured yeast*
Amount of yeast	–	*150 kg per washback*
Length of fermentation	–	*80 hours (shorts: week); 120 hours (longs: weekend)*
Initial fermentation temperature	–	*16°C*
Strength of wash	–	*8 per cent abv*
Number of wash stills	–	*3*
Wash stills built	–	*1974*
Wash still capacity	–	*35,345 litres*
Wash still charge	–	*18,000 litres (51 per cent of capacity)*
Heat source	–	*steam pans*
Wash still height	–	*23 feet (7 metres)*
Wash still shape	–	*plain*
Lyne arm	–	*gently descending (10°)*
Length of low-wines run	–	*c. 4 hours*
Low-wines collection range	–	*42 per cent abv – 1 per cent abv*
Number of spirit stills	–	*3*
Spirit still built	–	*1974*
Spirit still capacity	–	*29,549 litres*
Spirit still charge	–	*11,000–12,000 litres (37–41 per cent of capacity)*
Strength of spirit still charge	–	*c. 28 per cent abv*
Heat source	–	*steam coils*

Spirit still height   – *20 feet (6.09 m)*

Spirit still shape   – *plain*

Lyne arm   – *very gently descending (5°)*

Purifier?   – *no*

Condensers   – *six, internally sited, 10 feet 6 inches (3.2 m) long, each containing 171 one-inch (2.54 cm) tubes*

Length of foreshot run   – *around 25–30 minutes*

Length of spirit run   – *2^1/$_2$–3 hours*

Length of feints run   – *3–3^1/$_2$ hours*

Spirit cut   – *75 per cent abv – 65 per cent abv*

Distilling strength   – *70.5 per cent abv average*

Storage strength   – *63.5 per cent abv*

Average spirit yield   – *403 litres of pure alcohol per tonne of malt (2003)*

Disposal of pot ale and spent lees   – *dispersed in Sound of Islay*

Type of casks filled for branded malt   – *100 per cent second-fill and third-fill American oak hogsheads and barrels for Hidden Malts series*

Current annual output   – *3,500,000 litres of pure alcohol*

Number of warehouses   – *1 on Islay, but all stock now tankered off Islay for filling and ageing*

Type of warehouses   – *dunnage (on Islay); racked (on mainland)*

Storage capacity on Islay   – *3,000 casks and diminishing*

Percentage of branded malt entirely aged on Islay   – *almost none*

Vatting and bottling location   – *matured at Blackgrange, Cambus, Carsebridge, Menstrie or Leven; vatted and bottled at Leven (in Fife)*

Distillery expressions   – *10-year-old (approx) cask-strength (55 per cent, non-chill-filtered)*
  – *12-year-old*
  – *18-year-old*

Major blending roles   – *Johnnie Walker range; Bells; Black Bottle*

CHAPTER SIX

Nature

A foam of flowers,
dung, carrion, the gorged buzzard
chick: June's field of genes.

IT WAS GROWING DARK AGAIN. Dark – long before the evening news bulletins; long before any justification for a pre-dinner dram; long before the light inside the plastic pint of Guinness on the bar of the Bridgend Hotel had even been switched on. I looked out of the window, up to the last gleam in the sky. There were continents and countries mapped out up there: dark capes, mussel-shell promontories, sinister bluffs and chill grey plains separated by lighter flows of marine clarity. And, silhouetted with chill exactitude as they passed over the last breaks of pale blue, a dozen distant geese. They seemed minute from my tiny hotel room – and yet, from 500 feet up, as they trudged home across the familiar cold prairie of the sky, the building which hid me must have seemed to their wary eyes more insignificant still, a black void pricked out with a point or two of artificial light.

Something – a little spare time, a little restless sadness – then took me out, torchless, for a dusk walk into Bridgend Woods. I had left it too late; night had fallen; but the path was an even one, so I felt I could press on into this shady oblivion with relative safety. The geese were now invisible – but audible above me, skein after skein, whiffling home. They are supposed to bark. All I could hear was a sky full of rusty doors, swinging to and fro in the breeze.

The path reached a small footbridge over the river Sorn; beyond lie enclosed fields. Again I saw little – but I knew this was goose city, for a low sociable parping chatter filled the night air. The stars were bright; no moon, though. On a bright moonlit night, they will carry on eating all night. Life, health and happiness, for a barnacle goose, can be summed up in one word: fat. The acquisition of fat is the meaning of goosely existence. Islay provides.

To whom does Islay belong? To its three main landowners, Lord Margadale, Bruno Schroder and the Mactaggarts? Only by the letter of the law, as they would be the first to admit. To its 3,000 islanders? More persuasively, for sure, though the vast majority of land on the island will never see a booted human foot from one year's end to the next. Or does Islay belong above all to its animals and birds, its flowers, its rushes and bog moss? Only the most obsessive whisky lover could visit the island and fail to notice that the setting for its seven distinguished distilleries is a magnificent one. Nature frames Caol Ila; nature swaddles Ardbeg; nature invades Bunnahabhain. Nature, I have often thought, is so ubiquitously present on Islay that it tends to rise up like a tide between human beings themselves, sending them bobbing helplessly away from each other despite best intentions. Quietness and shyness, the burden of the unspoken, closes swiftly around human speech on Islay – even between those out for a companionable drink with each other, or sharing a married lifetime together. The breeze between beings never drops; the curlew's cry may lie dormant in every ear, but it never quite fades. This is an intimate part of the misery and bliss of life on Islay.

This chapter belongs to those Ileachs who may not be able to write or to speak, but who can fly from one side of the island to the other, make a home in its cow pats or lounge amongst its kelp; who may, perhaps, have no hearts at all, but instead flaunt spotty petals or lush green blades. Beginning with Islay's most celebrated winter visitors.

They've passed summer off the map. Most representations of Europe stop at Iceland and the northern reaches of Norway. Atlases, indeed, show their summer residence quite correctly as lying closer to the Canadian Arctic than it does to the nation which claims political dominion over it, namely Denmark. Islay's geese spend summer breeding in Greenland.

There are two species. The most abundant is the barnacle goose, some 35,000 of whom land at Loch Gruinart every October before spreading out around the island. It is a sociable, noisy and gregarious bird, elegant and dapper with its white underbelly, grey-and-black barred back and long black neck, vaguely recalling an Edwardian gentleman in evening dress. It has bred in small colonies on rocky ledges above large glacial valleys in Eastern Greenland; the young are called off their perches by the parents, and their first 'flight' is in fact a fluff-stiffening tumble into the void. Once fat permits, and as the north wind of winter begins to blow, they fly south to Iceland, feed again for two or three weeks, and then make off for Islay and other smaller Scottish islands, as well as to Ireland. Mostly to Islay, though, which is called home by two-thirds of the Greenland population; there is a smaller population from the Norwegian Arctic islands of Svalbard (Spitsbergen) which goes to the Solway Firth, while the Siberian population makes for the Hook of Holland.

The barnacle loves short grass, which Islay's extensive grazing farmland provides in abundance; it snips the blades deftly, up to 200 times a minute. Its natural foods are the clovers and grasses found on tidal islands and saltings. In common with many geese, it is, as Islay's most distinguished ornithologist Dr Malcolm Ogilvie explains, 'an inefficient feeder. Cows have gut bacteria which digest the cellulose; geese can't. So what geese do is eat seven or eight hours a day, but all they're getting out of it is the juices, the starches and sugars in the cells of the grass juice.' If you tease apart the small, green cylindrical goose droppings, you can still (with the aid of a microscope) identify the species of grass which it has been eating; all the goose has done is to break down the cell walls using grit in its gizzard. It does not require a great deal of deduction to work out that these prodigal eating habits put it in conflict with Islay's farmers, especially since barnacle geese numbers on Islay have risen threefold during the last four decades of the twentieth century.

Barnacles don't have Islay to themselves, though. Another goose shares its winter quarters; indeed were Islay not farmed, it would be this goose which would be the prime beneficiary, since it is equipped to graze the desolate peat bogs which leave barnacles nonplussed. It's a quieter, more placid, less sociable bird which breeds in the lonely lochs and marshes of Western Greenland, enjoying summer views of chill brilliance over the Davis Strait and Baffin Bay. It has further to come, of course, but it is bigger (3.5 kg, compared with 2 kg for the average barnacle goose). This meatiness (which translates into better eating) costs it dear in Iceland, where up to ten per cent of the population gets shot each year before reaching the protection of the European Union. (Those shooting it are chiefly the European Union citizens of Italy and Germany.) This is the Greenland white-fronted goose – a confusing name, since if any goose on Islay looks as if it has a 'white front', it is the barnacle goose with its white face and underbelly. The Greenland white-fronted goose has a preponderantly dark head and neck with a brown-flecked chest; the 'white front' referred to in its name is a very small white area at the front of its face and behind its orange bill. You can easily tell a white-front from a barnacle goose, though, since the two look so different (the white front seems to wear beige country casuals compared to the barnacle's dinner jacket) and the white front will nearly always form part of a smaller flock, and sometimes just an isolated family unit. Islay's 10,000–11,000 winter white fronts constitute some 40 per cent of the world population; others go to Wexford in Ireland. 'It's actually a digging goose,' says Malcolm Ogilvie; 'it's got a much bigger probing bill than a barnacle goose, and its natural feeding is on the roots and tubers of bog plants like cotton grass, bogbean and deergrass.' It has, though, learned to like grazing, and the fact that it uproots the entire plant rather than merely snipping the grass blade makes it even less popular than the barnacle goose with Islay farmers.

The barnacle geese tend to spend the nights in two enormous roosts, one at the head of Loch Indaal around Bridgend, and the other on the flats of the RSPB Reserve at Loch Gruinart, whereas the white fronts have smaller, more scattered and more private roosts. There are, suggests Malcolm Ogilvie, no great differences between the temperatures they experience in Greenland in summer and on Islay in winter: it is moderately cold all the time, which is fine for a fat goose. They feel the passing of time acutely, though, since they experience huge differences in terms of light; at the height of Greenland's short summer the sun will shine all night, whereas on a gloomy December day on Islay it barely seems to get light at all. Whenever they can feed, they will, since they need fat for their journeys north and south, and barnacle geese in particular return (in April) to an almost foodless environment; for half of the period of egg incubation above the cold glacial valleys, the female barnacle goose is living on her reserves. They encounter few if any humans in Greenland, and even on Islay are shy; any close approach will invariably send them clambering up into the sky with a universal cry woven of hundreds of individual yelps, preceded by a noise like a dry fire igniting suddenly, caused by their wings thrashing the air. The white fronts are slightly harder to alarm than the nervy barnacles, who station watcher geese on the outside of their flocks. No one who has ever seen a large flock descending will ever forget how moving the sight of a thousand shy heavy birds labouring out of the air can be. The vast skies of every winter dawn or dusk are invariably given perspective, too, by half-a-dozen gaggly braids or squadrons of geese (the white fronts fly more neatly), making brave headway into what seems to humans to be chill, lonely emptiness, but which to them doubtless feels a familiar and companionable void.

THE COW-PAT GOURMET

Islay has two other 'star' bird species. One is an exuberant extrovert, easy to see and impossible to dislike; the other is a petrified introvert, highly audible (to insomniacs), but desperately shy. The extrovert spends the year on Islay, whereas the introvert steals up improbably from Southern Africa in late spring. Let's start with the resident: the chough.

Islay has most of the Scottish population of this particular corvid, which means around 60 pairs (a quarter of the total British population; the rest are on the Isle of Man, in Wales and in Cornwall). It doesn't look starkly different from a crow or a rook – until you catch a glimpse of its beak and its legs, which are bright pillar-box red; moreover the beak has a debonair curve to it. It's a spectacular flyer, playing, wheeling, flopping and tumbling in the air, its splayed wing tips giving it a deliciously ragged look. Above all, though, it is its call which will attract your attention: lustily asthmatic, twangy and springing, occasionally sounding like the noise produced by 'death-ray guns' of the type favoured by exuberant seven-year-olds. Towards the end of June 2003 I was walking the track which leads from Octofad through the Rhinns forestry plantations to the coast road and beautiful Lossit beach. There's an old iron shed up on the hill above Octofad; it was improbably noisy inside, and that noise sounded like a technical rehearsal for a *Star Wars* battle scene. Eventually it stopped – and out flew two juvenile choughs, looking very pleased with themselves.

Why, when other family members have been so successful, are choughs now so scarce? 'Chough food disappears; choughs disappear. The link,' says Malcolm Ogilvie, 'is really very strong.' The clowning chough's one failing is that it is a picky eater. It likes . . . almost anything which might make the same martial seven-year-old say 'Yuk'. Leatherjackets (cranefly larvae) are a favourite, and few things can make a chough's eye light up like a five-day-old cow pat. Once it has stopped steaming, the nourishing pat is colonised by dung beetles and (in the summer) by dung flies, who lay eggs in the warm faecal matter. These eggs hatch into grubs, which choughs love; they tear the cow pats apart in their frenzy for these squirming morsels. Other insects will do, too – but the chough must have short grass; they can't find what they're looking for in the long grass.

The importance of the cow pat is one reason why Islay's farmers are paid money to keep their cattle outside all winter – especially Mark French at Rockside and Robert Epps at Ardnave, whose grassy sand dunes are the best place to see winter choughs. This outwintering has long been traditional on mild Islay. 'None but milch cows are housed,' wrote Thomas Pennant in 1772; 'cattle of all other kinds, except the saddle horses, run out during winter.' There had been no outwintered cattle on the Oa for seven years when the RSPB took over Upper Killeyan; sure enough, the choughs had disappeared. The RSPB put cattle back on the land in winter – and now there are three or four pairs of choughs nesting there. Their traditional nesting place is dark coastal caves, but of late they have decided that empty farm buildings are an acceptable substitute. In summer, the choughs (which are highly territorial) are dispersed around the island's coasts; in winter, by contrast, they flock. 'The winter flocks are very active,' says the RSPB's Land Operations Manager James How. 'It's a great time to watch them clowning. You can see them kicking each other, running round and nicking food off each other . . . though it's all pretty good humoured.'

A LONG, SEXY SUMMER

What a contrast to the introvert. The corncrake is just a little slip of a bird (five or six ounces, or around 160 g) whose flight is described by a leading ornithological guide as 'weak and fluttering' – though the nineteenth-century cookery writer Mrs Beeton said that it flew 'in an extremely heavy and embarrassed manner, and with its legs hanging down'. Weak? Embarrassed? Hardly. It manages to fly from Tanzania to the field in which it was born on Islay in April – and then back again in September. The corncrake should not be judged by appearances.

Not that you're likely to enjoy an appearance. No sooner has it touched down than it scuttles into long grass or nettles, and there it stays – 'skulking', as the bird literature has it, though that seems defamatory, too. It likes to live among grasses as woodlanders live among trees – and why not? The undulating blades are beautiful, cosy and seemingly safe, and it is a good place to find succulent earthworms, beetles, slugs and snails. The corncrake soon creates corridors, alleyways and secret passages there, too; 'it constantly skulks' – this is the traducing Isabella Beeton, again – 'among the thickest portions of the herbage, and runs so nimbly through it, doubling and winding in every direction, that it is difficult to get near it.' Since Mrs Beeton wanted to run it through herself with a skewer and roast it before serving it on fried breadcrumbs with a tureen of brown gravy, the little land-rail was well advised to keep moving.

In the nineteenth century, the corncrake was found throughout Britain, and its loud and distinctive night song was a familiar summer sound; indeed Stanley Baldwin (thrice British Prime Minister in the inter-war years of the twentieth century) declared this to be one of the most evocative sounds of England. Song? Call is a better word: it sounds like a credit card being dragged along the edge of a comb. The human ear interprets the call as a repetitive rasp, but acoustic analysis reveals that it is composed of two sound bursts a second, each of these 'crek' noises being composed of fifteen sound pulses, one-hundredth of a second apart. It is, like so much in life, a sexual invitation: the male makes his night calls between 11 and 3 in the morning, about the same time as lonely men in Chattanooga might dial up a late-night female radio host. Indeed if the male corncrake doesn't find a mate – and with barely 20 or 30 birds of both sexes making it to Islay each year, courting is a struggle – he may carry on all night, and even dare to show his face briefly in the light of day. (I have heard corncrakes calling well after dawn in May at the RSPB Reserve at Gruinart – though never yet seen one.) Seduction isn't accomplished by call alone; the male will also display his dappled, chestnut coloured wings (which must provide fine camouflage during his months on the savannah) in an elegant and obeisant bow to the female. The act accomplished, he shuts up – for a bit. Fidelity is not a corncrake trait, though, and pretty soon he starts all over again, hoping to father a second brood. So does the female, abandoning her chicks to their fate after no more than twelve days, still three weeks before they are able to fly – hence the importance of cover; she then goes male-hunting again. This two-brood promiscuity is perhaps what survival requires, for corncrakes are not long-lived birds; having been born on Islay, most will make it back for just one long, sexy summer. And never return.

There used to be many more on the island – James Brown of Port Charlotte remembers being kept awake by their din at night. The principle cause of their decline, according to the RSPB's James How, is 'the earlier cutting of silage and hay crops. They'd just find somewhere to sit on their nests, and then the mower would come through and churn them all up. The fact that hay meadows are generally cut from the outside in made it harder for them to escape, too.' Some of the other Hebridean islands (and especially Tiree) have more corncrake – up to 170 calling males each year. 'Early cover,' says Malcolm Ogilvie, 'is the absolute clue to it. In order to have early cover, you've got to have lots of areas where no grazing is going on. When the birds arrive in late April, they want to dive directly into cover. But Islay by the middle of April has been grazed by 50,000 geese, 10,000 cattle and 70,000 sheep. The place is quite bare.' The strategy on Islay is to create 'corncrake corners' of rough ground in which skulking is eminently possible, but success has been modest and costs high. Critics like Ian Mitchell, the local scourge of the RSPB, declare the exercise pointless – since at least 2.5 million calling male corncrakes fly north from Africa to Russia each year. 'It might have been reasonable,' wrote Mitchell in a February 2000 article for *The Oldie*, 'to spend the £8,000 per additional bird that has been expended over the last five years if the corncrake were about to go the way of the dodo or the great auk. But to spend public money on increasing the British corncrake population from 463 (the 1994 figure) to 571 (the 1999 figure), when the world population is well over 2.5 million, is absurd.' Perhaps – but I enjoyed my chance to hear one, and you might, too.

MOURNING SADNESS

Islay, of course, is not just a stage for star birds. 'The point about Islay,' says Malcolm Ogilvie, 'is the abundance and variety. There are over one hundred species on the island, always, continuously. One hundred and five species breed regularly. And at peak migration times it goes up to a hundred and twenty, a hundred and twenty-five species. It all goes back to the fact that in a small area we have got a huge variety of habitats. We've got sheltered sea; we've got a myriad lochs of different sizes, over two hundred of them; we've got hills; we've got old broad-leaved woodland and modern conifer plantations; we've got sand dunes; we've got big sea lochs and estuaries; we've got lush farmland; it's mild, because of the Gulf Stream; and it's all crammed into twenty miles by thirty.' A check list of the 105 breeding species would be worthy though dull; in its place, let me just tell you what an inept and relatively inexperienced bird-watcher like me, armed only with a small pair of binoculars in order to overcome myopia and a developing left-eye cataract, has been able to observe and hear on this island. (The binoculars are the key, by the way, and it is always worth using them, especially if myopic. In a rainstorm one autumn day, I noticed a flock of feeding starling making their way up the field next to my cottage. Boring . . . but something made me take a peek at this unexceptional sight – and I discovered that half the starlings were in fact redwing on their way to an Iberian winter. The residents and the migrants were having a merry sociable wet feed together.)

Oystercatchers are the first bird I think of when I remember Islay. Why? Because they are plentiful, absurdly cheerful, companionably noisy, and strikingly handsome both in flight (when the bold white wing bars flash in the light) and when prodding about with their bright red stockings and bills for something to eat. Wherever you are on the coast, there will always be a few around you, often piping dementedly over some obscure abuse of social protocol. Like cackling gulls and laughing kookaburras, once they get going a kind of internal trigger seems to be pulled and they cannot stop themselves until the piping fit naturally subsides. Which may take some time. Even at midnight.

The curlew, by contrast, is a much more poetic sort of shorebird. This is partly because of its beautiful lilting cry, rising and then falling like the wind itself, but also because it tends to stand stoically hunched and staring at the sea as if in mourning for some sadness that it has only half-remembered but can never quite succeed in forgetting. The lapwing is, like the oystercatcher, another showy bird to watch in flight – especially in the mating season, when it seems to lose its reason and indulge in paper-kite-like lunges and swoops, producing an astonishing electrical sound, like the tuning of a short-wave radio, as it does so. There are lots of pretty ducks (like scaup, shelduck, shoveler and pintail) splashing about, while the divers (red-throated and great northern) are sinister, exasperating and magnificent. Sinister because a close look through the binoculars will show you a sleekly feathered U-boat with tiny implacable eyes, every inch the natural born killer and a petrifying sight for any prawn or crablet out on a jaunt; exasperating because the damn thing keeps diving and it is impossible to predict where it will surface next, so it is hard to watch. And magnificent because it is often alone on a wide sea and appears serenely self-sufficient despite being condemned to a life of almost Sisyphean laboriousness.

The cormorant I saw beating its way up the Sound of Islay on a splendidly bleak morning from the Caol Ila distillery manager's office in the early 1990s was perhaps the first Islay bird to sear itself into my mind; it seemed, then, the very symbol of wilderness, insouciantly skimming the disquieting curls, licks and eddies which separate the island from Jura. I have often seen them since, perched on rocks, holding their wings out to dry in the chill wind, which in winter seems a bitter necessity and liable to result in flu. Their smaller relatives the shag favour congregation in lonelier spots, like the rock next to the lighthouse at Rhuvaal.

I have disturbed wading snipe on walks (usually ill-advised) across the boggier, more challenging sectors of Kidalton coastline: they fly zigzaggily off, yawing to and fro before dropping out of sight once again. One of the most poignant bird encounters I have ever had on Islay, meanwhile, brought me into contact with that aberrant wader who prefers moist leaf to seaweed and shell. Woodcock like Islay, Lord Margadale told me, because the mild climate means 'they can get their beaks into the ground. Come a cold winter, and they'll flock over to Islay.' The night in question was one of furious, roof-drumming rain. I had enjoyed dinner with Stuart and Jackie Thomson at Ardbeg, and was driving back along the lonely Kidalton road towards the Old Schoolhouse, near Aros Bay. The torrent tumbling out of the sky had cowed even the roe deer, who were loitering sheepishly by the roadside. Then, picked out by the headlights and just to the woodland side of the road, I saw a woodcock. At all times glum and heavy-jowled, it seemed to stare at me with particular balefulness on this occasion, willing me to stop, open the car door, and invite it to hop into the warmth and the dryness and escape from the miserable night. I drove odiously by.

A SOUND BROCADE

Islay has plentiful raptors; indeed many islanders think it is overburdened with these bulky killers and that the small birds suffer as a consequence – but it does mean that the island is a choice spot to view them. There are six breeding pairs of golden eagle on Islay – two on the Oa, two on the west coast of the Rhinns, a pair on the north coast and one on the east; the Oa is probably the best place to meet them. 'Go down to the American monument,' advises Malcolm Ogilvie, 'and just stare at the sky. You might be lucky. The problem with seeing Golden Eagles is . . . well, imagine you're an eagle. You get up in the morning. The weather turns nice. You take off; you see a hare. You kill the hare. You eat some of it – and that's your flying done for the day, and probably the next day as well. They're like lions; most of their time is spent lounging about.' (Quite a contrast to the tiny goldcrest – for whom a half-hour break from feeding on a cold winter day will be fatal.) Keen ornithologist Carl Reavey – who used to run the Port Charlotte Hotel – also stresses that most sightings of 'eagles' on Islay are in fact sightings of buzzards, which he nicknames 'the tourist eagle'. If it's perching in a prominent place like a fence wire or a telegraph post, he points out, it will be a buzzard; eagles don't perch visibly or prominently but retreat to their eyries if not on the wing. And if, in flight, you can see its head, it will also be a buzzard; flying eagles appear long and headless. In the past, eagles were poisoned or trapped on Islay – tales are rife of the former Islay Estates gamekeeper who used to sit in the bar of the Bridgend Hotel and boast of how many he had killed (I have heard the tally given as both 50 or 100, depending on who is telling the story). This persecution ended some decades ago here – though it continues on the Scottish mainland.

The buzzards are indeed numerous; Malcolm Ogilvie says there were 15 pairs on Islay when he moved to the island in 1986, whereas now there are between 45 and 50 pairs. Again, it is the decision by the large estates to stop persecuting them which has seen the numbers rise. 'Now they nest practically in the gardens of keepers' cottages, and are left alone. They weren't doing that much harm, anyway. It's the perception – that hooked beak. And it's a very easy bird to deal with, too; it's perching the whole time, the nests are low, and it comes into traps easily.' The main prey of buzzards is rabbit, though according to Lord Margadale they will also kill ground-nesting birds if the opportunity arises.

If Islay has a signature raptor, it is probably that master of the surprise kill: the hen harrier – formerly persecuted out of existence, because it preyed on the chicks and young of the precious grouse.

Grouse stocks on Islay, though, have either been shot to pieces or (more probably) destroyed by ticks and loss of habitat. In 1922 when Talbot Clifton bought the Kidalton Estate, the 'average game bag for the last seven seasons' on that estate alone included 800 red grouse and 150 blackcock (black grouse), while Lord Margadale told me that 1000 red grouse were taken on Islay in the best shooting year of the 1960s. No red grouse are shot today, though you will probably start the odd one when out walking on the hill; blackcock, meanwhile, are rare on Islay, with at the most three pairs on Islay Estates land in the lonely north of the island beyond Bunnahabhain. 'Hen harriers do well on Islay,' as Malcolm Ogilvie says, 'because there's no grouse-shooting.' A further reason why the hen harriers have flourished is because of Islay's unsuccessful conifer plantations. In the early stages of growth, the plantations attract voles and small birds, which is just what a hungry hen harrier wants to dine on. Normally, though, the canopy closes, shutting out all other life, as the plantation matures – but this hasn't happened on Islay, since the trees have struggled. There are consequently around 20 pairs of hen harrier on the Rhinns alone. Rabbits are also plentiful on the coastlands of the Rhinns, and raw, warm rabbit is another favourite hen harrier dish. These birds are smaller than buzzards, and fly low, their legs and posture making them resemble ski jumpers. Not everyone is a fan; Bruno Schroder says they are 'devils, because they chase to kill and not to eat', while Lord Margadale feels that they are another cause of the decline of the corncrake on Islay.

Hooded crows are relatively common, and unprotected: they may be trapped and killed (which is why they tend to be more frequent in unkeepered areas). They are voracious opportunists, but their natural inquisitiveness can be fun to watch – I spent ten happy minutes looking at one on the Oa as it explored every conceivable nutritional possibility offered by a white ceramic housing on an old, abandoned telegraph pole. Larger and gruffer are the ravens, which cruise upland Islay looking for prey and for carrion. Their intelligence can be used for what seem (to humans) vicious ends – pecking the eyes out of a lambing ewe, according to farmer John Edwards, and then eviscerating her while still alive using the rectum as a point of ingress. 'A raven will kill a ewe,' Lord Margadale confirmed, though he has heard tell of a different technique. 'It will split the ewe's tongue, and she will eventually die. And they know they've got lunch a week later. They'll also kill a lamb. They'll wait until it's asleep, and they'll go and peck its eyes out. I saw that happen last year; it's pretty unpleasant.' On Islay, though, the ravens have learned to feed at the council rubbish tip near Bridgend, perhaps lured there by the abattoir viscera, which has led to a population boom and fewer tales of brutality. There are, by the way, no jays or magpies on the island.

Barn owls are the most populous night-hunter on Islay. 'The habitat is really good for them and there's lots of prey species,' says James How, 'but if they can't fly to hunt then they suffer really badly. That's our problem. We've got the habitat, but the weather conditions aren't always what a barn owl is looking for. They can't hunt in anything above a light drizzle; their ears get waterlogged. If it's blowing a gale, they won't hear a thing. In a wet summer, their breeding success is not good at all.'

The skylarks alone are a reason to visit Islay, as anyone who has ever taken a summer walk on the hill will know; there are probably between 5,000 and 8,000 pairs on the island every year, adding much to the already distinguished human musical traditions of the place. The torrent of rolling, undulating notes spill out across the empty air like a gurgling burn. If you see a bird spiral down after a recital, or if you start one from its nest cup, it is hard to believe that such a tiny creature (18 cm or less) can fill the sky with this sound brocade. Other small birds like the rock pipit, the meadow pipit, the stonechat and the wheatear will keep walkers company, and the cuckoo's call often punctuates a late spring morning, but to compare their burblings, zittings and coos to the song of the skylark is like comparing a pub sing-along with *The Magic Flute*.

Or am I being unfair? Even the most mundane bird moments on Islay can turn swiftly sublime; you don't need fancy species to dazzle. Example: it is just after breakfast; 16 November 2003. Noticing the sun is up, I step outside, and there, on the roof of my cottage, are three nattering starlings. They proceed to produce such an astonishing repertoire of sounds that I am frozen in wonder for minutes. It's a non-stop patter of whistles, chirrups, glottal stops, tam-tam beats, twangs and squawks, full of imitative snatches – certainly a curlew, certainly the electronic mating call of the lapwing, certainly the throaty hacking of the gulls, all sewn together seamlessly and feeding off each other like a cockney vaudeville parody of a nightingale or a lyre bird, with occasional descents into rap. Their perky little beaks are silhouetted against the pale blue of the morning sky, and their feathers are typically akimbo. A small party of Greenland white fronted geese comes yapping over the hill and glides irresolutely down towards Loch Indaal; the starlings quieten down as that happens, but as soon as the geese have gone they start again. After a while they take to jumping over each other and landing on the other side of their neighbour, just to add a little physical playfulness to the inventive song. Meanwhile, two elegant monocled thrushes are working the lawn, cocking their heads as they do so; a stocky hooded crow struts up the track; and a neat wren darts around the woodpile. A sparrow on the fence wire catches the sun on its back, and suddenly I notice what a rich symphony of chestnut and beech leaf the feathers of this one common species reveals. No, you don't need the fancy birds . . .

THE SUDDEN SPLASH

There is, says Chloë Randall, the free-thinking estate manager of Dunlossit, 'something cold about them. It is almost as if they don't have a heart or a soul.' I have looked into their eyes, and I know what she means. Looking into their eyes is easy: if they see you, they will stare at you with an unbroken gaze for as long as ten or fifteen minutes. If you stay still, so will they. And thus you look at each other, seeking recognition, compassion – but only finding an empty, glassy stare. That is my experience of Islay's red deer – and it may well, of course, be their experience of me.

Warmth or its absence aside, they are magnificently autonomous creatures, and plentiful in Mountain Islay. I once took a winter photograph of Cnoc na Faire (Look-Out Hill), the most northerly peak of the island. It was covered in dry grass, and the low light threw expanses of it into shadow. That shadowland is pricked out in a dozen places by little points of light, which those to whom I show the photograph invariably take to be rabbits (the treeless scene lacks scale). In fact those points of light are red deer, the sun diagnostically catching their antlers, their underparts or their rumps. With binoculars, you can examine every rugged, sinewy inch of them in the motionless observing minutes they will, from a distance, afford you. You can count the tines on the stag's antlers: 12 make a Royal. Approach too close, by contrast, and they will be off, charging smoothly and low over the rutted, boggy ground despite their thudding weight. Much of Scotland is over-grazed by deer – but not, according to the lairds, Islay.

'We set up,' says Sir John Mactaggart, 'the first Deer Management Group in Scotland. By universally acknowledged consent, we are an example of how deer management groups should be run. The Deer Commission constantly quotes us as an example of how the thing can work well.' Bruno Schroder described the procedure to me. 'We count. On the basis of that, we decide jointly what we are going to shoot. We then divide that up between the estates, and it becomes a conservation objective. In other words, you have to shoot what you agree to – no more and no less. Then we have to show what we have shot to our neighbours and to a consultant, who not only recommends what we should shoot the following year but who also judges how well or badly the stags have been shot. There's usually a quality survey in Scotland as well, and I know that out of the dozen top heads each year, often as many as half are Islay's stags, but that does not come by accident. It's hard work and it's very, very careful shooting.' Price, Schroder stresses, plays no part in this. 'We don't make a premium otherwise you translate the quality of the stag into cash, and that makes it a temptation to shoot for cash rather than playing by the rules. The privileged get the chance to come to Islay and they behave themselves; they're told what to shoot and they don't argue, because they're paying no more than anyone else in Scotland. Their privilege is to see lovely heads – and leave them. You might march for a day about the place and see one good stag after another and go back empty. Not that you couldn't have shot them, but they are too good to shoot. If you complain, you don't get given the opportunity of coming to Islay again. Quite firmly.'

Schroder also stresses that the Islay Deer Management Group has got the ratio of stags to hinds at or near one to one, 'which is more or less how they are born. Where else in Scotland do you find a one-to-one sex ratio except on the southern part of Islay? Nowhere. Elsewhere there are many more hinds, which is why the deer are running riot. If you've got the hinds you've got the girls – and they will produce.' Lord Margadale says that the ratio of his estate at the northern end of the island has slightly more hinds (around 800) than stags (around 700).

'In principle,' says Malcolm Ogilvie from the conservationist's perspective, 'the red deer are confined to the eastern and northern hills, but in practice there are anything up to a hundred on the Rhinns. They're kept under control, though. The woodland in the south-eastern corner, from Lagavulin eastwards, has now largely been fenced against deer damage; that includes roe deer, and there may also be up to a hundred or two fallow deer that were introduced down there. That woodland is Atlantic oakwoods, native to western Scotland. If the historians are to be believed, seven thousand years ago it was largely oak forest up to about three hundred feet here, with understorey of hazel and birch, rowan, holly, that sort of thing; these are the little remnant patches. The deer have done a lot of damage in the past. As you can see: as soon as the fence goes up, it starts regenerating, very fast and brilliantly.'

Islay's mammal roll-call has some distinguished absentees: there are no foxes, no badgers, no weasels, no moles. Islay does have a unique sub-species of the field vole and the common shrew, but you need to be a mammalian dentist to appreciate the detail. Snakes lead the island's reptiles. 'Vipers swarm on the heath,' wrote Thomas Pennant in 1772, and they still do, the adder being Islay's key viper. A 'poultice of human ordure' was the traumatic eighteenth-century cure for a bite. There are cities of rabbits on the island; more noteworthy, though, are the lonesome hares; a walk on the hill usually means starting one or two of these strong, stringy furred athletes. The muscular run is nearly always preceded by a quizzical, psychiatrist's gaze.

Most of the mammalian interest, though, lies in the water – with the otters and seals. Nowhere in Scotland, according to Malcolm Ogilvie, has more otters than Islay. 'Shetland is always held up as the example, but we've got the same density (one or two every kilometre in the best bits, and one every three or four in the less good bits).' They are not easy to see, being lithe, slender and swift, and spending much of their time underwater, but that makes the sudden splash and its attendant brief glimpse even more of a treat. Gus Maclachlan of the RSPB on Oa saw five in a 2-km walk up the coast from the Carraig Fhada lighthouse one April mid-morning 'just hunting away. That time of the day was perfect for them.' Islay has mink, too, but the larger otters are the dominant species.

Seals, by contrast, are easy to see – grey seals (Britain's largest carnivore) lounge on the rocks in Portnahaven, and common seals sprawl and loaf on the skerries along the Kidalton coastline. There are probably more of the smaller (and, paradoxically, rarer) common seals than the greys around Islay. All seals, though, are hard to count – since they can spend up to an hour underwater without surfacing. The grey seals also have a colony on Nave Island, though you'd need a boat to go pup-spotting there.

No one could call a seal's eyes cold. They are so large, indeed, that they tend to have a vulnerable, imploring, childlike look; this is particularly true of the common seal. There is, though, something odd about those eyes all the same. They have no pupils. These undersea hunters need to see well in low light (they can dive to 200 m), so when they are on land, the eye is protected from sunlight by the pupils closing up, hence the abyssal gaze.

Islay's seal population has risen in recent years (as has that of Scotland as a whole since seal culling ended in the 1970s), and the seals have sparked a major controversy on the island. Fisher rivalry? Seals don't get blubbered up by nibbling on seaweed: the average grey seal wolfs down 1.8 tonnes of fish a year. Islay's professional fishermen, though, are only interested in scallops, lobster and crab; the two live in harmony. This is less true of the 'sporting' fishermen – Lord Margadale says that just one salmon was caught on the river Sorn in the summer of 2003, and he suspects the seals on Laggan Point and Gartbreck may know why that was. 'It was a dry summer and the salmon probably didn't run till later. If they're hanging around in the sea waiting to go up, the seals can just whip along, have a nibble and then go back to their rock. The balance has gone too far in their favour.' The main controversy concerning the seals, though, centred around whether the Kidalton coastline should be designated as a Site of Special Scientific Interest (SSSI), and more specifically whether or not it should win some sort of official recognition as a 'seal sanctuary', as George and Fiona Middleton of the Kidalton Estate wanted.

Fiona Middleton, or 'Fiona of the Seals' as she is styled on the copyright line of her 1995 book *Seal*, was born in the distant village of Seal in Kent, grew up in Sevenoaks, performed as a musician and songwriter, and first came to Islay in November 1976 with her future husband George (another Sevenoaks resident and sometime University of Kent radical student leader) by what they assured me were assorted fairy and supernatural machinations in the 1970s. The estate was apparently acquired by similar means: 'Fiona's fairy music helped us to get the estate,' George says; though having obtained shares in the 'Western Isles Development Company' – the last rump of Clifton ownership – George had the unfairy-like guile, as he told me, to call an emergency board meeting when his fellow directors were away on holiday, enabling him to become the laird of Kidalton. 'There wasn't anything they could do about it. That's life,' he said. 'I decided I was going to live here and make a wildlife sanctuary.'

Fiona spent a sizeable portion of her first two decades on Islay rescuing injured, sick or abandoned seals and nursing them back to health in tanks, in her bath, and in her living room (one photograph in the book shows a seal watching television with a Middleton family dog) before releasing them back into the wild. She has also been much snapped by newspaper photographers and television cameramen swimming and cuddling the seals – and playing her violin to them, too, just as Talbot Clifton used to play his flute to them. They are curious creatures, and seem to enjoy an impromptu concert; local boatbuilder and diver Gus Newman even gives them a blast on the bagpipes occasionally. The Middletons, together with the charity Animal Concern, were the prime movers in the 'seal sanctuary' plan; George Middleton told me that his philosophy was that 'the rights of animals predominate' on his estate, and that the seals 'have prior call' to the use of the house. 'Some people would say that that's going too far, but that's not how we feel about it.'

Local opposition to this plan was widespread, both from the Mactaggart family (who own a larger section of the coastline than the Middletons) and from the local community, who tend to see all official land designations and support for particular wildlife species as the unwanted meddling of outsiders in Islay affairs. The seal controversy forms part of a larger debate about wildlife on the island (see Chapter Eight), but what is worth noting here is that no one on either side of the dispute actually wished the seals harm. Gus Newman opposed the SSSI designation as Chairman of the Kidalton and Oa Community Council – but he also leads seal-viewing boat trips out among the Kidalton skerries. 'I'm not in favour of it being called a seal sanctuary,' he told me. 'But it's one of the natural assets of the island, so if they're there, we may as well educate people in them rather than ignoring them. So I'm on the fence and I'm staying there.'

The outcome was a kind of stalemate. The SSSI designation was rejected on appeal, so Scottish Natural Heritage then sought and won the right to have the area designated (under European and not British law) as a 'Special Area of Conservation' (eSAC). This was castigated by Islay's maverick anti-environmentalist Ian Mitchell, in his best pugilistic style, as 'a defeat for democracy by a cynical and malignant bureaucracy'. Nothing much seems to have changed, though, and both the Ileachs and the seals continue to enjoy life under the 'cynical and malignant bureaucracy' much as they did before.

Dolphins can be seen from Islay on occasion – though those occasions are hugely unpredictable. So many were seen off Islay in 2001 that the Hebridean Whale and Dolphin Trust (based on Mull) decided that Islay should be part of their routine monitoring in 2002. Observations, says Malcolm Ogilvie, were made by one of their staff and two PhD students from May through to September, 'and they hardly saw a dolphin. Whereas I'd seen eight of them in front of my house one Boxing Day when it was snowing. They were upended about ten yards offshore, and they were grabbing little flatfish off the bottom. It was so shallow that their tails were out of the water. They stayed for about an hour, and people stood watching them along the road.' The day Bruichladdich reopened (29 May 2001) was another celebrated dolphin moment: they leapt serendipitously in the sunshine on Loch Indaal within view of the crowds at the distillery.

The island's wild goats, by contrast, attract no attention whatsoever, though they seem a remarkable if whiffy bunch to me.

They are impressively shaggy, and their colours are wildly variable; they often look down at you from horrifying precipices on the Oa or the north coast with insouciant curiosity, their horns making them look professorial rather than diabolical. The island population is thought to be over 500, with most on the Oa and the north coast and a few on the Rhinns (Gus Maclachlan has counted over 400 on the Oa alone). They graze whatever is up on the hill, and often come down on to the beach for a slimy meal of seaweed, too.

THE BURIED HEAD

You can photograph, without too much difficulty or skill, a chough or a barnacle goose, a stag or a storm, a copper still or a bronze sunset. What visitors to Islay routinely fail to capture on film or disc is the subtle flecking majesty of the island's wild flowers. Agreed, you could snap a springtime splash of yellow wild iris on the marshlands, since the plant is fleshy, eye-catching and easy to frame; but this is little more than a single brushstroke compared to the epic, pointillist canvas of the coastal grasslands in June. A million tiny petals seethe amongst the tangle of grasses, stretching away triumphantly beyond the grasp of any lens other than that of the emotional human eye. There is nothing unusual about many of these flowers; but to see buttercups, daisies, clovers, meadowsweet and bedstraw in such carpeting profusion, and to smell them sweetening the brilliant clarity of the summer air, sends the soul soaring.

'Our total higher plant list including grasses is fifteen to sixteen hundred species; this compares with Argyle, which is well over three thousand.' Malcolm Ogilvie's statistical analysis makes Islay seem almost dull. 'But, having said that, we have some plants which are decidedly scarce. They've become established here, and have been left alone; they haven't been cultivated out of existence. If you've ever been here in late June or early July, the orchids are fantastic . . .' And he's right: the delicate pink freckles of the heath spotted orchid mingle with pretty yellow tormentil stars up on the hills to give colour and life to the heather even before its own flowers have broken cover. The more elegant common spotted orchid and the early purple orchid, plus the smaller northern marsh orchid and early marsh orchid are all profuse on Islay too, though they tend to favour lowland limestone and sand rather than upland peat; telling them apart is not easy, since they not only resemble each other but happily hybridise, too.

The gypsy flamboyance of ragged robin – the same pink as the orchids, but a taller plant whose petals seem to have been torn apart by some night sprite – also strides through the grasslands, and foxgloves (with smaller, daintier flowers than in southern mainland Britain) are ubiquitous, despite the absence of foxes. Another cheerfully chaotic flower adding to the dabs of mauve, lilac and violet which dust every summer walk is the devil's-bit scabious – and you won't be the only one to notice it. The marsh fritillary is Islay's prize butterfly, and it is on the leaves of the devil's bit scabious that the female will pile her glossy yellow egg clusters (they later turn red); the caterpillars are black and hairy, and spend the winter in silk-wrapped colonies. This pretty though shy butterfly has orange and brown chequerboard wings. Look out for the male flitting and skimming its delicate way about the bogs in June; it may pause on yellow flowers like dandelion and bird's foot trefoil. Walk the rockier headlands of the coast and you will find cheerful, nodding colonies of honey-scented thrift contributing a paler, milkier pink to the summer paint box; succulent yellow stonecrop creeps around the stones, too. In September, heather lights the hills.

Bridgend woods provide a profusion of species (many introduced) including the cools blues of bugle and brooklime; in January and February, a white hush of snowdrops rises from the cold ground. Lichens, mosses and liverworts, too, are all magnificent on Islay, thanks largely to the gentle dampness of the air and the lack of pollution, and all the island woodlands nourish them; they hang like green satin drapes from the branches of the stunted trees, and flare from tombstones and walls. The island, in sum, may not have as long a species list as elsewhere, but you will rarely feel the lack.

No account of nature on Islay would be complete without an introduction to two very small species which will be keen to meet you. Any walk on Islay undertaken with partially bare arms or legs is likely to arouse the interest of the eight-legged nymph (or female adolescent) tick, which before you happen along will be about the size of a pinhead.

(This will probably be *Ixodes ricinus* or the sheep tick, though there are at least 12 other biting species in Britain, too.) It's sightless – but it clings to the top of a plant or blade of grass with its six hind legs, waving a front pair in the air. This front pair of legs has sensors which can detect changes in temperature, humidity and odour: your presence, in other words. As you walk by it will grab you and scuttle, with remarkable and generally imperceptible agility, towards the softest spot it can find: up to your groin or down to the back of your knee would be ideal, though a soft thigh or upper arm will do. It then gets out a pair of sharply toothed skin cutters; once through your precious epidermis, it buries its barbed headpiece (called a hypostome) inside you, secretes a little glue to cement its head to your skin and ensure you can't give it the brush-off, then begins drinking. It also secretes anti-inflammatory chemicals to ensure you don't notice it, and anti-clotting chemicals to keep the blood flowing. By the time it has finished, it is rather bigger than a pin-head. You will probably be entirely unaware of its presence until you take your clothes off for a shower after the walk.

Ticks are the reason why anyone intending to walk on Islay should put a pair of tweezers into their suitcase. Press the two points of the tweezers to each side of the tick's embedded headpiece, and draw the whole lot out; if you just try to rub or scratch the creature off, it will probably break in two, leaving its glued headpiece firmly inside you. Most tick bites will have no adverse health consequences, but there have been cases of Lyme disease on Islay, so if you experience flu-like symptoms any time during the month after a tick bite, seek medical help. If you think humans have problems with ticks, meanwhile, talk to those vets and scientists who have looked closely at sheep, grouse, deer, mice and seabirds, none of whom possess tweezers. Chronic tick affliction may mean smaller animals and birds bleeding to death or dying from a multitude of tick-borne diseases, while larger animals can suffer enormously. 'Tick is terrible on Islay,' says Bruno Schroder, who cites this as a major cause of reduced grouse stocks. 'If you see a little grouse with tick all around its eyes, you can understand why the poor thing dies.' Lord Margadale agrees. 'The deer are covered in ticks. And it's one thing for a deer, bigger than you or I, to have twenty ticks on it, but imagine if you're just something the size of a bantam. If you get covered with ticks before you can fly, it's going to kill you. Wild red deer, unlike farmed sheep, are not treated against tick. I think that is one of the big reasons why we have so few grouse now on Islay.'

The other small species which demands mention is *Culicoides impunctatus*, or the Highland midge. Once again, its size is unintimidating (a wingspan of 1.4 mm); once again, it is the female which is more trouble than the insignificant, non-biting, nectar-eating male. Ticks must imperatively drink blood to breed; for midges it is optional, though breeding is much more successful if they can do so. The second half of June until early September is peak biting season (though I have been bitten as late as 18 November); perfect conditions mean still air and low light, either due to heavy cloud cover, woodland shade, or the long hours of twilight which sandwich the desultory northern summer nights. Islay furnishes ample low light and lots, too, of the moist boggy ground which provides ideal larval breeding sites for the midge. Only the wind – that cool Islay breeze – is on the side of the humans. If the wind drops under a covered sky, beware. Numerically, the midges are likely to have the upper hand: a hectare of wallowing bog can support up to 24 million midge larvae.

The midge bites less neatly than the tick (it scissors its way in), though once it has rolled its mouthparts into a food canal and plunged this into the wound it will take its ten-millionth of a litre of your nutritious blood more swiftly than the tick will: a minute or two should be ample. There is no glue involved this time, but the salivary strategy is different; in place of anti-inflammatories, midge spit induces an allergic response which sends histamine to the wound, causing vasodilation and giving the midge a food surge before antibodies kick in to repair the wound and staunch the flow of blood. By then, of course, the midge will have danced off to find a nice wet spot to lay her eggs, leaving you with an irritating itch – but not, generally, anything worse. One bite is supportable, but when you see midges advancing in clouds, then a hasty retreat (accompanied, if possibly, by copious pipe smoke) is advised. The weather, though, is key. In bright and breezy sunshine, Islay is yours.

SIXTH GLASS

Lagavulin

The castle: ruined;
sea-scattered: the bruised clan.
Salvaged: the spirit.

LAGAVULIN (PRONOUNCED 'LAGGA-*VOOL*-IN') IS NOT the oldest legally established distillery on the island: that honour is Bowmore's. No other Islay distillery, though, has quite the same seigneurial quality as this great white milestone on the Kidalton road. Come to the spirit, or come to the place, and in both cases you will feel the breath of the past at the nape of your neck. Nothing could be less new than Lagavulin; nothing could be less vulgar. Time works a patina into the spirit; time has dripped dignity in every stone of the place.

There is no more evocative setting for a distillery in the whole of Scotland. The road dips down almost to sea level at this point, and crosses the distillery burn: 'mill hollow' is the translation of the Gaelic name Lagavulin, and the site feels snug. It is as you walk down through the distillery buildings towards the sea, though, that the location begins its subtle work on you. There is a little rocky summit to the right of the distillery topped by Lagavulin's former church bell (the clapper has been removed to stop the wind and the under-14s from disturbing the peace of the hamlet); in spring, this natural rockery glitters with daffodils. It's called Goat Hill, though the island's shy and shaggy wild goats seldom venture here any more. The brown burn which provides the distillery's process water tumbles in a white-washed channel to your left as you walk seawards. You pass a tombstone on a wall, of which more later; there is a warehouse to your right, and a pier straight ahead, its lanky finger dipped into Lagavulin Bay. Before you, straight ahead, guarding the head of the bay, hunched like a cat against the fierce enigma of the sea, is Dunyvaig Castle. It was demolished by the cannon balls of Sir Oliver Lambert in the opening days of February 1614 and has been gently softening under the Islay rain ever since.

Astonishing, really. There is no Macdonald (however spelled) anywhere in the world today whose roots do not tug him or her back to this place. It was the sea fort of the Lords of the Isles during a period when the Macdonalds challenged the Stewarts and the Plantagenets as equals, and when Islay and Finlaggan could be spoken of in the same breath as Holyrood, Scone, Canterbury or Westminster. More remains of it than of Finlaggan. Yet it's an unexcavated ruin. 'Warning: Dangerous Building', says the only explanatory notice you will find there. 'Please keep clear'. It belongs to the world's biggest drinks company, Diageo, the owners of Lagavulin; it is subject to the adminis-tration, however, of Historic Scotland. 'We agonise about it,' says Donald Renwick, Lagavulin's manager. Diageo, he says, spent £100,000 on it in 1998: just enough to shore up the ruins. 'When we got involved,' says Peter Smith of Diageo, 'the pile of rubble was literally about to fall into the sea and our main aim at the time was to prevent the collapse and hopefully slow the general weathering. Historic Scotland were extremely helpful with this and we worked within their guidelines. We had looked into what might be needed to improve access and I had had various meetings with the local council and community representatives with a view to opening it up as an asset to the island. However, Historic Scotland was understandably cautious about any activity of this kind as it would accentuate the decay. We got the message loud and clear that any further development would run counter to [their] objectives.' The official view, thus, seems Kafkaesque: that an evidently decaying and unexcavated site of great historical significance should be left alone in case investigation causes further decay. The state of Dunyvaig is, in sum, a disgrace; along with Kilchoman Church, it is one of the two saddest sights on Islay. Is there a wealthy, whisky-loving, bureaucratically adroit Macdonald reading these lines who can help?

It's not hard to see why the Macdonalds chose this spot for their sea fort. Dunyvaig itself sits atop a promontory which shelters the bay from the south-east. Surnaig, the twin promontory to the other side of the bay, shelters it even more effectively from the south-west (it also bears the remains of a fort). Across the water's mouth, moreover, are a group of blocking rocks which provide further shelter, while undersea hazards make this a treacherous bay to enter for those without knowledge or charts. Even the prosaic Alfred Barnard couldn't help but acknowledge the 'rocks of fantastic shape' which 'rise abruptly from the sea; in some places detached masses have fallen in such a position that they rise from the sea like weird monsters of the deep, and by moonlight produce startling effects on the surface of the waters.' The navigable water channel passes close to Dunyvaig itself. A reconstruction of the castle (by W. Ashley Bartlam) during its years of glory hangs inside the distillery: it shows the laird's house high at the top of the rocks, with a drawbridge over the natural V-shape of the rocks adjacent to the bay. The castle proper, meanwhile, spreads itself amply out across the flatter land below the rocks. The sea gates were found in front of these rocks, and boats were hauled up on to the narrow beach there, their sails being used at night (according to the artist) as tents.

It's not hard, either, to see why, in the eighteenth century, there were once some 10 or 11 little 'black pots' scattered around the bay, making this one of the earliest known sites for distilling on the island. Fresh water would always have been plentifully channelled off the hills into this natural hollow, hence its vocation as a mill site; barley, too, would have grown well in the sunlight and shelter provided by southerly Kidalton's gentle microclimate. Peat was to hand above the field systems of the lower ground, and once (as the nineteenth century dawned) the Excisemen began taking an interest in proceedings this would have remained, as it still is today, a private and sheltered place. By 1816, though, no ambitious distiller could afford not to have acquired a licence, and the first one here was granted to John Johnston, father of the two brothers who were later to found Laphroaig, and (according to one source) one of a successful trio of incomers from Ardnamurchan. No family was more important than this one in the early history of distilling on Islay, since Johnstons had a hand in Lagavulin, Laphroaig, Tallant and Bowmore distilleries at various times, yet all too little is known about them. There is even a tombstone set in a wall of the distillery commemorating one Angus Johnston, who died in 1836. Not only was he a very old man for the times (over 80), but he was important enough to be buried on the offshore island of Texa. As his funerary stone was being loaded on to a boat to follow the corpse over to the island, it fell into the water. This aroused such superstitious horror that it lay there for many years, its inscription read only by crabs and shrimps, before finally being rescued and becoming part of the distillery fabric. Was Angus the father of John, or his brother? No one seems to know.

A second distillery called Ardmore was licensed here in 1817 by Archibald Campbell (whose family had distilled at Lagavulin, informally or illicitly, for over 30 years); this licence, though, seems to have passed into the hands of the laird, the young and optimistic Walter Frederick Campbell, soon afterwards.

When John Johnston died in 1836 (the same year as the Texa-bound Angus), the two distilleries were united. Unlike Laphroaig, Lagavulin passed out of the hands of the Johnston family. John had built up debts with Alexander Graham, a Glasgow whisky merchant who, thanks to his Ileach wife's connections, specialised in selling the whiskies of the island, and it was Graham who acquired the now-united distilleries. His two sons Walter and John ran the distillery, with Walter doing the distilling himself. (Walter also distilled for Laphroaig for a decade after the fatal 1847 pot-ale burning of Donald Johnston, until Donald's son Dougald was old enough to take over.)

ARRIVAL OF AN ALPHA MALE

By 1861, a new name had become associated with Lagavulin, a name which in due course was to make the distillery a famous one. That name was Mackie. While Walter Graham distilled, his brother John continued to cultivate his father's merchant business in Glasgow (called 'The Islay Cellar') as well as running the administrative side of Lagavulin. John Graham had met James Logan Mackie in Glasgow; the two obviously hit it off, and Mackie was invited to become a partner. At the same moment, new leases were drawn up with the laird – who, by now, was not the easy-going and generous Walter Frederick Campbell but the quietly punctilious John Ramsay, himself a distiller. A squabble ensued about the valuation of the property, with the leaseholders feeling that the laird had been sharp with them. These disagreements were eventually resolved, the proof being that further leases were granted by Ramsay. In the 1881 census, the manager was J.C. Graham, described as 'resident partner' (though temporarily absent) when Alfred Barnard visited; but by 1889, the Grahams had faded from the scene, and James Logan Mackie's nephew, Peter Mackie, who had learned his distilling under the Grahams at Lagavulin, became sole partner.

Peter Mackie was to become Islay's first 'celebrity distiller'; indeed it was not until Jim McEwan began his ambassadorial work for Bowmore that Mackie's achievements in taking the name Islay around the world were rivalled. Mackie, moreover, was an astute and ferociously energetic businessman, and his promotion of the White Horse blend (created and named, after the White Horse Inn in Edinburgh's Canongate, by his uncle) made him a minor Edwardian whisky baron. John Ramsay may have been more financially astute, but he was a far quieter man and his prodigious organisational energies were expended on his Islay estate itself rather than Port Ellen's whisky. Mackie, nicknamed 'Restless Peter', was a proud peacock. There is no photograph of this tall and handsome Scot that doesn't suggest overweening amour-propre. An 1896 snap of the distillery staff taken on a bright summer day, for example, shows 11 bemused and rustic workers, every one with cap and prodigious beard; a middle manager in a suit – and Mackie in full highland dress, his chin jutting forward, his magnificent moustache neatly trimmed, his hands grasping his sporran in proud, alpha-male style. The group are standing underneath a large plaque which reads 'Mackie & Coy.'

Off the island, Mackie's great achievements lay in his becoming a founder-shareholder in Craigellachie Distillery on Speyside in 1891 (then sole owner in 1916), and in turning White Horse from a minor project of his uncle's into a blended whisky of world renown. He launched himself into most controversies of the day, not the least of them the celebrated 'What is Whisky?' controversy of 1905–9. This arose because Islington Borough Council in London had brought and won a case in the North London Police Court convicting local licensees of mis-selling Scottish grain spirit as 'whisky'. Islington's case had its origins in the council's worthy attempts to outlaw the adulterated and often noxious brandies of the post-phylloxera era, which were finding their way into local pubs. As the zealous officials from the Angel investigated, it occurred to them that much 'Scotch whisky' of the time, too, was a queer sort of product produced in a far-from-traditional manner. Their contention was that only pot-distilled Scottish malt whisky should be called 'Scotch whisky'. Huge vested interests were, naturally, at stake, since it was the new-fangled grain whisky which was powering the boom in Scotch sales worldwide. The mighty DLC (Distillers Company Limited) quickly financed an appeal, which was inconclusive, then pushed for a Royal Commission – which duly if languidly found in their favour. Ever since then, Scottish grain spirit has been allowed to call itself 'whisky' (which the Commission oddly decided to spell 'whiskey').

Mackie was preoccupied, almost obsessed, with the question of maturity in whisky, and he deplored the many young, poor-quality blends which were flooding the market at the time. His early efforts with White Horse, indeed, had been unsuccessful, losing him £8,000, despite it being 'a brand of the highest age and quality, second to nothing that had ever been offered to the public'. Why did it flop at first? Because Mackie had 'not calculated the immense sum required for advertising', nor had he correctly gauged 'the ignorance of a large section of the English public in regard to quality'. Despite being a blender, therefore, he supported the initial judgement of the Islington magistrate: 'I think it will be the means of the public's getting better whisky, because the brewers will buy better whisky for their tied houses than they have in the past.' He was not against the use of grain spirit in blends ('Had the trade in whisky been confined to malt, unmellowed by grain spirit, the trade would not have been a tenth of what it is today'), but he pressed hard for a three-year minimum maturation period before sale for all Scotch whisky. Prescient, in other words, since that is the rule today, but ahead of his time (the three-year rule was not adopted until 1933, nine years after his death). Mackie, meanwhile, carried on fulminating. 'It is in the interests of the working man, many of whom are not judges of whisky, that they should be protected from the young, cheap, fiery whisky which is offered. Experience teaches that most of the riotous and obstreperous conduct of drunks comes from the young and fiery spirit which is sold, while men who may over-indulge in old matured whisky become sleepy and stupid, but not in a fighting mood.'

So much for Mackie abroad. Mackie at home was no more emollient. His Glasgow business held the agency for Laphroaig as well as Lagavulin, and it had been obvious for many years (Barnard noted as much in 1887, for example) that both of these distilleries produced exceptionally fine malt. Mackie coveted Laphroaig, and he had made offers to John Ramsay for the lease. Perhaps this was why he didn't try as hard as he might have done in marketing and selling Laphroaig. After some years of frustration, the Johnstons withdrew the Laphroaig agency from Mackie in 1907 – and Mackie was furious. Access to water was a repeated source of strife among the Kidalton distilleries (there is no shortage of it up on the hill, but it descends via a thread-work of wandering, filigree streams), so Mackie's retaliation took the form of some 'rearrangement' of the water supplies. The outraged Johnstons took Mackie to court over the matter, and won. Mackie was not to be outdone. He decided to build himself a second, miniature Laphroaig at Lagavulin. This he did, calling it Malt Mill; it ran from 1908 until June 1962.

THE BOTTLE AT THE BACK OF THE CUPBOARD

What was Malt Mill like? None of Lagavulin's present-day workers was employed in Malt Mill days, but some have distant childhood memories of the distillery installations. Malt Mill had its own malt floors, malt kilns, washbacks and stills; the only element of production it shared with Lagavulin was the mash tun. It was meant to imitate Laphroaig closely, and was therefore robustly peaty; one former Ardbeg manager, Hamish Scott, claimed that the Malt Mill kilns used as much peat for one firing as the Lagavulin kilns used in a week. Former general manager Grant Carmichael also recalls that nothing but peat was burned in the Malt Mill kilns, whereas smokeless coal and anthracite were also used for Lagavulin. 'You could almost chew Malt Mill,' Grant told me; 'I'd never tasted anything so peaty.' It would be gratifying, of course, to locate an old cask or two of this lost warhorse. There are 7.4 million casks of maturing whisky in Diageo's inventory, so it is not inconceivable that some Malt Mill may be lurking at the back of a warehouse somewhere, though it is probably even more likely that zealous stock controllers will have tipped the last of it into a batch of Johnnie Walker Black a couple of decades ago. What is certain is that, at the back of manager Donald Renwick's sample cupboard at Lagavulin, there is a half-litre bottle of clearish spirit labelled 'Malt Mill last filling June 1962'. The neck is heavily encrusted with sealing wax; it would seem that no one has sampled it since it was drawn. Malt Mill is not yet extinct.

There is, moreover, a collection of old whisky bottles from the Mackie era kept at Lagavulin, and these suggest that both Malt Mill and Lagavulin were bottled separately as well as vatted together and used in blends. There are almost certain to be old, unopened bottles of Malt Mill lying forgotten in cupboards and cellars around the world (the two Mackie-era brands which mention Malt Mill alone, in this collection, are 'Lammas Brew' and 'Old Highland Whisky'). It should also be remembered, though, that there are few finer incentives for the unscrupulous forger than this lost, peaty gem from Islay.

Mackie's final years were, like those of many of us, a mixture of pleasure and pain. His only son was killed during the First World War, a grievous blow which made the award of a baronetcy in 1920 almost ironic. This vigorous conservative, fervent imperialist and passionate field-sports enthusiast died a painful death from cancer in 1924. One of his quirkier endeavours was the creation of a personal patent 'flour' called, rather sinisterly, 'Brain, Bone and Muscle', or B.B.M. for short. Mackie wanted every Highlander to cut as fine a figure as he did, and B.B.M. was a means of achieving this. It was given to all White Horse and Lagavulin workers as a dietary supplement which they were required to eat daily. B.B.M. was milled, in best Sweeney-Todd style, from obscure and unspeakable ingredients in a cellar at Craigellachie. The day after he died, according to Donald Renwick, the mill was turned off, and the unloved B.B.M. followed its creator into oblivion.

Three years later, in July 1927, White Horse Distillers Ltd, Lagavulin and Craigellachie were acquired by the Distillers Company (this was the very same month, as it happened, in which Caol Ila had also been sold to DCL by Robertson & Baxter). In common with every other distillery on the island, Lagavulin was closed in the Depression (there were only two operational malt distilleries in Scotland in 1933), as well as during the two World Wars (for one season in 1918, and between 1941 and 1945). Apart from that, though, Lagavulin has never faced even partial redundancy, and seems unlikely ever to do so. This, manager Donald Renwick claims, is Scotland's busiest distillery; it regularly scraps with Laphroaig for the accolade of 'most popular Islay malt'; as I write, sales have been going so well that it is on allocation in all markets. Over 80 per cent of production is used for pure-malt bottlings, with a small percentage going into its traditional blending role for White Horse. There are also some outstanding contracts which will not be renewed when they expire, but the malt which leaves Diageo's hands in honouring these contracts tends to get bottled as pure malt rather than used for blends.

THE HILL

It was a still day of mist-filtered sunlight towards the end of March 2003 when I set off with Donald (who's a keen walker in his spare time) to visit Lagavulin's water source: the two Sholum Lochs. (On the Ordnance Survey map, the upper loch is marked 'Lochan' – 'little loch' – despite being almost as large as the lower loch.) They lie below Ardbeg's Uigeadail, and at about the same height as Laphroaig's Beinne Brice; indeed Donald and I set off from Kilbride Farm, above Laphroaig, crossing the burn which runs down from Beinne Brice as we made our way up the hill. It had been a dry late winter; the papery grass stems were blond; the hillside dun and desert-like. The heather's purple August glow was long since lost, and the plants either cropped back to their wiry stems by deer teeth, or staining the hillside in brown winter abeyance. The land seemed strangely parched, surprised by the light which eased from the mist. The clockwork of springtime was as yet unwound. Water was the key.

When we reached Sholum Loch, Donald was shocked by its low level. The water had retreated far from the vegetable banks, leaving great rubble beaches of bleached quartzite; it barely cleared the sill for the outflow, and had fallen to eight units below point zero on the level indicator stick. A few more weeks of drought, and Donald would have had to close the distillery.

It was, though, an exquisite sight. This relatively shallow loch occupies four sprawling lobes, making it seem almost landscaped: easy and unfolding on the eye. From its eastern end, the pale blue of the sky was mirrored on the motionless water, while the misty sunlight sheathed the falling land to the west into gentle silhouettes. We turned and climbed to the lochan, following the deeply incised and sometimes reinforced channel between the two, its banks often hoof-trampled. This upper loch is rounder, and proved to be more amply filled (indicating depth). Donald took out some miniatures of Lagavulin 16-year-old from his pockets, and a couple of glasses, and we enjoyed the rich, lustrous malt cut with its own loch water, under the wilderness of a wide March sky.

The descent is far from straightforward, and the path followed by the main watercourse almost impossibly difficult to follow, passing, as it does, through several areas of woodland, under a number of fences, and between the small sills and hills so typical of lowland Kidalton. (It is, though, called Abhainn Smithil, *abhainn* meaning 'river' in Gaelic, whereas most of the Kidalton burns are called *sruthan*, 'little stream'.) When Barnard visited in the 1880s, he was told by his driver that 'the Lagavulin water has a hundred falls before it reaches the Distillery, and that it travels over moss and peat lands all the way down, which is said to give the pronounced flavour to the Lagavulin whisky.' Nowadays this driver could have looked forward to a blossoming career in the marketing department. There are no falls at all worth the name, though there is moss and peat aplenty – exactly like Ardbeg, and exactly like Laphroaig. Donald showed me the small, rough dam where the water is gathered before travelling the final half-mile to the distillery in a pipe; this isn't marked on the Ordnance Survey map, but lies next to the small strip of woodland under Druim Mór (or 'great ridge'). There was once a distillery pool, and its walls and rusting pipework are still visible – crowned, on that bright March day, by the cheery yellow prickle of gorse.

Good water? It certainly is. Different water from Laphroaig and Ardbeg, its two neighbours? It certainly isn't. It is the same: brownly peaty, flowing over hard quartzite and through banks of heather, cottongrass, bog myrtle, bedstraw, bog asphodel – and, of course, the peat which these exquisite, lonely, hardy, shy plants come to compose in decomposing over the centuries ... A water, in other words, very low in mineral content, but high in vegetable content. I have already quoted the Diageo view that the influence of water is (in the words of Douglas Murray) 'the biggest myth which we, as an industry, have perpetuated', and that the influence of peat in the water on Islay's peaty whiskies is (in the single word of former Lagavulin and Caol Ila manager Mike Nicolson) 'baloney'. I disagree with that, as I will describe in writing about Laphroaig (see page 328). Before leaving the matter for now, though, we might note that Mike Nicolson, in remembering his Lagavulin days, described it as an easy distillery to run ('it's hard to get it wrong at Lagavulin,' he said). The only exception to this, he said, was the uncertainty of the water supply. As it came directly from the clouds in the sky via two pools on a distant hillside, and had to make its own way down through bogs, woods and dead animals, it was subject to both seasonal vagaries and physical hazards. 'I'd like to plug Lagavulin into the mains,' said this blues-playing, Gitanes-smoking pragmatist. 'If there were any mains.'

Barnard mentioned the chaotic layout of Lagavulin; the mash-house and distilling room, he said, was 'a sombre building, which brings our memories back to the middle ages', and he said he would have muddled his way had a manager not guided him and his famous tape-measure around. The distillery is still rather chaotic; like the street plan of medieval city centres, it has evolved rather than been designed. A milling explosion in 1952 (tiny stones can cause sparks in the mill plates, and flour dust can be explosive) caused part of the site to catch fire, and there were more major changes in 1962, when the Malt Mill distillery ceased operation. At that point, both distilleries had one wash still and one spirit still each; they were then moved in together, and for four years 'Lagavulin' became a combination of the four, which would certainly have changed its character. In 1966, though, the old, coal-fired stills were taken out and four new, steam-fired stills put in, all of them designed on the Lagavulin models – which was when the Malt Mill trace, thus, was finally lost. The last major change came in 1974, when malting stopped at Lagavulin, and Port Ellen took over the relay.

Lagavulin, as it happens, still owns its former peat banks up on the Machrie, though peat is no longer cut there (the Port Ellen supplies come from the Castlehill moss – or from the Scottish mainland, as they did during 2003 following the wet summer of 2002). The peating specification for Lagavulin's malt is around 35 parts per million phenols, giving finished phenol levels in the new make spirit of between 16 and 18 ppm; as we discovered in the Caol Ila chapter, identical levels there give a very different final result. The recovery of the original phenols in the malt at Lagavulin is good, and no one smelling and tasting the whisky at any moment from new-make infancy to 25-year-old old age can be in any doubt as to the rich peatiness of this Islay grandee.

Lagavulin's mash size, like that of Ardbeg up the road, is relatively small, and the pressure on the distillery to produce as much as possible means that the mash tun is filled no fewer than 20 times a week (the mash cycle lasts five hours). It's a new steel tun, installed in 1996. The 10 larch washbacks, by contrast, are 60 years old. Why have they not been replaced with new steel ones? 'If you ask any manager who has wooden washbacks,' says Donald, 'he will put his hand on his heart and say that these wooden washbacks add something to the process, although he can't prove it. Ask a manager who's got stainless steel washbacks and he'll enthuse about them because they're easy to clean, they're easy to seal – all this kind of nonsense. But if you pin him up against the wall after a long night's drinking, he will openly admit that he'd prefer wooden washbacks.' This may well be so – but it contradicts the message given out by Diageo's tutors on its Malt Advocates' course, where the choice of wood rather than steel is said to be (in Mike Nicolson's words) 'show business – it's just cosmetic.'

'It doesn't make any difference,' says Douglas Murray. 'The wash is in there for such a short period.' The Diageo policy, I was told on that occasion, was to replace wooden washbacks with stainless steel if it was a little-visited or unvisited distillery – but to keep the wooden wash-backs if it was a distillery which received hordes of camera-snapping visitors every year, like Lagavulin. Construe that how you will.

The Diageo experts were agreed, though, that one of the things which did impart a major difference to the character of the spirit was the length of fermentation, which varied throughout the whole group from between 40 hours at the shortest to 160 hours at the longest. In principle, the shorter the fermentation, the more nutty or spicy would be the character of the final spirit (Blair Atholl being the classic example of this nuttiness and spiciness, obtained by a rapid fermentation followed by distillation of the turbid beer). Lighter, finer spirit needs a longer, slower fermentation, or a period for the newly made beer to rest and clarify completely after fermentation. I was told by Douglas Murray and Mike Nicolson that the 55-hour fermentation period which Lagavulin undergoes is relatively slow ('Lagavulin uses heavily peated malt but we try to run the place like a light site,' said Mike), though comparison with some of the other Islay fermentation times suggests that this is not necessarily so: most are longer than 55 hours. And the fact, too, that Lagavulin works right through the weekends means that there are no fermentations left dawdling through a quiet two days, as at less busy distilleries. The fine, sinewy spirit of Bunnahabhain, for example, ferments for between 60 and 80 hours, while the 'long' weekend fermentations at sister distillery Caol Ila last for no less than 120 hours.

Once fermentation is over, the contents of each washback is split into two, and used to fill the two wash stills with 10,500 litres each. This equates to 85 per cent of capacity: a full charge, which is what one would expect for this relatively rich, pungent spirit. The four-hour run through the wash still, however, is slow for this quantity, working some coppery finesse into the vapour. The wash stills are taller than those at Laphroaig and much taller than Ardbeg's squat wash still; the sharp downward angle of the lyne arm from the wash stills is worth noting, as is the fact that their shape is plain rather than ball or lamp-glass. To summarise, we could say that despite the full charge, the low wines will be vaporising slowly and making copper contact as they rise – but once they are over, there is no going back, and there may well be a little carryover. All the reflux, in other words, takes place in the still itself.

The spirit stills at Lagavulin are less tall than the wash stills, but rather broader, which is why (uniquely on the island) they have both a larger total capacity and a larger charge. The aim, according to Donald Renwick, is to have 'a very long and slow spirit run' of ten hours in total, the longest of any of the Kidalton distilleries. A vital reason for this slow and stealthy distillation is that the spirit stills are filled extremely full, to 95 per cent of capacity: the biggest percentage charge on the island, and a further means of creating Lagavulin's pungent, rich spirit. The contrast with Caol Ila, whose spirit stills are given the smallest percentage charge on the island, is dramatic. As already noted, too, Lagavulin's cuts are much 'wider' than Caol Ila's: the spirit comes on at 72 per cent and goes off at 59 per cent, yet another way of creating its more richly peated, congener-influenced style. The shape of the still, too, is a very plump and accommodating version of the 'plain' design, while the lyne arm descends from the top of the still, although more shallowly than for the wash stills. There are of course no purifiers at Lagavulin, and the condensers are smaller and contain fewer tubes than at Caol Ila, another significant character-building difference between the two distilleries. Combine all these factors (especially the rapid fermentations, the full charges, the descending lyne arms and the wider cuts), and you have the full explanation as to why Lagavulin is so different from Caol Ila, despite the fact that it uses identical malt.

Lagavulin's new make is pungent and splendid: a rich, oily emulsion of peat, soap and cereal. It is collected at an average strength of 68.5 per cent abv, and is as usual diluted to 63.5 per cent abv before going into the casks. All of the pot ale, spent lees and washing waters at Lagavulin have to be taken over to Caol Ila by road. They were formerly piped into the bay and had been for over a century, but because the bay is (as the Macdonalds noted a millennium ago) naturally protected and sheltered, these arrangements could not meet current legislation for dispersal rates. This means three tankers per day have to travel the 70-km round trip carrying 21,000 litres each: a heavy financial cost for the company and environmental cost to the island's roads and those who live alongside them. From Caol Ila, the waste goes into the briskly tidal Sound of Islay.

Diageo has no fewer than 29 differently coded cask types in its system to cover everything from a first fill of a freshly imported cask, to the fourth fill of a rejuvenated cask (one which has been mechanically scraped inside before being retoasted and recharred). In principle, though, none of this complexity is relevant since almost all Lagavulin new make goes into third-fill 250-litre American ex-bourbon hogsheads. In other words, these casks have been broken and exported from the USA once their charge of bourbon has been emptied; they are remade in Scotland, and then take one fill of grain whisky, followed later by another fill of another malt whisky, before finally making room for Lagavulin. This is a discreet oak regime – far more so, for example, than down the road at Laphroaig, where the spirit goes straight into freshly imported ex-bourbon casks. 'The aggressiveness,' says Donald, 'of American oak has been smoothed out quite considerably.' And sherry? 'We do fill the odd sherry cask,' Donald says, 'but the wood is exhausted. And we do it less and less nowadays, So far as I'm concerned, there's more or less no sherry any more in Lagavulin.' In times past there was more sherry wood used, as head warehouseman Iain McArthur, known as Pinkie, remembers. 'We used to get a lot of bodega sherry casks, but they were nothing but leaks, nothing but trouble.'

And then? Then, for the lucky few, it's a quiet decade-and-a-half on Islay, with one ear cupped to the sea. There are 7,000 casks in Lagavulin's three warehouses, and another 7,000 down in the very old dunnage warehouses (some of the oldest in the industry) at Port Ellen. A further 2,000 are aged at Caol Ila (there is more Lagavulin aged at Caol Ila than Caol Ila itself). But that's it. The vast majority of the whisky in every bottle of Lagavulin has been aged not on Islay, but on the Scottish mainland. Lagavulin and Caol Ila are the two big exceptions to the general principle that Islay whisky is aged on the island – and to the general belief that island-ageing has a profound influence on the quality of the spirit.

For me, this is a shame. Jonathan Driver of Diageo, the man charged with selling the 'Classic Malts' series into which Lagavulin fits, has spoken of them as 'small château malts using a geographical notion of *terroir*'. If this is so, no opportunity should be missed at any stage to reinforce that stamp of *terroir*, of placeness, in the malts, and passing 16 or more years in Islay's damp, cool maritime climate, with its undulating barometric pressure and its blustering westerlies, is a major opportunity; indeed it is arguably more important than the mere fact of its having been distilled there in the first place. The whisky, let's not forget, evaporates at a rate of two per cent a year, so with every month that passes there is more space in the cask. On Islay, that space is filled with what one distillery manager described to me as 'the air of the sea'. There is no shortage of land on Islay on which to build whisky-storage warehouses, and it would bring more jobs to an island which needs work, especially for the young.

Diageo's experts, however, claim it makes no difference where whisky is aged – provided it is in Scotland. 'Our findings,' says Douglas Murray, 'show that it is Scotland and its climate that is the important thing. It's irrelevant to us whether Lagavulin is aged on Islay or in Central Scotland. Almost all Oban, for example, is warehoused in Central Scotland and yet people still find a 'sea salt' character in it. There is no scientific evidence to show that whiskies aged in different places in Scotland are significantly different from one another, and in some ways quite the opposite.'

Perhaps. Yet I have stood in Macallan's warehouses on Speyside and Dalwhinnie's warehouses on the roof of the Highlands, and even a few minutes in each 'feels' utterly different to the moist, almost misty coolness of Laphroaig's number 1 warehouse or Ardbeg's gloomy number 3. Macallan's warehouses have a much dustier and dryer feel, while Dalwhinnie's are often bone-crackingly cold and still. Obviously weather conditions vary in each location, but I don't doubt that storms (which are frequent) on Islay feel different to storms (less common) on Speyside, or that a bright summer's day at Lagavulin feels different to a bright summer's day at Dalwhinnie. If the Scottish environment makes such a difference compared to that of England, Kentucky or Cognac, then it is counter-intuitive to argue that different locations within the large and wildly various geography of Scotland will have no influence at all. If it doesn't matter, why bother to keep the warehouses at Port Ellen? If it doesn't matter, why evict Caol Ila from its own warehouse to make room for Lagavulin? Perhaps the key word in what Douglas Murray told me was 'significantly'. Pressed on this point, Douglas said in the end that the issue was simply 'not significant enough for us as a company to worry about'. Drinkers, of course, may disagree. If enough drinkers begin to disagree, then it may become significant enough for Diageo to worry about.

TASTING LAGAVULIN

There can be no disagreement, though, that Lagavulin is a very fine dram, even if most of it is aged on the mainland. The youngest variant (aside from those which might be offered by independent bottlers) is the 12-year-old cask strength version, bottled without chill-filtering at around 58 per cent. As you would expect, this is as near as Lagavulin gets to wildcat ferocity: toffee, peat smoke and engine oil tumble over one another in a slitheringly energetic Gaelic knot. Interestingly, when Lagavulin was first released as a single malt, it was a 12-year-old, but when the time swung round to incorporate it into the Classic Malts series in 1989, the blending team felt that, in Donald Renwick's words, it 'just wasn't ready at that stage. So we tried it at sixteen, and sales shot through the roof.' Releasing the 12-year-old as a cask-strength version (with the attendant expense) targets it fairly and squarely at the aficionado, which is a good idea. Do you need to love Lagavulin to get the most out of it? Perhaps, but the choice of casks used in this surprisingly pale blend seems to put some interesting and unexpected notes into the mix: dewy mint, angelica and liquorice. Once watered, elegance is not unthinkable.

The 16-year-old (bottled at 43 per cent) is, of course, the classic. This is a brilliantly constructed whisky. Its aromas without water are rich and multilayered, the elegant oxidative notes of age having muffled the raw roar of peat and conjured some raisiny fruit from a secret recess; leave it in the glass awhile and you will begin to catch a hint of hessian at one moment, a whiff of toasted nuts at another, and the viscous bubble of tar and oil at a third. Water seems to let it breathe a little, freshen it all up, and suggest yet another note: the caress of soft leather. Sip, and you run into a wall of flavour – yet the encounter is less bruising than you might expect. The fact is that, even neat, this powerful whisky opens sweetly and creamily, drawing you in disarmingly before bearing down with a swinging thurible of smoke and spice. With water, it's gentler: a big beast, yet well fed, at ease, inclined to play. I would love to know if Islay-maturation could add the final, moist kiss of perfection to this engaging dram.

The Distiller's Edition version of Lagavulin bears the legend 'double matured' on the label, this being Diageo's way of alluding to what others call a 'finish'. It has, in other words, been put into sherry casks at the very end of its maturation period – and not just any sherry casks, either, but casks containing Pedro Ximenez. What is Pedro Ximenez? It's a grape variety which, in Jerez and Montilla, is laid out on mats once it has been picked to become concentrated and raisin-like; the fortified wine produced from these sticky, juice-less grapes is in truth closer to a food than a drink, and is usually used for sweetening dry sherries. It's black; it's as thick as crude oil; and it's heart-stoppingly sweet. The pores of casks which have contained such a wine will be gorged with this syrup of raisins, and that, sure enough, translates itself into the whisky, as we'll see in a moment. This version of Lagavulin bears a distilling date rather than an age statement, though it is usually around 16 years old as well; it is also bottled at 43 per cent. How long did the spirit spend in the PX butts? 'As you know,' said Donald, 'sherry can take over the character very quickly, and we wanted to leave as much distillery character as we could. It's months rather than years.' The finish is a clever one, since the casky bite of the wood itself is matched perfectly by the moist raisiny qualities of the ghostly wine, making it a wonderful and toothsome after-dinner dram. Even those (like me) who almost always prefer their whisky watered will find a compelling case to take this grand old gypsy Islay neat. If anything, the blenders have grown more daring since the series began, upping the length of time the malt spends in the wood to add an extra bangle, another earring, a further spoonful of toffee, crushed fig and sultana paste.

Finally, a Lagavulin well into its third decade of life: the 25-year-old cask strength (released as a limited edition of 1,000 numbered bottles). It's a complex, harmonious dram in which the raw allusive urgency of the earlier years has been buffed and polished; no one would sniff this old-gold dram and think of the engine room of a fishing smack. The oxidative scents hint at the dried fruits of Madeira or the *rancio* of old Cognac, though there is plenty of hessian and damp earth there, too, to make those who have visited the dunnage warehouses of Scotland smile in fond recognition. Add some water, and it settles down into the glass like a hen on to her nest. The flavours are dryer and deeper than both the 16-year-old and the Oloroso-finished Distillers' Edition, providing a long, rich, meditative mouthful in which the peat of the early years has become a kind of dark, antique oak backbone to stiffen the whisky as the years sink about it. In its notes and allusions, no Lagavulin is less Lagavulin than this. In its dignity and grandeur, by contrast, none is more typical.

Lagavulin   DISTILLERY FACTFILE

Distillery operating hours	– *7 days a week @ 24 hours a day*
Number of employees	– *15*
Water source	– *Sholum Loch and Lochan*
Water reserve	– *not known*
Water colour	– *brown*

Peat content of water – *trace*

Malt source – *Port Ellen*

Own floor maltings? – *no*

Malt type – *Optic*

Malt specification phenols – *average 35 ppm*

Finished spirit phenols – *average 16–18 ppm*

Malt storage – *360 tonnes*

Mill type – *Porteus, installed 1963*

Grist storage – *4.32 tonnes*

Mash tun construction – *stainless steel, Lauter*

Mash size – *4.32 tonnes*

First water – *16,400 litres at 69°C*

Second water – *continuous process (5,000 litres at 68°C added to washback)*

Third water – *continuous process (18,000 litres at 68°C–78°C returns to hot water tank)*

Number of washbacks – *10*

Washback construction – *larch*

Washback charge – *21,300 litres*

Yeast – *Mauri and Quest cultured yeasts (50/50)*

Amount of yeast – *50 kg per washback*

Length of fermentation – *55 hours*

Initial fermentation temperature – *18°C*

Strength of wash – *8.9 per cent abv*

Number of wash stills – *2*

Wash stills built – *1966*

Wash still capacity – *12,300 litres*

Wash still charge – *10,500 litres (85 per cent of capacity)*

Heat source – *steam coils and pans*

Wash still height – *22 feet 6 inches (6.89 m)*

Wash still shape – *plain*

Lyne arm – *steeply descending*

Length of low-wines run – *c. 4 hours*

Low-wines collection range – *50 per cent abv – 0.1 per cent abv*

Number of spirit stills – *2*

Spirit stills built	–	*1966*
Spirit still capacity	–	*12,900 litres*
Spirit still charge	–	*12,200 litres (95 per cent of capacity)*
Strength of spirit still charge	–	*c. 25 per cent abv*
Heat source	–	*steam coils*
Spirit still height	–	*18 feet 10 inches (5.73 m)*
Spirit still shape	–	*plain*
Lyne arm	–	*gently descending*
Purifier?	–	*no*
Condensers	–	*internally sited, 9 feet (2.74 m) long, each containing 121 1-inch (2.54 cm) tubes*
Length of foreshot run	–	*30 minutes*
Length of spirit run	–	*5 hours*
Length of feints run	–	*4 hours 30 minutes*
Spirit cut	–	*72 per cent abv – 59 per cent abv*
Distilling strength	–	*68.5 per cent abv average*
Storage strength	–	*63.5 per cent abv*
Average spirit yield	–	*405 litres of pure alcohol per tonne of malt (2003)*
Disposal of pot ale and spent lees	–	*tankered to Caol Ila, then dispersed in Sound of Islay*
Type of casks filled for branded malt	–	*99.5 per cent third-fill American oak hogsheads; 0.5 per cent third-fill sherry butts*
Current annual output	–	*2,300,000 litres of pure alcohol*
Number of warehouses	–	*3 at Lagavulin (numbered 1, 2, 3); 9 at Port Ellen (numbered 4, 2, 3, 7, 8, 12 to north of road, with 5 and 6 to south of road); plus 1 at Caol Ila*
Type of warehouses	–	*dunnage*
Storage capacity on Islay	–	*7,000 casks at Lagavulin; 7,000 casks at Port Ellen; 2,000 casks (and rising) at Caol Ila*
Percentage of branded malt entirely aged on Islay	–	*well under 50 per cent*
Vatting and bottling location	–	*non-Islay stocks matured at Blackgrange,*

near Alloa; vatting and bottling at Leven
in Fife

Distillery expressions   – *12-year-old cask strength (58 per cent*
  abv, un-chill-filtered)

  – *16-year-old*

  – *Distiller's Edition (approx. 16-year-old,*
  finished in ex-Pedro Ximenez sherry
  casks)

  – *25-year-old cask strength (57 per cent*
  abv, un-chill-filtered)

Major blending roles   – *none; small role in White Horse*

CHAPTER SEVEN

Shipwrecks

Wide water steppes: grey . . .
grass-green. Shearing air. Then fear:
a spire, the long fall.

T HE FARE – AND THIS DURING a year when Islay's laird found himself more than £750,000 in debt – was two pounds and ten shillings for an adult, and children (two to a bed) at half price. The sum took each passenger across the Atlantic from the port of Derry in the north of Ireland to Canada's Quebec. Nineteen had raised the money from the village of Kilmacrenan, including the McDermott and the McGettigan families, who travelled with their ten children and one infant. There were 25 from Strabane, one of them 'an infant at breast'. From Omagh came one woman: Ann Alone.

Two pounds and ten shillings brought them the chance of a new life. They hoped they would never again have to look on rats rummaging inside the ragged skirt of an old woman's corpse by the roadside. Never again, they hoped, would a winter week pass with only turnips boiled with a dog bone and a few morsels of rotting donkey meat to keep them warm. They wanted an end to mockery funerals and grief-hollowed eyes. They wished, in the quiet of their despair, for clothes to wear, and a roof through which rain would never drip; they hoped for dry wood for a hot fire. Their passage-money pittance made them the lucky ones. A strange luck, it was: the luck never to look on the rest of the family again; never again to walk the place in which they had taken their first steps in life; never again to smell hay cut in Ireland.

Were a pestilent equivalent of *Phytophthora infestans*, the fungus that caused potato blight, to strike today's Britain with the force that it struck Ireland in the mid-nineteenth century, it would leave seven million dead. The scourge of the blight fell on a people already traumatised, as were the Highlanders, by the injustice of eviction and clearance. It was to do no more than stay alive that the McDermotts and the McGettigans and the 25 from Strabane travelled to Derry. It was to stay alive that Ann Alone stood shivering on deck at dawn under a thin brown shawl, after a sleepless night in the packed hold, and watched the squally shoreline of Loch Foyle recede behind her forever. There were 230 passengers and ten crew alive on the *Exmouth of Newcastle*, a weatherbeaten 36-year-old former whaler registered to carry just 165, as it dipped its way towards the North Channel during that late Sunday in April 1847, a brisk westerly breeze filling its canvas sails. Land eyes would have seen her depart. Two of them, we might imagine, belonged to James McKibben, the owner of Bushmills Distillery in Antrim, visiting family members at Portrush. As darkness drew on and under thickening skies, he reached home, stabled his horse, and went inside to a waiting tea. As he ate a precious egg or two, he looked up at the barometer on the wall. He paused between mouthfuls, surprised by what he saw. Clutching a napkin, he walked over and tapped it. To his astonishment, instead of jolting to the right, it would have sunk a little further to the left, indicating lower atmospheric pressure than he ever recalled noting. And, as he resumed the eggs of good fortune, his windows would have begun to stir in their frames.

The sea is Islay's environment. For most of human history, the only way to reach or leave the island has been by boat, and under sail. Islay itself, indeed, is a kind of stationary stone boat, anchored by its mineral roots to the sea bed. Stationary? That depends on the time frame. Measure these things against the ticking of the geological clock, and Islay is indeed in movement, leaving Europe behind it. Watch the currents racing down the Sound of Islay, or between Orsay and Portnahaven, and you might almost imagine the island to be in palpable motion, making visual progress across the vast, wind-harried wilderness of the North Atlantic. Nothing, remember, divides Tormisdale, Kilchiaran or Kilchoman from howling Labrador but sea water.

Storms, sometimes severe, are a part of Islay life. At such moments, the seas roar; they climb tree-high; they fall like masonry in an earthquake. On 18 December 1991, for example, part of the bridge of the substantial Russian fish factory ship *Kartli* crumpled like foil when two thirty-foot waves pounded down on it, killing three of her crew members instantly. She was nine miles off the south coast of Islay at the time.

Little surprise, then, that there are over 250 known wrecks and strandings around the coast of Islay, and many more lost to record and memory. Is the island, thus, a paradise for wreck-divers? Not necessarily, as Islay diver Gus Newman points out. 'If you go down to Weymouth [on Britain's south coast], the wrecks are in forty metres of water, they're all intact, and you can swim right through them. Here they're all smashed to a pulp.' Islay's sea swells, buffered by no land mass for 1,700 miles, are remorseless. 'The *Otranto*,' says Gus, 'was 12,000 tons. It's not recognisable as a boat now.' A 2,000-ton steel steamship called the *Belford*, wedged (and photographed) underneath Smaull just north of Tormisdale and Kilchoman on 11 February 1916, had entirely vanished, dismembered and digested by the pounding waves just four days later. Her crew of 13 were all lost, the second mate's body being the only one washed ashore and buried. Gus Newman was in charge of the party of divers from Lancashire that recovered her spare bell. 'Completely flattened, like a bit of paper.'

The rich harvest of catastrophe, though, means that there is always something new to discover. 'You could spend a lifetime on Islay diving, and you'd never discover everything you were looking for.'

The compass of one chapter is not, of course, adequate to do justice to this dossier of loss. There is not space, here, to provide all the details of the night in February 1937 when the fishing trawler *Luneda* ground on to rocks which would normally have been within sight of Ardbeg – but with snow falling so thickly that the crew had no idea where they were. They spent the night in an open boat like twelve snowmen, before the puffer *Pibroch* rescued them in the morning. There are the remains of two railway trains lying beneath the swirling tides which tear past Orsay island at the bottom of the Rhinns: this was where the becalmed *Thomas* was sucked down in August 1857. Their brass, sea-polished and rock-bonded, makes the gully sides 'glitter like a goldmine,' according to Gus Newman. A little further up the Rhinns, and there is more railway wreckage: a number of locomotive chassis, lying off Kilchiaran Bay, scattered amongst jeeps, tyres and Iraqi coinage, marking the spot where the *Floristan* went down in January 1942. Kilchiaran Bay, too, was where the iron barque *Ocean* was wrecked in a storm on 4 November 1911. More than half the crew got off via the fallen mast before the ship was churned to pieces, but not the oldest crew member, who sat for four hours on the stern hatchway waiting for the end, and since it was slow in coming hurried down below decks to meet it there. A little futher north from Kilchiaran, between Coul Point and Saligo Bay, lies another of Islay's wrecked curiosities: the submarine that fought on both sides in the Second World War. U-570 had been on her maiden patrol from Norway when she was captured by British forces, seeing service later as *HMS Graph* (and sinking a sister U-boat in 1942). By 1944 her useful career was over and she was being towed up to the Clyde from Chatham to be used for depth-charge practice when (in the usual heavy weather) her tow line parted and she eventually drifted to her wrecking place.

Islay, as an island, has always relied and still relies on boat traffic for its supplies: the island has seen its ferries wrecked (the paddle steamer *Islay III* ran aground on Sheep Island – Eilean na Caorach near Port Ellen in thick fog on 15 July 1902) and its fuel boat wrecked (the

Eileen M ran aground perilously close to the high cliffs of the Oa on 12 January 1966). How many Ileachs have perished in small sea journeys from one part of its coastline to another is impossible to say, but the historical total would certainly run into thousands. The great-grandfather of Christine Logan of Bowmore Distillery was one: like Christine's father and grandfather, he worked as boatman to Islay's lighthouse-keepers until a squall claimed him off McArthur's Head. Islay has often troubled the trawlers of Fleetwood in Lancashire: the wreck of the *Wyre Majestic*, the most easily visible of any on the island today, has already been described on pages 209–10, but others which have fished no further than Islay include the *Cormoran* (five of whose crew had to spend three January days and nights in the open in a leaky boat before being washed ashore, frost-bitten and starving, on Tiree), the *Criscilla*, the *Anida*, the *Exmouth*, the *Ida Adams* and the *San Sebastian*, as well as the snow-bound *Luneda* with which this little synopsis of mishap opened.

The two most beautiful boats ever to be wrecked on Islay were probably the French barque *Guethary* which ran aground on Cairn Island (Eilean a'Chuirn) packed with nickel from New Caledonia which it was taking to Glasgow; and the graceful sailing ship *Harald*, returning in ballast from Cardiff to Sandefjord, which was another victim of the Oa and its fierce tide rips. Storms of near-hurricane (Force 11) strength have been behind many of the island's wrecks, including two of the most tragic of all, described in detail below. One wild storm, that of 23 November 1893, wrecked 38 fishing boats on Islay alone; 'the whole Sound of Islay,' reported the *Campbeltown Courier*, was 'a boiling cauldron of seething foam and water.' The Islay lifeboat, naturally enough, has been involved in many rescues, and none more dramatic than the 11-hour rescue of the crew (including the Captain's wife and nine-month-old baby daughter) of the Dutch coaster *Regina*, which sank off the Rhinns in a gale on 12 November 1971. The most mysterious of all Islay's wrecks, finally, is that found scattered among Frenchman's Rocks – if indeed it is a wreck at all. There is a cannon down there, and cannon balls, and a broken anchor; a hinge has been found, and navigational instruments, and carpenter's tools, and a silver coin. The most attractive theory was that it was the wreck of one of the missing Armada ships, the *Santa Maria De La Vista*, but the fact that the silver coin was dated 1688 makes this impossible. Despite several RAF Sub-Aqua Federation expeditions, the mystery remains. The objects may have been off-loaded from a ship in difficulties which sank elsewhere – or survived.

The prime purpose of this chapter is to describe the circumstances surrounding Islay's three most tragic wrecks. No fewer than 837 human lives were lost in these maritime disasters. Those 837 people had, like you or me, but one life, and it ended prematurely and in terror among the wild waters and unforgiving rocks of Islay. The vast majority of those 837, interestingly enough, had no business (under what we call normal circumstances) to be making the journeys they found themselves embarked on. None wished to sail past Islay. Most, indeed, had no wish ever to climb into a boat of any sort. All, apart from the professional sailors who crewed these three boats, were there under duress, forced into the danger and discomfort which eventually snatched life itself away from them. By whom? By what? By the arrogance and greed of England's ruling class, which became translated during the nineteenth century in Ireland into famine and eviction; and by the arrogance and greed of Europe's ruling elite, which soured during the early twentieth century into the most pointless of all wars. With which thought, I will swiftly return the reader to the darkening night of Sunday 25 April 1847.

'. . . THE COMMOTION OF THE ELEMENTS'

The *Exmouth of Newcastle* was captained by Isaac Booth of South Shields and manned by nine other Tynesiders, including the captain's 15-year-old son. A seaman's life in the age of sail consisted of miseries and privations; the trial they were about to go through, however, would scar the strongest mind, though only three survived it. A fresh wind had, as we've seen, taken the boat out of Loch Foyle on Sunday afternoon; by midnight, the ship was labouring in a severe storm. Black waves lifted the wooden boat, while the rain flew in bolts. The crew climbed the masts and made their way out along the spars to furl the fore and main sails as the ropes howled in the rain and darkness, their clinging bodies tracing bird-like arcs across the sky as the boat was lobbed by the waves. Later, as the storm worsened, they went up again higher still, to furl the topsails. Provided two catastrophic events are avoided, a seaworthy ship would expect, somehow or other, to weather even conditions like this. If she becomes disabled, though, or if her crew lose or mistake her position, then the situation becomes grave.

It is hard to figure the fear of Ann Alone, the McDermotts and the McGettigans. There were 230 human beings packed in below decks, including 63 children and nine babies. Many would never have stepped into a ship before. All would have been weakened and harrowed by the famine years. The adults would have known this journey was the pivotal one in their lives, and would have spent everything they possessed to be locked into this nightmare prison which took them from their home to the cold enigma of Canada; the children would know little other than terror. After some hours of violent rolling and pitching, the floor would have been slippery with vomit, urine and faeces; the air stinking; the darkness filled with groans and screams.

The storm, a northerly of near-hurricane force, did not beat itself out overnight; if anything, it grew worse on Monday. The ship laboured all day out of sight of land, with never a glimpse of the sun to take any observations. A moonless doomy darkness again fell; again the crew spent the night trying to master and conserve the boat against the abrasions of a mountainous sea. By dawn on Tuesday, both catastrophic events had occurred. The sails were in rags, the longboat and lifeboat away, and the bulwarks stove in; and the master and crew no longer had any idea where they were. The unfortunate Captain Booth, assuming the ship had made headway to the west, set a course south-east, hoping to find shelter along the fractured Donegal coast. Still the storm continued. How was Ann Alone coping, down in the hold? Perhaps she was losing her mind, and ranting aimlessly; perhaps she had joined others in lip-biting prayer; perhaps she was now silent and hopeless, wishing only for an end to a life she had every right to curse.

As Tuesday night drew on, even the crew must have been losing hope. They had not slept nor eaten since Sunday. All their dwindling strength was bent towards keeping the ship afloat, and scouring a violent horizon for a light of some sort. Finally, amid the chaos of rising and falling waters, the lookout saw a glimmer to starboard. It was around 11 at night. Captain Booth's heart thudded; it was what he had been hoping for: Tory Island light, some 50 kilometres west of Malin Head, and still a chance of shelter. He took the boat towards the light.

This was the final deception. As the light grew closer, and when the sea allowed more than a momentary view of it, Captain Booth noted it was flashing every five seconds rather than shining steadily. It must, therefore, be the Orsay light at the tip of the Rhinns of Islay. Far from sailing west, the *Exmouth of Newcastle* had in fact journeyed east. For his ship to meet the rocky coast of the Rhinns in high-running seas, he knew, would be disastrous, yet that was precisely where the storm was now dragging her. He set his remaining sails, attempting to ride the ship off the land, and climbed up to the maintop himself in order to monitor the coast and shout orders to the crew. Midnight passed; it was now Wednesday 28 April; and the *Exmouth of Newcastle* was well north of the beach which might have been its last hope: Saligo Bay.

I've walked Glen Tuath (North Glen), which runs from the tiny, pretty beachlet at Am Miadar (the Meadow) down to the messier, rubbish-strewn pebble shore of Tràigh Bhàn (Fair Strand). At the edge of the glen on the northern side runs a high ridge of hills. Climb them, and you will see the sea far below you, walloping and kettling up against the rock in a series of dizzyingly deep gullies. Even on a calm day, you can see the submarine muscle at work as a football-field full of water is thundered against the rock five times a minute. It was into one of these marine slashes, Geodha Ghille Mhóire or Gilmour's Creek, that the *Exmouth of Newcastle* was hurled at midnight-thirty.

The crew, by this time, were mostly in the tops, hoping that one of the masts would come down on to rocks and give them a bridge to land which might help get any other survivors ashore. The boat struck the rocks four times in all before disintegrating entirely, and three apprentices – William Coulthard, George Lightfoot and John Stevens – who had been with Captain Booth in the maintop succeeded in scrambling on to the rocks. The Captain followed them, but a huge wave took him off the mast as he was crossing; the mast then disintegrated. 'The ship was ground and crunched so frightfully,' according to the report in *The Scotsman* of 5 May, based on the survivor's accounts, 'that she must have broken up almost instantaneously. There was no cry of agony from the multitude of God's creatures cooped up within the hull of the ill-fated brig; or at least it was unheard; for the commotion of the elements was so furious that the men on the top could scarcely hear each other at the top of their voices.' The three young man lay, half-dead, in the pouring rain in a slit in the rock until first light, when they staggered up the hills and across the rough ground to some cattle-grazings. There they collapsed again, hoping someone would come to tend the cattle. No one did. After a while, they struggled on. Having spotted Sanaigmore Farm from a rise at the glen's edge, they made for it, and were fed and put to bed there by farmer Robert White and his family of seven. Did those young men ever go to sea again?

Recovery of the bodies was arduous and harrowing. Even in those more populous times, this was a remote part of the island, and the rescuers had to abseil down into the treacherous gullies to bring up the naked remains, mostly of women and children. Of the 240, 108 rock-mutilated bodies were recovered, and now lie buried under the undulating turf of Tràigh Bhàn, though no stones other than a recently built cairn mark the place. Captain Booth is among them; perhaps Ann Alone, alone forever, too. The laird's son, the many-talented John Francis Campbell, helped in the recovery, and made sketches of the wreck and burial sites. The terrible incident provoked an editorial in *The Times*, which pointed out how poorly trained many of Britain's sea captains were. A far greater indictment, though, came from the fulminating pen of another of the rescuers, who was none other than the great Land Leaguer and radical John Murdoch, at that time working as an Exciseman on Islay. 'They lost their course and, before morning, the *Exmouth* was dashed against the rocks and her unfortunate cargo of living beings shared the fate of the thousands of other evicted Celts who were shipwrecked in rotten vessels to be out of the way of more highly favoured sheep and cattle. The vessel was literally reduced to atoms – for she was an old craft fit only for the timber trade. She had, in fact, been chartered to bring a cargo of timber from Canada. But it was turning a double penny to take out a cargo of "mere Irish". Their passage was paid. And although they and the ship went to destruction, the owners were no losers. And the landlord who cleared out the people thought no more about them than if they had gone quietly to rest in their beds. In Ireland they were in the great man's way. At the bottom of the sea they ceased to trouble him . . . There they rest – well on to 200 of the millions missed in the Irish census of 1851. And when the day of reckoning and retribution comes, the loss of these people will be laid at the door of the supporters of the British feudal land system. And these supporters, coronetted and gartered though they may be, will be arraigned at the bar of justice for the murder of these poor Irish men, women and children.'

'LIKE A WOUNDED BIRD OF THE FLOCK . . .'

The *Tuscania* was mighty and modern: 14,348 tons, almost 550 feet long, twin funnels, four decks, with cabin space for almost 2,500 passengers. Her misfortune was that she was built (for the Cunard-Anchor line, by Alex Stephen & Co of Glasgow) in a dark year: 1914. She never sailed a peacetime journey; most of her working life was spent ferrying troops from their North American homes to a gas-choked death in France; and this modern, mighty ship slid, stern-first, to the bottom of the ocean just 24 hours before her third birthday. There she lies today, about four miles south of the Mull of Oa, in 80 metres of water. The 166 victims who lost their lives on the cold night of 5 February 1918 make her the third most costly of Islay's wrecks in terms of flesh, blood, lost hopes and bitter memories. Of the dismal three, she was the only ship to meet her end on a relatively calm night. Had the weather resembled the storm of 28 April 1847, the night the *Exmouth of Newcastle* was dashed against Islay's rocks; or had it prefigured the hurricane which came eight months later on 6 October 1918, when the name *Otranto* and that of Islay became tragically intertwined, then the *Tuscania*'s toll would most certainly have been much worse. There were 2,397 people (and 30 mules) on board her at the moment at which her destiny changed, which was twenty to seven on the evening of the 5th, and the vast majority of those were saved.

Lt Cpt Wilhelm Meyer had found 5 February a busy and nerve-jangling day. He captained U-boat UB77, which had left Borkum on 29 January. At seven in the morning of the 5th, UB77 had to dive to avoid destroyers. At 8.20 it found a large vessel to attack but the swell meant the giant tube kept breaking water; with the arrival of more destroyers, the attempt had to be abandoned. UB77 had to surface at around 10.30 to recharge its batteries; it dived at 14.18 to avoid a patrol. It reconnoitred with another U-boat at around 15.30, and the two decided, like a pair of pike, to move to the head of the North Channel, the strip of water which separates Ireland and Scotland, and wait for prey. 'With surprise and trembling,' Meyer remembered later, 'at 16.50 in the west I noticed heavy clouds of smoke. We hurried towards these.' UB77 had spotted convoy HX20.

'The submarine service,' Meyer later told one of the survivors of the *Tuscania*, Leo V. Zimmerman, 'was arduous and dangerous work. It required the fullest coordination of the person, in battle against the elements, and the threatening dangers of the enemy. A U-boat that left its home port had to reckon with the 50 per cent probability of never returning. Mines and nets underwater, destroyers, motorboats and armed fish steamers, 'subchasers' on the water's surface, flying machines and airships above: all combine to exterminate us. It was a serious and novel duty that the fatherland required. For us, it was a life of struggle and self-denial. But we were proud of it, so to serve the German people by sea in their struggle for existence, against almost all the nations of the world.'

Meyer chased the convoy for an hour, in gathering darkness. 'I cruised above water back and forth and in front of the advancing transports in order to determine the course and speed of the *Tuscania*. There was constant danger that we might underestimate the speed of the ships and be run down in their path.' He knew he had to attack soon, and decided at 18.05 to do it from the surface on the starboard side. However he suspected a destroyer had seen the U-boat (it hadn't: the convoy was entirely unaware of the danger it was in) and he dived, using the periscope only for the next half-hour. 'Finally do I see gliding into the periscope an indistinct, befogged shadow; only until over this shadow a smoke stack makes its appearance do I recognise the sought-for ship. Thereupon at 18.40 do I fire number one tube, and immediately after the torpedo from number two tube is released. We dive to 30 metres, and the crew and I listen in suspense. One minute and ten seconds later a very violent explosion is felt.'

'It felt,' wrote Zimmerman himself, on board the *Tuscania*, 'like running into a sandbar.' Then came 'the roar of the explosion, the crashing of steel and timbers and also the racket from scattered breakables. Like a wounded bird of the flock, the *Tuscania* whistle incessantly shrieked its call of distress. Up into the sky, like two spurts of blood, climbed and quivered two red stars, submarine warning rocket signals. The night was clear, there was a slight wind blowing, and visibility for about a mile.'

Meyer, his duty to the fatherland done, watched the stricken boat from a safe distance. 'It looked like a spectre of a horse rearing on its hind legs. It was like sitting in a motion picture theatre, viewing a silent film drama, except that we could not see a single human soul.' They listened, forensically, to the radio traffic. 'The position given by the radio signals from the *Tuscania* differed from our calculations by one half a degree North and one fourth a degree West. We put this down to the probability that the *Tuscania* officers were greatly excited.'

As no destroyer pursued them, UB77 let off a third torpedo to hasten the demise of the *Tuscania* at 19.49. It missed. The *Tuscania* was fully abandoned by 20.40, and sank an hour later. She went down, remembered Meyer, 'stern first, the bow but for a few minutes protruding above the sea like a monument'. With her, of course, went the unlamented mules. (She still lies, as Gus Newman says, at 'eighty metres to the deck' – a deep, difficult and dangerous descent which has claimed the life of at least one diver in recent years.)

Three of the eight destroyers in the convoy had instantly turned to assist in the evacuation of the *Tuscania*: HMS *Grasshopper*, *Mosquito* and *Pigeon*. Those taken aboard the destroyers were the lucky ones. Others found themselves in lifeboats in the cold darkness. Theirs was a far greater danger. The propagandist newspapers of the day provided largely fictitious, morale-boosting accounts of the evacuation: the *Daily Record and Mail* of 9 February 1918 had Americans lining up on one side of the boat singing 'The Star-Spangled Banner' while Britons were on the other side singing 'God Save The Queen.' 'The destroyers took off our men in splendid style, and with perfect order,' an anonymous Amercan officer was quoted as saying.

'Writing,' confessed Arthur J. Siplon, a retired policeman in Muskegon, Michigan, 'is a hobby of mine though I have no training in the field.' The modest Siplon's talents meant that, many years later in retirement, he provided an excellent account of what actually happened on that February night. 'The ship's crew evidently had little training in the handling of the lifeboats. In addition, the ship almost immediately listed badly to starboard, thus making it difficult to release lifeboats on the opposite side. Some men attempting to take boats down were spilled into the chilling water like dice from a box. This was caused by lines getting fouled, and then some excited person would cut loose one end with disastrous results. One lifeboat was chopped loose on both ends, and dropped down on a loaded one already in the water. Some of the men thrown from the lifeboats were caught in the wash of the propeller; others were lost between ships.' Siplon grimly watched the 'sights of death, and drowning from those jumping overboard'.

There was no room for him on any of the destroyers, nor for his shipboard friends, 'Ragfoot' Smith and Wilbur Clark. At nine, those remaining on board were told that it was every man for himself. Arthur and Ragfoot found a final lifeboat on the listing starboard side, and managed to get it into the water. Built for 48, there were soon 60 desperate men in it. 'It appeared that this was the last boat to get away, and we were the last men to leave the ship.' They watched it sink. 'Our mighty ship was leaving us. Just a few short hours ago she was moving majestically towards Liverpool, England. Now the bow was lowered, throwing its monstrous stern into the air. [Siplon's recollection conflicts with Meyer's in this respect.] There it briefly paused, in stark silhouette against a stormy sky – then with a muffled explosion slid ignominiously below darkened waters. It left us with an eerie and lonesome feeling.'

The night was a chill one. Waves were breaking over the boat, and it had to be baled out continuously. There were only three oars on board, and none of the 60 men had any idea where they were or where they were going. 'We could not control the boat, and it was caught and moved sideways in the trough of the waves, and pitched from crest to crest.' Midnight came and went. One passenger died of exposure. Through the gloom, some of the sharper-eyed men thought they could make out land – land which turned out to be the vast and sinister mass of the Oa. 'Some time later, we could faintly hear the roar of the surf. The sound of it increased as we went closer, like a dire warning of imminent disaster.' Even on a calm day, the waves which beat against the rocky shore of the Oa are huge and rangy, full of the lazy power of the open ocean, and it was one such which tipped the overloaded lifeboat against a rock in the small hours of the morning, emptying its human contents into the sea. Arthur Siplon and Wilbur Clark managed to clamber again on to the now-upturned lifeboat, but were washed off by a second huge wave. 'It was then just a matter of being buffeted about against the bruising rocks, washed in with the waves and out with the undertow. Just how long this pounding lasted there is no way to determine. When it seemed my last breath was reached . . . I was struck forcibly in the chest [by a rock]. I grabbed it with both hands.' Siplon found himself out of the water at last, battered and bleeding, together with another survivor, a boy. They found a tiny cave. 'Here we tried to protect ourselves against the bitter cold. We snuggled up into each other's arms like a couple of cub bears, to keep from freezing to death.'

As dawn broke, they heard a call and saw a light. 'It proved to be a kindly farmer, who lived close by in the headlands. He said he thought something had happened last night off his rocky shore, and came to take a look around. He told us we were on the island of Islay, and had landed on the most rocky and dangerous part of the whole coastline. When daylight arrived, a terrible sight met our eyes. Many dead bodies were washing about by the sea. A number of men were badly injured with broken arms and legs, or other injuries. My close pal, Wilbur Clark, who shared a brief moment with me on the upturned boat, was among the lifeless forms, and Ragfoot Smith, too, was numbered among them.'

The farmer took the pair to his croft, where Siplon smelled peat smoke for the first time. 'His wife made scones on an ancient fireplace, fired with peat. With the scones, she served hot invigorating tea, until the supply was completely exhausted.' They were eventually taken to

Port Ellen, where they learned that, of the lifeboat of 60, only six had survived. 'The kindly folks of Port Ellen proved to be angels of mercy. Many of the mothers gave up the best clothes of husbands and grown sons, most of them away to war.' The White Hart Hotel was used as a hospital for the injured, who lay three to a bed.

The man charged with recovering the bodies of the dead and looking to the needs of the living was Police Sergeant Malcolm MacNeill, who was about to endure a year which must have haunted him for the rest of his life. He was, as it happens, the maternal grandfather of George Robertson, the Ileach who became British defence minister in the Labour government of 1997, and later (as Lord Robertson of Port Ellen) Secretary-General of NATO. Sergeant MacNeill's punctilious records of the recovery of the bodies, typed up in purple ink, have remained in the Robertson family and have now been permanently loaned by Lord Robertson to the Library at Islay's Museum of Rural Life.

Burials were an urgent priority, but survivors like Siplon were distressed that there was no American flag to be found on Islay. 'It didn't seem proper,' Siplon remembered, 'to bury a soldier so far from home without the comfort of the Flag for which he had given his life. The answer was not slow in coming. It came from the generous-hearted mothers of the village of Port Ellen. They would make a flag, even as Betsy Ross had made the first one, with their own hands. They searched their homes, and found the necessary red, white and blue. They cut out the white stars and tenderly sewed them on the field of blue.' Mary Armour, Florence Hall, Jessie MacLellan, Catherine McGregor and (no mother, but no matter) John McDougall were the five who made the flag, and it is today kept at the Smithsonian Institute in Washington. Siplon saw his friend Wilbur Clark buried on the Oa: he was just eighteen, and 'the 1917 honour student of his class in Jackson, Michegan. The folds of the homemade flag whipped smartly in the winter's chilling wind.'

Most of the bodies were eventually repatriated or re-buried at the American cemetery at Brookwood, Surrey. Not, though, all. In Kilnaughton Military Cemetery, facing the sea between the Oa and Port Ellen, is one of Islay's most famous tombstones.

Unknown Negro
S.S.Tuscania
5th February 1918
Known Unto God

It has been the source of much speculation. (It has also, shamefully, been defaced and inadequately cleaned.) The *Tuscania* survivors reported that, although there were some American Indians and many Mexicans aboard the ship, none could remember any black troops. (Many of the victims of the *Otranto*, by contrast, were black.) Amid a crowd of 2,397, however, no one could remember everyone; the unknown victim might in any case have been a crew member. What is certain is that he was someone's son, quite probably someone's brother, and quite possibly someone's father. He grew up far away, and may never have known that the island of Islay existed; yet his bones have lain there now for 85 years, and they will lie there until they become part of the island itself.

'. . . LIKE PAPER IN A WHIRLWIND'

They chose satin-wood for the music room; Italian walnut was felt to be more appropriate for the lounge. 'The ceiling of hand-modelled plaster,' wrote the correspondent for *The Syren and Shipping*, having looked over the first-class dining saloon in Workman, Clark & Co's yard in Belfast, 'is extremely interesting, and, being lit by large and lofty domes, an effect of lightness and airiness is achieved far beyond what is usually associated with ship furnishing, making most successful rooms for travelling through the tropics.' The *Otranto* was destined to see a lot of the tropics: it was intended to work out its days cruising to and from Australia on the mail run, which was why Australian wine, and not Champagne, spilled from the broken bottle swung against her bows as she was launched in the summer of 1909. Her maiden voyage took her from London to Brisbane, sailing on 1 October. Cigar smoke, doubtless, drifted out from a bridge party in the first-class smoking room as she glided past the Azores, while star-gazers picked out Pegasus in the winking night sky. The following day, under a balmy sun, the ship's photographer recorded for eternity the ladies' potato race, the egg-and-spoon race, and pillow fighting on the spars.

Nine years later, and the satin-wood and the Italian walnut had been removed. So had the first-class smoking room; so, indeed, had been the cabins where the 1,400 fare-paying passengers passed their tranquil nights. In their place were row after row of bunks; indeed according to one account, the ship had been fitted out to transport 18,000, which suggests not bunks but hammocks. Few, though, were filled; there were just 665 American soldiers on board. Many were black, from the central southern states; most had never stepped into a ship before. The *Otranto* was to take them to fight, with resigned bewilderment, Europeans in Europe. Among them was Shellie Webb from Ray City, Georgia, who had lost the big toe on his left foot but had a good watch; among them was David Roberts, who knew the Kentucky mountains; among them was Ira Garland, Lewis Shuets and Rivil Parker. Edgar Shepherd from Augusta Georgia joined the *Otranto*, too, with grave misgivings: he saw rats jumping into the sea from the ship as he boarded, and was later to write that he was 'born to undergo tragedy'. He did, nonetheless, find enough cheer to wave at the girls standing on the Statue of Liberty as the ship passed. The *Otranto*, under the command of Ernest Davidson, became Commodore vessel to Convoy HX50, which formed in the Lower Hudson and left Hoboken, New Jersey on 24 September 1918. There were thirteen ships in the convoy, escorted by two US cruisers and a destroyer.

Convoys powered unlit through the night, and there was in 1918 much other maritime traffic on the sea relying on sail alone. Seven days into the crossing, the dark mass of the *Otranto* bore down on just such a ship, a French barquentine called *Croisine*, on its way back across the Atlantic from the still-teeming Grand Banks. The crew of 36, including its Captain Jules Le Hoerff, were rescued and taken on board the *Otranto*; so too was Captain Le Hoerff's Newfoundland dog. The *Otranto* then turned her searchlights on, and its gunners sank the *Croisine* so that she would present no further danger to shipping. One of the French fishermen told Edgar Shepherd that it was the sixth time he had been wrecked.

The convoy eluded the U-boats and their torpedoes which had proved fatal to the *Tuscania* just eight months earlier that year. The weather, though, worsened, and soon the convoy found itself in a storm as severe as that which broke the *Exmouth of Newcastle* and its huddled emigrants. By the night of Saturday 5 October, the wind measured storm force 11 and Edgar Shepherd saw waves 40 feet high break over the masts of this large ship. Shepherd wrote later that, being largely empty, the ship had been rolling and listing throughout the voyage. 'This within itself,' he recalled, 'kept all frightened.' With the worsening weather, though, the movement of the ship became violent. One soldier committed suicide during the crossing; another died of the Spanish flu which was soon to kill millions; all were seasick; most were terrified. At which point, matters became very much worse.

As with the wreck of the *Exmouth of Newcastle*, catastrophically bad weather combined with errors in navigation had much to do with what followed. Land was seen shortly after dawn on Sunday. Most of the convoy identified this as the south-west coast of Scotland, though few if any thought it was Islay; the *Otranto*'s watch officer, by contrast, thought it was the island of Inishtrahull, off Malin Head in Northern Ireland. The *Otranto* therefore turned to port, and to the north, at a time when the other ships (and most notably the adjacent *Kashmir*) were turning to starboard. All of the ships, in any case, were having great difficulty steering a course through the violent seas. To his horror, Captain Davidson suddenly saw the *Kashmir* surging on a wall of water towards his own ship. What followed was rapid and confused, though the enquiry (under Lord Justice Hill) later decided that both ships changed direction when they saw they were on a collision course, but that both of these orders were in turn countermanded. Thus it was that, amid 40-foot waves and in a force 11 gale, the 8,985-ton *Kashmir* ploughed into the side of the 12,124-ton *Otranto*. It was about 8:45 in the morning. The ships fell away from each other and were soon lost in the furious gloom; no other ships in the convoy were within view. After the collision, the *Kashmir* found herself seaworthy and limped on, assuming that the *Otranto*, a larger and stronger ship, would be in better shape.

She wasn't. She shipped a huge amount of water which eventually extinguished her engines; she dropped her anchors but they failed to find or hold the bottom and were lost. She sent out an SOS.

On Saturday, the convoy's American escort had dropped away and a British escort was scheduled to take over the protective relay. The demonic weather, however, meant that the convoy was scattering and the escort failed to find its flock; most gave up and returned to port. One destroyer, however, continued the search, though one of its own crew, Gunner Fred Robinson, admitted later that 'we hardly knew where we were.' This was the 896-ton HMS *Mounsey*, whose acting captain was Lt Francis Craven. The *Mounsey* spotted some straggling ships at first light, and sighted land (Lossit Point on the west coast of the Rhinns, they learned later) around 8.30. 'The weather can't get any worse than it is, Gunner,' Robinson recalled Craven saying to him. Robinson himself never saw a severer storm in 26 years at sea.

The *Mounsey* picked up the *Otranto*'s SOS call, and located the ship at 9.30. Davidson, realising that the disparity in size between the two ships in such a sea would make any rescue attempt all but impossible, warned Craven not to bring his ship alongside. Craven, however, was a man of temerity. He refused the order (for which he could have been court-martialled) and pushed his ship head into the wind behind the powerless bigger vessel, so that the wind itself would bring the drifting *Otranto* alongside for a few critical moments. This gave the soldiers the chance of a jump, though timing was everything: at one moment the waves put the decks within five or ten feet of one another, but a few seconds later the deck of the *Mounsey* would drop down forty feet below that of the *Otranto*. The *Otranto*'s lifeboats were used as fenders to stop the two boats grinding each other. They were reduced to tinder as the *Mounsey* attempted to come alongside no fewer than eight times, four of those successfully. This astonishing feat of seamanship no survivor ever forgot.

Nor did they forget the terrible scenes which punctuated the rescue. According to the patriotic, truth-bending reporter of the *Belfast Telegraph*, the American soldiers 'lined up as if on parade, and at the word of command stood to attention like statues. They never wavered. They remained there in military formation, exemplifying during the crisis the noblest traditions of the Army for heroism and discipline. The same thing applied to the seamen.' Edgar Shepherd, who was there, remembered terror and panic, with the older troops 'running up and down the deck crying and wringing their hands'. Some of the troops timed their jump badly and fell into the sea; others broke legs as they smashed down on to the *Mounsey*; others made it safely on to the destroyer's deck but were then washed off again by the waves. Some fell between the boats and were cut horribly in two by the deck plates; one man actually fell into the forward funnel of the destroyer. Shepherd himself got off on the *Mounsey*'s final attempt to come alongside. The *Croisine*'s captain Jules le Hoerff mistimed his jump and fell into the sea; his Newfoundland dog leapt into the waves after him. Another vivid memory was of the *Otranto*'s young bugler who, having played the notes of 'Abandon ship' clearly and loudly, threw his instrument in a wide arc into the water, as if he knew he would never need it again. A fellow officer on the *Mounsey*, Lt Warner, remembered Craven's eerie bravery, for which he was awarded the V.C. and America's Distinguished Service Medal. 'During the whole of this operation he never showed the slightest excitement, and during the worst of the business he was laughing. To use an Americanism, he "scared the pants off me".' The *Mounsey* eventually made for Belfast around midday in such a battered state that it never went to sea again; the ship's engineer said later that he considered Craven's seamanship in nursing the ship back was even more outstanding than the rescue itself. The bridge had been smashed beyond recognition, and the port side was crumpled. No fewer than 313 injured and shocked soldiers from the *Otranto* together with 239 crew-members and 30 fishermen from the *Croisine* (some now wrecked for the seventh time) filled every inch of the little destroyer and were lashed to her deck; there was water down below, a heavy roll which frequently took the ship to the edge of capsizing, and vomit everywhere. Meanwhile, on the damaged bridge, Craven and his fellow mariners ate ham and drank sloe gin. (The fearless Craven, as it happened, didn't have long to live. He joined the Royal Ulster Constabulary after the War, and was killed by a landmine in the Irish uprising of February 1921.)

Despite the *Mounsey's* best efforts, there were still almost 450 people on board the *Otranto*, which now drifted helplessly towards the Rhinns coast. The storm was not abating, and in the early afternoon the ship ground on to a reef about half a mile off the cliffs known locally as Granny's Rock and marked on the map as An Crois-sgeir (Cross Reef). On a calm day, Machir Bay is within easy reach, but some measure of how impossible the conditions were can be gauged by the fact that out of the 450 only 20 men (17 soldiers and three crew members) made it to shore, and of those four died shortly afterwards. The total death toll on the *Otranto* was 431, making it the worst convoy disaster of the First World War.

It was around five in the afternoon when news of the wreck reached Sergeant Malcolm MacNeill of Bowmore Police Station. Was Lord Robertson's maternal grandfather a man of strong mental constitution? One must hope so, since the trauma of dealing with the battered and mutilated bodies washed ashore after the *Tuscania* disaster was about to be revisited on him, and with redoubled force. Once again, his meticulous notes on the victims, typed in purple ink, make sober reading. Ira Garland's body was washed ashore with $1 and 50 cents, a testament and some papers; Lewis Shuets had just 10 cents and a razor; Frank Loughran had a whistle; Rivil Parker had nothing. At least they could be identified. Of victim 265, MacNeill wrote 'Head crushed and gone except scalp and all from waist down missing. Description, light brown hair. From appearance of upper part of trunk – ordinary build. No other description possible.' Victim 305 was simply 'in a bad state of decomposition', while Victim 357 was 'much decomposed, description impossible'. Despite the ship going down within half a mile of Machir Bay, two bodies were found on Coll, two on Colonsay (including the 'nude body of a man, about 5' 6½", ordinary build, no hair, flesh dropping off head and feet') and that of Victim 376, Corporal James Williams, was found on Mull. The final body, that of Frank Dismore, was not recovered until the following March, long after the War he left his home to fight had concluded.

One of the 16 survivors who had made it off the *Otranto*, David Roberts, wrote a short but vivid letter to his mother from the Bridgend Hotel. He told her how the colour of the sea changed on Sunday from blueish black to grass-green; he said the waves looked 'just like the Kentucky mountains'. It was those waves, he remembered, which 'carried me away from the ship, then one came about me high as a house and whirled me around like paper in a whirlwind. Believe me,' he continued with a plain man's understatement, 'we live high. Your loving son David Roberts.'

Captain Davidson went down with his ship, and his grave, together with those of a number of his crewmen, can be found today in a small, quiet enclosure just above Machir Bay over which the setting sun falls. As with the *Tuscania* victims, the American bodies were initially buried in Islay's earth, but later most were taken either back home to America, or to the American cemetery at Brookwood in Surrey. Those, that is, that were found. In January 1920, Sergeant MacNeill was awarded the MBE for his harrowing work.

In June of that year, he took delivery of a letter, initially received and then forwarded to him by a survivor from New York.

> *Kind Sir,*
>
> *We lost a dear Boy on the ship Otranto (Shellie L. Webb) and your name has been given to me as one who was there at the time and I am writing to you to see if I can get any information as to my dear Boy. We can't find where he was ever picked up. There are fifty-one unidentified buried there and my boy could be identified very well as his big toe on his left foot was off; also he had a scar on his left hand caused by a burn also he had a good watch that I would be so glad to get. It would be some relief to my heart-broken family to know that he was buried. Now Kind*

Sir if you can help me in any way I assure you it will be appreciated.

Hoping to hear from you real soon I still remain a heart-broken mother.

Mrs J.T. Webb, Ray City, Ga

Sergeant MacNeill was unable to help.

POSTSCRIPT

Whisky Galore! are the two words (and a punctuation mark) which evoke, for many, the spirit of the Hebrides. They constitute the name of a popular novel by Compton Mackenzie which was first published in 1947, and of a much-loved film (from the Ealing Studios) of that novel which appeared in 1949. The event which both novel and film reworked in fictional form was the wrecking of the SS *Politician* on 5 February 1941 off the bleak Outer Hebridean island of Eriskay (or 'goblin island': it lies between Barra and South Uist). The *Politician*, attempting to evade the attentions of Germany's highly effective Second World War U-boats, had unwisely attempted to nose through the Sound of Eriskay, foundered near the islet of Calvay, and broken in two. She carried plumbing fittings, motorcycle parts, fine silks, £3 million's worth of uncirculated Jamaican currency – and 264,000 bottles of The Antiquary, White Horse, King's Ransom, Johnnie Walker Red and Black Label, Mountain Dew, MacCullum's Perfection, Old Curio, Spey Royal and other choice Scotch whiskies. Compton Mackenzie was living on Barra at the time, and his novel was a warm-hearted account of how the islanders, having first seen to the safety of the crew of the 'Polly', subsequently saw to the safety of the spirit, concealing it with great ingenuity from the over-dutiful Excisemen Charles McColl and Ivan Gledhill. Mackenzie omitted from the narrative the fact that 36 islanders were subsequently prosecuted by the ever-humourless Customs & Excise (including a 14-year-old boy), and that 19 of them were subsequently imprisoned in Inverness.

Less well known is that Islay had its own *Politician* – called the *Mary Ann*. The story took place almost a century earlier, towards the end of May 1859. The *Mary Ann* was a wooden brig which set sail, under Captain Pryce, from Glasgow to New Brunswick with 300 tons of pig-iron – and a substantial cargo of brandy, whisky, gin and wine in both boxes and puncheons. The *Mary Ann* appears to have been barely seaworthy: she immediately sprang a leak, and put into Dublin for repairs. These effected, she set off again, only to spring a new leak, this time off the west coast of Islay. As she was beginning to sink in a fresh offshore wind, the crew abandoned ship. The wind then changed to a westerly, which enabled local fishermen from Portnahaven to give her a tow into the soft and sandy embrace of Machir Bay (called Kilchoman Bay in contemporary accounts).

The year 1859 was not a happy one on Islay. The island was thickly populated, and many of those once engaged in farming had been evicted from their homesteads to make way for sheep. The potato blight, and its attendant miseries, were an anguished recent memory. Some of those pushed off the land had made for America or Canada, lost to their relatives forever; but those that remained had been settled by the laird in the planned villages which now delight the tourist eye, and told that they should fish. So fish they did, in huge numbers. Even by the time of the Royal Commission 35 years later, there were 50 fishermen in Port Wemyss and a further 80 fishermen at Portnahaven. Neil Macnab, a 67-year-old from Port Wemyss, had (by April 1894) been a fisherman for 40 years; he had been forced into it ('it is not for the love of it'), and for 40 years he and his fellow fishermen had cast a yellow eye on 'the farm that is a desert and uncultivated' called Ballymony sheep farm. 'Do the fishermen at Port Wemyss make a fair living at the fishing one year with another?', he was asked by the commission chairman, the crofter's MP Angus Sutherland. 'There is not a fisherman at Port Wemyss,' replied Neil Macnab, 'that will support himself by fishing alone.'

These are the facts that should be remembered as you read of what happened on the long, sunlit May evenings following the beaching of the *Mary Ann*. 'Hundreds of people,' learned the readers of the *Argyll-shire Chronicle* on 27 May, 'flocked from all parts of the neighbourhood, especially the Portnahaven fishermen, who turned out to a man. Boxes were seized as soon as landed, broken up, and the contents were carried away and drunk. Numbers could be seen here and there lying amongst the rocks, unable to move, while others were fighting like savages.' The police arrived – Sergeant Kennedy and Constable Chisholm – and established some order, until the summer dusk drew on. 'When,' continued the reporter, who seemed to imagine himself describing a colonial skirmish in darkest Africa, 'night came on some of the natives showed some evidence of their disapproval of the police being there at all, and on the latter preventing a fellow knocking out the end of a puncheon, in order, as he said, to "treat all hands", they were immediately seized upon by the mob, and a hand-to-hand fight ensued, which lasted half an hour, and ended in the defeat of the police.' Kennedy and Chisholm legged it up the hill to Coull Farm, 'closely pursued by about 30 of the natives, yelling like savages'. James Simpson and his wife, who farmed Coull, took the police in, and supplied them with guns of some sort, at sight of which the drunken fishermen returned to the beach to prolong their unanticipated party.

'Next morning the scene presented was still more frightful to contemplate. Donald McPhayden, a fisherman from Portnahaven, was considered the strongest man on Islay; but the brandy proved to be still stronger. He has left a wife and family. Others apparently in a dying state were conveyed to the nearest houses, where every means was used to save life.' James Simpson made a coffin for Donald McPhayden, the fallen Goliath of Portnahaven, and buried him the next day. 'At the time when the corpse was being taken away, some groups could be seen fighting, others dancing, and others craving for drink, in order, as they said, to bury the man decently.' There were two further deaths over the weekend.

SEVENTH GLASS

Laphroaig

The hopes of gold grains
die in smoke. Night falls. Outside:
sleek otters slip home.

LAPHROAIG (pronounced 'La-*froig*') is both savage and pretty. Savage,
for its malt encapsulates better than any other the aerial boisterousness
of this edge of the southern Hebrides. Smoke and seaweed are more
than distant allusions, here, winking distantly through taut staves and
grains; they provide the drink's caustic, billowing matter. The ocean
bears down on Laphroaig with unrivalled glee; its warehouse walls are
regularly flayed with kelp, and the distillery manager's sitting-room
windows have been, on every occasion I have visited, sticky with brine.
Laphroaig's peat, part of it dug from the moss near Islay airport and
sent billowing through the grain in one of the island's two working
kilns, floats no less palpably through the finished spirit; the stubby little
stills sublimate those raw materials with fierce fidelity. Laphroaig
10-year-old is Islay's most exuberant and uncompromising dram.

And pretty, for its site ('the place of the hollow') is the neatest and sweetest of all of the island's distillery settings. The Kidalton road climbs out of Port Ellen, bumping over hills left by the sea and crossing a line or two of the distinctive hard-rock sills which lend so much intrigue to the landscape of this south-eastern part of the island. The road comes within splashing distance of a wild sea at one point, then straightens and makes its way inland. The first clue that Laphroaig is nearby comes as its three most modern warehouses slide into view; they are sited, dully if practically, up by the road. Shortly after them, in the middle of a conifer plantation, is the right turn to the distillery. Follow the drive down, and you will soon come to a little white community of buildings divided by neat lawns; the Prince of Wales's crest is proudly hammered into the wall of the office buildings on the left, for this is the favourite whisky of today's Lord of the Isles, the hapless aviator Charles Windsor. (It was when visiting his beloved Laphroaig on 29 June 1994 that he guided his plane off the runway and into the comforting Islay mud. He was on Islay for four hours, eventually leaving in a red helicopter; the plane remained for six weeks.) If you're in luck, the wind will be trouncing peat smoke about the yard when you visit, and it will mingle with the brighter, estery urgency of distillation. The focal point of all is the bay itself. It is sheltered, being a U-shaped inlet scoured out of the quartzite between two higher, harder banks of metagabbro; yet it meets, to a greater extent than its neighbours Lagavulin or Ardbeg, the full force of the westerlies. To the peat smoke and distillery vapours, then, you can add a heady marine lungful or two.

This, mind you, was once a forbidden view.

THE LAST DESCENDANT

'He wouldn't have allowed you into this place,' former distillery worker Iain Maclean told me. 'There was a notice at the road end. "Strictly private. No admittance except on business." I'll always remember that notice. In the summer months, when the distillery was silent, all the doors had to be locked; every place had to be locked. I don't know what his reason was. There's no secret in making whisky; everybody makes whisky by the same process. Now why he should have all the doors locked I don't know; he was very secretive in his ways.'

The secretive man was Ian Hunter, Laphroaig's last family owner. He arrived in 1908: a brisk young engineer with neatly oiled hair, the son of a whiskery Leith seed merchant, sent to look after his plump mother's interests on the island. He died in 1954, wifeless, childless and sick (some say with arterial sclerosis, others say with cancer). 'The poor man,' recalls Iain Maclean, 'was more or less an invalid. I used to take him out along the main road in a chair. That was a good job; I didn't mind that at all. It was lovely. That was better than the distillery work. I enjoyed taking him out in the invalid chair, away up the road.'

Ian Hunter's management style was typical of its place and its period. 'He was difficult,' says Iain Maclean, who began work for Laphroaig in November 1927, aged 14. 'No matter what it was, he always found fault. But of course there was nothing you could do about it; there was no other place you could go. No other work, nothing. He took advantage of that.' Maclean, sacked and reinstated twice by Hunter, was one of the few who was not intimidated by him. 'One night he landed up at my house, all togged up with this big heavy scarf round his neck. One of the men had got drunk during the day, and of course he blamed me for it, you know? He knocked at the door. "I want to see you down at the office," he said. "Aye right," I said. "That's fine." It was pitch dark. I followed him down the road. When I came to the garden gate, I took a short cut through the garden; he walked round. When he landed up at the office, I was standing in front of the door. He got the shock of his life. He thought I was going to be scared stiff of him, you see, but it was the other way around. So in we went. "Now listen," he said; "that man was the worse for drink." "Yes," I said, "I know that." "You're responsible," he says. "I'm nothing of the sort," I said. "I warned you once before that you shouldn't take that man on, and you didn't take any notice of me. You're entirely to blame yourself." He was stuck for words; he couldn't answer me. I was in a hell of a mood, and no bloody wonder. So when I was going out of the door, I gave it one hell of a belting. He got a fright. You could put up with so much, but not more. He always had to blame someone.'

Maclean remembers one way by which distillery workers could

avoid him. 'He used to wear . . . I don't know what the stuff was on his hair, brilliantine or whatever; it was heavily scented, you know? And when you were up on the malting floor or near the kiln door, you see, there was always a certain amount of draught. If you were going in there and you caught a whiff of that scent, you'd know he was in there and you'd better turn back. It was a giveaway. You'd turn back. No matter wherever you were and you got a whiff of it, you'd turn back.' Whisky alone mellowed him. 'The only time that he was really happy was when he had a good dram on him. Oh yes. If you met him with a dram on him, everything in the garden was lovely. But if you met him the day after or the night before, you avoided him.'

For all Hunter's failings, he was a sound and committed steward of the distillery through difficult times. Laphroaig's popularity as a single malt mirrors its historical popularity among blenders (who even today continue to take 90 per cent of production). 'Hunter never advertised Laphroaig in the papers or anything like that,' confirms Iain Maclean. 'And yet he was never without work. The place worked. There was always a demand, yet he never advertised it. The demand was for blending. There's not a whisky in Scotland that doesn't have Laphroaig in it.' In earlier times still, too, this was a much-coveted distillery. 'The place of the hollow', it would seem, was destined to distil.

SCENT OF THE PAST

Its history is a complicated one – and sometimes tragic. One owner died after being horribly burned by falling into a vat of hot still waste; two have died heirless; another died leaving three wills. Its final owner, Bessie Williamson, had no children either, and chose to sell it rather than pass it to her own relatives. It became the property of a once-great but eventually myopic brewer (Whitbread); now it is a small cog in the giant drinks machine of multinational Allied Domecq.

All of this would, likely as not, be wholly beyond the comprehension of its founder-farmers, Donald and Alexander Johnston, who began distilling here (according to one of the many conflicting accounts of this vitally important but little-recorded family) between 1810 and 1816. Their father John, some sources say, had come with his two brothers

Roland and Duncan to Islay for quiet refuge and a name change (from MacIan); the trio had backed the English against Bonnie Prince Charlie in 1745, and had felt it politic to leave their home on the Ardnamurchan peninsula, north of Mull, as a consequence. Islay was where they began anew. They farmed at Lagavulin, Laphroaig and at Tallant, which lies just inland from Bowmore (indeed Bowmore's distillery lade, connecting the river Laggan with the distillery, passes close to little Loch Tallant). John Johnston was Lagavulin's first licensed distiller.

Donald seems to have been in charge by 1826, and he became sole owner in 1836 on the death of his brother. 'Owner', of course, signifies walls and slates rather than land: the rock and peat belonged to Islay's laird, which at this moment meant Walter Frederick Campbell. Not for the first or last time, the laird's interests didn't necessarily coincide with those of the tenant. Little Laphroaig, it would seem, was producing impressive whisky; it attracted envious attention; and this, moreover, the moment of Islay's population explosion, with every morsel of cultivable land being hungrily eyed. In 1837, Campbell leased the neighbouring property to two entrepreneurial brothers called James and Andrew Gairdner; they promptly established a rival distillery alongside Laphroaig, handing over its management to a second brace of brothers who (by another of the confusing coincidences in which Laphroaig's history abounds) were also called James and Andrew. The surname in this case, though, was Stein. The pair were experienced lowland distillers from Clackmannan, close to Stirling. This second distillery was named Ardenistiel and, crucially, it relied on the same water source as Laphroaig: at that time, the Sanaig burn, a westerly forerunner of today's little Kilbride. Donald Johnston was aghast, and went to law, assuring the court 'of the impracticality in the dry season of two distilleries being properly supplied with water. There is scarcely enough for one. I am at a standstill,' he continued, 'and cannot carry on with any improvements.' In the event, though, Ardenistiel barely achieved adulthood as a project; Andrew Stein died suddenly in 1846, and his brother James moved to Port Ellen to work with his cousin, a bright young man very much on the up: John Ramsay. (James eventually became Ramsay's brother-in-law, too, marrying another cousin: John's sister Margaret.)

Ardenistiel maundered on until the 1860s. One manager, John Morrison, had occupied himself more assiduously with pig farming on Texa, the 48-ha island which lies directly south of Laphroaig, than with distilling across the water, and Ardenistiel never seems to have been in full production. John Morrison, in any case, had a poor track record, since it was his failings as manager of the nascent Port Ellen distillery which originally brought John Ramsay to the island. Eventually the meticulous Ramsay, whose unstoppable rise meant that he was now the laird of Kidalton, sensibly merged it with Laphroaig.

The threat from Ardenistiel must have clouded what were to prove the last days of Donald Johnston, for it was he who tumbled into the simmering residues of his own apparatus in June 1847. His agony lasted two days, and he died intestate. He had, from two marriages, one son and four daughters. The son, Dougald, was just eleven at the time – so the Lagavulin distiller, Walter Graham, ran the business until Dougald took over in 1857. Graham made a good job of it, doubling its still-minute production. Dougald continued for 30 years, duly dying, childless, in 1887. One of his four sisters, Isabella, had married a cousin called Sandy (Alexander on his birth certificate), also a Johnston, from the branch of the family which farmed Tallant near Bowmore; Isabella's maiden name was thus identical to her married name. Sandy Johnston ran Laphroaig until he himself died in 1907, his wife having predeceased him; he left three wills and two squabbling branches of the Johnston family. The lawyers got to work.

When the legal ink had dried, Laphroaig belonged to Sandy's sisters Catherine Johnston and Isabella Hunter, and his nephew, a mainland tram engineer with the chaotically reverberative name of John Johnston Hunter Johnston. Ian Hunter was another nephew, the son of Isabella and the whiskery Glasgow seed merchant who also (by another of the celebrated Laphroaig confusions) happened to be called Hunter. Young Ian inherited everything, in the end, from the three devisees on whose behalf he had arrived on Islay in 1908 – and more than that, bought the lease to Laphroaig from the laird, who by that time was Captain Iain Ramsay, unsuccessful son of the prodigiously successful John Ramsay. Ian Hunter also succeeded in acquiring both Texa and Ardenistiel House, the main property adjacent to the distillery; both were bought from Iain Ramsay, who found himself in such straitened circumstances that he had to sell the entire estate in 1922.

Laphroaig was obviously worth squabbling over. Its desirability is underscored by the fact that the Mackie family of Lagavulin made repeated attempts to acquire the lease from the Johnstons. A bitter dispute over water rights in 1907, following the severance of an agency agreement between the Johnstons and the Mackies, saw the establishment of a micro-distillery at Lagavulin called Malt Mill which attempted, deliberately though unsuccessfully, to duplicate Laphroaig itself. Laphroaig was, in short, a fine and covetable malt. It saw its production increase under successive owners, and by the time that the touchstone whisky chronicler Alfred Barnard arrived in the last year of Dougald Johnston's life, Laphroaig was recognisably itself. 'The Whisky made at Laphroaig,' wrote Barnard, 'is of exceptional character, being largely sought after for blending purposes, and is a thick and pungent spirit of a peculiar 'peat reek' flavour.' A sentence or two later come perhaps the most provocative 73 words in Barnard's great book. 'The distilling of Whisky,' he writes, 'is greatly aided by circumstances that cannot be accounted for, and even the most experienced distillers are unable to change its character, which is largely influenced by accidents of locality, water and position. No better instance of this can be given than the case of the Lagavulin and Laphroaig distilleries, which, although situated within a short distance of one another, each produce Whisky of a distinct and varied type.' Yes, in other words: Barnard himself believed that what the French call *terroir* (the stamp of place) is an element in the creation of great whisky flavour just as it is in the creation of great wine.

BESSIE

After the chaotic swirl of the Johnston genes, Elizabeth ('Bessie') Williamson marked a singular and unexpected change of ownership. She was, unusually for a woman at that time, a graduate – in chemistry, from Glasgow University. She came to Islay with a friend for a holiday in 1934; they boarded, ironically, in Port Ellen's Temperance Hotel. She had some secretarial experience; Ian Hunter, as it happened, was looking for secretarial help. 'Oh yes, she came here in 1934,' recalls Iain

Maclean. 'I remember that very well. She was just a young office girl in those days. The years don't wait, do they?'

Hunter noticed Bessie Williamson's intelligence; her knowledge of chemistry, too, would have primed her for distillery comprehension. Eventually (in 1945) she became Hunter's manager and, as Iain Maclean remembers, she was the only one who lasted. 'I forget how many managers I worked under here. A manager's lifetime here was roughly eighteen months. And they were all good men. But it made no difference. If there was an argument, he wanted his way. There was only one way, and it was his way. Whether it was right or wrong.' Why did Bessie succeed where the 'good men' had failed? 'I suppose being a woman was a big help. And she was a good boss. She just let the workers carry on with their work; it was the proper thing to do. Everybody knew his job, anyway. She couldn't improve on anything there. She never had any bother.'

There is, of course, one question which has to be asked. Ian Hunter was single; Bessie Williamson was single. He gave her a job; eventually, on his death in 1954, he left her the distillery, Ardenistiel and the island of Texa, though he had blood relatives to whom he could have left these valuable assets had he wished. What exactly was the nature of their relationship? I asked Iain Maclean, who watched them over the twenty years during which they knew one another.

'What was Bessie like?'

'She was nice, a very attractive young girl.'

'Was there any romantic attachment between them?'

'Oh God, I don't know. I can't go into that, no. But she was a very attractive woman.'

'Ian Hunter never got married.'

'No, but he liked the company of women.'

'Did he have a housekeeper?'

'Aye.'

'Did Bessie have suitors?'

'Oh no, no, none of that. No no, I think that was forbidden.'

'By Ian Hunter?'

'I think so, yes. I don't think he was fond of her going to dances or anything like that.'

'So he saw himself as a father figure to her?'

'Aye, I think he did. He taught her the job, you see. And she was very clever, an educated woman.'

Former distillery manager Iain Henderson, who arrived at Laphroaig in 1988, had asked this question himself, too, on a number of occasions to those who knew them. 'Some people say there was, and some people say there wasn't. They were different generations, remember. That wouldn't be a barrier now, but it might have been a barrier then.' My own guess is that Bessie Williamson became the most important person in Ian Hunter's life, and he in hers, though without this relationship ever losing the physical formality imposed by their different ages (he was some twenty years older than she), the precedents of the epoch and perhaps their own personalities. We should not assume it was any the less rewarding for all that, despite the taciturnity of the early twentieth-century Scots. When Bessie wrote the chapter on Kidalton for a short book on Islay published in 1968 by the Scottish Women's Rural Institutes, she referred to Ian Hunter as no more than 'the last descendant' – and failed to include any reference to her own management and ownership of Laphroaig.

Whatever the truth, Bessie did eventually marry after Ian Hunter's death – in 1961, to Wishart Campbell, a Canadian singer and accordion player whose grandfather had emigrated from the Oa, after which she styled herself Mrs Wishart Campbell. Viewed from a distance, it seems a puzzling relationship, and there are mixed verdicts on how successful it was. 'He was a queer mixture, to be honest,' remembers Iain Maclean. 'I knew him by sight. Sometimes he'd have a conversation with you and talk to you for hours; other times he wouldn't know who you were. That was the sort of man he was.' Rumour had it that he was bisexual. 'She would,' says Iain Henderson, 'have found that abhorrent. But she was bowled over by him originally; he was a good-looking guy. When he came to Islay, all he had was a suitcase and a white grand piano. The piano is still in Ardenistiel House.' In the short text on Kidalton alluded to above, there is an enigmatic reference to 'a Canadian' who 'started a horticultural project in recent years' at Ardenistiel (here called 'Ardenistle') to sell 'fresh vegetables, tomatoes and flowers to the local village. It is proving a success and a great boon to the local shops and hotels.' Mrs Wishart

Campbell's 'Canadian' was none other than Mr Wishart Campbell.

Bessie sold Laphroaig in three stages (in 1962, 1967 and 1970), initially to Long John, which was owned by the American company Schenley. Why? 'I don't know,' said Iain Maclean. 'I don't know why she did that. That was a strange thing to do, right enough.'

'She had a philosophy that she came to the island with nothing, and she was determined to leave the island owning nothing as well,' according to Iain Henderson. Others claim it was to prevent Wishart Campbell acquiring and mis-managing the distillery if she should pre-decease him (which she did, in 1982). Schenley was not, in fact, Bessie's first choice: the distillery was offered to the Mactaggart family, owners of the Ardtalla estate (the major part of Ramsay's old Kidalton estate), and it is a matter of some regret to Sir John Mactaggart that the offer was declined. 'My father and my uncles were offered Laphroaig, in nineteen sixty-three, for eighty thousand pounds, by Mrs Williamson. My uncle Sandy said "We shouldn't be making our money in that kind of business." He had reservations about the booze business full stop. I think I could have swallowed my moral scruples, given that the distillery is probably worth fifty million pounds nowadays or something like that.' Bruno Schroder of Dunlossit also recalls his father Helmut taking an interest, nine years earlier, in Laphroaig. 'When Ian Hunter died my father said there will probably be estate duty to pay. So he drove over to see Miss Williamson and offered her help; he was happy to be a sleeping investor. She thanked him, but said no. I think at that time she wanted industry assistance, whereas my father could only provide money.'

Bessie herself finally retired as a director in 1972, Whitbread having taken over Long John in 1971. Since the takeover, it has had seven managers, of which Iain Henderson (1988 to 2002) has been the longest serving. It is now run by Robin Shields, a former Bass brewer and long-term whisky enthusiast.

THE HILL

With a production of two million litres of spirit a year, Laphroaig is at present the third most productive distillery on the island after huge Caol Ila and industrious Lagavulin.

Its water comes from the Kilbride reservoir, with what Iain Henderson called 'the strategic reserve' at Loch na Beinne Brice, up on the rugged quartzite hill land which dominates Islay's picturesque, woody, cove-strewn south-eastern coastline. Is it the water which creates the differences between Laphroaig, Lagavulin and Ardbeg? Absolutely not, according to Iain Henderson. 'There's a lot of rubbish talked about the water. I know from having run Ardbeg, and from having sampled the water at Lagavulin, that there's absolutely no difference between them. The bedrock here is impervious: metamorphosed quartzite. It's fused by heat; you're not picking up much in the way of minerals or trace elements. The water's all just sitting in peat bogs. What's remarkable is its softness: the hardest I've ever seen here is about five parts per million of calcium, and the lowest about 1.5 parts. It never varies. The only thing that varies is the flow rate, and even then not often.' Henderson was absolutely right: in terms of topography, catchment areas and geology, the water sources for the three Kidalton distilleries mirror each other closely: a loch or two high on the hill (Beinne Brice for Laphroaig, Sholum for Lagavulin and Uigeadail for Ardbeg) tumbling down to the distillery across identical terrain, and collected via holding pools (the Kilbride reservoir for Laphroaig and Loch Iarnan for Ardbeg; Lagavulin only has a small, roughly built dam serving this function).

The walk from Laphroaig up to Beinne Brice is a slightly easier one than from Ardbeg to Uigeadail or from Lagavulin to Sholum, not least because you can drive halfway by taking the road to the Kilbride Farm, and parking there. (The reservoir, which as well as being fed from the hill also gathers a lot of ground water, lies between the farmhouse and the distillery.) From the farmhouse, it's the usual rough and boggy yomp across rising ground until you come to the burn which runs from the loch, called Sruthan Goirtean na Beinne. Follow this up the hillside – and if you do it in early July, as I did, you can expect a quivering halo of juicy brown flies to accompany you (a piece of live meat on the move, after all). Just as you are beginning to think that the loch is a mythical one, it appears before you, bowl-like and bright, gathering light from a wide sky. Perhaps my eyes misled me, but the rich leather brown of the water there certainly seemed some of the darkest I had come across on the island. The view on the way up is dominated by the Kidalton coast, the rocky sills lending it depth and perspective, as scenery wings do for a stage forest or village. Beinne Brice, though, lies alongside a little summit (Beinn Bhreac), and from this hinge in the hills you can look down on to the twin Leorin Lochs, once the water source for Port Ellen's distillery, and still the pools from which the water needed to swell the barley grains in Port Ellen maltings is drawn. The corner, in other words, of the island has been turned, and a descent via the Leorin Lochs takes you towards the Oa.

Could the prodigiously peaty water of Beinne Brice affect the flavour of the whisky? 'Och it's fractional, tiny,' Iain Henderson told me, echoing his other Kidalton colleagues. The distillers' consensus is that the peatiness in their whiskies is entirely due to their use of peated malt, not peated water. They should know. John Thomson of Port Ellen Maltings pointed out (in Chapter Four) that peat has to be burned in order to create the characteristic phenolic reek we recognise in classic Islay malts. And yet . . . while staying in the Machrie Hotel I have tasted a glass of the peat-brown tap water which flows off the island's largest area of peat moss, comparing it with a glass of clear Strathmore mineral water. The difference was stark: the water which runs from the taps of the Machrie Hotel has, beyond question, a vegetal presence. It is not a reek or a smoke, but the ghostly print of bog plants. Smoked malt is of course the dominant note, but the water cannot truly be said to be neutral either. Where flavour exists, it will leave its trace.

The debate surrounding yeast takes a similar form. Ask beer brewers about the importance of their yeast strains, and they will tell you it matters a great deal. The former brewer for Fuller's of Chiswick, Reg Drury, once told me that he calculated that yeast accounted for as much as 70 per cent of the distinctive flavour of an individual brewer's ale. Scotch whisky distillers, by contrast, contend that flavour neutrality and simple efficiency in the fermentation process is all they are after (though their Bourbon-producing counterparts disagree). Iain Henderson reckoned that 'under five per cent' of the flavour of Laphroaig came from its yeast. It uses either Mauri or Quest. 'It makes no difference; it's the same product,' he claimed. 'They were both developed for the baking industry. We don't use brewer's yeast; we don't want character and flavour. The yeast has no flavour; I don't even associate yeast with flavour. We're going to get forty per cent of our flavour from the cask, and the rest will come from the malt and the distilling process. The yeast doesn't distil, remember. It's all left behind. It's what we feed the fish with.' Beer is essentially a fresh product in which the print of yeast will figure large; indeed in British real ale the yeast is still working to 'condition' the beer as you drink it. The primeval Laphroaig beer, by contrast, will not only have exploded through distillation but also have seen out ten damp Islay Christmases by the time it moistens your lips. Within it, the argument runs, yeast is no more than a fading childhood memory.

I asked Robin Shields if he, as a former brewer, took a different view to Henderson. He is keeping an open mind on the matter, but nothing he had seen so far had led him to challenge Henderson's assertions. The chief question he was addressing in 2003 was whether or not it might be possible to switch to the much lighter dried yeast, as the distillery on Jura has already done, without losing Laphroaig's precious character.

WALKING LAPHROAIG

Laphroaig is, with Bowmore, one of only two Islay distilleries still to do its own malting. Even then, around three-quarters of its requirements come from the Port Ellen maltings, with the 1,500 tonnes malted here every year providing just a quarter of its needs. 'If you were an accountant,' Iain Henderson told me prior to his retirement, 'you wouldn't do this. Our malt is twenty per cent more expensive than Port Ellen malt, and that's already among the most expensive in the industry. We do it for three reasons. First of all, because it's part of the heritage of the distillery. Secondly, because there's a flavour consideration, which I'll tell you about in a minute. And thirdly, because it's great PR. People like to see the old processes working.'

Indeed they do; indeed I do. Steeped barley is raked out across the floor like a thick carpet of dull, beaded gold. When the sunlight spills through the windows, as it occasionally does, lozenges of brilliant white-gold gleam below the wall apertures. This is a living, growing carpet; a mass of soft seeds which wishes, urgently, to become a field in its own right, to grasp at the sky, to consume its light, and thus to make seeds of its own. The pillars which support the malting floors stand like neat trees among the grain. The effect is as calming as the interior of Córdoba's Mezquita, though the architecture of the Laphroaig's maltings (which date from 1923) is as frumpily industrial as the former mosque's is exquisite. You can catch the sappy vapour of growth as the tiny rootlets push urgently for life; the grain itself begins to smell creamy. The air is full of moist, burgeoning anticipation – which, of course, it is the maltman's job to defeat utterly.

Each malting run is composed of eight tonnes of grain dry weight in the winter, and seven in the summer. It is steeped in water from Beinne Brice (at 15.5°C) for 48 hours before being raked over the floors to form a foot-thick carpet. 'It's a very physical job,' Alec Gunn told me. So I could see, by Alec's muscular breadth; he had done it for 32 years. 'Every aspect of it is physically hard. What you're doing is fighting the weather. You have to adapt tonnages, thickness, temperatures, steeping times: it can all change from day to day.' The heavy, steeped grain needs to be spread across the four separate malting floors, then turned every eight hours as it chits, and then finally gathered up about a week later for kilning. Growing grain doesn't recognise the human need for a weekend break. On the day I spoke to Alec, the barley variety on the floor was Optic from East Lothian; Iain Henderson recalled having used an Australian-grown variety called Clipper in the past. 'You wouldn't tell the difference.'

'If you put sugar in your coffee,' said Alec by way of support, 'you wouldn't know if it was cane or beet.'

Laphroaig's peat is cut (by Iain Brown) from the Glenmachrie moss, just south of the island's little airport, where the company owns a 185-acre plot. 'Unfortunately,' Robin Shields told me in November 2003, 'there's only four to five years' supply left there. That's our big issue at the moment.' The distillery needs between 300 and 400 tonnes a year. It's cut in April; dried over the summer; then brought back to the distillery in September. The fire is begun with dry peat, then moister bricks and the loose caff is put on to produce maximum smoke.

Is Laphroaig's malt different to that produced by Port Ellen? 'Theoretically,' Iain Henderson told me, 'they are to the same specification, but there is a wee difference. We do the peating first, and then the drying afterwards. At Port Ellen there is more overlap. We had a chemist here who worked out that that does give you a flavour difference.' The peat, according to Iain, accounts for little of the drying effect; it is, if you like, a kind of 13-hour flavouring before the grain is dried to a crunch for the final 18 hours over warm air (obtained by heat exchange from the stills). The end result of this is that the phenols in Laphroaig's own malt are slightly higher (43 ppm) than they are for the malt purchased from Port Ellen (40 ppm). Malt from the two sources is ground separately (in a Porteus mill – at night, when the electricity is cheaper) before being mixed in the grist bin. And then, of course, this sweet, smoky flour needs to be fermented.

Laphroaig's brewing facilities date back to July 1986 and the Whitbread era, and it shows: this is steely clean, big-brewers' kit. The mash tun is a full Lauter, so extraction rates of sugar from the malt are highly effective, and in contrast to every other distillery on the island Laphroaig's washbacks are stainless steel, too, giving brisk fermentations. (These metal washbacks date back to Laphroaig's American ownership in the early 1970s, and were installed in place of the previous pine washbacks, according to the manager of the time John McDougall, 'because they were considerably cheaper'.) I put it to Iain Henderson that other distillers on the island continually stressed the benefits of wooden washbacks: Donald Renwick at Lagavulin told me that the wood gave the wash a pleasant lactic character, while Jim McEwan of Bruichladdich claimed that wooden washbacks mean the finished spirit has more floral notes. Iain laughed. 'I've run distilleries with both, and to be honest I don't think it makes a blind bit of difference. Except ours are much easier to clean.' Who's right? There's no doubt in my mind that Laphroaig has a more precise, rumbustious and straightforward style than its Islay peers; perhaps the use of stainless steel fermenting vessels makes a minor contribution to that focused pungency.

The relatively brisk fermentations and the fact that the distillery was until recently working six-and-a-half days a week meant that the fermented wash didn't have long to wait before it met the wash stills: this again would tend to increase the boisterous style of the spirit. The switch to a five-day working week in 2003, though, has meant that some fermentations now linger over the weekend, which might in the long run have a slight refining effect.

There are three wash stills, each around 19½ feet high (6.02 m), and filled with a charge of 10,500 litres. Laphroaig has not been able to tell me the total capacity of these stills, so I cannot work out what percentage of capacity this charge represents, though it must be fairly high since Robin Shields says that 'the most you could safely get into the wash stills is twelve thousand litres'. Past visitors should note that the 'contents' figures displayed for many years on the notice above each wash still and spirit still were, mysteriously, incorrect.

The spirit stills are small – or at least most of them are. Three are just 14 feet 5 inches (4.4 m) and filled to just 4,700 litres (once again, the total capacity figure has proved to be unobtainable, so I can't provide a percentage figure for the charge). These are the famous 'teapots' of Laphroaig. Back in 1972, though, a much larger 'coffee pot' appeared alongside them (17 feet 9 inches, or 5.41 m), as former manager John McDougall recalled in his book of memoirs *Wort, Worms and Washbacks*. 'When it came to increasing the capacity of the stillhouse at Laphroaig in 1972 there was quite a confrontation, because the engineers and the distillers came to the situation with views which were poles apart. Increasing the number of wash stills was comparatively simple, because there were already two, and the installation of one extra wash still could take care of the extra capacity required. When it came to the spirit stills, however, two new ones were needed, but on grounds of cost-effectiveness it was decided that one double sized still would be installed. The engineers and bosses of Schenley were warned that to do this would inevitably change the character and style of Laphroaig from its traditional heavy, peaty, oily, smoky, phenolic, iodine-like form. Unfortunately,' McDougall concludes, 'the spirit did change. . . . At the end of the day, I would have to say that economic considerations mattered more than maintaining the quality and tradition of one of Scotland's finest and most distinctive whiskies.'

Nor was this the only moment at which Laphroaig's character 'evolved'. When I talked to Iain Maclean about whether Laphroaig today had changed from the Laphroaig of his youth, he said, 'It has, I'm convinced of that.' The larger spirit still wasn't the cause, though, for Maclean. 'The biggest change was when they changed to steam coils from coal-fired stills. I remember the first filling day, from the steam coil; I could recognise right away that there was a big change. It seemed to me like burnt toast, with the steam. Before it was entirely different. It was a very pleasant smell; it smelled to me like whisky. But this, no. Of course it's much easier work; coal was a lot of extra work. But in my opinion, yes, it changed it.' Maclean (who retired as head warehouseman) also remembered that 'in the olden days, it was all sherry casks'; the switch to bourbon wood came with the transfer to American ownership. These three factors mean that Laphroaig in 2004 is certainly a very different spirit from Laphroaig in 1904, 1934 and even 1964.

It does, though, remain Laphroaig. The distillery's spirit cuts are distinctive, in that foreshots are run here for a full 45 minutes, followed by a relatively short spirit run and a long, slow feints run. This, according to Iain Henderson, went back to Bessie's times. 'We do forty-five minutes on foreshot runs here. That's because the first part is very sweet and estery. We're not interested in that part. We want the peaty phenolic part, and that's further down the spirit run. It's just a tradition that Bessie Williamson started out doing, and we've carried on. You don't change a winning recipe, and that was her recipe.' So what, I asked Iain, would happen if the stillmen switched to the spirit run a little earlier – after 15 minutes, say, as at Ardbeg? 'Your whisky would become sweeter; that would be what would happen. You'd take away that pungency from Laphroaig.' That was Henderson's belief – though it's worth noting that the only other distillery on Islay to run foreshots for as long as Laphroaig, Bruichladdich, has a very different (and much less pungent) style, even for its Port Charlotte spirit.

The still size and shape may, I suspect, be more important: Laphroaig's spirit stills are squat, and are the only ones on the island apart from Ardbeg's to have a lamp-glass design. All are as usual equipped with an anti-collapse valve (Iain Henderson recalled seeing

stills collapse at both Dufftown and Braes of Glenlivet). None of the Laphroaig spirit stills, though, has a purifier. One of the great enigmas of the three Kidalton distilleries is the way that Laphroaig, whose malt has always contained lower phenols than that of Ardbeg, actually tastes 'more peaty'. The answer to the enigma can probably be assigned to three facts: Laphroaig's three relatively small spirit stills (the figures I have been given suggest they are a little taller than Ardbeg's spirit still, but the charges and presumably the total contents are substantially lower); its slightly wider spirit cuts; and above all the lack of a purifier. The fact that Laphroaig has two-stage condensing – via both warmer-than-usual condensers and a sub-cooler – may also eventually prove significant for its flavour profile, though this is a recent development following the installation of a heat-recovery system in the late 1990s, and the spirit made in this way has not yet gone to market. These are the elements which mother that brusque, bruising and boisterous spirit so many of us love. There is finesse there, too, of course, and the fact that the lyne arms ascend rather than being horizontal or descending, thereby adding an element of reflux, may account for that. 'Ninety per cent of the lyne arms in Scotland go down,' said Iain Henderson to me. 'And all the famous ones go up.' He was teasing, of course. Macallan's spirit stills, for example, are as small or smaller than Laphroaig's teapots – and have steeply descending lyne arms. Lagavulin's lyne arms descend, too.

Once the spirit is condensed and diluted to its filling strength of 63.5 per cent abv, all Laphroaig to be used for distillery bottlings is put into first-refill bourbon casks, and preponderantly 180-litre barrels. Most of these, Iain Henderson told me, come from Maker's Mark, which uses only high-quality air-dried wood, but I have also seen casks from Claremont Springs, Heaven Hill and Jim Beam on the premises. Wood quality was something which, quite rightly, Iain Henderson felt very strongly about. 'I've fought for years for that, and often created a fuss about poor-quality wood. Sometimes I've been made to fill it, but on other occasions I haven't. It's even gone as high as director level, because I refused to fill the casks. We take so much trouble here to make our whisky and if they send us rubbish to fill, it's just not worth it.' All the spirit to be used for distillery bottlings, I am assured, spends all its maturation time on the island, as does a proportion of the Laphroaig fillings to be used for the Ballantynes blend. The only young Laphroaig to be tankered off the island is for other blending customers, Henderson told me.

Laphroaig has six warehouses of its own, holding a total of 55,000 casks; there are also a further 11,000 casks stored at Ardbeg. (Laphroaig's warehouses are numbered, with customary island illogic, 1, 7, 8, 9, 10 and 11.) The best and briniest warehouse – indeed, perhaps the most propitiously sited warehouse on the whole island – is warehouse number 1, a classic damp, soft-floored dunnage warehouse with space for 12,000 casks perched next to a strip of narrow beach in Laphroaig bay. Its walls are regularly showered by the sea, and you can almost feel the surreptitious brine in its cool, arthritic air. Warehouses 7 and 8 also offer low-lying dunnage storage close to the sea. This, according to Iain Henderson, is where 'we deliberately age our single malts. We also try to put the best wood here, close to the beach.' Warehouses 9, 10 and 11 are modern warehouses where the casks are stacked on racks 11 high, located up next to the Kidalton road.

TASTING LAPHROAIG

There cannot be many readers of this book who reach this point never having smelled or tasted a drop of this grand malt whisky. What, though, is it like as new make, before it has ever met the vanilla charms of the bourbon barrels or had the Hebrides tattooed into it via the intricate needles of the sea air? The immediate impression from Laphroaig's new make is of oily peat smoke, frank and fierce, plus what Allied's Master Blender Robert Hicks calls Laphroaig's 'iodine'. There is, though, a depth there, too, and as you continue to search its scents you'll find a natural spirit sweetness which, mingled with the soapiness of all new make, contrives momentarily to suggest bluebells in cool spring woods or hyacinths in a moist conservatory. It is a complete new make, not a limping or halting new make. It is ready to be engraved and ornamented by time and by wood, but it doesn't need them, as some whiskies do, as a crutch.

I haven't yet had a chance to taste the new make for what Robin Shields is calling 'the ultimate Laphroaig' – in other words the 100,000 litres of spirit distilled for two weeks in August 2003 from Laphroaig's own malt alone. Before Iain Henderson left Laphroaig, he told me that his one regret was that he never had the chance to produce a run of spirit made exclusively from Laphroaig malt. 'When we made it,' says Robin, 'Robert's comment was that the iodine which, for him, is the typical note of Laphroaig had gone missing. It was smoky – but just smoky. My mission now is to understand why.' It couldn't, I suggested, be the peat itself – since otherwise all the distilleries using Port Ellen's malt would have an iodine character, too. 'That's right. It could be the fact that we did it in August, when you have peak temperatures for fermenting and condensing; it could also be the fact that the peat was too dry by then. Or it could be because we didn't use the big spirit still for that run; we just used the teapots. And we cut down the wash-still charges to nine thousand litres instead of the usual ten thousand five hundred.' I got the feeling that Robin was looking forward to teasing out the conundrum.

The main aged expressions of Laphroaig are the 10-year-old (in two versions); a 15-year-old, and (for the time being) a 30-year-old. The standard 10-year-old, when tasted against its island peers, is sweeter than in the past; it seems likely that this is a consequence of the uniform use of top-quality first-refill bourbon barrels. The gruffness has gone, and in its place is a seductive quality; the peat lurking behind it adds a visceral note. On the palate, that old note of salt, smoke and iodine is more palpable, but the sweetness of the wood closes around it nonetheless, like a fierce throat lozenge dusted with sugar.

My preference is for the cask-strength 10-year-old, bottled at around 57 per cent and un-chill-filtered. This, to me, is the whisky which lets the beast out of the cage. I love Laphroaig young, because that is when its fierce frankness emerges with most gusto. I remember, one night in early January 2003, driving in the darkness past the (rented) farmhouse at Bun-an-uillt on the shores of Loch Gruinart. As my car rounded the field corner just beyond the buildings, I suddenly knew there were peat fires burning inside; that scent – which is so much more savoury and nourishing than coal smoke, just as Havana cigar smoke is several worlds richer than cigarette fumes – filled the car for a quarter-mile or so. And I thought of Laphroaig. No other whisky on the island combines the savoury warmth of a true peat fire with the thrown salt of a wild sea like Laphroaig, and this cask-strength 10-year-old at present is the best place to find it. The wood sweetness is still there, of course, but this time the peat smoke seems to have the upper hand. The sweetness, thus, now has the dignity of scented moss, or of young seaweed freshly uncovered by the tide. The oily peat, meanwhile, slaps the tongue with a calving seal's strength; the salt is tightly packed; there is a blackness there, almost a bitterness. Even the spices are black: liquorice, clove. This is grand, stoic malt.

The older expressions are very beautiful but less primeval. The 15-year-old is creamy and mellow in scent, the peat smoke beautifully incorporated and more or less completely tamed; on the palate the malt is soft and fruitcake-rich. This is a fine, full, toothsome dram. The 30-year-old is almost Madeira-like in scent and its flavour is winey, too, with lots of liquorice toffee sweetness – though the slight hardness and stiffness of over-aged whisky is just beginning to creep in. The throb of peat and the pounding of the sea are now distant, like childhood memories in old age. (You are not imagining this, remember: the 40 ppm in the malt has become 25 ppm in the new make, 8–10 ppm in the 10-year-old and 15-year-old, and just 6 ppm in the 30-year-old.) This blend owes its existence to the dedicated collecting work of an American called Jack Gross, who assembled an extensive collection of older casks of Laphroaig (including many very rare sherry casks); when

Gross died, his widow sold the collection back to Allied. These stocks will not last much longer, and future bottlings are likely to contain a lower proportion of sherry-aged Laphroaig. From time to time, too, there are single vintage special editions; the 2004 Feis Ile saw the release of a prodigiously aromatic cask-strength 17-year-old (one cask only, distilled in 1987); and while visiting the distillery I have had a chance to taste fine individual barrels. It's always there in the best of them, no matter how close the attentions of the wood: that boisterousness, that wind-blown quality, that salt-caked, smoke-stack style of the irreducibly exuberant Laphroaig.

Laphroaig   DISTILLERY FACTFILE

Distillery operating hours	*5 days a week @ 24 hours a day*
Number of employees	*24*
Water source	*Kilbride reservoir, fed from Loch na Beinne Brice*
Water reserve	*est. 5 million gallons*
Water colour	*brown*
Peat content of water	*sizeable trace*
Malt source	*approx. 75 per cent Port Ellen; approx. 25 per cent own malt*
Own floor maltings?	*yes*
Malt type	*Optic*
Malt specification phenols	*Port Ellen malt: average 40 ppm;* *Laphroaig malt: average 43 ppm*
Finished spirit phenols	*25 ppm*
Malt storage	*284 tonnes*
Mill type	*Porteus*
Grist storage	*25.5 tonnes*
Mash tun construction	*stainless steel, Lauter*
Mash size	*8.5 tonnes*
First water	*37,000 litres @ 67°C*
Second water	*16,000 litres @ 85°C*

Third water	–	*32,000 litres @ 85°C*
Number of washbacks	–	*6*
Washback construction	–	*stainless steel*
Washback charge	–	*42,000 litres*
Yeast	–	*Mauri cultured yeasts*
Amount of yeast	–	*125 kg per washback*
Length of fermentation	–	*55 hours (shorts: week);*
		90 hours (longs: weekend)
Initial fermentation temperature	–	*18–19°C*
Strength of wash	–	*8.5 per cent abv*
Number of wash stills	–	*3*
Wash stills built	–	*2: not known; 1: 1972*
Wash still capacity	–	*information not supplied*
Wash still charge	–	*10,500 litres*
Heat source	–	*steam pans*
Wash still height	–	*19 feet 8 inches (6.02 m)*
Wash still shape	–	*plain*
Lyne arm	–	*ascends*
Length of low-wines run	–	*c. 6 hours*
Low-wines collection range	–	*45 per cent abv – 1 per cent abv*
Number of spirit stills	–	*4*
Spirit still built	–	*1: not known; 2: 1972*
Spirit still capacity	–	*3 smaller: information not supplied;*
		1 larger: information not supplied
Spirit still charge	–	*3 smaller: 4,700 litres;*
		1 larger: 9,400 litres
Strength of spirit still charge	–	*26 per cent abv*
Heat source	–	*steam coils*
Spirit still height	–	*3 smaller: 14 feet 5 inches (4.40 m);*
		1 larger: 17 feet 9 inches (5.41 m)
Spirit still shape	–	*lamp-glass*
Lyne arm	–	*ascends*
Purifier?	–	*no*
Condensers	–	*all internally sited, and two-stage:*
		condensers run warm, then condensing
		finished in a sub-cooler. Each condenser

is 10 feet (3.05 m) long, and contains 280 copper tubes with an outside diameter of 1 inch (2.5 cm) and an internal diameter of $^3/_4$ inch (18 mm)

Length of foreshot run	– all stills: 45 minutes
Length of spirit run	– 3 smaller: approx. $2^1/_4$ hours; 1 larger: approx. $3^1/_2$ hours
Length of feints run	– all stills: approx. 2 hours
Spirit cut	– 72 per cent abv – 60.5 per cent abv
Distilling strength	– 67.5 per cent abv average
Storage strength	– 63.5 per cent abv
Average spirit yield	– 406 litres of pure alcohol per tonne of malt (2003)
Disposal of pot ale and spent lees	– piped into Laphroaig Bay
Type of casks filled for branded malt	– 100 per cent first-fill bourbon (chiefly ex-Maker's Mark, air-dried wood, barrels rather than hogsheads)
Current annual output	– 2,000,000 litres of pure alcohol
Number of warehouses	– 6 (numbered 1, 7, 8, 9, 10, 11)
Type of warehouses	– dunnage and racking
Storage capacity on Islay	– 55,000 casks plus 11,000 at Ardbeg
Percentage of branded malt entirely aged on Islay	– 100 per cent
Vatting and bottling location	– Kilmalid, Dumbarton
Distillery expressions	– 10-year-old
	– 10-year-old cask strength (57 per cent, un-chill-filtered)
	– 15-year-old
	– 30-year-old
	– special releases (e.g. 17-year-old at 2004 Islay Whisky Festival)
Major blending roles	– Ballantynes, Teachers, Long John, Islay Mist

CHAPTER EIGHT

Islay Today

A life on the edge:
fought, bare-hand; fraught with knowing
and sudden moonlight.

JAMES BROWN'S morning was going badly. I was sitting in his tractor
cab, listening to the Gaelic station to which the radio was permanently
tuned; James was 200 metres away, struggling with a chainsaw which
wouldn't start. A woman was singing, unaccompanied; the song was
tide-slow, floating, sad.

The sun had just come out; it was spilling across the water
of Loch Indaal. The air was spotless after months of rain. The
grasses nodded gently in the wind. The low sunlight bouncing off
the water silvered their stems. I looked more closely, soothed by
the music and the warmth of the winter light in the cab. The base of
each stem was green, and the top of each stem was brown, but it
was the silver in the middle which caught the eye, shimmering, as
the wind ruffled it. In my glass cave, I felt ruffled, too – by the

snowdrop Hebridean voice flowing out of the sky, out of history.

James's wife Sheila teaches at the school in the village. It was 4 December, and he had promised to cut the children a Christmas tree. He'd taken his chainsaw up to the plantations on the hill, found a suitable candidate, begun cutting – and the chain had come off. So he'd gone back down to fetch a handsaw, come back with it, attacked the same tree – and the blade had broken. He'd gone back down yet again and put an old chain back on the machine . . . which was the moment when I arrived, so he took me back up the hill with him in the tractor. I wanted to walk over to watch his eventual triumph over the sappy wood, but I wasn't wearing boots so he told me not to; I'd ruin my shoes.

He'd got the saw started again now. The hour must have turned; a man was reading the news. I could make out the odd word amid the sibilant flow (Indonesia . . . Abbey National . . . kerosene-diesel . . . Saddam Hussein). Eventually James came over with the tree. 'This chain's blunt. I burnt it down more than cut it.' We drove off the hill again, put the tree in the back of the van, and taxied it round to the school. By the time we got there, the months of rain had returned, but the job was done; I could imagine the unseen children smiling with excitement. Then back to the farmhouse where, since it was lunchtime, James put some venison burgers under the grill and heated a tin of baked beans.

The world knows Islay through its whiskies, but if you live and work on the island, then you are more likely to spend your days looking after sheep and calves than filling casks. There are seven distilleries, but around 120 farm units. Distilling on Islay was originally a farming sideline; as we will discover in the Postscript, it may become so again. Distilleries take up little space on the low, green island; farms occupy much. All of the distilleries save Bruichladdich are owned off the island, and their futures decided at boardroom tables many hundreds or thousands of miles distant from Bowmore or Port Ellen; Islay's farms, by contrast, provide the social spine of the island. Distillery profits, unlike corncrakes, have only the very weakest homing instincts; few find their way back to their birthplace. While Islay's whiskies are sipped with reverence by expensively dressed derivatives traders in leather-scented hotel bars in Tokyo, London and New York, Islay's farmers are dealing with darkness, mud, wind, rain, the blood of calving cows and electricity bills printed in red ink.

Meet four of them. None, perhaps, is more typical than the first, James Brown. Physically: he's built like a Caledonian pine. If he's not the strongest man on the island, then he's certainly a contender. I asked him about his Islay roots. 'On my father's side,' he said, 'back to Viking days. Probably.' With his blond hair and fair complexion, the claim is easily credited. He's got a resilient sense of humour, one proof of many being the fact that he once challenged me (a man built more like a playing card than a pine) to a bout of arm wrestling. He's an optimist, too, of course. Ask him how things are going, and the answer, even when delivered in the gloom of a wet winter afternoon as his muddy, penned cows low gravely around him like chanting Tibetan monks, is invariable: 'Every day's a bonus.'

His father was one of seven children, and the whole family lived on a 40-acre (16-ha) croft at Carn, just to the south of Port Charlotte. 'Everything would be grown in the garden, fish out of the sea, rabbits, kill a hen. Selling an animal, too, but it wouldn't be a lot. The croft would have only had half-a-dozen cows.' This way of farming – a tradition which goes back to the time of the Lords of the Isles – no longer exists on Islay.

'We came here in 1960,' says James, alluding to the move up to Octomore, on the hill to the north of the village. 'We walked the cows from one end of the village to the other. I was eight.' He left school at 16, and worked for and later in partnership with his father (who died in 1995). They were tenants of the Foreland Estate, but in the mid-1980s got the chance to buy their farm, which at 500 acres (202 ha) was much bigger than the original croft. 'Now we own it. As in the Royal Bank of Scotland. "The bank that cares". No, they're very good. No complaints.'

Like all the farmers on the island, James says that without subsidies (known on the island as 'little brown envelopes') and without his other, non-farming activities, he would quickly fail. He has two holiday cottages, converted from former farm buildings, and he works as a part-time lighthouse keeper (for the Port Charlotte light) and a part-time policeman on the Rhinns, as well as supplying Bruichladdich distillery with his clear, unpeaty spring water and playing the bagpipes for local functions. He has a JCB digger, and does a bit of contract work with that; he has, finally, 300 beef cattle, some sheep – and a stationery cupboard. 'The only way to farm now is with paperwork. If the paperwork's not right, it doesn't matter how good your animals are, it'll just cost you money to get them burnt.' He gets around £10,000 a year from Scottish Natural Heritage (SNH) in 'goose money' – compensation for the damage the geese do to his grazing grass; a further £7,500 a year for farming in an Environmentally Sensitive Area (ESA money); 'and we have a management agreement with SNH for choughs and things which is worth around eight-and-a-half thousand pounds a year as well. Then there are the subsidies on the beasts, like the suckler cow premium and the beef national envelope and so on. That probably comes to about one hundred and ninety pounds per cow, so if you've got one hundred cows, it's a fair bit. Oh, and there's also something called the LFA, that's the Less Favoured Area Support Scheme, and in our case it comes to about another ten thousand pounds.'

Blair and Margaret Rozga farm 300 acres (121 ha) at Kilmeny, in the core of the Heartland. Blair is a shyer man than James Brown, and more quietly spoken; his father was a Pole from a farming family who found himself stationed at Inveraray as the Second World War came to an end. He wanted to go back – but, like many Poles, his parents wrote to him and said 'Don't come back: we're still occupied. The Germans have gone but the Russians are here.' So he saw an advert for a farm worker in the *Oban Times*. He applied for it and got it – at the north end of Jura. He never saw his parents again.

Unlike James Brown's Octomore, Blair's farm is a tenancy – from Islay Estates. 'It's good land. Between Ballygrant and Bridgend is the best farming land on the island, though I'm slightly on the margin of it. It's good green ground on limestone, which gives you stronger grass. Not all of this farm is limestone, though; I've also got some slate, and there's peat below on the meadow.' Blair, like James, raises beef cattle. 'The main farming income is the sale of calves. Calves and little brown envelopes.' He and Margaret showed me how prices had lurched up and down over the last two decades, particularly at the height of the

BSE (or 'mad cow disease') crisis – which affected Islay as a part of the United Kingdom, though no cow there had ever eaten anything apart from a strict vegetarian diet of grass, draff and silage plants. The best average price the Rozgas ever got for bullocks was £473 in 1995, just before the BSE scare; by 1998 they were only getting £287 per bullock, and heifers were fetching just £170. Prices have recovered somewhat since. They receive nearly £3,000 goose money plus ESA and chough money, as well as all the usual beef subsidies. Which they accept . . . thoughtfully.

'Part of me,' says Margaret, 'thinks that if you are running a business that is not sustainable – in other words if you are relying on subsidies – then you should not run that business. Fine. But then we would all have to move to the mainland, to the cities. And that would add to all the problems which you already have in the cities – overcrowding, unemployment, and all the social problems which go with that. And what would happen here? Really it's a better idea to spread people out, and to encourage them to make a living from different things. But if you want to have people like us, in a difficult place like Islay where transport costs so much and everything costs so much, then we need those subsidies. And if people like coming to Islay, to see the geese and to eat our food and to have somewhere nice to stay, then maybe the subsidies are good value for money.'

In any case, Margaret is an impressive businesswoman in her own right. 'When my children were little, my brother-in-law was working at Bunnahabhain distillery and they needed some electricians to come over urgently, and there was nowhere for them to stay. He rung me up and said, "Could you look after these guys? You've got a bedroom or two there." I said, "I couldn't do that", but then he told me how much they were paying and I thought, "Oh right, well, maybe I can." So I helped, and that was very good. Three months later the same thing happened, and then I had some tourists . . .' Now Kilmeny Farm not only offers the most luxurious guest house accommodation on the island, but some of the best in Britain, and Margaret has a cupboard full of awards to prove it. She limits it to six guests at a time; the house is immaculately clean and tidy; the giant kettle is always on the hob; her cooking is superb. As I interviewed Blair and Margaret, I was plied with Scotch pancakes served with home-made bramble jelly and carrot cake, and I still remember the succulent roast Islay lamb I ate there on the night I stayed in August 1999. The guest house makes as much as the farm; without the subsidies, it would make more. The only problem Margaret faces is identical to that of the island's annual Whisky Festival: the same people keep coming back every year. 'The draw to Islay is that there's peace and there's freedom. Every corner you turn and there's a beach. Every other door you pass there's a distillery. You gaze up and you've got mountains; you gaze across and you've got the sea. Doors are never locked. Anybody who's got anything for me will always leave it at the end of the road. Nothing's ever gone missing. We all wave to each other. When I go shopping, it's sixty per cent talking, forty per cent shopping. There's three ferries a day and two flights. I do think, "Why do they keep coming back year after year? Are they not fed up?" Yet for somebody who wants a bolt-hole, Islay is the perfect place to come. It's a special place.'

The fact that the Rozgas don't own their farm is one reason why both Blair and his son Tony are strong supporters of land reform in Scotland. 'Bruno Schroder does a lot for the island,' says Blair, whose farm borders Dunlossit. 'He employs a lot of people; he's a bit more unusual than the typical absentee landlord. But if the rest went tomorrow, the landowners and factors and what have you, to be honest we wouldn't miss them. I should have written letters supporting the land reform. The bill's going through, but the bit about reforming the tenancy act is going to be scrapped; the landowners and factors have been scaremongering too much. If the estate is going to be sold, the tenant farmers will have first refusal, but not the outright right to buy. And these estates don't change hands; they're held in trust for centuries. Nothing will really change.'

Did Blair think that farming land on Islay was used well? 'Absolutely not. A lot of the farms are not let any more. Compare here with Kintyre. The Duke of Argyle had to sell off the whole of that area for death duties, and it's now all owner-occupied. The land is very similar to Islay. Go and see the farms there, compared to the farms hereabouts.' I pointed out that Islay Estates, the Rozgas' landlord, had at least sold them the farmhouse. 'Aye, well,' said Blair, 'they got to realise some of their capital, and all the liabilities went at a stroke.'

'They're very decent people,' adds Margaret. 'But they go along with what isn't socially and morally correct, in our view.'

'It's the system which needs to change,' Blair said. 'We bought the farm, but they still have what is called a feu superior on it. They can stipulate what we do. We had to get written permission from them to run a guest house. It's not allowed to be licensed. They still have the mineral rights; they could mine underneath the house if they wanted. But the system carries on, because the tenant farmers don't like to speak out. People are a wee bit fearful of the estate and the factor, and that's the same all over Scotland.' The 'great, dark cloud' to which John Murdoch referred (see page 149) may have lightened and thinned during the twentieth century, but it still exists.

I asked Lord Margadale of Islay Estates about the future of tenant farms like that of Blair and Margaret Rozga. 'It is tough. I appreciate that if someone has been a tenant on a farm for as many generations as we have owned it for, I can understand them feeling rather aggrieved that they don't own it. But we don't want to create islands within the estate. In a year or two's time, the Scottish Assembly may give tenants an absolute right to buy, and then we would not be in a position to turn them down. That uncertainty is very destructive. It discourages us as landlords from investing more money in buildings and things which are needed. If you build a new shed, and two years later the tenant gets the absolute right to buy . . . it feels like you might as well be writing a cheque out to the guy and saying goodbye to it.' Lord Margadale said that the 30–40 tenant farms owned by Islay Estates currently run at a loss, though other aspects of the Estates activities (like stalking and shooting, or like the 'enterprise zone' of Whin Park) were profitable 'and you can balance things. I'm positive about agriculture, too. I think it's over the hump now, and Islay farms and farmers produce excellent sheep and cattle. It's just tragic that there is no longer a dairy industry on the island.'

There's no doubt that, of the three major landholders on the island, Islay Estates is the least popular among Ileachs – but perhaps that is inevitable, given that it is the landlord of the best farming land on the island, and the estate is run from Wiltshire. Neither the Schroder family's Dunlossit nor the Mactaggart family's Ardtalla have any tenant farms any more: both estates bought their last tenants out in anticipation of the Scottish Executive's land reforms, and they now farm their own land. Not that it makes it any more profitable: Chloë Randall of Dunlossit says that 'the farm has lost half a million quid in five years'; her aim is to make it break even. One of the more colourful strategies has been the acquisition of pigs 'as foresters: they are employees, not livestock. The only difference is that I can sell pig carcases for about eighty pounds each, whereas I have to pay pensions to the other forestry workers.' The use of pigs to clear overgrown woodland and control bracken on the hill has been a long-cherished project of Bruno Schroder's: he personally flew the first two boars up to the island in his private plane.

Bruno Schroder himself pointed out to me that without the dividends from the 200-year-old Schroders Private Bank, keeping the estate would be difficult. 'I told my daughter long ago that Dunlossit would yield about two per cent if you were very lucky, whereas banking should make twenty-two per cent pre-tax. As a young child she told me that the difference was eleven times, and I said to her "Never forget the eleven times." Without the bank you will never keep the estate in the long term.' Sir John Mactaggart quoted, with a weary smile of assent, the often-used simile that owning a Scottish estate 'was like standing under a cold shower tearing up fifty-pound notes'. The estate, he confirmed, was subsidised by the family's other business interests 'but we have no debt on it, and one of our axioms is that we never shall.'

When I visited Islay in August 1999 and stayed at Margaret and Blair Rozga's Kilmeny Farm, it was to make a radio programme about food production on the island. I couldn't understand back then why the Islay name never followed Islay meat to market. Whisky, after all, had made Islay world-famous; yet the island's beef and lamb was every bit as good as its malt. Post-BSE, British consumers were desperate to buy beef they felt they could trust; yet no supermarket and few butchers ever seemed to sell beef under its name of origin. Scotch beef, perhaps; Islay beef, never.

There are practical problems, I learned. Islay has a fine reputation for its breeding stock and its calves (called 'the store trade'), but they leave the island at between nine and 12 months old to be 'finished' elsewhere – generally fattened up in north-east Scotland before being slaughtered at between 18 and 30 months. You can't sell a fillet steak as 'Islay beef' if the bullock from which that steak was cut spent half its life eating turnips in Fife. The prevailing view on the island is that Islay doesn't have enough feed to finish its cattle properly, especially since the geese are guzzling more and more of the rich grass every year; and with just one small slaughterhouse at Ballygrant, it doesn't have the slaughtering facilities, either. Everyone agrees, though that it's still a good idea. 'It's something that should be done,' says Blair Rozga, 'to cut down on the travelling for the animals. And add the value here.'

James Brown did it for a while, albeit in a small-scale way. After the radio programme was broadcast, London restaurateur John Torode got in touch with butcher and slaughterhouse-owner Gilbert Mactaggart, and they set up a system for some of James Brown's bullocks to be finished on the island, slaughtered and hung at Ballygrant, then packed and dispatched direct for Torode's London restaurant (Smith's of Smithfield), where it sold under the Islay name, and proved popular. The slaughterhouse, though, closed, and the arrangement lapsed.

There is one Islay farmer who finishes all his cattle on his farm – and sells all the meat under his own 'Islay Fine Food Company' trademark. He also takes and processes all the venison shot by the sporting estates on the island, and sells that under the Islay name. This paragon of initiative has other plans, too.

I well recall the first time I saw Mark French. I had made a four-o'-clock appointment with him; it was a June day of heavy rain. There was no one in the house, so I made my way over to the barns. An enormous bull was standing in a courtyard, surrounded by Mark, his wife Rohaise and what I assumed were their two sons. Farmer French, a man of substance, wore a greatcoat; he tapped the bull with a stick. His wife looked at him; the boys looked at him; the rain poured down. No one said anything much. For a moment, I felt I was staring at an eighteenth-century farming portrait, save that followers of

Gainsborough or Reynolds would have been instructed to choose better weather in which to frame their subject. 'Is it 4-o'-clock already?' he said, noticing me. The desultory discussion came to an end, and the boys led the bull slowly away.

French is an Englishman, an incomer. 'I first came here about twenty-five years ago; my father-in-law had bought the Foreland Estate. Rohaise's father and my father were very good friends; they actually farmed next door to each other, on top of the North Downs, near Maidstone in Kent.' French's farm, Rockside, was once part of the Foreland Estate; after his father-in-law died, he and Rohaise inherited it. He remembers Rod Dawson arriving at the Ellister Estate; he remembers how Jane Dawson ensured it was broken up and sold to the tenants. 'It's nice not having major estate ownership on the Rhinns; it's made a huge difference. If everybody owns their own farms, they tend to look after them. If you own your own house, you'll repair the gutters. If you rent it, you'll ring up and wait for someone else to do it. I think there were one or two hiccups, in that some of the farmers sold their hill land for forestry, and the way that the subsidies work it has left them a little bit short of extensive grazing. But they had to do it to buy the farms.'

Every time I asked a farmer to name the best farm land on the island, Rockside was always mentioned. It's a big farm of around 2,500 acres (1,012 ha), magnificently sited on the Rhinns under the crags of Granny's Rock, overlooking boggy Loch Gorm and the pale sands, wild flowers and tumbling choughs of Machir Bay. A wild spot on a stormy day, of course: the remains of the *Otranto* lie out in the bay – and the war cemetery where Captain Davidson and some of his crew lie is reached via a path across some of Rockside's fields. But the farm has sheltered arable land as well as exposed land, and the nourishing shell sand blown in from the sea makes fine grazing pasture.

The starting point for Mark French's initiative actually came from United Distillers, the antecedent of Diageo. 'They had this idea of producing something they called "whisky gold beef". Basically it was a PR thing on their part to try to get people to buy more draff. The distilleries were pumping it out, and they couldn't get rid of it. So they held some finishing trials on Islay and Speyside whereby cattle were given different feeds. We just fed ours on draff, and that got us started on the idea.' Mark's cattle, by the way, produce different growth rates depending on whose draff they are eating. 'They do well on Bunnahabhain; they're not so keen on the high phenol ones from Laphroaig and Lagavulin. It's not a huge difference, just a few kilograms, but we just notice it because we're weighing fat cattle every week.'

Mark calculated that if he were going to succeed with his Islay Beef, he would have to aim at the top of the market. Transport and other associated costs are so high on Islay that the end result would inevitably be expensive. 'I got this idea that we ought to be smoking beef, because I'd never heard of anybody else doing it. And because it was coming from Islay, we thought we ought to marinade it in Islay whisky, too. So we spent about two years doing trial work with Rannoch Smokery [on the Scottish mainland]. We supplied the raw materials; they did the trials. I used to go over every month and we'd have tastings, see how much whisky we could add to it, see how drunk we could get. Then we decided to give it a go, and formed the Islay Fine Food Company in 2001.' French uses three-quarter-bred Aberdeen Angus cattle (Angus cross cows mated with pure Angus bulls) which give a well-marbled, open-textured beef ideal for absorbing smoke and whisky flavours. Once slaughtered, French and his staff cut them up at Rockside: 'It's not conventional butchery. We tend to use individual muscles rather than joints.' The whisky-marinaded version is soaked and injected with Bruichladdich (whose logo also appears on the packs), then it is all sent off to Rannoch to be smoked for two days, before coming back to Islay to be packed and dispatched – in 100 g packs. In the long run, Mark hopes to build a smoker of his own on the island. The beef has sold well so far: about half a tonne every two months 'to all four Harvey Nichols shops, Harrods, Selfridges, airport shops, independent delicatessens . . .' though to Mark's surprise the non-whiskied version largely outsells the whisky-marinaded one. He is also now supplying fresh beef, and both smoked venison and fresh venison. The farm, too, has 30 ponies and horses used for trekking across the fields, dunes and beach in the summer – but despite all this, Mark says he still needs his little brown envelopes and goose money to survive. 'I don't think any farm on the West coast of Scotland is viable without subsidies.'

Our fourth farmer is the least typical; and at 250 acres (101 ha), his property is the smallest of all. Toby Roxburgh worked for 27 years as a London publisher, latterly for Macdonald – at the point at which it was bought by the fraudster Robert Maxwell, who pinched most of Toby's pension. He and his wife Harriet (who had a dairying degree) decided they wanted to farm their way towards retirement – so, 'out of the blue', they bought Ballivicar Farm, at the southern end of the Low Road before it turns towards Port Ellen. It was, let's say, a courageous decision. 'If I had known back then just what it was going to be like, I might not have had the courage to do it. I was a fool, to be frank, but I didn't know and I don't regret it. I wouldn't live anywhere else now. Though every so often I remember the fact that my disposable income is now less than my expense account used to be sixteen years ago. This is not a business where you are going to make money, and as a return on capital it's absolutely pathetic. My neighbour down the road at Kintra says that in order to survive as a farmer on the island you must be at least twenty-five per cent more efficient than you would be on the mainland. I think if anything he is underestimating that. It's a wonderful place to live but it ain't no Shangri-la.'

Writer and campaigner Ian Mitchell told me that Toby Roxburgh (whom he nicknames 'Uncle Tobes') had a London publishing reputation as 'a formidable luncher'; with his Pickwickian silhouette, high colour and bright, exclamatory eyes, I guessed the reputation was well earned. None of this, though, seemed to have checked the range of activities undertaken at Ballivicar, which is as ingenious as any. Toby calculates that 55 per cent of his total income comes from the farm (including subsidies, environmental schemes and the sale of animals), while around 45 per cent comes from the holiday flats on the farm, a pony trekking business run by Harriet, a paper-shredding scheme, and his editorship of the *Ileach*, the island's local newspaper. The balance is about to change slightly: Roxburgh has just retired from the newspaper. He also has a small aggregate quarry which makes him no money but wins favours ('and on the island you are going to need them').

Roxburgh, needless to say, is well-qualified to talk about some of the island controversies – such as the tension between environmental organisations and the islanders. Put at its simplest, the issue is as follows. Everyone who visits Islay is struck by its natural beauty. If it is beautiful, the islanders reason, then it proves that they have looked after it very well over the last three hundred years. Yet the last thirty years have seen a proliferation of organisations arriving on the island and issuing or implementing environmental instructions and directives. Not only that, but the RSPB has become a sizeable landowner on the island (it now has 4,120 acres or 1,619 ha), and many islanders – and all of the lairds – believe that this 'green lairdship' has altered the species balance on the island for the worse. 'Islay is a very tolerant community,' says Toby. 'But if the island gets sufficiently annoyed, it's better not to be here. It doesn't happen often. The classic example was David Bellamy and the Battle of Duich Moss. When they came back from their public meeting, they found all their luggage in the court yard outside the Machrie Hotel. They asked for police protection but the police told them to forget it. "You make your own way, mate," was the message.'

These events took place back in August 1985, when the now-retired Grant Carmichael was General Manager for Lagavulin, Caol Ila and the Port Ellen maltings. 'We were hoping to secure a new peat moss,' Grant remembers. 'The Wildlife and Countryside Act had come into force in 1981, but none of us paid a lot of attention to that. We negotiated with Laggan Estate to use Duich Moss – there was a good supply of peat up there, and a solid road which we could use for access. That's always the big difficulty: you can cut peat anywhere, but getting it out isn't so easy. Then along came something called the Nature Conservancy Council. Nobody knew who the hell they were. What right had they to tell us on Islay what to do? But we soon realised the power these people had. They came in and argued that we were disturbing the roosting grounds of the Greenland white-fronted goose. Which was a load of nonsense. Okay, there were a few up there, but not where we wanted to cut. They were very arrogant in their approach; it got people's hackles up right away. Then Rentamob came over, in the shape of David Bellamy and Friends of the Earth. Nobody on Islay had ever heard of Friends of the Earth. Who were Friends of the Earth? They began picketing and demonstrating and whatnot; people were horrified. They didn't take kindly to it. It didn't go down well.'

The battle came to a head with a meeting in Bowmore Hall attended by no fewer than 650 people, and adroitly chaired by Jonathan Porritt, who at that time was Director of Friends of the Earth. Television environmentalist David Bellamy was greeted with laughter when he suggested that it was birdwatchers who kept the ferries going to and from the island, but when he called the outside demonstrators a 'brave young band of people' who 'faced down an angry crowd' the mood changed. 'It was this miscalling of the Islay people which upset most islanders,' as the *Ileach* reported.

'I'm used to being the cuddly good guy,' Bellamy later told the *Daily Mail*, 'but listening to what went on last night, one begins to realise why there are problems in Northern Ireland.' The public meeting of Ileachs overwhelmingly endorsed the decision to go ahead with peat cutting on Duich. By then, though, the decision-making process had moved far from Islay. Although Dr Bellamy and the protesters made a hasty exit, the Battle of Duich Moss was lost, and Port Ellen had to switch its peat extraction to Castlehill.

After such a start, the various environmental organisations and nature charities have had to struggle to achieve public support on Islay. This is sad, since my experience of Ileachs is that they have an instinctive feel for nature; they understand that you have to work with it rather than fight it or manipulate it; they observe it closely; and they appreciate it more intimately and care for it more solicitously than, for example, Londoners seem to appreciate or care for London. The ordinary British domestic gardener is far more lavish in his or her use of herbicides and pesticides than any impecunious Islay farmer, and the greatest killers of British birds are not quiet, observant Hebrideans but speed-crazed mainland motorists and Britain's colossal army of pampered domestic cats. The islanders and nature charities, in other words, should be close allies, not enemies.

Birds, moreover, fly to Islay heavily laden with government money. The geese alone, according to Rae Mackenzie of Scottish Natural Heritage, bring £750,000 from the British taxpayer to the island's farmers; it is hard to imagine a few dozen Italian goose-shooters doing that. Additional money is brought to the island and spent on the island by those who come to look at the birds, though this revenue stream tends to be talked down on the island. 'The thing with the birdy folk,' – Ian Mitchell's attitude is typical – 'is that they are all mean as cat's pee. They come along with their little flasks and sandwiches; they don't go into the pubs; they don't spend any money; they're all kind of "pure" people.' He contrasts this with whisky enthusiasts and shooting enthusiasts and yachtsmen who, he says, are 'fun' people who put up in the hotels and spend lavishly. 'Islay would be far better off if there were fewer boring charities from Bedfordshire buying up half the island and pretending that we all love looking at choughs, which we don't particularly. Nobody's got anything against choughs, but it doesn't lift the duvet for anyone, really, choughs.'

Mitchell's invective may be amusing, but my own observations suggest that he may be wrong. Many visitors to Islay – like the exuberant Alan Watson, a Consultant Paediatric Nephrologist from Nottingham City Hospital who I met on a late autumn visit with his wife at the Machrie Hotel – come to enjoy both the whisky and the birds. Bowmore Distillery (the most visited on the island) gets up to 10,000 visitors a year, yet the RSPB Reserve (despite being far less conveniently sited) still gets up to 7,000. Read the comments in the visitors' books of those using the island's holiday cottages (which are as important a source of revenue as hotel bookings) and you will find them to be preponderantly nature-orientated. These guests may not raise the rafters of the Lochindaal Hotel every night, but they are still buying food, drink, film, postcards and petrol on the island, and handing over substantial weekly rents. Many return, too, year after year.

Icy antagonism, though, is beginning to melt. The early arrogance of the RSPB and other environmental organisations has gone; they farm more intelligently than they used to do; and they employ islanders to help with the farming and to build fences. 'We don't go and tell people how to farm,' says the RSPB's James How. 'I'd soon be chucked off any farm as a short hairy Englishman trying to tell an Islay farmer what to do. What we try to achieve is small tweaks in timing and things like that.' Even Ian Mitchell seems to have decided that the 'absolutely disastrous situation where you have these arseholes from Lancashire coming here and telling people how to plough their fields' has ameliorated. 'It has become apparent to me,' he now says, 'that after a

lot of kicking and beating they have actually changed their approach.'
He still considers the aim of the RSPB is to 'disrupt the relationship
between people and nature', which will come as a surprise to RSPB
members, but 'the organisation is definitely trying to behave on Islay.'

The thoughtful Chloë Randall of Dunlossit Estate owns to being
puzzled by the 'venom' some of those on the island expressed for the
RSPB. 'The RSPB are the richest charity in the country; they are a
source of income for us. We have a good relationship with them. We
are trying to develop the variety of wild life we have, and that's all they
want us to do, so why fight them? They're not against shooting. And a
lot of the opposition to geese doesn't make sense. I get twenty-three
thousand pounds a year from the goose management scheme. That
makes the geese a better crop than sheep.' Ornithologist Malcolm
Ogilvie has also observed an improvement in relations between farming and wildlife interests on the island. 'There are a number of reasons
for that, but perhaps the prime one is that the farmers and crofters are
getting money for conservation – and that money is often their profit.
SNH is now dispersing the better part of one million pounds every year
on the island – and if we didn't have that one-million-pound add-on,
we would be in dire straits, there's no doubt about it.' Many parts of
Islay have been designated as Sites of Special Scientific Interest (SSSIs),
something that originally aroused 'vehement opposition' according to
Ogilvie: 'They were seen as restrictive, as stopping people doing what
they've always done or what they wanted to do with their land.' This,
he says, has also changed, once the islanders 'saw that there was actually
a positive benefit. That meant that instead of being able to do exactly
what you wanted on your land, you accepted the restriction but you
were paid what, by and large, is quite a reasonable amount of money.
There are farmers without the SSSIs who look with some jealousy at
what's going on with their colleagues who are just inside the line.'

The real reason for this disharmony is as much to do, perhaps, with
history as with present-day practicalities. The fact is that, ever since the
Macdonalds were chased from the island in the early seventeenth
century, Islay has been predominantly owned by outsiders and not
Ileachs. The first branch of the Campbell family to own the island were
notorious absentees; the second branch were better, though the more

native they became the less businesslike they were, with the result that Walter Frederick died in Normandy and his son Iain Og Ile, 'Iain of Islay' – a man the Ileachs could readily accept as an Ileach – died in Cannes owning less of Islay than do today's Friends of Laphroaig (all 200,000 of whom are apportioned a square foot of the island each). Then came James Morrison, 'the Napoleon of shopkeepers', and his various heirs and successors, including today's Lord Margadale and his brother Hugh Morrison (a Wiltshire farmer and a trainer of race-horses respectively); the Mactaggarts, a property family with bases in Mayfair, the Caribbean and Canada; and the Schroders, City of London merchant bankers. Viewed from Islay, the RSPB was merely the latest and least familiar of these rich outsiders, arriving on the island and telling Ileachs how to behave, albeit an outsider whose fortune was based on the modest annual subscriptions of widowed blue-tit-feeders rather than vaults of private capital. Distillers, of course, are another sort of laird: corporate, shareholder-owned, faceless, but respected (when they run distilleries rather than close them or demolish them) because of the employment they provide. In any case, if opportunities to buy land do come up on Islay, genuine Ileachs are seldom wealthy enough to take advantage of them. 'I'm afraid it is a fact of life on Islay that money comes in with the incomers,' says Toby Roxburgh. 'If we put Ballyvicar on the market, we wouldn't expect to sell it to an Ileach. We would advertise it in *Country Life* and it would sell off the island. That's the way it is. The local just gets pushed aside. I don't know what the answer to that is.'

Matters are not helped by what we could call the democratic deficit on the island. There is no Islay Council and no Mayor of Islay. Instead there are three 'community councils' (Kidalton and Oa, Kilmeny and Kilchoman) on to which, according to Toby Roxburgh, serving councillors 'have to be dragged kicking and screaming'. Real power, in any case, resides with Argyll and Bute Country Council to whose mainland chamber Islay sends just two councillors, one of whom, Robin Currie, co-represents Colonsay and Jura. Islay, thus, is neither owned nor run by Ileachs.

The result is a general feeling of powerlessness which has two ways of manifesting itself. The first is an instinctive opposition to schemes and proposals which come from outside, no matter how beneficial they might be; and the second is a kind of long-standing lassitude and fatalism among islanders. Initiative on the island is often said to come from incomers (like Mark French) rather than Ileachs – though I would contest this cliché. Margaret Rozga, for example, has created one of the best businesses of its type in Britain, and Jim McEwan is perhaps the most charismatic distiller in the whole Scotch whisky industry; both are Ileachs with plenty of peat in their veins. Another Islay saw is that 'all those who have any get-up-and-go have got up and gone' – or, as adoptive Ileach Grant Carmichael puts it, 'Our biggest export is not whisky, but brains. It's young people. The youngsters all go away for further education, and many of them do well. But they don't come back. There's not the jobs here. We're an ageing population.'

I chatted to two pupils from Islay High School, Ben Harrison and Kirsten MacIntyre, both of whom knew that they would have to leave the island to further their education. They liked the safety and security of Islay – but at the same time they were looking forward to having more privacy and independence on the mainland. Neither expected to have a career on the island – because, apart from farming and distilling, there aren't any. (Many tourist jobs are part-time since tourism is so seasonal on Islay.) Farming is, as we have seen, a struggle, and distillery jobs are few and far between – when two vacancies came up at Bowmore in 2002, there were 54 applicants, and 90 per cent of those were from the island. Even if you get a distillery job, there isn't necessarily much career progression; of the seven distillery managers on Islay at present, only four are Ileachs, with the most recently appointed manager (Robin Shields at Laphroaig) being an incomer.

But I also talked to chemistry teacher Stephen Harrison (no relation of Ben) at the High School, and he pointed out that while talented young Ileachs were leaving the island all the time, bright incomers with children were arriving on the island, too, so he felt the 'genetic drain' was an exaggerated problem. And Islay, he stressed, was a wonderful place to bring up children – for ambitious mothers and fathers. 'Parental involvement is the key. If the parents are involved, you can create very well-rounded individuals here.' Ben – an enthusiastic and talented mathematician and sportsman who plays trombone, piano and guitar – was, he said, a good example. A less happy situation for the island was that there was a drift of 'problem families' to Islay, either moved to the island by social services 'for a new start', or who moved themselves to the island for the same reason.

The idea that Islay is an idyllic spot untouched by the difficulties and ills of the world is, of course, a myth. While researching this book, I learned about an alleged rape; the obscure and tragic death of a baby in Port Ellen; a stabbing in the Ardview pub; the circumstances behind the November 2002 gas-explosion fire at the Port Charlotte hotel which burned out the kitchen and dining room and which – had the wind been a normal westerly rather than an abnormal northerly – might well have burned the guests in their bedrooms; and a long history of domestic violence on one of the island farms which, too, had tragic consequences. You won't read about these events in the *Ileach*, of course. Police, too, find convictions hard to obtain.

'If,' says Toby Roxburgh, 'the *Ileach* was a hard-headed newspaper and I was a hard-nosed journalist, then we would have splashed these things, but you just can't do that here; it's not fair. There is no point,' he said, referring to the rape case, 'in making that kid's life any worse than it already is. Everybody knows about it anyway. If you publish it, all you are doing is compounding the problem.' Roxburgh confirms, too, that there are drugs on the island: 'If you know where to go, you can buy drugs anywhere on Islay. Hard drugs included. Ileachs are certainly smoking pot; they are taking heroin. There is far more in the way of drugs on the island than anyone is willing to admit to. The trouble is that in a community like this, it is very hard for the police to get the evidence.'

The worst substance abuse, in any case, concerns that drug which lies at the heart of this book; which is, indeed, the reason why this book exists. Ethanol; alcohol; whisky. We have seen from the history chapters how deeply rooted whisky distillation is on Islay, and how fickle a friend it has sometimes proved to the population. Colossal drams of neat, raw spirit were administered, within living memory, three times a day or more to the workers in every one of Islay's distilleries. Jim McEwan and Ian McPherson both remember what a risky business it was to leave empty barrels in the open air at Bowmore, for they were often disturbed at night by those upending them to extract the semi-toxic dregs – called 'bull' – to drink. Alcoholics Anonymous meets every Sunday night at Islay Hospital. If the driver of every car using Islay's roads after dark were to be breathalysed, the motoring population of the island would be substantially reduced. Most Islay families have been affected at some point by the ill-effects of alcohol, and if a worker, a brother or a husband disappears for two or three days 'on the spree', this is still regarded as normal and even acceptable behaviour. 'People fall on and off the wagon,' says Jackie Thomson of Ardbeg. 'You tend to book a tradesman for the third Wednesday of the month, because that's when he does his best work. No one's being judgmental; it's just because . . . that's the way it is.' Both Ben Harrison and Kirsten MacIntyre had seen the problems of alcohol in their communities, as a result of which Kirsten only drinks occasionally and Ben doesn't drink at all. On what we might call ancestral Islay occasions – the 'coffining' of a neighbour (a pre-funeral vigil), for example, or at the wake afterwards – the peer pressure on Islay men to consume whisky in dangerously large quantities is intense.

So no, Islay is not idyllic. Even visitors can readily understand how claustrophobic it must feel to spend month after month on the island. Almost everyone I spoke to stressed the importance of getting away. 'There are difficult moments,' says Jackie Thomson. 'It tends to come to flashpoints with me and Stuart, then I just have to get away. I want a bit of pollution. I want to stand in a huge supermarket. I need a fix of anonymity, of looking at all the food in the supermarket, of driving in traffic and not waving at everybody . . . so you have that, and then you come home, and it's lovely again.'

The heartening thing about Islay is not that it doesn't have problems, but that those problems tend to be predominantly social rather than criminal, the product of human frailty rather than human wickedness. 'Oh yes,' said Iain Maclean, in his 89th year, sitting in the distillery manager's drawing room at Laphroaig, 'it's a happy place, because we know each other. Look at the freedom. There's no break-ins or anything like that. I'm here with you now, and the door's not locked at home. When I go to bed at night, the door's not locked. Aye, there's the difference for you: no crime at all.' Really, Iain? I queried. Eighty-nine years, and you've never been the victim of crime? 'No, never,' he replied. There was a pause. 'Well, wait a minute now.' Behind his pale, watery eyes, a chill memory was stirring. 'I remember a garden fete here once; Miss Williamson, as she was then, used to have a garden fete here, to raise money for charity. And I had my boat down on the beach down there, and somebody pinched a rowlock. So I was left with only one rowlock, which wasn't much use. That was the only time, I think. It wasn't too bad.'

When Iain Maclean died in 2003, the island lost another of its native Gaelic speakers. 'It's dying out,' he told me. 'It's a lost cause. I met a woman down in Port Ellen recently. She was born here; I knew that. So I decided to speak to her in Gaelic, out of curiosity; I thought I'd try it out. So I said, "It's a cold day." And she looked a bit puzzled. "Don't you speak Gaelic?" I asked. "Oh, well, a little," she said. "I don't under-stand it very well." Now if that's what's happening here, it's dead, it's a finished language. I speak it very seldom now. I go shopping in Port Ellen practically every day in life, and I'm lucky if I speak half-a-dozen Gaelic words when I'm there. Which is a shame; I prefer to talk in Gaelic. The words seem to come more natural to you. But it's played out, now; it's finished.' Iain McArthur of Lagavulin agrees. 'I still speak it to my father, but not otherwise. I listen to the Gaelic radio, too – but a lot of that is different to what we had on Islay. It's Gaelic from Lewis and up that way; it's a different dialect.' I asked him if he'd like to see it become the language of the islands again. 'No fear,' he said. 'It's a different scene now to what it was. My mother would always speak to me in Gaelic, but I'd always answer her back in English.' Margaret Rozga remembers the same thing. 'My mother was a Gaelic speaker first and foremost; to start with, she hadn't a word of English. But then English speakers came on to the island, and oh, it was the way forward; you must speak English. It wasn't the done thing to be seen speaking Gaelic to your children. We were brought up non-Gaelic speakers. I regret it desperately, and I think my late mother would regret it now, too.' Ben and Kirsten at the High School only knew one pupil whose mother tongue was Gaelic, and where Gaelic was still spoken at home. They'd like to speak it, but in year five of school, when they got the chance to choose to learn either Gaelic or French, they both opted for French.

For all that, on 16 August 2002, a £2 million education centre for Gaelic language, culture and heritage called Ionad Chaluim Chille Ìle (the Islay Columba Centre) opened at a scenic spot called Garnatra between Bowmore and Bridgend. It offers courses in Gaelic language, arts and history – and a wonderful sea view. I anticipated an enthusiastic reception from the islanders, but the postwoman driving the post bus down to Bridgend soon put me right. The islanders, she said, considered it a scandal. The old people's home on the island was next to the hospital, she said, and it had no sort of view at all; everyone thought the Gaelic centre should in fact have been a new old people's home. I decided to visit the hospital and old people's home tucked away behind Bowmore, and found that the postwoman was absolutely right. It's hard to find anywhere on Islay with a really dull view, but that's what these buildings have, looking as they do on to a half-developed, light-obscuring hillside and Bowmore's back streets. Perhaps Islay's older Gaelic speakers would welcome the Gaelic Centre, though?

'An absolute waste of money that is,' said Iain Maclean. 'How on earth can you make people talk the language? I don't see it working at all. It's finished. And it's of no earthly use to you anyway. You can't go to Glasgow and talk to people in Gaelic. It's crowded out.'

'The Centre?' said Iain McArthur. 'Waste of money. I don't see what it's going to do. It would be nice if it was the old folk's home. It's an ideal spot for an old folk's home.' Once again, I began to get the feeling that no one had asked the Ileachs what they wanted.

The only enthusiast I found for the Centre among those I talked to (though it has plenty of support on the letter pages of the *Ileach*, often from those living in Vancouver or Queensland) was Margaret Rozga, who was using it to recapture her lost cultural birthright. Why, I wondered, was everyone so opposed to it? 'I'll tell you why. It's because it hasn't come from the inside but the outside.' It was, in other words, the democratic deficit at work once again.

Despite this local scepticism, the Centre has been busy since it opened, with almost 100 students attending its first Awards Ceremony on 14 February 2004. The 2001 census revealed that 34 per cent of Islay's population understood Gaelic: exactly the same figure as in the 1991 census despite the death of many native Gaelic speakers during the decade, suggesting perhaps that the historic decline may have been arrested. Gaelic medium teaching (in which all classes are taught in Gaelic) is available in Bowmore Primary School, and a small number of pupils take advantage of it. Islay certainly lags behind the Western Isles, where 72 per cent of the population speaks Gaelic, but predictions of its extinction are premature. I count myself lucky to have heard Gaelic used casually and naturally on Islay – as when, one sunny June evening, I was out with Bowmore's Christine Logan on the road from Port Wemyss to Portnahaven and she met her friend Flora Hutton walking up to an evening bingo session in the village hall. The pair chatted effortlessly before (recalling my presence, but greatly to my regret) switching to English. Christine told me later how her parents had always talked to each other in Gaelic. She remembered the summer Sundays of her childhood, when her mother and father would take her off in their boat for a picnic, and the soft, thick lap of Gaelic would mingle with the splash of the oars. Her father would fish from the boat for a sea-trout or two, while her mother would sit on the beach playing her practice chanter. Sunday afternoons rarely unravel like that now on Islay.

Even if the language remains out of reach for many, Ileachs of all ages speak Gaelic in their souls. Christine's mother Lily had begun her career in Glasgow as a 'Kleeneze girl', walking the housing estates selling brushes and dusters on a door-to-door basis. 'Very rude people on the mainland,' she told me. 'I would mention Kleeneze and they'd slam the door.' You'd not find anyone with a Gaelic-speaking soul behaving in such a fashion to a diminutive and plucky Kleeneze girl from Islay. I have travelled the world meeting wine-makers, brewers and distillers for the last decade and a half, but nowhere have I met such gentleness and patience as you'll discover if you meet Ileachs like Billy Stitchell of Caol Ila or Duncan McGillivray of Bruichladdich. It is the gentle who are the true aristocrats of the earth. It takes a while, and perhaps more than a lifetime, to learn Islay ways; Bruno Schroder – who 'adores Islay . . . because it is totally non-hierarchical' – admits he is still studying, and does not, in 2004, yet count himself an Ileach. 'It was beautifully summarised for me about twenty-five years ago, back in 1977, when I was walking with some friends down by Caol Ila one day. I saw this chap I had known for years. He was moving some barrels around and we got talking. "How long have you been on the island?" he said to me. "I arrived here in nineteen thirty-seven, and it's now nineteen seventy-seven, so I think I've been here about forty years." "Och, Bruno," he said, looking me straight in the eyes, "you'll soon be becoming one of us."'

No Ileach alive has had a more successful career than Lord Robertson of Port Ellen, born (on the first floor of the Port Ellen police station in 1946) plain George Robertson. Or George Islay MacNeill Robertson, to give him his full name. 'I knew his father well,' remembered Iain Maclean. 'A very nice friendly man; a policeman. I used to take him over in the boat to Texa when they were dipping sheep; that's how I got to know him. All the farmers were under supervision by the police when they dipped sheep, to check that they were done.' After a General, Municipal and Boilermakers' Union career (he makes two appearances in John McDougall's book of memoirs *Wort, Worms & Washbacks*, journeying from Glasgow to Islay at the request of sacked Laphroaig workers; McDougall describes him as 'an absolute gentleman'), he became Labour MP for Hamilton; Defence Secretary in the Labour government of 1997; and Secretary General of NATO in August 1999. Perhaps, in that job, he took the gentle Ileach Gaelic-speaking soul to places where it was badly needed. His house on Islay is a modest one; everyone on the island (which he visits often) knows him as 'George'. 'He's one of the best-known men in Europe,' says Bruno Schroder, 'but when he's up there he helps quite quietly, absolutely like anybody else, and I admire that enormously.' 'George,' Iain Maclean confirmed, 'is a fine fellow right enough. Oh, George is top of the pops here on Islay.'

The world is thirsty for Islay's malts, but in truth it is even more acutely in need of Islay's spirit. That, in other words, which is gentle; that which is quiet; that which is observant. That which is unrancorous, despite the long history of dispossession; that which is tenacious – as uncomplainingly tenacious as Ian McPherson was, when he took that crazy author on a fly-harried walk through the impenetrable thickets which line the Bowmore distillery lade; or as tenacious as Duncan McGillivray was, as he counted (for the same crazy author) the number of tiny copper tubes in the old condenser out in the yard in the pouring rain at the end of a long day. Minor tenacities, both – but they are merely the ones I know about. There will be many others, more heroic and more secret.

This spirit is another reason why those who come to Islay find the island so hard to forget. No one expressed this soul-haunting to me more memorably than Sandy Mactaggart, as we sat next to an open coal fire in Ardmore House on 1 July 2003. 'I've found at a certain point in your life you get imprinted with some piece of ground and you can't get it out of you, you just can't. I like Canada; I've done well there; but how do you get Islay out of your heart? The songs are right. I find it full of ancientness. How do you forget it? How do you leave? You can't. You've probably felt it for yourself.'

He's right; I have. Many times. The hidden times, stepping gently among Kidalton's wind-tortured oaks, fingering their lichen, dazzled by the sunlit raindrops which line every twig; watching the horned rams of Ballychitrigan charge at each other and fight head-crackingly as the Atlantic ploughs the rocks below them; marvelling at a shooting star plunge down behind Octomore as the dawn light grew. More social times, too, of course. Islay has a remarkable stock of fine musicians and singers; they perform at ceilidhs, stepping up modestly before launching with the poise and assurance of gale-riding kestrels into unaccompanied song of grave beauty which leaves no one in the hall unruffled. But I think, too, of my friend Ivor Drinkwater, an Ileach by adoption only. Ivor was born in the English Midlands, and his accent still has the twang of the hop yard and the apple orchard about it. He was a promising footballer, playing for Worcester City in a distant sporting past; just as his Port Charlotte drinking partner, former Sheffield vet turned Rhinns farmer John Edwards, possesses an unlikely musical past as a Worcester Cathedral choirboy. Ivor's longer-term talents were for painting, though; he admired the Norwich school, and for many years his carefully observed and skilfully executed nature and wild life paintings have sold well, usually to commission, on

Islay. He smokes a pipe, and has a long, tobacco-tinged beard and moustache which, when combined with his pale colouring, high forehead, exuberant eyebrows and sparse, energetic and wilful hair contrives to make him look as if he had just stepped into the bar of the Port Charlotte Hotel from the pages of *The Brothers Karamazov*. After a life spent in choppy waters of various sorts, he found a home on Islay. His own gentleness is not misplaced here; he has the chance to turn his own acute observations on the hill into paintings which others treasure and love.

When the mood takes him (which is rare and beyond solicitation), Ivor will draw a harmonica from his pocket, stand up and play. To say he plays with passion is to understate the case. His whole body trembles with hand-induced vibrato; he seems to find great gales of inner wind; he taps his own soul and the souls of all those listening. There are a number of melodies in the repertoire, but a tune called 'Dark Island' is the one no one ever forgets. He may be a wandering Midlander, I may be a rootless southerner, James Brown standing at the bar with a glass of Bruichladdich may be a distant blood relative of Somerled, and you sitting at the table in the corner over an Ardbeg or a Lagavulin may be a brief visitor from Malmö, Belfast or Tallinn – yet on that instant, nourished by the vapours of great malt, we are all Ileachs, joined in Dark Island fellowship.

Distilleries Past and Future

A hiss in the night.
Scent: on the black water. In
the byre: ghost spirit.

DISTILLATION PROBABLY began on Islay in the late thirteenth or early fourteenth century, and became a commonplace farming activity during the 300 years which followed. Martin Martin, Thomas Pennant and the Reverend Archibald Robertson all observed grain being used to make whisky throughout the Hebridean islands during the eighteenth century – and on Islay to excess, according to the visitor Pennant and the resident Robertson. Children went hungry while their parents drank the harvest. As the nineteenth century dawned, the Excisemen arrived, and the long list of 233 Islay names of those contravening the Excise Act in 1801 (researched by Neil Wilson for his book *The Island Whisky Trail*) proves just how ubiquitous farm distillation was.

It rapidly became less so; the final conviction for illegal distilling on Islay came just 49 years later. By 1833, there were twelve licensed distilleries on the island. Bruichladdich and Bunnahabhain hadn't been built by then, but in addition to the five in existence today there were distilleries at Newton, Daill and Lossit in the Heartland, at Octomore and Port Charlotte on the Rhinns, at Port Ellen itself – and Ardmore, sited next to Lagavulin. When Alfred Barnard arrived in the mid-1880s, the number was down to nine: all the Heartland distilleries had gone, as had Ardmore and Octomore – but bright new Bruichladdich and Bunnahabhain had just opened for business. The Port Charlotte distillery (latterly called Lochindaal) was eventually closed by DCL, the ancestor of Diageo, in 1929; and Port Ellen was closed by the same owner in 1983. Which leaves our seven survivors.

Lochindaal, according to Barnard, was something of a hotchpotch, and at that stage very much dominated the village of Port Charlotte, which the author described as 'of little importance and interest except for the large distillery'. The sea-front warehouses occupied the buildings which are now home to the Wildlife Centre, while the distillery itself lay back across the road where there is now a garage and a fire station; the higher warehouses, by contrast, still exist as such and are used by Bruichladdich. Lochindaal took its water supply from two nearby lochs, which Barnard called 'Garroch' and 'Octomore'. Garroch is the present-day Gearach, a pretty loch lying up the valley behind Port Charlotte, while Octomore would presumably have been the same source which fed the defunct Octomore distillery – though according to the present-day owner of the land, James Brown, this is in fact just a dam. There were eight washbacks and 'three old Pot Stills'; all the drying of the malt was done using peat fires, so the whisky would have been a robustly peaty one. Despite Barnard's description of it as 'large', its annual production of 127,068 gallons (or 577,651 litres) put it in sixth place out of the nine functioning distilleries at the time; it produced about half what the biggest distillery, Ardbeg, was distilling; and only Bruichladdich, Lagavulin and the then-tiny Laphroaig produced less. The distillery was owned at the time of Barnard's visit by J.B. Sherriff, later to own Bowmore.

Lochindaal spirit is, today, a great rarity, if indeed any still exists at all. Peter Pearce, a Yorkshireman who used to farm Sanaigmore at the bleak northern end of the Rhinns, is said to have had a bottle of 'Port Charlotte' among his collection. He lived alone in circumstances of considerable disarray ('He was a very good farmer, but his skills didn't lie in housekeeping,' I was told by another farmer's wife), and was for some years in conflict with the landlord, Islay Estates, over the dilapidated state of his house. 'I'll never leave Sanaigmore; they'll never get me out of Sanaigmore,' he used to tell his fellow islanders when he met them at the Co-op. He died of a heart attack while out tending sheep in the mid-1990s – and was rumoured to have left two instructions regarding funeral arrangements. The first was that he was to be buried on Sanaigmore itself, thereby ensuring that he remained unevicted for eternity; the second was that every bottle of whisky in the house was to be consumed at his wake. Both wishes were executed – and some of those who attended this now-legendary Islay funeral think they remember helping to drink the bottle of 'Port Charlotte'.

DEATH OF A SIXTEEN-YEAR-OLD

By contrast, spirit from Port Ellen irrefutably still exists and, as I write, is still plentiful enough to be on sale. It's an outstanding whisky. The cask-strength Port Ellen distilled in 1979 (and bottled in 2002), for example, is a pale sand-gold in colour, and there's something in the scent which reminds me of damp sand, too – the white sand of Port Ellen bay over which the peat smoke from the maltings drifts, or those rust-coloured grains created when the peaty waters which seep off the Machrie meet the storm-pounded edge of the Big Strand. It's frankly peaty, yet graceful, too; less seaweedy than Laphroaig, less antiseptic than Caol Ila, less richly oily than Lagavulin – but more perfumed and heathery than any of them. In the mouth, the style is one of soft refinement and burnished elegance, yet for a 23-year-old the peat retention is excellent, balanced by notes of angelica root.

The distillery's origins go back to 1825. It was built as a malt mill by Alexander MacKay, but converted to a distillery soon afterwards, passing rather shakily through the hands of a number of different owners, leaseholders and managers before the redoubtable John

Ramsay arrived to investigate how matters stood at Port Ellen on behalf of his uncle (who had an interest in it) in 1833. He was just 18. Seven years later, the distillery was in effect his. The laird of Islay, Walter Frederick Campbell, may have ordered his own affairs dismally, but he recognised business acuity when he saw it – and he re-acquired the lease on behalf of Ramsay when it came up. Ramsay speedily repaid him, and the distillery became the foundation stone of his colossal fortune. When Barnard visited in the 1880s, Ramsay was not there to meet him – which was a pity: what would the effusive journalist have made of the punctilious, penny-counting but now lairdly distiller? Production, from the two pot stills, was about the same as at Caol Ila, and greater than at Bruichladdich, Laphroaig and Lagavulin. When Ramsay died in 1892, the distillery lay at the centre of his vast estate, and was ably managed for some time by his widow, Lucy. After the First World War and the introduction of Prohibition in America, though, distilling looked less rosy; John Ramsay's son Iain sold the distillery on to a Buchanan-Dewar partnership, which was in turn absorbed into the nascent DCL in 1925. The distillery fell silent again in 1929 and was closed as the Depression set in, in 1930.

And closed it remained for long decades – until 1967. At that point, whisky was booming once again, and the blenders were looking for suitable top dressings to carry their anodyne grain whiskies. Port Ellen not only reopened, but reopened in brisk and modern style, after a refit which saw two new stills installed, doubling potential production. Present-day Lagavulin worker Iain McArthur began his career at Port Ellen, and remembers that he was one of 33 workers there at the time. The spirit was, of course, peaty; its malt spec was 35 ppm, the same as at Caol Ila and Lagavulin. Distilling continued until the 1980s, at which point the future Diageo was faced with a looming crisis of overproduction. 'Twelve distilleries were closed on the mainland,' remembers Grant Carmichael, then the General Manager on the island with responsibility for Lagavulin, Caol Ila, Port Ellen and the bonds on Kintyre at Campbeltown, too. 'So one had to go on Islay. It was a blenders' decision, really, and they chose Port Ellen rather than Caol Ila or Lagavulin. It had only been on the go since 1967, remember; the oldest spirit was only just approaching its sixteenth birthday. That made it something of an unproven quantity by comparison with the others. Now we know it's a wonderful single malt. We liked it at the time, but . . .' Several distillers on the island have told me that they feel that Port Ellen is a slow-maturing malt; it only comes into its own at around the 20-year mark. Yet there was no 20-year-old Port Ellen in existence when the distillery was closed in 1983; the decision thus acquires tragic allure.

'It was a very modern distillery, very well designed,' remembers Grant Carmichael. 'The water came down from the Leorin Lochs – there was a pipe to the reservoir behind the distillery. The cooling water came from there, too. We had a sea-water cooling system, but it never really worked properly. Beautiful washbacks, and lovely shaped stills – quite tall for Islay, though not as tall and narrow-necked as Caol Ila. There was nothing special about the cuts; thirty minutes on foreshots, as far as I remember, and about four hours on spirit.' (That's actually quite a long, slow run; among the island's present-day distilleries, only Lagavulin and Ardbeg take longer.) 'We had no purifier; normal condensers. It was fine spirit – not as pungent as Laphroaig or Lagavulin. After about eighteen years it takes on a soft, chocolatey flavour. We used more sherry than you get nowadays – up to about twenty per cent, I think, though the better butts always went to Lagavulin. And there was much less first-fill bourbon. There was even a shortage of casks back then, because overall production was so high; the filling strength went up to sixty-eight or sixty-nine per cent abv for a few years. There wasn't enough wood to be got. That's why some of the cask-strength bottlings today seem high. Personally, I like Islay best when it's bourbon-matured. I think that combination is absolutely super. They don't need sherry; they already have the body.' Production was, Grant thinks, around 1,700,000 litres of pure alcohol per year ('Port Ellen produced about half of what the rebuilt Caol Ila produced'). Its fine, listed warehouses, thought to be some of the oldest in Scotland, now contain Lagavulin.

It was Grant who had to tell the workers that the distillery was to close in 1983, and that all their jobs would be lost – though in the end, those who wanted to carry on working were found new jobs in the maltings or (like Iain McArthur) up at Lagavulin. The stills were removed from the island during the 1990s, and what remained of the distillery was knocked down in 2003. 'With hindsight,' says Grant, 'it could have been different. Ardbeg closed at the same time as Port Ellen, and look at the success story there.' Had Port Ellen managed to remain in independent ownership, it would certainly have known hard and perhaps silent years. Would it, though – as a major, historic distillery producing peaty single malt whisky of proven quality on the isle of Islay – have been reduced to rubble? It seems unlikely.

PALACE MEDICINE

Times change. In the same year in which what remained of Port Ellen was broken for eternity, a new project got underway which aims to return the distilling of whisky on Islay to its earliest roots. Indeed the two were nearly linked by a physical souvenir. 'I tried to get one of the old pagoda roofs from Port Ellen before they pulled it down, but unfortunately we weren't quite ready for it in time.' The speaker is Mark French of Rockside Farm where, perhaps by the time you read these words, farm distilling will resume on Islay after a 200-year break.

The enterprising French's plan is conceptually simple but in practice challengingly complex. He intends to grow and malt barley on his farm, Rockside, at Kilchoman; he will then grind it, mash it and brew it himself; distil it on site; then age it on the farm, too, exposed to the full force of the westerlies which come tumbling in, fresh from Labrador, across the shell sands of Machir Bay. Now that Bruichladdich has a bottling line up and running, the final stage of the process could be completed on the island, too. Production will be tiny – just 40,000 litres of pure alcohol a year initially, which is less than what Caol Ila produces in a week. The eventual total production capacity will be 180,000 litres a year.

Among French's collaborators are managing director Anthony Wills, a whisky bottler with family connections to Islay (his wife's family were the former owners of the Laggan Estate) and John McDougall, a former distiller at both Laphroaig and Springbank (and the author of *Wort, Worms & Washbacks*). Cask and wood-ageing expert Jim Swann is also on the consultative team, as is writer Charles MacLean. French's vision does not go back just two hundred years but six or seven hundred. 'The summer palace of the Lord of the Isles was up at the church here. Angus Og [an ally of Robert Bruce and the father of 'Good John of Islay'] married an Irish girl who was part of Clan Macbeatha [also known as the Beatons]. They then became the hereditary physicians to the Lords of the Isles. They were distilling whisky as a medicine originally – so it is possible that Kilchoman was where whisky distilling first started in Scotland.' Possible indeed.

More practically, Rockside (the farm lies underneath the peaks which form the saddle of land separating this hamlet from Bruichladdich, and overlooking Loch Gorm) has some of the best potential barley fields on the island. 'There has only been one year in the last twenty when we didn't get a barley crop because the weather was too bad. The soil is mainly blown sand. Which for malting barley is actually quite good. If you try to grow barley in high-rainfall areas on a fertile soil, you end up with too much nitrogen, which is just what you don't want for malting. Our soil is basically a neutral growing medium, so we can control the amount of nitrogen we put into it.' French is already harvesting Optic and Challice. 'It would be nice to grow Golden Promise, but you'd have to spray it such a lot: its resistance has broken down completely. It's not an easy crop to grow.' The idea, French explains, is to follow the rhythm of the seasons. 'We want to take it back to the historical way of distilling. You'd harvest in August or September, then get ready to malt in late autumn or winter. Distilling' – and the Kilchoman team intend to use 'a live flame' to heat the wash still – 'will take place in the spring.' How peaty will the new spirit be? 'We'll probably do a variety of different spirits, including peaty ones, yes. That's the joy of being so small: you can do whatever you want.'

As I write in spring 2004, work on the distillery is finally beginning (the original plan envisaged completion by 2003). Another pioneering farm distillery on the Scottish mainland, at Daftmill in Fife, is further advanced: the concept is a timely one. It is very hard to build a new distillery of 'normal' size and find the blending contracts needed to keep it working for week after week, year after year; when you are distilling at a farm scale, by contrast, blending contracts are irrelevant. As, in truth, is time – especially on Islay, which runs to a different and more leisurely clock to the rest of the world. We've waited 200 years for the return of farm distilling on Islay, so there is no reason why we shouldn't wait one or two more.

Glossary

of Scottish words, whisky terminology
and other technical and curious matters
found in this book

abv	*Alcohol by volume: the percentage of pure alcohol in a given liquid or drink*
acrospire	*The initial shoot which develops within a grain of barley during the malting process*
acrotelm	*The upper (hairy) layer of peat in a peat bog or moss*
auld	*Scots spelling of 'old'; also means 'usual'*
American barrel	*Ex-bourbon barrel containing 180–200 litres*
angels' share	*The portion of stored spirit lost annually by evaporation. In Scotland, two per cent per year is allowed by Customs & Excise rules*
aftershots	*Another word for feints (q.v.)*
barque	*A three-masted sailing vessel*
barrel	*See American barrel*
black pot	*An illicit still*
blended whisky	*A mixture of malt whisky (q.v.) and grain whisky (q.v.)*
boll	*A measure of capacity formerly used in Scotland for grain, roughly equivalent to six Imperial bushels or 0.22 cubic metres*
break	*The 'break point' is that at which the stillman switches from foreshots (q.v.) to spirit (q.v.). It is also the point during malt kilning at which all the surface water has dried off the malted barley grains*
brig	*A two-masted sailing vessel*
bull	*The whisky dregs left in empty barrels, drunk in the past by the desperate, impoverished or ruffianly*
butt	*A cask (usually though not invariably ex-sherry) containing 500 litres*

caff	The crumbled fragments, dust and sweepings found at the base of a pile of dried peat bricks or sausages
carryover	The undesirable passage of liquid (rather than vapour) from a wash or spirit still into the lyne arm and thence to the condenser
cask	A general term for the wooden container (of various sizes) in which Scotch whisky must by law be aged for at least three years
cask strength	A whisky bottled without dilution, at the same strength at which it finished its cask maturation, and often without chill filtering (q.v.)
catotelm	The lower (smooth) layer of peat in a peat bog or moss
ceilidh	An organised evening's entertainment with music and dancing
charge	The amount of wash (q.v.), or low wines (q.v.) plus foreshots (q.v.) and feints (q.v.), put into a wash still (q.v.) or a spirit still (q.v.)
chill filtering	A cold filtering process which ensures that whisky bottled at below 46 per cent abv (q.v.) will not throw a haze. It does, however, involve some loss of flavour and texture, so many whiskies bottled at 46 per cent abv and above are now not chill filtered (and declare as much on the label)
chitting	The point at which a grain of barley produces rootlets or culms during the malting process
clearances	The eviction of the indigenous Highland farming population from rural regions during the nineteenth century to make way for sheep (described as 'hooved locusts' by John Muir, the Scottish-born father of America's national parks)
clan	Originally a local or family group; now regarded as a loose association of those sharing the same once-Scottish surname
clegs	Horseflies
colorimetric analysis	The most common means of measuring the phenolic levels (or 'peatiness') of malt or spirit; less accurate than HPLC (q.v.)
condenser	The item(s) of equipment responsible for turning the spirit vapour which rises from a still into a liquid. The lyne arm (q.v.) connects the still to the condenser
congeners	General term used to describe the flavour- and aroma-bearing impurities found in malt whisky
corvid	A member of the crow family
cottar	Housed agricultural worker: the lowest tier of non-vagrant existence in the rural Highlands

cratur	Shortened form of 'creature': humorous yet respectful Scots term for whisky
croft	Small farmstead
crofter	Small-scale (and often part-time) farmer
culm	The rootlets which protrude from a grain of malted barley. They are removed and processed into animal feed
cuts	The points during distillation in a spirit still when the stillman switches from foreshots (q.v.) to spirit (q.v.), and then from spirit to feints (q.v.). The cuts vary from distillery to distillery, and are an important means of creating the character of an individual malt
diver	The steel receptacle used to take samples of wort (q.v.) or wash (q.v.)
double maturation	Diageo's term for what other distillers call a finish (q.v.)
draff	The spent remains of the malted barley after the mashing process is completed. Draff can be used as animal feed
dram	A measure of whisky of indeterminate and variable size. The Oxford English Dictionary states that it originally referred to half a fluid ounce (2.8 cl) of medicine, and thus by extension became 'a small draught' of any liquor taken on medicinal grounds. Charles MacLean suggests that a dram equated to one-third of a pint (18.9 cl) in the taverns of early nineteenth century Edinburgh, and to one gill (14.8 cl) as the standard issue in the distillery dramming (q.v.) tradition
dramming	The practice, now illegal but formerly ubiquitous, of supplying free new-make (q.v.) or cask-strength (q.v.) whisky to distillery workers at regular intervals throughout the day and night
dump hogshead	Another name for a hogshead (q.v.)
dunnage	Traditional, low-ceilinged Scotch whisky warehousing with an earth floor on the ground level giving damp, dark storage conditions. While ideal for maturation, dunnage warehouses rarely make the best use of available space and are impossible to mechanise. Modern warehouses are larger, dryer and cleaner and use mechanised racking systems for positioning the casks
ethanol	Alcohol
exciseman	An agent of Customs & Excise, formerly resident on each distillery site but now making only occasional, unannounced supervisory visits at any time of day or night

factor	The resident manager of a large estate, reporting to the (often absent) owner
fank	A Scots word for 'sheepfold'
feints	All of the distillate produced by a spirit still (q.v.) after the stillman has finished running spirit (q.v.). On Islay, the commencement of the feints varies between 65 per cent (at Caol Ila) and 59 per cent (at Lagavulin). A large volume of feints is produced, and the run takes up to $4^1/_2$ hours (at Lagavulin)
feints receiver	The tank in which the foreshots (q.v.) and feints (q.v.) are gathered. The contents of this tank is then mixed with the low wines (q.v.) produced by the wash still (q.v.) to provide the next spirit still (q.v.) charge (q.v.)
feu	A feudal tenancy, initially considered advantageous because it did not require the performance of military services and gave the tenant more security of tenure than other types of tenancy; in more recent times regarded as anachronistic and onerous. In 2000, the Scottish Executive passed a Feudal Abolition Act (effective from 28.11.2004) extinguishing feu duty and mitigating the power of 'superiors' (those who had issued the feu)
feuars or fewars	Those holding feus, and thus considered members of the rural middle-class in seventeenth and early eighteenth-century Islay
finish	A malt whisky which has undergone the final stage of its maturation process in a highly active cask of named type and origin, thereby stamping the malt with palpable cask-derived characteristics
foreshots	The first distilled vapour to cross the lyne arm and be condensed from a spirit still (q.v.) once it has been charged and heated. Since the oily foreshots contain unpleasant and noxious alcohols, they are separated and mixed with feints (q.v.) in the feints receiver (q.v.) before being in turn mixed with low wines to form the charge for the next spirit run. On Islay, the foreshots are concluded and the spirit cut (q.v.) made at between 75 per cent (Caol Ila) and 72 per cent (Bunnahabhain, Lagavulin and Laphroaig). Bruichladdich's spirit cut varies between 76 per cent and 71 per cent. The standard practical test to distinguish between foreshots and spirit is to mix the distillate with an equal quantity of water. If the emulsion is cloudy, the foreshots have not finished; if it is clear, the spirit has commenced. Foreshots usually take

	between ten minutes (Ardbeg, Bunnahabhain) and 45 minutes (Bruichladdich, Laphroaig) to run
gauger	An informal and mildly derogatory term for an Exciseman, though formerly an official job description (the 1660 Excise Act empowered 'gagers' to enter distilling premises 'at all Times, as well by Night as by Day')
grain whisky	Whisky distilled from mixed grains (malted barley usually represents about 11 per cent of the grist) in a continuous still. There is no grain whisky produced on Islay
gralloch	The hillside disembowelling of a dead deer
grist	Ground malt, ready for the mash (q.v.)
heads	Another word for foreshots (q.v.)
heart	Another word for spirit (q.v.)
hogshead	A cask of 250 litres capacity, usually (though not invariably) of American oak
HPLC	High Pressure Liquid Chromatography, a more precise means of measuring the phenolic levels (or 'peatiness') of malt or spirit than colorimetric analysis (q.v.)
Ileach	A native of Islay, and in its purest sense, one born on the island or whose family is long established there; also the name of Islay's fortnightly newspaper
jo	An informal term for wash (q.v.)
keeper	A shortened form of the word 'gamekeeper', meaning an individual responsible for the practical management of game and wildlife on an estate
lade	A channel bringing water to a distillery (or to a mill)
lamp-glass	Double-waisted still design (see diagram on page 15). The only lamp-glass stills on Islay are Laphroaig's spirit stills and Ardbeg's wash still and spirit still
lauter tun	An enclosed and fully mechanised type of mash tun (q.v.) with rotating sparging arms (for spraying hot water on to the grist), fully adjustable revolving knives or rakes (for mixing the water and the grist) and a slotted false bottom out of which the finished sweet wort (q.v.) drains at the end of the process. The draff is then emptied automatically and the tun cleaned automatically before receiving the next charge of grist and hot water
lazy-beds	A system of strip-cultivation once widespread in rural Islay in which a raised rig (q.v.) is created by cutting and lifting turfs from either side. This rig was manured (on Islay with both quarried lime and seaweed or 'sea ware') and used to grow crops, generally potatoes. Despite its name, lazy-bed

	cultivation was laborious. Islay's former lazy-beds can easily be seen from the air as intricately ridged ground
low wines	*The product of the wash still (q.v.) which, when mixed with the contents of the feints receiver (q.v.) forms the charge for the spirit still (q.v.). Low wines have an alcoholic strength of just over 20 per cent which the contents of the feints receiver raises to about 28 per cent*
low wines still	*Another name for a spirit still (q.v.)*
lye pipe	*Another name for a lyne arm (q.v.)*
lyne arm	*The connecting pipe which leads from the top of the spirit still (q.v.) to the condenser (q.v.). Whether the lyne arm rises, is straight or descends will affect reflux (q.v.) and perhaps carryover (q.v.), and is therefore influential in the creation of the character of an individual malt*
malt	*Barley which has germinated and begun growing, then had that growing process arrested by heat. The purpose of malting is to convert unfermentable starches into fermentable sugars*
malt floor	*In those distilleries (like Bowmore and Laphroaig) which still do their own artisanal malting, the barley grains are laid out in deep carpets on malt floors to germinate*
malt mill	*A mill used to grind malt (q.v.) for brewing purposes*
malt whisky	*Whisky made from malted barley (q.v.) alone, and double distilled in pot stills. All of Islay's whiskies are malt whiskies*
malted barley	*Barley which has undergone conversion into malt (q.v.)*
marriage	*The period of time a blend (including a blend of casks for a single-malt bottling) spends together before bottling*
mash	*A mixture of grist (q.v.) and hot water which produces sweet wort (q.v.)*
mash tun	*The vessel in which mashing takes place. Older mash tuns, like that at Bruichladdich, are open and often made of cast-iron, with the hot water being poured on through a spout and a system of rotating rakes used to mix the grist and the water. Modern lauter tuns (q.v.), like that at Laphroaig, are enclosed and fully automatic. Semi-lauter tuns (q.v.) also exist, sometimes converted from older tuns*
middle cut	*The central part of the spirit run (q.v.), during which the spirit (q.v.) is produced and collected*
moss	*A peat bog (chiefly formed of sphagnum moss)*
murrain	*The general name for any plague-like disease affecting cattle*
mutskin	*Alternative form of 'mutchkin': a liquid measure equating to*

	one-quarter of an old Scotch pint, or about three-quarters of an Imperial pint (3 gills or 43 cl). Even half a mutskin, in other words, was quite a dram (21.5 cl: see page 131)
new make	The high-strength, colourless spirit (q.v.) which runs from the spirit still (q.v.)
och	All-purpose Scots word often indicating sorrow, pain, regret, annoyance, weariness, surprise, contempt or disagreement, but also used to lubricate utterance more generally
oxidative	Implying exposure to oxygen. Oxidation is an important aspect of malt-whisky maturation, contributing complexity of aroma and flavour
phenols	The portmanteau term used to describe peaty aromas and flavours in whisky: a complex spectrum of chemical compounds which includes phenol (carbolic acid: C_6H_5OH) but also includes many other chemical compounds, too
plain	The simplest, single-waisted still design (see diagram on page 15). All of the stills on Islay are plain in design except Ardbeg's two stills and Laphroaig's spirit stills
pot ale	The residues left after the wash (q.v.) has been distilled into low wines (q.v.) in the wash still (q.v.); a waste product on Islay. The amount of pot ale produced vastly exceeds the amount of low wines
pot still	Descriptive term for the distinctively rounded, full-bellied stills in which malt whisky (and other fine spirits such as Cognac) are produced
ppm	'Parts per million': in the context of this book, the expression of measurement of peatiness in a spirit. The standard means of arriving at a ppm figure are colorimetric analysis (q.v.) and HPLC (q.v.)
puffers	The deep-bellied little steam boats which formerly serviced the inaccessible West Coast of Scotland – including supplying all of Islay's distilleries with coal, barley and empty casks, and taking full casks off for blending and bottling. The celebrated fictional Vital Spark, captained by Para Handy, was a puffer ('Ye'll be in Bowmore before it's ten o'clock, in time for a refreshment', the captain tells his mate Macphail in Running the Blockade). Now, alas, replaced by charmless heavy goods vehicles
puncheon	Another cask of around 500 litres, though rounder in shape than a butt (q.v.)
purifier	A large pocket-shaped item of equipment fitted to the lower half of the lyne arm (q.v.) in certain distilleries. It

removes the heavier alcohols before they reach the condenser and returns them via a tube at the bottom of the purifier to the main spirit still pot for further distillation and reflux. Ardbeg is the only Islay distillery with a purifier on its spirit still. The effect, according to manager Stuart Thomson, is to move the distillation regime halfway between standard double distillation and triple distillation (as formerly practised at many Lowland malt distilleries, but nowadays only practised by Auchentoshan; triple distillation is still, however, widely practised in Ireland)

recovery temperature The temperature at which the condenser operates: another important factor in the creation of individual malt-whisky character. Lower recovery temperatures suit more heavily styled malts; higher recovery temperatures more lightly styled malts

refill Industry term for the second fill of a cask once it has reached Scotland. Much malt is put into refill casks; freshly arrived casks tend to be filled initially with grain whisky. An Islay exception is Laphroaig, invariably filled in freshly arrived bourbon casks

reflux Term describing the tumbling back down of condensed or partly condensed spirit vapour before it reaches the condenser itself. The more reflux, the more copper contact; and the more copper contact, the more polished and refined the spirit. There are, though, many different ways of achieving reflux: lamp-glass (q.v.) still designs as at Ardbeg or Laphroaig; tall and slender still necks, as at Bruichladdich; large stills with modest charges, run slowly, as at Bunnahabhain or Caol Ila; rising lyne arms, as at Ardbeg or Laphroaig; or the use of a purifier, as at Ardbeg.

rig A strip of cultivated land such as that created by lazy-bed (q.v.) farming

runrig A communal landholding system in which each tenant was given several rigs (q.v.) to cultivate each year, those rigs being chosen by lot

rut The period of sexual excitement and reproductive activity among male deer, corresponding to the period of oestrus in female deer. A noisy and violent time out on the hill

sea ware Seaweed, formerly used as manure on Islay

semi-lauter tun A mash tun with some of the operational advantages of the lauter tun (q.v.), such as automatic sparging of hot water on to the grist or mash, but without adjustable rakes

shieling	A Scots word for summer pasture with shepherd's hut or huts
single malt whisky	A malt whisky coming from one distillery alone
skein	A flock of wild geese in flight
skerries	A Scots word for sea rocks, especially those covered at high tide
sludge	A deposit formed at the bottom of the feints receiver, and removed at regular intervals
sorning	A practice common in the Hebrides in medieval times whereby bands of young men on informal military service would demand board and lodging of local populations by force
sparging	The sprinkling of hot water over grist during the mashing process, especially in a lauter tun (q.v.)
spent lees	The residues left in the spirit still after distillation. Like pot ale (q.v.), a waste product
spirit	The heart or middle cut of a spirit run, following foreshots (q.v.) and preceding feints (q.v.). This spirit is collected and becomes the new make (q.v.) and eventually, after ageing, the single malt itself: the point and purpose of all Scotch malt whisky distilling activity. The word 'spirit' is also used more generally to describe any distillate
spirit cut	The point at which the stillman switches from foreshots (q.v.) to spirit (q.v.)
spirit run	The second half of the double distillation process, in which the low wines (q.v.) are heated in the spirit still to produce foreshots (q.v.), spirit (q.v.) and feints (q.v.)
spirit safe	A beautiful and securely locked copper-framed glass box in which sampling, testing and cutting of distillate can take place without the distillery workers having tempting physical access to the spirit itself. Partly developed on Islay at Port Ellen by John Ramsay, the spirit safe eased the administrative burden of formerly resident Excise officers. Nowadays, the spirit safe is a purely decorative distillery adornment, and the keys are generally kept in the distillery manager's office rather than in the waistcoat pockets of Excisemen
spirit still	The still in which the low wines (q.v.) are distilled into spirit (q.v.): the second stage in the two-stage process of pot-still distillation. The spirit still is usually slightly smaller than the wash still (q.v.), though Lagavulin is an exception to this rule
splashing	Informal Islay term for the poaching of salmon using nets

positioned near the mouths of salmon rivers such as the Laggan or the Sorn

steam coils	One of two potential heating elements positioned in the bottom of a still; sometimes used on their own and sometimes in conjunction with steam pans (q.v.)
steam pans	The second of two potential heating elements positioned in the bottom of a still; usually used in conjunction with steam coils (q.v.)
steeps	Containers in which barley grains are soaked at the beginning of the malting process
still	A piece of apparatus consisting of a pot, a neck (or swan neck, q.v.), a lyne arm (q.v.) and a condenser (q.v.) used for the distillation of alcoholic liquids. Copper pot stills (q.v.) are used for malt whisky distillation on Islay
strand	A beach or shoreline
swan neck	Term sometimes used to describe the neck of malt whisky stills, though rarely with any ornithological accuracy nowadays. Not so in the past: see Bowmore chapter
switchers	Devices fitted to some washbacks (q.v.) and wash stills (q.v.) to stop excessive frothing
tacksman	An agricultural middleman in the rural Hebrides, holding a sizeable tenancy from the chief or laird (to whom the tacksman was often related) and in turn sub-dividing and sub-letting it to tenants or cottars
tailings	Another word for feints (q.v.)
tails	Another word for feints (q.v.)
tanist or tanister	The appointed heir under a system of tanistry (q.v.)
tanistry	The system (commonplace in the medieval Hebrides) whereby the heir of a chief was not his eldest son (primogeniture) or nearest male descendant but the worthiest of his kin, chosen prior to his death
terroir	A French (wine) term, adverting to the fact that the chief element in creating the scent and flavour of a wine or other comestible is a profoundly local and individuated matrix of soil, topography, climate and custom
township or toun	A small community of crofts. The less accessible parts of Islay are scattered with abandoned townships or touns; there were 170 on the island as mapped by Stephen MacDougall in 1740
traik	A Scots word for murrain (q.v.)
trestarig	According to Martin Martin's late seventeenth-century observations, this Gaelic word meant a triple distilled spirit,

	as opposed to the four-times distilled usquebaugh (q.v.)
tun room	The room in which the washbacks (q.v.) are sited
uisge beatha	The Scots Gaelic equivalent of the Irish Gaelic word usquebaugh (q.v.)
underback	The vessel in which wort (q.v.) is collected from the mash tun (q.v.) prior to being pumped to the washbacks (q.v.)
usquebaugh	The (Irish Gaelic) original of our word 'whisky'. According to Martin Martin's late seventeenth-century observations, usquebaugh (or usquebaugh-baul) was a four-times distilled spirit (as opposed to the triple-distilled trestarig, q.v.). In the 1770s, Thomas Pennant claimed that usquebaugh was a flavoured spirit, the unflavoured alternative (pure malt) being called aqua vitae (or 'water of life' in Latin), a distinction drawn nearly 50 years earlier in George Smith's The Compleat Body of Distilling (1725). Johnson's Dictionary (1755) also stated that usquebaugh was 'drawn on aromaticks'; he further added 'by corruption, in Scottish they call it whisky'. The Scots Gaelic equivalent of usquebaugh is uisge beatha; both mean 'water of life'. Charles MacLean suggests that, by the mid-eighteenth century, usquebaugh routinely described a flavoured spirit, whereas whisky, uisge beatha and aqua vitae were all terms commonly used to describe unflavoured pure spirit
vatted malt whisky	A blend of malt whiskies from different distilleries
vents	Stills are equipped with vents, partly to stop them collapsing or exploding under emergency circumstances (such as a blockage) and partly to allow highly volatile substances produced during distillation to escape from the still
wash	The name for the fermented beer, ready for distillation, which forms the raw material of whisky
washback	The large wooden or steel vat (on Islay, only Laphroaig uses steel) in which fermentation takes place
wash still	The still in which the wash (q.v.) is distilled into low wines (q.v.): the first stage in the two-stage process of pot-still distillation. The wash still is usually slightly larger than the spirit still (q.v.), though Lagavulin is an exception to this rule
water	A vital requirement for malt whisky distilling, used in copious amounts not only for brewing but also for cleaning, steam heating and condensing. All of Islay's distilleries use a 'wild' water source for their brewing water. In six cases, this is brown peaty water gathered in hillside lochs or reservoirs; in the case of Bunnahabhain, this is clear unpeaty spring water

wee	*A Scots word for 'small'*
whiffling	*Term used for the noise made by wild geese (and by Lewis Carroll's Jabberwock) in flight*
wormtub	*A primitive alternative to the use of condensers (q.v.) for condensing. There are no wormtubs on Islay*
wort	*The warm sweet malty liquid produced in the mash tun (q.v.). Once fermented, the wort becomes beer or wash (q.v.)*

Bibliography

HISTORY

Blair, W.N., *Reminiscences of Islay in the 19th Century* (Islay: Museum of Islay Life, 1995)

Bold, Alan, with Drake, Jane, *Scottish Clans* (Andover: Pitkin, 1994)

Caldwell, David H., *Islay, Jura and Colonsay: A Historical Guide* (Edinburgh: Birlinn, 2001)

Clifton, Violet, *The Book of Talbot* (New York: Harcourt, Brace and Company, 1933)

Dodgshon, Robert, *The Age of the Clans: The Highlands from Somerled to the Clearances* (Edinburgh: Birlinn with Historic Scotland, 2002)

Driscoll, Stephen, *Alba: The Gaelic Kingdom of Scotland AD 800–1124* (Edinburgh: Birlinn with Historic Scotland, 2002)

Gatty, Richard, *Portrait of a Merchant Prince: James Morrison 1789–1857* (Northallerton: Pepper Arden, n.d.)

Hawkes, Christopher and Jacquetta, *Prehistoric Britain* (Harmondsworth: Penguin Books, 1952)

Hunter, James (ed.), *For the People's Cause: From the Writings of John Murdoch* (Edinburgh: Her Majesty's Stationery Office, 1986)

MacDonald, William, *Descriptive & Historical Sketches of Islay*, with Murdoch, John, *A New and Ready Way of Disposing of The Interesting Island, which would Pay the Debt, Restore the Late Proprietor and Give the Best Return to Large and Small Capitalists* (Islay: The Celtic House, 1997)

Maclean-Bristol, Nicholas, *Murder Under Trust: The Crimes and Death of Sir Lachlan Mor Maclean of Duart, 1558–1598* (East Linton: Tuckwell Press, 1999)

Marsden, John, *Somerled and The Emergence of Gaelic Scotland* (East Linton: Tuckwell Press, 2000)

Martin, Martin, *A Description of the Western Islands of Scotland Circa 1695*, with Monro, Donald, *A Description of the Occidental i.e. Western Isles of Scotland* (Edinburgh: Birlinn, 1999)

Minutes of Evidence taken before the Royal Commission (Highlands and Islands, 1892) Vol II (Edinburgh: Her Majesty's Stationery Office, 1895)

Moffat, Alistair, *The Sea Kingdoms: The History of Celtic Britain & Ireland* (London: HarperCollins, 2002)

Murdoch, John, *see* MacDonald, William, and Hunter, James (ed.)

Paterson, Raymond Campbell, *The Lords of the Isles* (Edinburgh: Birlinn, 2001)

Pennant, Thomas, *A Tour In Scotland and Voyage to the Hebrides, 1772* (Chester: John Monk, 1774)

Prebble, John, *The Highland Clearances* (Harmondsworth: Penguin, 1969)

Ramsay, Freda, *John Ramsay of Kidalton* (Toronto: Peter Martin Associates, 1969)

Ritchie, Anna, and Breeze, David J., *Invaders of Scotland* (Edinburgh: Historic Scotland, 2000)

Sinclair, Charles, *A Wee Guide to Macbeth and Early Scotland* (Musselburgh: Goblinshead, 1999)

The Statistical Account of Argyleshire by the Ministers of the Respective Parishes (NSA), (Edinburgh, 1845)

Smith, G.G. (ed.), *The Book of Islay* (Edinburgh, 1895)

Storrie, Margaret, *Islay: Biography of an Island* (Islay: The Oa Press, second edition 1997)

Thompson, Francis et al., *Lamplighter and Story-Teller: John Francis Campbell of Islay 1821–1885* (Edinburgh: National Library of Scotland, 1985)

Twigger, Robert, *Inflation: the Value of the Pound 1750–1998* (London: House of Commons Library Research Paper 99/20, 1999)

Way of Plean, George, and Squire, Romilly, *Clans & Tartans* (Glasgow: HarperCollins, 2000)

GEOGRAPHY AND THE POLITICS OF LAND OWNERSHIP

Callander, Robin, *How Scotland Is Owned* (Edinburgh: Canongate, 1998)

Cramb, Auslan, *Who Owns Scotland Now?: The Use and Abuse of Private Land* (Edinburgh and London: Mainstream, 2000)

Haswell-Smith, Hamish, *The Scottish Islands: A Comprehensive Guide to Every Scottish Island* (Edinburgh: Canongate, 1999)

Lees, George, and Duncan, Kathy, *Coasts: Scotland's Living Landscapes* (Perth: Scottish Natural Heritage, n.d.)

McEwan, John, *Who Owns Scotland?* (Edinburgh: Polygon, 1981)

Mitchell, Ian, *Isles of the West: A Hebridean Voyage* (Edinburgh: Birlinn, 2001)

Newton, Norman, *Islay* (Newton Abbot: The Pevensey Press, 1997)

Nicolson, Adam, *Sea Room* (London: HarperCollins, 2002)

Slatterley, Glyn, *The Highland Game: Life on Scottish Sporting Estates* (Shrewsbury: Swan Hill Press, 1999)

Wightman, Andy, *Who Owns Scotland* (Edinburgh: Canongate, 2000)

GEOLOGY AND NATURAL HISTORY

Anonymous, *Boglands: Scotland's Living Landscapes* (Perth: Scottish Natural Heritage, 1995)

Bell, Pat and Wright, David, *Rocks & Minerals* (London: Chancellor Press, 1994)

Cribb, Stephen and Julie, *Whisky on the Rocks: Origins of the 'Water of Life'* (Keyworth: British Geological Survey, 1998)

Cruwys, Elizabeth and Baxter, John, with Harwood, John, *Seals* (Perth: Scottish Natural Heritage, 1996)

Dawson, Jane, *Old Squaw* (Islay: Lochindaal Press, 2003)

Dunning, R.W. et al., *Britain Before Man* (London: Her Majesty's Stationery Office/Institute of Geological Sciences, 1978)

Dunning, R.W. et al., *The Story of the Earth* (London: Her Majesty's Stationery Office/Institute of Geological Sciences, second edition 1981)

Elliott, Richard E., *Birds of Islay* (London: Christopher Helm, 1989)

Feltwell, John, et al., *Field Guide to the Butterflies and Other Insects of Britain* (London: Reader's Digest, 1993)

Fiona of the Seals, *Seal* (Edinburgh and London: Mainstream, 2000)

Green, Rhys, and Riley, Helen, *Corncrakes* (Perth: Scottish Natural Heritage, 1999)

Hayman, Peter, *Birdwatcher's Pocket Guide* (London: Mitchell Beazley, 1998)

Hendry, George, *Midges in Scotland* (Edinburgh: Mercat Press, 1994)

Hendry, Georges, and Ho-Yen, Darrel, *Ticks: A Lay Guide to a Human Hazard* (Edinburgh: Mercat Press, 1998)

Maltman, Alex, Elliott, Richard, Muir, Roderick and Fitches, Bill, *A Guide to the Geology of Islay* (Aberystwyth: Institute of Geography and Earth Sciences, University of Wales, second edition 2000)

Newton, Norman, *Islay: A Geological Guide* (Highlands and Islands Development Board, 1988)

Ogilvie, Malcolm, *The Birds of Islay, including when and where to find them and lists of other fauna and flora* (Islay: Lochindaal Press, 2003)

Ogilvie, Malcolm, *The Wild Flowers of Islay: A Checklist* (Islay: Lochindaal Press, 1995)

Pellant, Chris, *Rocks and Minerals* (London: Dorling Kindersley, 1992)

Press, J.R., Sutton, D.A. and Tebbs, B.R. et al., *Field Guide to the Wild Flowers of Britain* (London: Reader's Digest, 1997)

Scott, Michael, *Scottish Wild Flowers* (Glasgow: HarperCollins, 2000)

Taylor, Andrew and Nortcliff, Stephen, *Soils: Scotland's Living Landscapes* (Perth: Scottish Natural Heritage, 1996)

Thackray, John, *The Age of the Earth* (London: Her Majesty's Stationery Office/Institute of Geological Sciences, 1980)

Thomas, J.A., *Butterflies of the British Isles* (London: Hamlyn, 1992)

ISLAY LOCAL INTEREST

Booth, C. Gordon, revised and extended by Ogilvie, Malcolm and Perrons, Margaret, *Guide to Places of Interest on Islay* (Islay: The Museum of Islay Life, 1997)

Booth, C.Gordon, *An Islay Notebook* (Islay: Islay Museums Trust, n.d.)

Booth, C.Gordon, *Islay Worthies* (Islay: Islay Museums Trust, 1979)

Booth, C.Gordon, *The Islay Woollen Mill Story* (Islay: Islay Woollen Mill Company Ltd, 1983)

Committee of the Finlaggan Trust, *Finlaggan* (Islay: The Finlaggan Trust, 1998)

Earl, Peggy, *Tales of Islay: Fact and Folklore* (Islay: The Celtic House, n.d.)

Ferguson, Katie and Perrons, Margaret, revised by Ogilvie, Malcolm, *Place Names of Islay* (Islay: The Museum of Islay Life, 2002)

Jupp, Clifford, *Dunyveg* (Islay: The Museum of Islay Life, 1998)

Lamont, W.D., *Ancient & Medieval Sculptured Stones of Islay* (Glasgow: John Smith & Son, 1988)

Lenton-Halsall, Patricia, *Nerabus: The Story of a Small Hebridean Settlement Since 1850* (Glasgow: Russell Design, 1991)

MacDougall, Dougie, *As Long as Water Flows* (Islay: The Celtic House, 2002)

Maceacharna, Domhnall, *The Lands of the Lordship: the Romance of Islay's Names* (Islay: Argyll Reproductions Ltd., 1976)

Storrie, Margaret, *Continuity and Change: The Islay, Jura and Colonsay Agricultural Association, 1838–1988* (Islay: The Oa Press, 1988)

Trevorrow, Rev. J.A., *Kilarrow Series Volumes One to Five: Patterns of a Christian Past in a West Highland Parish* (Islay: Bowmore Parish Church, 1999)

Various, *An Islay Miscellany* (Islay: The Museum of Islay Life, 2002)

Welsh, Mary, *Walks on the Isle of Islay* (Doune: Clan Books, 1999)

WHISKY

Andrews, Allen, *The Whisky Barons* (Glasgow: The Angel's Share, 2002)

Arthur, Helen, *Whisky: Uisge Beatha, The Water of Life* (London: Apple Press, 2000)

Barnard, Alfred, *The Whisky Distilleries of the United Kingdom* (Edinburgh: Birlinn, 2003)

Bruce Lockhart, Robert, *Scotch: The Whisky of Scotland in Fact and Story* (Glasgow: Neil Wilson Publishing, 1995)

Cooper, Derek, *A Taste of Scotch* (London: André Deutsch, 1989)

Gunn, Neil M., *Whisky & Scotland* (London: Souvenir Press, 1977)

Hills, Phillip, *Appreciating Whisky* (Glasgow: HarperCollins, 2000)

Hills, Phillip (ed.), *Scots on Scotch: The Scotch Malt Whisky Society Book of Whisky* (Edinburgh and London: Mainstream, 1991)

Hume, John R. and Moss, Michael S., *The Making of Scotch Whisky: A History of the Scotch Whisky Distilling Industry* (Edinburgh: Canongate, 2000)

Jackson, Michael, *Malt Whisky Companion* (London: Dorling Kindersley, 1999)

Jackson, Michael, *Scotland and Its Whiskies* (London: Duncan Baird, 2001)

Jackson, Michael, *The World Guide to Whisky* (London: Dorling Kindersley, 1987)

MacLean, Charles, *Malt Whisky* (London: Mitchell Beazley, 1997)

MacLean, Charles, *Scotch Whisky* (London: Mitchell Beazley, 1998)

MacLean, Charles, *Scotch Whisky: A Liquid History* (London: Cassell Illustrated, 2003)

McCreary, Alf, *Spirit of the Age: The Story of 'Old Bushmills'* (Bushmills: The 'Old Bushmills' Distillery Company Ltd, 1983)

McDougall, John and Smith, Gavid D., *Wort, Worms & Washbacks: Memoirs from the Stillhouse* (Glasgow: The Angel's Share, 2000)

Murray, Jim, *Classic Blended Scotch* (London: Prion, 1999)

Murray, Jim, *The Complete Guide to Whisky* (London: Carlton, 1998)

Schobert, Walter, *The Whisk(e)y Treasury* (Glasgow: The Angel's Share, 2002)

Smith, Gavin D., *A to Z of Whisky* (Glasgow: Neil Wilson Publishing, 1997)

Steadman, Ralph, *Still Life with Bottle* (London: Ebury Press, 1994)

Townsend, Brian, *Scotch Missed: The Lost Distilleries of Scotland* (Glasgow: The Angel's Share, 2000)

Wilson, Neil, *The Island Whisky Trail: An Illustrated Guide to The Hebridean Distilleries* (Glasgow: The Angel's Share, 2003)

SHIPWRECKS

Baird, Bob, *Shipwrecks of the West of Scotland* (Glasgow: Nekton Books, 1995)

Blackburn, Steve, *Dive Islay: Wrecks, Transits, History, Photos, Launch Sites* (Stoke-on-Trent: Bucknall Publications, 1986)

Moir, Peter and Crawford, Ian, *Argyle Shipwrecks* (Inverclyde: Moir Crawford, 1997)

Wiggins, J., *The Exmouth of Newcastle 1811–1847* (Islay: Ileach Teleservices Ltd, n.d.)

MAPS

British Geological Survey Scotland Sheet 19: South Islay

British Geological Survey Scotland Sheet 27: North Islay

Ordnance Survey Explorer 352: Islay South

Ordnance Survey Explorer 353: Islay North

Ordnance Survey Landranger 60: Islay

Ordnance Survey Road Map 2: Western Scotland & The Western Isles

Index

Note: The letter *g* appended to page numbers indicates a glossary entry. Page numbers in *italic* indicate illustrations.

200–201, 379*g*
Humbrecht, Margaret 222
Humbrecht, Olivier 222
Hume, John 107
Hunter, Ian 318–20, 322, 323–5
Hunter, Isabella 322
hunting 261
Hutton, Flora 363

ice ages 84–5
Ida Adams (trawler) 296
Ileach (newspaper) 359
illegal distilling 132–5, 272–3,
  367–8
  see also crime
Inge, King 89
Innse Gall 88
Invergordon Distillers 172
Iona 88
IRA (Irish Republican Army) 159
Ireland 87, 88, 159, 293, 301
Irish Republican Army (IRA) 159
Islay 1–4, 26–58, *26*, *220*, 341–66
  administration by outsiders 356–8
  early history 82–105
  Fault, the 38–41
  geology 29–31, 55–6, 84
  Heartland, the 41–4
  Kidalton 54–8
  Moss, the 48–50
  Mountain Islay 44–8
  nature 246–69, 354–6
  Oa, the 50–54
  recent history 124–68
  Rhinns 29–38
  weather 23, 84–5, 220–29
Islay III (steamer) 295

Jabour, Roy 166
James I, King of Great Britain and
  Ireland (James VI of Scotland) 91,
  95, 96, 99
James IV, King 131–2
James VI, King of Scotland (James I
  of Great Britain and Ireland) 91,
  95, 96, 99
J.B. Sherriff 112, 368
Jefford, Steve 184
Jennings family 163

Jim Beam Brands 61, 172, 173, 184
John Strachan (boat) 60
Johnson, Wally 166
Johnston (family) 273, 276, 322
Johnston, Alexander 320
Johnston, Alexander ('Sandy') 322
Johnston, Angus 273
Johnston, Catherine 322
Johnston, Donald 273, 320, 321, 322
Johnston, Dougald 273, 322
Johnston, Duncan 321
Johnston, Isabella 322
Johnston, John 107, 273, 320–21
Johnston, John Johnston Hunter 322
Johnston, Roland 321
Johnston, Willie 199–200
Jones, John Paul 130

Kartli (ship) 294
Kashmir (ship) 309–310
Kennedy, Sergeant 316
Kenneth I, King (Kenneth
  MacAlpin) 87, 88
Kidalton 54–8
Kilarrow 128
Kimble, Norrie (Norman Campbell)
  190–93

lades 108–9, 113–14, 379*g*
Lagavulin distillery 270–91, *270*
  blends 291
  bottling 290–91
  casks 22, 23, 284, 287, 290
  condensers 17–18, 283, 290
  cuts 13, 283, 290
  expressions 286–8, 291
  factfile 288–91
  feints 14, 290
  fermentation 282, 289
  foreshots 290
  history 273–8, 281
  low wines 283, 289
  lyne arms 17, 283, 289, 290
  malt 281, 289
  mash 281, 289
  maturation 285–6, 290
  peatiness 281, 289
  production 290
  spirit run 283, 290